ISRAEL'S DAY OF LIGHT AND JOY

Israel's Day of Light and Joy

The Origin, Development, and Enduring Meaning of the Jewish Sabbath

JON D. LEVENSON

EISENBRAUNS | University Park, Pennsylvania

Library of Congress Cataloging-in-Publication Data

Names: Levenson, Jon Douglas, author.
Title: Israel's day of light and joy : the origin, development, and enduring meaning of
the Jewish Sabbath / Jon D. Levenson.
Description: University Park, Pennsylvania : Eisenbrauns, [2024] | Includes biblio-
graphical references and index.
Summary: "Explores the origins and development of the Jewish Sabbath and the
rich and diverse range of theological and ethical meanings and characteristic
practices it acquired over the centuries"—Provided by publisher.
Identifiers: LCCN 2024000109 | ISBN 9781646022717 (hardback) |
ISBN 9781646022731 (paperback)
Subjects: LCSH: Sabbath—History.
Classification: LCC BM685 .L48 2024 | DDC 296.4/1—dc23/eng/20240126
LC record available at https://lccn.loc.gov/2024000109

10 9 8 7 6 5 4 3 2 1

The Pennsylvania State University Press is a member of the Association of Univer-
sity Presses.
It is the policy of The Pennsylvania State University Press to use acid-free paper.
Publications on uncoated stock satisfy the minimum requirements of American
National Standard for Information Sciences—Permanence of Paper for Printed
Library Material, ANSI Z39.48–1992.

This day for Israel is light and joy, a Sabbath of serenity.

—Traditional Friday evening table song

To Asher, Avner, Eliana, Graeme, Lila, Sarit, Shai, and Teaghan,
with a wish for lives filled with Israel's special days of light and joy.

CONTENTS

PREFACE

Of the making of books about the Jewish Sabbath, there is no end. So, why another one?

The answer lies in an unfortunate bifurcation in the existing literature. On the one side lie volumes that seek to introduce the potential practitioner to the observance of this all-important holiday. Some speak poetically and evocatively about the underlying theology and the spiritual meaning of the occasion; others give detailed instructions about just how to practice it, what must and must not be done in order to honor it properly; and still others combine these two essential dimensions.

On the other side lie the multitudes of specialized studies by biblical scholars and historians of Judaism. These, too, speak to dimensions of the subject I find essential—scholarly rigor, intellectual honesty in the study of religion, awareness of historical change and the corollary disinclination to harmonize across periods, and, finally, the placement of the material in its wider cultural context and the parallel forbearance from caricaturing other cultures and traditions. Given their thoroughly historical orientation, such studies are understandably disinclined to address the "Jewish Sabbath" in its fullness but rather focus on one period—the biblical, for example, or the early rabbinic—and do not attempt to speak to the larger sweep of the Jewish tradition or the meaning the institution might have for contemporary Jews.

What has been in short supply are books that speak to both sides of this divide—that is, studies alert both to the theological, ethical, and aesthetic dimensions of the subject and to the vitality of the Sabbath today that can also pass muster in the discourse of historical-critical scholarship. It is in order to fill this worrisome gap that I set about writing this volume.

Such a lofty goal, together with my own limitations, has compelled me to be selective in the subjects addressed and the materials interpreted. Though keenly aware that so much has been left out, I nonetheless hope that the present book will offer a productive framework for understanding the broad outlines of the theologies and practices of the Jewish Sabbath as they gradually assumed their long-lasting shape in antiquity, came under attack in modernity, and have experienced a renaissance among some Jews and, *mutatis mutandis,* some Christians in our own time.

The most difficult challenge I faced in research was simply the burgeoning bibliography on so many of the passages and subjects discussed. It seemed that in the notes of every article were references to probably half a dozen more that I needed to consult, but at some point a researcher working on a subject that has been investigated in detail for a good century and a half and on at least three continents has to stop reading and start writing. That there are, consequently, some questionable omissions is again something of which I am painfully conscious and for which I beg the reader's indulgence.

Also challenging has been the evaporation of many of the points of consensus in biblical studies in which I was educated in graduate school in the early 1970s (CE). One need only consider the erosion (but hardly disappearance) of classical nineteenth-century thinking about the delimitation and dating of Pentateuchal sources, for example, to realize how thoroughly the basic assumptions have been cast into an uncomfortable flux. In this volume, I have tried to steer clear of arguments that depend too strongly on precise and contentious claims about the contours and dates of sources and have instead concentrated on the ideas and texts themselves, considered in a broad chronological framework that is widely accepted among historical-critical scholars.

The difference between the two sorts of studies to which I referred at the outset corresponds to deeper differences in the goals for studying classical religious literature and in the communities of interpretation in which such study takes place. The authors who focus on spiritual meanings and religious practices tend to speak in the present tense. For them, all the texts and traditions converge in the present and are available to the reader or can be readily made so. Scholars who stand on the other side of the divide are careful to speak of each text or institution in the context of the period in which it appeared, even if passages from different periods have been woven together, as indeed they have. Sympathetic to both perspectives and, as it were, with a foot in each camp, I have on occasion stepped back to elucidate the differences in approach in hopes of helping both interested laypersons and academic scholars to appreciate the logic and objectives of the other group.

A number of institutions and individuals have proven immensely helpful to me in the process of researching and composing this study. I thank Harvard Divinity School and its generous dean, David N. Hempton, for the sabbatical year they granted me in 2019–2020, much of which I devoted to elucidating the sabbatical day. Over the years, five talented doctoral students helped me with bibliographic matters and proofreading—Michael Ennis-Villarreal, Ryan Gregg, Allison Hurst, Byron Russell, and Andrew P. Hile. My learned, wise, and eagle-eyed editor at Eisenbrauns, Maria J. Metzler, saved me from more than a few errors, stylistic and substantive alike. In addition, I owe a debt of gratitude to the various scholars who aided me on specific points as indicated in the notes. Needless to say, the mistakes that remain are solely my fault.

Finally, I must express my thanks to my long-suffering and ever-supportive wife, Beverly, for bearing with me during the periods when I was working on the Sabbath six days a week. On occasion, late on a Friday afternoon, I would hear her say, "You only have an hour." "What?" I would say to myself. "I only have an hour?! Why didn't the doctor tell me that?" Then I would realize that I had become so involved in writing about the Sabbath that I had momentarily forgotten it was coming. It was always a delight to take one day off from the Sabbath every week, especially in her company.

Unless otherwise noted, the translations from the Hebrew Bible are taken from the Jewish Publication Society *Tanakh,* as it appears in the *Jewish Study Bible.*

The transliterations from Hebrew correspond to the format most commonly used among American academic scholars, except that I have rendered the consonantal *vav*/*waw* as *v* and the fricative *b*, *k*, and *p* (*vet, khaf,* and *feh*) as *ḇ*, *ḵ*, and *p̄*, respectively.

As in the Jewish Publication Society *Tanakh* and in accordance with a widespread practice, I have rendered the four-letter proper name of God, which Jewish law forbids to be written or pronounced with its own vowels, as "the Lord," which I have put in brackets in quoting authors who do not adhere to this convention.

ABBREVIATIONS

Primary Sources
Rabbinic Literature

ʾAḅot R. Nat.	ʾAḅot de Rabbi Nathan
b.	Babylonian Talmud
B. Bat.	Baba Batra
Ber.	Beraḵot
Beṣah	Beṣah (=Yom Ṭob)
ʿEruḅ	ʿEruḅin
Gen. Rab.	Genesis Rabbah
Ḥul.	Ḥullin
Ketub.	Ketubbot
m.	Mishnah
Mak.	Makkot
Meg.	Megillah
Mek.	Meḵilta
Pesaḥ	Pesaḥim
Pesiq. Rab.	Pesiqta Rabbati
Pesiq. Raḅ Kah.	Pesiqta de Raḅ Kahana
Pirqe R. El.	Pirqe Rabbi Eliezer
Roš Haš.	Roš Haššanah
Šabb.	Šabbat
Sanh.	Sanhedrin
Šeḅu.	Šeḅuʿot
S. Eli. Rab.	Seder Eliyahu Rabbah
Sukkah	Sukkah
Taʿan.	Taʿanit
Tg. Ps.-J.	Targum Pseudo-Jonathan

y.   Jerusalem Talmud
Yoma   Yoma

Other Ancient Sources
1 En.   1 Enoch
Ag. Ap.   Josephus, *Against Apion*
Ant.   Josephus, *Antiquities*
Hist. rom.   Dio Cassius, *Roman History*
Jub.   Jubilees
J.W.   Josephus, *Jewish War*
Macc   Maccabees
Spec. Laws   Philo, *On the Special Laws*
Wis   Wisdom of Solomon

Qumran Scrolls
4Q41 (4QDeut^n)   4QDeuteronomy^n
4Q264 (4QS^j)   4QRule of the Community^j
4Q421   4QWays of Righteousness^b
11Q19 (11QT^a)   11QTemple^a

Journals, Series, and Reference Works
AB   Anchor Bible
AEL   Miriam Lichtheim. *Ancient Egyptian Literature*. Vol. 1,
                          The Old and Middle Kingdoms. Berkeley: University of
                          California Press, 1975.
AOAT   Alter Orient und Altes Testament
AYBRL   Anchor Yale Bible Reference Library
BDB   Francis Brown, S. R. Driver, and Charles A. Briggs.
                          A Hebrew and English Lexicon of the Old Testament
BZAW   Beihefte zur Zeitschrift für die alttestamentliche
                          Wissenschaft
CBQ   *Catholic Biblical Quarterly*
COS   William W. Hallo, ed. *The Context of Scripture*. 3 vols.
                          Leiden: Brill, 1997–2002
FAT   Forschungen zum Alten Testament
GKC   *Gesenius' Hebrew Grammar*
HALOT   Ludwig Koehler, Walter Baumgartner, and Johann J.
                          Stamm. *The Hebrew and Aramaic Lexicon of the Old Tes-
                          tament*. Translated and edited under the supervision of
                          Mervyn E. J. Richardson. 4 vols. Leiden: Brill,
                          1994–1999

HTR	*Harvard Theological Review*
HUCA	*Hebrew Union College Annual*
JBL	*Journal of Biblical Literature*
JSOTSup	Journal for the Study of the Old Testament Supplement Series
LCL	Loeb Classical Library
LJI	Library of Jewish Ideas
NJPS	New Jewish Publication Society *Tanakh*
OTL	Old Testament Library
PAAJR	*Proceedings of the American Academy of Jewish Research*
TSAJ	Texte und Studien zum Antiken Judentum
VT	*Vetus Testamentum*
ZAW	*Zeitschrift für die alttestamentliche Wissenschaft*

CHAPTER 1

The Two Origins of the Week

> ⁸Remember the sabbath day and keep it holy. ⁹Six days you shall labor and do all your work, ¹⁰but the seventh day is a sabbath of the LORD your God: you shall not do any work—you, your son or daughter, your male or female slave, or your cattle, or the stranger who is within your settlements. ¹¹For in six days the LORD made heaven and earth and sea, and all that is in them, and He rested on the seventh day; therefore the LORD blessed the sabbath day and hallowed it.

—Exod 20:8–11

This familiar injunction, traditionally counted as the fourth commandment of the Decalogue,¹ presupposes an institution that is so familiar to modern people that we forget it has an origin at all and is not, in fact, natural or self-evident. That institution is the week—a regularly and continuously recurring series of seven days with a defined beginning and ending. The week, however, has a historical origin, or, to be more precise, two diverse historical origins. The first of these lies in biblical texts like the one cited above, which speak of the ancient Israelite Sabbath, the seventh day of the series and the one that culminates and concludes it. No other day is so much as named here, and, in fact, in the Hebrew Bible, no other day *has* a name. In David M. Henkin's words, the biblical week is not conceived as "a set of seven distinct days" but as "a binary set of two kinds of days"—the Sabbath and the other six.² Even when, much later, the Hebrew language comes to individualize the days of the week, it refers to them by ordinal numbers rather than proper names. There is, for example, no "Sunday," only a "first day," and no "Wednesday," only a "fourth day." This is the case with Modern Hebrew even now. In the Hebrew Bible, the week is thus a bit of an illusion, or, to put it differently, to speak of a week is something of a misstatement. What recurs here is the seventh day, defined as "Sabbath." (As we shall explore in our third chapter, not every biblical text makes an explicit equation between "the seventh day" and the "Sabbath," and many scholars now believe the two institutions were once separate.)[3] In a text like this, the Sabbath makes the week; the other days are simply nameless, faceless units counted off one-by-one until the Sabbath arrives.

What complicates the picture is the clear evidence from ancient Israel for the existence of a unit of seven days apart from the sabbatical week. There is, for example, the "week" (šābûaʿ) of celebration following a wedding (Gen 29:27, 28), or the period of "two weeks" (šəbūʿayim) during which a woman who has borne a girl remains in a state of ritual impurity (Lev 12:5). Or, to give one last and, to practicing Jews, better known, example, there is the set of seven "weeks" (šābūʿôt) that the Deuteronomic liturgical calendar specifies must pass between the time that "the sickle is first put to the standing grain" and the ensuing holiday that is thus most commonly known today as "Shavuʿot," or the Feast of Weeks (Deut 16:9–10). There is no reason to assume that any of these units of seven days begins on the first day of the sabbatical week and ends on the seventh. In fact, as Jeffrey H. Tigay points out, in both biblical and rabbinic texts the word for "week" (šābûaʿ) "refers only to non-sabbatical weeks and to septennia," the latter being sets of seven years rather than days, as in Dan 9:24.[4]

In short, in ancient Israel, including Rabbinic Judaism, what is today the standard Hebrew term for "week" (šābûaʿ) could be used for any number of specialized series of seven consecutive days, but not for the institution, so familiar to us, of regular, recurrent series of seven days culminating in a distinctive ending. That institution, rather, owes its origin to the notion that the last of those days was special and thus to be honored in special ways.

If the week is not a natural unit, the month is, or, to be more precise, used to be. In ancient Mesopotamia, the land in which some highly familiar biblical texts claim the people Israel had their origin, the calendar was lunar, and aspects of the lunar calendar remain alive among the Jews to this day. Thus, in ancient Mesopotamia every month began with the new moon and found its midpoint at the full moon. In some texts, certain numerically designated days of the month held special significance. In one suggestive instance, a particular sacrifice (the neo-Babylonian ḫitpu) is to be offered on the seventh, fourteenth, twenty-first, and twenty-eighth days of the month.[5] The pattern obviously evidences not only a practice of counting off sets of seven days but also, given the lunar character of Mesopotamian months, correlates with the phases of the moon.[6] But precisely therein lies the outstanding problem with the parallel. Given that the period between consecutive new moons (the synodical month) is a bit more than 29.5 days, there is no clean division of the lunar month that can yield the seven-day week or any other regularly recurring series of days. Henkin, writing of the closeness of the number of days in the synodical month to thirty, suggests that a lunar origin would be "more likely to have suggested a week of five, six, or ten days"—that is, six, five, or three weeks in each month.[7] But, if so, that pesky missing half day would still raise a problem even for such a division. In the case of the seven-day week, since in every lunar calendar there are always more than seven days between the twentieth-eighth of one month and the seventh of the next, such a derivation of the week from the month is even less likely.

The more general practice of regularly counting off sets of seven days may possibly lie in the deep cultural background of the ancient Israelite Sabbath, but the Neo-Babylonian *ḫitpu* offers scant evidence for anything even vaguely approaching a seven-day week in ancient Mesopotamia.[8]

According to Eviatar Zerubavel, the ancient Egyptians, another group very much at the center of the biblical account of Israelite origins, were "the first people to have established a continuous weekly cycle that was entirely independent of the lunar cycle."[9] Although claims of originality are always vulnerable to new discoveries, it is certainly the case that ancient Egypt early on devised and implemented a calendar in which the months had lost their lunar connections. As Janice Kamrin describes the matter:

> By at least the middle of the Old Kingdom (ca. 2450 BC), and quite possibly several centuries earlier, the Egyptians had developed a "civil" calendar composed of twelve months of thirty days each (360 days), divided into three seasons—Inundation (*Akhet*), Emergence (*Peret*), and Harvest (*Shemu*)—of four months each, with five epagomenal days (days outside the regular months) added at the end of the year.[10]

To be sure, the lunar calendar did not disappear but continued in use for agricultural and ritual matters. "Some ancient Egyptian festivals were therefore determined by the moon," writes Anthony J. Spalinger, "and quite a number of significant religious events were solely set to a specific lunar day, such as the new moon."[11] More to the point of our discussion, Margaret A. Murray notes that "each month [was divided] into three ten-day weeks. The beginning of each week was indicated by the rising of the *decan*-star; the names of the decans are often given in the lists."[12] Of course, a "week" as we have been using the term cannot consist of ten days, but the important point here is the division of the month into recurrent subunits, which was made possible only by the replacement of the lunar month of 29.5 days with a nonlunar month of thirty days. The ten-day Egyptian week, like the later phenomenon of the Israelite sabbatical week, was independent of the lunar cycle, although, unlike the Israelite parallel, one could claim that it was still based on an astronomical phenomenon—namely, the solar year.

In the case of the Romans, by contrast, there existed for many centuries a unit of eight days called the *nundinum*, the last of which was a market day (*nundinae*[13]). Like the Sabbath of ancient Israel, the eight-day Roman week, apparently of Etruscan origin, was independent of the month and not determined by astronomical observation or calculation (though, when Roman months were still lunar, special days marked phases of the moon).[14] The market day exhibited certain affinities with the Jewish Sabbath (with which the early Romans had no familiarity), as can be seen from this description of it by a British classicist:

> People spruced themselves up, after seven days of hard work on the farm, before they went to market. It was a regular school holiday, eagerly anticipated by the children in the elementary and grammar schools. As Varro wrote, "The ancients devoted seven days to work and the eighth to business in town." Business could involve lawyers, who were to be found in towns. So the day was a *dies fastus* [one on which it was proper, or even auspicious, to conduct business], on which legal transactions could be effected. On the other hand, no public meetings could be held, since they would have interfered with the proper business of the day.[15]

Fancier clothing, cessation of regular work, and a holiday atmosphere on the last day of a regular series are all reminiscent of the Sabbath as it was eventually to develop in Rabbinic Judaism and are highly familiar to Sabbath-observant Jews today. Responsible historiographic method prevents us, however, from assuming that the full pattern was already in practice in biblical times. The same classicist also mentions inviting friends for a festive meal, another familiar aspect of the Jewish practice, and notes that, as in the seven-day week, the eight days of the *nundinum* were "identifiable in writing and conversation" by their relationship to the market day at the end of the sequence.[16] Here, too, the parallel with rabbinic practice is striking, whether there is a genetic connection or not. The rabbis of the Talmudic era, like their biblical antecedents (and, as mentioned, speakers of Modern Hebrew as well), had no names for days of the week other than the Sabbath; they designated them simply by their numerical relationship to the culminating day of the series, which they termed *šabbāt*, of which the English word is essentially a transliteration.

Despite these similarities, some of them conceivably owing to Roman influence on Rabbinic Judaism, we must not miss the telltale differences between the two special days. Whereas the Roman *nundinae* was especially devoted to conducting business, on the Jewish Sabbath business transactions seem to have been forbidden from early on, as seen from this oracle of around 500 BCE:

[13]If you refrain from trampling the sabbath,
From pursuing your affairs on My holy day;
If you call the sabbath "delight,"
The LORD's holy day "honored";
And if you honor it and go not your ways
Nor look to your affairs, nor strike bargains—
[14]Then you can seek the favor of the LORD.
I will set you astride the heights of the earth,
And let you enjoy the heritage of your father Jacob—
For the mouth of the LORD has spoken. (Isa 58:13–14)

Similarly, when Nehemiah, the Persian-appointed Jewish governor in Jerusalem in the fifth century BCE, spotted merchants bringing their products into the city to sell on the Sabbath, he ordered the gates closed and guarded "to preserve the sanctity of the sabbath" (Neh 13:22), not to be reopened until after the holy day was over.[17] Legal transactions, needless to say, could not be performed on such a day. In a later period, rabbinic law would, in fact, altogether prohibit courts from meeting on Sabbaths and festivals.[18] The Sabbath was thus not the conclusion of the workweek; it was the *opposite* of the workweek, a day that was protected from labor, production, and commerce—all of which it radically relativized. No wonder that, as one classicist put it, "the idea of a regularly recurrent day on which all work was suspended had no appeal for the pagan Roman, and Roman writers generally stigmatized the Jewish observance of the Sabbath as a decadent glorification of sheer idleness."[19]

It is also important to remember that in the Roman system different regions observed different market days.[20] There was no assumption of national synchrony. To be sure, it is not impossible that in early Israel a parallel situation obtained with regard to the Sabbath. Perhaps the members of a given household devoted themselves to work for a set of six consecutive days and to sabbatical rest on the seventh—without, that is, any expectation that the entire House of Israel was working and then resting simultaneously with them. In support of such a speculation, one might note the analogy suggested by the law of the "Hebrew slave" as it appears in what historical scholars generally take to be its earliest form: "When you acquire a Hebrew slave, he shall serve six years; in the seventh year he shall go free, without payment" (Exod 21:2). Now, it is inconceivable that every eligible slave was bought in the same year and thus went free at the same time six years hence. In this form, the law thus differs from the version in Deut 15:12–18, in which the release of the slave has become associated with the septennial national year of remission of debts (*šəmiṭṭâ*), mandated in the first eleven verses of the same chapter. Were we to reconstruct an analogous process with regard to the seventh day, we should have to say that the same standardization and synchronization came into effect with respect to the week only gradually. In any event, if there ever was variation, regional or other, in the day Israelites marked as the seventh in the sequence, all traces of this have disappeared in the literature that survives, wherein it seems assumed that the whole nation acts as one in regard to the sabbatical observances.[21] Although aspects of the annual calendar, especially the dates of festivals, were hotly debated in ancient Judaism, what day of the week it was and on what day the Sabbath falls seem never to have been an issue.

The antiquity and security of the sabbatical week in Judaism and its well-nigh worldwide scope today should not blind us to its recency in cultures that are neither Jewish, Christian, nor Muslim in heritage. Nor should those factors cause us to forget that, as the term itself suggests, the origin of the sabbatical week lies in the special and radically separate nature of the last of its seven days. Regarding China and Japan, for example, Henkin points out that "it was not until the second half of the nineteenth century that the seven-day week gained purchase in either country as an instrument for organizing work, social life, or popular timekeeping." In both countries, rather, the traditional calendars knew of a ten-day sequence that "bore little structural or functional resemblance to the Western cycle of rest and work." In Japan, its "practical role was even more limited," and the urban communities "observed a five-day work schedule that more nearly approximated the Western week."[22]

We have been examining the ordering of time in calendrical systems through units that, like the week as that institution is conventionally defined, are shorter than the month but, unlike the week, are composed of a number of days other than seven. These are systems from societies in which the week, as we have been using the term, had not yet taken firm root, if it was even known there. We should be remiss, however, if we failed to mention the existence of societies that, knowing the week, devised and implemented systems to replace it.

In the Bahá'í religion, the "week" consists of nineteen days, which, as Zerubavel points out, "is the closest approximation of the square root of the annual cycle."[23] That is, nineteen squared equals 361, which is not too far from the number of days in the solar year (365.2422). Four intercalary days, or five in leap years, are added to coordinate more exactly with the solar year. Bahá'í, which originated in the mid-nineteenth century CE, contrasts with other modern replacements of the week in that its calendar encodes religious messages rather than obviously political ones.

In the case of the French revolutionaries of the end of the eighteenth century CE, by contrast, the new calendar was intended to replace and rationalize the traditional Christian calendar, with its supposedly retrograde features such as the Sunday Sabbath. Thus, instead of the seven-day week—and in unwitting imitation of the ancient Egyptian solar calendar—the revolutionaries set up the *décade*, a recurring unit of ten days. Three of these constituted a month, and twelve months constituted a year of exactly 360 days. Here, too, extra days—five in ordinary years and six in leap years, all of them festive in character—were added to synchronize the calendar with the solar cycle. The last day of each *décade*, known therefore as *décadi*, served as the day of rest and celebration, thus replacing Sunday—and, needless to say, vastly complicating the lives of any Christians (or, all the more so, Jews) who sought to uphold the day of rest that their tradition mandated. Zerubavel puts it well. The goal of the reform, he writes, "was obvious—to pull the entire social and economic life of France outside the sphere of the traditional Christian weekly rhythm, so as to make the latter absolutely irrelevant to daily life."[24]

A similar motive underlay various calendrical reforms implemented in the Soviet Union in the twentieth century, except that here the impetus was not Enlightenment Deism but rather the uncompromising atheistic materialism of the Communist system. In one version, introduced in 1929, the new calendar replaced the seven-day week with one of five days, with workers resting on the fifth and thus having a day without labor more often than had been the case under the older, Christian arrangement.[25] But the days off did not coincide for the entire populace. Again to quote Zerubavel, the Soviet workers "certainly did not rest together, as one society, since 80 percent of the entire Soviet working population would be at work on any given day."[26] There was, in other words, a day off but no Sabbath, no day that testified to anything as universal and consequential—or, as the Communists would see it, as superstitious and reactionary—as God's creation of the world: "As in France 140 years earlier, the main purpose of abolishing the seven-day week in the Soviet Union was to destroy religion there."[27] Nonetheless, the Gregorian calendar never disappeared, and Soviet efforts to replace the week ultimately proved short-lived, themselves disappearing by the time World War II broke out.[28]

If in ancient Israel the week, unlike the month, corresponds to no natural event—to nothing, that is, in the heavens—the same cannot be said for the other of the two origins of the seven-day unit, the planetary week. This system seems to have emerged in the second century BCE in Hellenistic Alexandria, whence it spread widely, becoming well attested in Rome by the end of the next century.[29] It rests, in brief, upon two pillars: an older Egyptian division of the day into twenty-four hours and the well-known fact that seven heavenly bodies are visible to the naked eye.

If one assigns each hour of the day successively to one of those visible bodies (or, in Greek usage, "planets," that is, "wanderers" through the heavens)—the sun, the moon, Mars, Mercury, Jupiter, Venus, and Saturn, to give the order generally familiar to speakers of many Western languages today—the pattern repeats itself after the last hour of the seventh day, and so a new planetary, or astrological (in contradistinction to sabbatical), seven-day week begins.[30]

The actual order of the days in this Alexandrian system, each one named for the planet that governs its first hour, is more complicated. Based on the time it takes for the seven heavenly bodies to orbit the sun—actually, as these pre-Copernican thinkers saw it, for the planets, including the sun, to orbit the earth—the sequence from the longest to shortest (according to their calculations[31]) would be Saturn, Jupiter, Mars, sun, Venus, Mercury, moon. As often noted, the actual series involves the skipping of two planets at a time, so that, for example, we move from Saturn to the sun, skipping Jupiter and Mars. If we include all the planets in this curious process, we thus end up with the familiar sequence: Saturn, sun, moon, Mars, Mercury, Jupiter, Venus.[32] The notion that Saturday is the first day of the week must surely sound strange. It is, after all, the last day of the Jewish week and thus the Sabbath (though, according to the rabbinic law, the Sabbath begins at sundown the previous evening and ends when three stars have appeared the next night). Even in contemporary secular discourse, Saturday begins the "weekend" (a revealing term, as we shall see),[33] not the "week-start." But the reasons that the week begins on Sunday (which, again, in the traditional Jewish reckoning starts on Saturday night) are of biblical origin and would not have held force among pre-Christian gentiles in Hellenistic Egypt.

In origin and essence, the planetary week was not about a seven-day sequence at all. The astrological character of each day was a function, rather, of the planet that governed its first hour. "The fact that the planetary type is properly one of hours rather than days," writes Colson, importantly, "and that it is part of a general system of time sovereignties makes it impossible in my mind to look on it as a mere variation of the Jewish or Sabbatical type."[34] This is not to say, however, that the two distinct sources of the seven-day week, the Jewish and the planetary, did not eventually come into a productive interaction. Indeed they did.[35]

The point of connection was the fact that the Sabbath fell on Saturn's Day. Leaving aside the complicated and multifaceted figure of the god Saturn after whom the planet was named, we can safely say that ancient astrology associated the latter with gloom and ill-omen.[36] In one of his elegies, the Roman poet Tibullus (ca. 55–19 BCE), having fallen ill on a trip, speaks of how he had sought to delay his departure from his lover Delia: "My pretext would be birds or dire prophecies, or Saturn's holy day was keeping me" (*Elegies* 1.3.18).[37] In what sense Tibullus regards Saturn's day as "holy" (*sacram*) is less than obvious. Colson is convinced that the elegist is "primarily alluding to the

Sabbath." He is less certain, however, that this shows a knowledge of the planetary week. Rather, "the belief that the Sabbath was a Jewish form of reverencing the planet *may* have originated independently of the planetary week and indeed be anterior to it."[38] On this reading, then, Tibullus would have wanted to avoid setting sail on the Jewish Sabbath because the day was associated with the ill-omened planet. In the background of this reasoning would lie, in turn, a serious misunderstanding of the Jewish institution. "Then the Gentile world observing the Jewish abstention from work and misreading the day of rest and rejoicing as a day of superstitious dread of activity," Colson speculates, "may have evolved the theory of its connexion with Saturn."[39] More likely, though, is the position that Colson actually prefers, that Tibullus does indeed associate a particular day with Saturn because of his familiarity with the planetary week. As we shall soon see, Colson also stands on solid ground in suspecting that something more than the coincidence of the Sabbath with Saturn's day accounts for the belief among pagan Romans that the Jews were thought to reverence the planet.

Whether Tibullus's "dread of activity" on that day is also associated with the Sabbath is, in my view, less certain than Colson thinks, but a point in favor of that association is the poet's use of the term "holy," which regularly describes the character of the day in the Jewish scriptures and was perhaps also on the lips of any Jews with whom the poet came into contact.[40] But we should not ignore the possibility that "holy" is a mistranslation of the Latin term in the elegy, since the Latin *sacer* can sometimes mean "accursed, wicked, execrable," and the like, and may refer here simply to the bad luck associated with the planet Saturn.[41] Alternatively, the words *Saturniue sacram . . . diem* may simply mean "the day [that is] sacred to Saturn," again with no reference to the Sabbath.

Whatever the relationship of Saturn's Day and the Jewish Sabbath in Tibullus, a connection would become explicit in the work of the Roman historian Tacitus (ca. 56–120 CE). Connecting the Latin word for "Jews" (*Iudaei*) with that for the residents of Mount Ida on Crete (*Idaei*), Tacitus relates a tale to the effect that "the Jews were originally exiles from the island of Crete who settled in the farthest parts of Libya at the time when Saturn had been deposed and expelled by Jove [i.e., Jupiter]" (Tacitus, *Histories* 5.2 [Moore, LCL]). As for the Sabbath, Tacitus (no admirer of the Jews or Judaism he) first connects it with a legend that the Jews, a "race . . . hateful to the gods" (Tacitus, *Histories* 5.2 [Moore, LCL]), were expelled from Egypt to bring about the end of a plague and then

first chose to rest on the seventh day because that day ended their toils; but after a time they were led by the charms of indolence (*blandiente inertia*) to give over the seventh year to inactivity (*ignaviae*). Others say that this is done in honour of Saturn, whether it be that the primitive elements of their religion were given by the Idaeans, who, according to tradition, were expelled with Saturn and became the founders of the Jewish race, or is due to the fact that, of the seven planets that rule the fortunes of mankind, Saturn moves in the highest orbit and has the greatest potency; and that many of the heavenly bodies traverse their paths and courses in multiples of seven. (Tacitus, *Histories* 5.4 [Moore, LCL])

Note that, though he stresses the connection of the Sabbath to Saturn, which in his view reflects, in turn, the importance of the planet to the Jews, Tacitus does not explicitly connect Jewish "inactivity" on the seventh day to the nature of the planet in the regnant astrological thinking of his time.[42] Rather, unless a belief in the inauspiciousness of Saturday is one of those "primitive elements" that the Jews supposedly received from the Idaeans, their "inactivity" on Saturday is actually owing to the planet Saturn's having "the highest orbit and . . . the greatest potency" and thus serving as the fittest celestial correlative to their one and all-powerful God—"that supreme and eternal being [who] is to them incapable of representation and without end" (Tacitus, *Histories* 5.5 [Moore, LCL]), as Tacitus eloquently puts it elsewhere.

In the case of Dio Cassius (ca. 155–ca. 235 CE), a Roman historian and statesman who wrote a massive history of Rome in Greek, the issue of the association of Saturn with the Jews' not working on the Sabbath is, however, more complex.

Like his Latin forerunner Tacitus, Dio presents the Jews as having "dedicated to [their God] the day called the day of Saturn, on which, among many other most peculiar observances, they undertake no serious occupation" (Dio Cassius, *Hist. rom.* 37.17 [Cary and Foster, LCL]). Indeed, in Dio's telling, it was the Jews' reverence for Saturday that accounted for the Roman general Pompey's momentous capture of their Temple in 63 BCE. The Temple, Dio reports,

was on high ground and was fortified by a wall of its own, and if they had continued defending it on all days alike, he could not have got possession of it. As it was, they made an exception of what are called the days of Saturn, and by doing no work at all on those days afforded the Romans an opportunity in this interval to batter down the wall. The latter, on learning of this superstitious awe of theirs, made no serious attempts the rest of the time, but on those days, when they came round in succession, assaulted most vigorously. Thus the defenders were captured on the day of Saturn, without making any defence, and all the wealth was plundered (Dio Cassius, *Hist. rom.* 37.18 [Cary and Foster, LCL]).[43]

Whether the Jewish refusal to fight on the Sabbath is here connected to the astrological character of the planet that governs that day is unclear. Perhaps that "superstitious awe of theirs" refers to the native Jewish account of why Saturday is different from all other days, whatever the pagan Dio Cassius understands that native account to be. For, as we shall see at greater length in chapter 6,[44] Second Temple Jewish sources speak of uncertainty about whether warfare is licit on the Sabbath. According to 1 Maccabees, after a group of Jews who, during the uprising against Antiochus IV (ca. 167 BCE), died because they would not desecrate the Sabbath by defending themselves, others resolved that such national suicide must not continue: "So they made this decision that day: 'Let us fight against anyone who comes to attack us on the sabbath day; let us not all die as our kindred died in their hiding places'" (1 Macc 2:41, NSRV). But the Book of Jubilees, which dates from after the period described (but is not necessarily later than 1 Maccabees itself), still calls down a curse of death on any who would conduct warfare on the Sabbath (Jub. 50:12–13). Eventually, Rabbinic Judaism, by contrast, allowed even offensive war to be conducted on the Sabbath, though with limitations and precautions.[45]

It is highly doubtful, however, that Dio Cassius has a sophisticated understanding of Jewish thinking on the issue.[46] It would seem more likely that the Roman historian assumes that the inauspicious associations of Saturn are so culturally pervasive that his readers will reflexively—and properly—connect the Jews' abstention from "serious occupation" on Saturn's day with the latter's astrological character, rather like Tibullus's resistance to setting sail on that day. In support of this, one could note that Dio's account of Pompey's capture of the Temple provides him with an opportunity to speak of the origin and nature of the planetary week in some detail. "The custom," he writes, "of referring the days to the seven stars called planets was instituted by the Egyptians, but is now found among all mankind, though its adoption has been comparatively recent; at any rate the ancient Greeks never understood it, so far as I am aware." Tellingly, Dio Cassius, writing in the early third century CE, notes that the planetary week "is now quite the fashion with mankind generally and even with the Romans themselves, and is to them already in a way an ancestral tradition" (Dio Cassius, *Hist. rom.* 37.18 [Cary and Foster, LCL]) and thus deserves the substantial account of it that he then provides. It would seem likely (though by no means certain) that, as Dio sees it, the Jews' devotion to the planet Saturn as emblematic of their sole deity has caused them to devote Saturn's day—itself a phenomenon derived from the planetary week—fully and without compromise to their God.

What we have now determined is that the modern seven-day week is a more complicated phenomenon, both in definition and in origin, than first seems the case. One of its sources lies in ancient Israel, specifically in the notion that the last of the seven days of the continuously repeating sequence has a special character, different from and in some important ways opposed to that of the other six. Another, and later, source lies in the observations and calculations of astrologers and astronomers—the two were not yet distinguishable—of Hellenistic Egypt who, arranging the seven visible planets (a term that for them included the sun and the moon) in the descending order of their orbital periods, assigned each of the twenty-four hours of their day to the regency of the successive planets, thus yielding the sequence of seven days that has now become dominant across the world. As Henkin points out, "the understanding of the week as a set of seven distinct days, rather than simply a binary set of two kinds of days" is a legacy of the astrological rather than the sabbatical week.[47] For in the latter, in its pre-Hellenistic form, the only distinction was between the six workdays and the sacred seventh day.

That these two sources of the seven-day week would interact was inevitable, given the presence of so many Jews in the Greco-Roman world and the spread of the planetary week throughout it.[48] Pre-Christian and non-Christian gentile writers more than occasionally remarked on what was to them the baffling institution of the Jewish Sabbath, and some of them, as we have seen, were intrigued by its coincidence with the Greco-Roman Day of Saturn. Perhaps some also attributed Jewish inactivity on that day to its association with bad luck in their astrological system. For their part, some Jews also took note of the coincidence of the two days and may possibly have drawn conclusions about their Sabbath from it. Consider this passage from the Babylonian Talmud:

> "And do not go out alone at night." For it was taught: One should not go out alone at night, neither on Wednesdays nor on Sabbaths, because 'Agrat the daughter of Maḥalat and eighteen myriads [i.e., 180,000] of destroying angels go forth, and each has permission to cause destruction on his own. In the beginning, they were present every day. One time, she ['Agrat] encountered Rabbi Ḥanina ben Dosa and said to him, "Had an announcement about you not been made in heaven, 'Be careful of Ḥanina his Torah!' I would have put you in danger." He said to her, "If I have any importance in heaven, I decree against you that you shall not pass through the settled areas of the world." She said to him, "Please do me a favor and leave me a little space." He left her the nights of Wednesdays and of Sabbaths. (b. Pesaḥ. 112b)

Despite the several uncertainties in this passage, it would seem clear that it identifies Wednesday and Friday nights as occasions when demons range over the world and thus as times when it is especially dangerous to set out alone.

Why, strictly according to the logic of the passage itself, this should be the case for either night is not addressed. If we turn to the larger cultural background, however, and note the importance of astrology in the Greco-Roman world (including, with certain qualifications, the Jews), a ready answer appears. The danger of the night of the Sabbath is connected to the regnant planetary influence. As Vettius Valens, an astrologer writing in the mid-second century CE, put it, Saturn was associated, *inter alia*, with "violence and hidden malice"[49]—certainly an apt characterization of 'Agrat bat Maḥalat and her eighteen myriads of destroying angels ranging the world on the nights of what in the rabbinic reckoning was already Saturday.

The interaction of the sabbatical and the planetary weeks (complete with the astrological connotations of the latter) can also be found in a Talmudic passage that correlates each of the seven days of creation with the temperaments or destinies of those born on it (b. Šabb. 156a). Thus, for example: "One who is born on the second day of the week [i.e., Monday] will be quarrelsome. What's the reason? Because that is when the waters were divided" (Gen 1:6–8). And what about one who is born on the Sabbath? Here, we might expect an uplifting correlation, one that reflects the sanctity and blessedness of the day. But what the passage actually relates is something quite different: "He who is born on the Sabbath, on the Sabbath will he die because they desecrated the great day of the Sabbath on his account." The reference here is to the medical procedures associated with childbirth that override the ordinary restrictions of Sabbath observance. In characteristic Talmudic fashion, however, a dissent is immediately offered, one that, by picking up on that term "great," suggests that such a birth augurs that the child will instead partake of the magnitude and holiness of the special day whose strictures have been overridden to bring him into the world: "Rava ben Rav Sheyla said: And a great saint [literally, holy man] he shall be called."[50] A bit later in the same discussion, we find a variant account of the ill fortune that will overcome one born on the Sabbath, only with an explicit reference to Saturn: "He who is born under Saturn (*Šabbətā[']y*) will be a man whose plans will come to nothing (*bəṭēlîn*)" (b. Šabb. 156a).

Here, the great medieval commentator Rashi (1040–1105) helps us understand the wordplay. The key is the overlap between the Aramaic verb *bəṭal*,[51] among whose meanings are (1) "to come to an end" or (2) "to amount to naught, be void or annulled," and the Hebrew *šāḇat*, which can convey the first meaning (though probably not the second) and is connected with "Sabbath" (*šabbāt*), which, in turn, has therefore generated the rabbinic term for "Saturn" used in this passage.[52] The plans of the man born on the Sabbath will come to an end, the Talmudic passage first asserts, though, sadly, not in the positive sense in which the seventh day brings the primordial week to an end, consummating and crowning the first six, but in the negative sense of proving to be null and void.

In the Middle Ages, the connection between the Jews' observance of the Sabbath and the astrological influence of Saturn becomes explicit. Rabbi Abraham ibn Ezra (ca. 1089–ca. 1167), one of the major figures of the period (and, not coincidentally, the author of several volumes on astrology) explains the connection in detail when discussing the Sabbath commandment in the Decalogue:

> The sages who taught on the basis of experience say that for each of the planets there is a particular day of the week in which its power appears and in which it is in charge of the first hour of the day and the first hour of the night. They say that Saturn and Mars are harmful stars, and anybody who starts work or goes on a journey when either one of them is in power will experience harm. Therefore, our predecessors, of blessed memory, said that permission has been granted to work destruction on the nights of Wednesday and the Sabbath, and, actually, throughout the week you will not find another instance of a night and a day, one after the other, in which these two harmful planets are ruling, except for this day [i.e., the Sabbath]. For that reason, it is not appropriate for one to occupy himself with worldly matters on it, but exclusively with the fear of the Lord.[53]

Here, the ostensible inactivity of the Jews on the Sabbath is interpreted as a rational response to the malign planetary influences that rule the day. Instead of occupying themselves with quotidian activities by which one earns a living on a day unlucky for such things, the Jews are to devote themselves to the highest power, the God of Israel, creator of the world.

In a highly instructive study, Shlomo Sela argues that ibn Ezra's concern with the astrological meaning of Saturn in several of his works reflects, in part, a response to the anti-Semitic implications of the association of the Jews with that maleficent planet that had by then attained venerable antiquity and wide currency. We have already seen the association in the works of the Roman historian Tacitus; Sela notes its presence in the enormously influential Christian theologian Augustine (354–430) and later in medieval Muslim and Christian sources.[54] "The natural inference from this view," he writes, "was that the Jews, being astrologically connected to and governed by Saturn, should be contaminated by the malignant and wicked nature of Saturn. Therefore, it is not surprising that this posited connection was a welcome addition to the arsenal of anti-Semitism and was used by hostile elements in society to harass the Jews and to associate them with some particularly negative attributes."[55] What this prejudice misses, according to ibn Ezra, is that God has graciously given the Jews collectively a way to *escape* the malignant influence of Saturn[56]—and, we should add, to put the otherwise ill-starred day in which that planet reigns to the highest imaginable use, the worship of God and obedience to his will. The notion that the Sabbath was associated with bad luck and malign influences will surely seem bizarre to those familiar with the Jewish institution as it has been practiced now for millennia. For the latter is a day associated with joy, celebration, spiritual replenishment, camaraderie, and good will. And yet, as we shall see in chapter 2, although the particular connection with the god Saturn is of Roman origin, there are aspects of the biblical Sabbath that have suggested to some scholars a more complicated spiritual orientation than can be accommodated by the handy dichotomy of joy versus avoidance.

Although it is correct to speak of two sources of the seven-day week, one Hebraic and one Hellenic, it is essential to notice that the two yield very different institutions. The planetary week of the Hellenistic astronomers/astrologers was an endlessly recurring set of seven days, each named for the "planet" that reigned over its first hour. There was nothing particularly eventful about its beginning or its ending. If, as we saw in Tibullus, there was a sense that the day ruled by Saturn was inauspicious, this had to do not with the week per se but rather with the deep mythological background of the god for whom the planet was named (including his Greek predecessor Kronos). Among the Greco-Roman gentiles, there was, so far as I am aware, no communal celebration, whether festive or apotropaic, that routinely characterized a particular day of the week or honored the god for whom it was named.

In the case of the Hebrew Bible, by contrast, six of the days of the seven-day unit are totally lacking in proper names and identifying characteristics. Although the available evidence does not permit us to reconstruct the historical practice of ancient Israelites,[57] biblical texts about the Sabbath give the impression that each of the other six days was the same as all the others, with only the seventh and last different in kind. The first six have no distinct theological meaning; they are not associated with any god. The seventh, by contrast, is "a Sabbath of the LORD" (Exod 20:10), the particular God of Israel and, as a multitude of biblical texts affirm, also and not coincidentally the lord and master of the whole world. The special character of the last day is owing not to any astrological influences but rather to the commandments that God issued to his special people; it makes sense only within the larger narrative about the unique relationship of that singular Deity and his unparalleled people.

Both ancient sources of the seven-day week involve metaphysical assertions; neither reflects straightforward empirical observation. Although the Greco-Roman astrologers surely thought that longstanding human experience testified, to one degree or another, to the predictive value of their complicated system of hours and days, the planetary influences in which they believed were invisible and transcended ordinary human observation. Many centuries later, modern astronomy would, of course, undermine the picture of the universe that underlay their system. As Eviatar Zerubabel notes, "Had they been able, with the help of some sophisticated telescopes, to also observe Uranus, Neptune, and Pluto, the week might have evolved as a ten-day cycle. On the other hand, had they accepted our heliocentric model of the planetary system, where the sun is considered a stationary star rather than a planet, this cycle might have been only six days long."[58] So, unlike the sabbatical week of Judaism (and, later, Christianity), the seven-day planetary week had always been contingent on the state of science in the ancient world. Although in many languages the names used for some or all days of the week derive from the names of the seven so-called planets identified by these ancient astrologers/astronomers, modern science destroyed the underpinnings of that week—and ancient astrology more generally—several centuries ago. In secular society, the seven-day week is now merely a convention, surviving because of inertia and tradition. It lacks metaphysical authorization.

The same cannot be said for the sabbatical week. Whatever doubts about the God of Israel modern science may have elicited among philosophers, no empirical observations, nothing visible to the telescope or apparent to any of the senses, undermines its claim of transcendent authority. For, according to the theology of the biblical text itself (again, whatever the preceding or contemporary social reality), the origin of the recurring seven-day unit lies in the mysterious will of God, who set the last day radically apart from the first six, investing it with transcendent meaning and ensuring that, among Jews and Christians who hear the voice of God in the sabbatical laws, the seven-day week can never be merely a human convention surviving because of nothing more than cultural inertia. For them, the Sabbath and thus the week to which it gave birth is like the God who authorizes them—utterly invisible and yet a palpable reality in the routine of their communal life.

But our notice of these important theological constructions should emphatically not be taken to deny that the Sabbath has a human history and, for that matter, a human prehistory. It is, in fact, to the pressing question of the origins and early history of the Sabbath that we turn in our next chapter.

CHAPTER 2

From Seventh Day to Sabbath

ALTHOUGH THROUGHOUT OUR DISCUSSION we have been referring to the seventh day of the week as the "Sabbath," that name does not actually occur in what historians generally regard as the earliest texts about the institution. Consider this paradigmatic instance: "Six days you shall do your work, but on the seventh day you shall cease from labor, in order that your ox and your ass may rest, and that your bondsman and stranger may be refreshed" (Exod 23:12).[1] Here, what we have been calling the "Sabbath" is designated not with that term (*šabbāt*) but rather as simply "the seventh day." The difference is significant. "Sabbath" is a proper name; it denotes a holiday. "The seventh day" simply indicates a day that follows six others. It may refer to the special day that concludes a sabbatical week, but it does not have to. In the Decalogue, for example, the equation is explicit and beyond doubt: "the seventh day is a sabbath of the LORD your God" (Exod 20:10). But in many other cases, such an equation is unlikely or impossible, as in the law of Passover (or, to be biblically precise, the Festival of Unleavened Bread): "You shall celebrate a sacred occasion on the first day, and a sacred occasion on the seventh day" (Exod 12:16). In context, it is clear that "the first day" refers here to a date in the lunar month, the fifteenth, so that "the seventh day" is not, or not necessarily, a Sabbath but rather simply "the twenty-first day of the month" (v. 18), regardless of the day of the sabbatical week on which that date falls in any given year.[2]

In the previous chapter, in connection with the law of the male debt slave in Exod 21:2–6, we had occasion to note the possibility that, just as every slave owner would not have purchased his slave the same year and thus released him after six more, so not everyone working for six days and resting on the seventh would have necessarily done so at the same time.[3] Applied to Exod 23:12 (the passage quoted above), this observation raises the possibility—nothing stronger than that is, alas, warranted—that, in the period in which these verses originally appeared, "the seventh day" on which their addressees must cease from labor may not have referred to a synchronized occasion (Saturday, as it were) but rather to a regularly recurring pattern of six days of labor and one of rest. Here, one might make an analogy to the Soviet experiment with a five-day week that we mentioned in our previous chapter. In this arrangement, work ceased on the last day of the "week," but, to quote Eviatar Zerubavel again, the Soviet workers "certainly did not rest together, as one society, since 80 percent of the entire Soviet working population would be at work on any given day."[4] Under such a system, there is no "Sabbath" as that term has come to be used in Jewish and Christian tradition and even earlier, at some point in the history of biblical Israel—quite apart, of course, from the obvious and massive difference that the state-sponsored atheism of the Soviet Union made.

The great difficulty posed by the whole enterprise of dating biblical texts effectively renders certainty in questions like this impossible. The Pentateuch itself ascribes all its legal collections to the same period, that of the revelation to Moses just before Sinai, at Sinai itself, during the wilderness wanderings afterward, and, of course, at his great Deuteronomic summation (and, truth to tell, revision) across the Jordan from the promised land. This Mosaic ascription has long provided a powerful rationale for harmonizing the many discrepancies between laws in the Torah, and rabbinic midrash provided a rich and creative resource for doing just that. Without harmonization, it is hard to see what it would mean actually to observe the Torah, since practicing one law might well mean not practicing another in the same corpus. And so, for the purpose of the lived religious life, the leveling of differences is essential.

For historians, however, the matter is very different. For them, the discrepancies serve as telltale and thus precious indications of the uneven processes of development that have resulted in the text now in our possession, and the midrashic enterprise of harmonization effaces the true historical picture by substituting—often at great cost to the plain sense—a largely static image of uniformity across time. Whereas religious practitioners are committed to bringing the text alive and keeping it that way, historians are committed to placing it in its ancient contexts (which, in the case of the Hebrew Bible, may comprise a period of something approaching a thousand years), contexts that are vastly different from those of the historians' own times or those of the traditional practitioner. Thus, whereas religious traditionalists prize textual unity, historians suspect it. Both act for good reason.

All that being the case, the historical investigation of the terms "Sabbath" and "seventh day" on which we are about to embark will necessarily provide a view not only different from but at odds with the picture almost all readers of the Bible have. As we have been at pains to point out, the new picture is far from certain (though many scholars treat it as established fact) and not without formidable objection from some within the guild of historians of ancient Israel. A respectable case can be made for it, though, and, if it is valid, it explains a great deal—even as it inevitably raises new questions. At the end of this chapter, we shall provide a more direct evaluation of the proposal and outline counterarguments that have been offered.

If, as some scholars have maintained,[5] in the preexilic period (that is, before the Babylonian Exile began in 586 BCE), or at least in a large part of it, the antecedent of the Sabbath was known simply as "the seventh day" and was not necessarily practiced synchronously throughout the society, a major conundrum confronts us: What is the origin of the word "Sabbath" (*šabbāt*) and the calendrically defined occasion that it came to denote? For the historical record is clear: If "Sabbath" ever was an uncommon term or referred to something other than a weekly event, it has nonetheless come to be equated with the term "the seventh day" in the sense of the day of cessation from labor that the latter term has in texts like Exod 23:12 and the Exod 34:21, the two texts that are usually paired in historical-critical discussions of the weekly Sabbath in preexilic Israel.[6] If, in other words, the two terms had different meanings at some point, the discrepancy was eventually harmonized, so that the conjecture that the two terms once referred to different things, or that one of them ("Sabbath") was at some point not yet in circulation consequently strikes most modern Bible readers as exceedingly odd.

Initially, the question confronting us appears to have an easy answer: at first glance, "Sabbath" (*šabbāt*) would seem to be simply a noun formation from a verb that occurs in both those two exemplary verses—the verb *šābat*, meaning "cease, come to an end." To be sure, the existence of such a verb in Biblical Hebrew is beyond doubt; most of its occurrences have nothing to do with the Sabbath.[7] Thus, in the little poetic version of the promise given to Noah after the flood, we read:

So long as the earth endures,
Seedtime and harvest,
Cold and heat,
Summer and winter,
Day and night
Shall not cease (*yišbōtû*). (Gen 8:22)

The same verb can also be used of human beings who cease to perform an activity, as in the introduction to the Elihu speeches in the book of Job: "These three men ceased (*vayyišbətû*) replying to Job, for he considered himself right" (Job 32:1). These examples of verbal forms of the root *šbt* are all in the simple (or *qal*) stem, but the verb also occurs in other common Hebrew verb formations, with the meaning one would predict for a root whose *qal* means "cease, come to an end." Here is an example of the *niphal* stem:

Fortresses shall cease (*wənišbat*) from Ephraim
And sovereignty from Damascus;
The remnant of Aram shall become
Like the mass of Israelites
—declares the LORD of Hosts. (Isa 17:3)

Since the *niphal* usually has a passive meaning, perhaps "be brought to an end" or the like would be more accurate (if less fluent) here.

Similarly, the *hiphil*, which most frequently yields a causative sense, means "to bring to an end," as in this inspiring verse in praise of the LORD:

He puts a stop (*mašbît*) to wars throughout the earth,
breaking the bow, snapping the spear,
consigning wagons to the flames. (Ps 46:10)

It is also worthy of mention that at least one noun other than *šabbāt* (Sabbath) from the same root is attested:

All the precious things she had
In the days of old
Jerusalem recalled
In her days of woe and sorrow,
When her people fell by enemy hands
With none to help her;
When enemies looked on and gloated
Over her downfall (*mišbattehā*). (Lam 1:7)[8]

More complicated is the word *šebet*, which some scholars think can denote the act of refraining or desisting, as in this proverb: "It is honorable for a man to desist (*šebet*) from strife, / But every fool becomes embroiled." (Prov 20:3) Quite apart from the ambiguities of the second half of the verse, it is possible that the root of *šebet* in the first half is not *šbt* at all but rather *yšb*, a very frequently attested root whose *qal* verbal form means to "sit, dwell," and the like.[9] *šebet* is, in fact, its most common infinitive,[10] and, so understood, means "to sit," "to dwell," "the act of sitting or dwelling," and the like. If that is the form in this verse, the sense would be that one should, as it were, "sit tight" in the face of strife and not, as the next verb (*yitgallā'*) is perhaps better rendered, "burst out." Here, an analogy with the rabbinic expression *šēb və'al ta'āśeh* commends itself. The idiom, which literally means "sit and don't do," is employed to contrast a course of (in)action to a positive action that one undertakes to perform.[11] If, on the other hand, *šebet* in Prov 20:3 derives from *šbt*, it speaks in praise of one who, feeling the urge to engage in strife or perhaps having already begun to participate in such a quarrel, instead "stops," whereas the fool allows himself to get embroiled in it.

The same ambiguity is found in Exod 21:19, which specifies that an assailant is obligated to pay for his victim's "idleness" (*šibtô*). Is that the time during which the recovering person had "ceased" (*šbt*) working or the period during which he "sat" (*yšb*) at home, disabled from the assault?[12] In practice, there would be scant or no difference, but for the semantics of the root *šbt* and the implications for the history of the Sabbath, the question matters.[13]

In the previous section, we have explored one ostensibly commonsensical answer to the question of how the term *šabbāt* in reference to the weekly day of rest originated. It derived, according to this thinking, from the well-attested Biblical Hebrew verb *šābat*, which in the *qal* means to "stop," "cease," "desist," or the like and in the derived stems has the meaning one would accordingly predict, to "be brought to an end or to "bring to an end."[14] If so, *šabbāt* is analogous to the noun **mišbāt* in Lam 1:7[15] and to *šebet* in Prov 20:3, Exod 21:19, and Isa 30:7—if, that is, *šebet* is indeed from *šbt* and not from the much more common root *yšb* ("sit," "dwell," and the like) in these last three verses. It is important to note that in no instance can the verb *šābat* by itself, without a connection to the noun *šabbāt*, be taken naturally to mean anything like "rest" or "be refreshed." There is no reason to suspect any intrinsic semantic connection of this word with that for Sabbath (*šabbāt*). In cases like those we have been discussing, it simply means "stop," "cease," or the like, without sabbatical implications.

The overall picture, it turns out, is considerably more complicated. For the verb *šābat* also has a specialized and much less commonly attested meaning to "celebrate the Sabbath or a similar festal day." Thus, in the law about Yom Kippur in the liturgical calendar in Leviticus we read:

> It shall be a sabbath of complete rest (*šabbat šabbātôn*) for you, and you shall practice self-denial; on the ninth day of the month at evening, from evening to evening, you shall observe (*tišbətû*) this your sabbath (*šabbattəkem*). (Lev 23:32)

It would be senseless to translate that last phrase to mean "you shall cease / bring to an end this your sabbath." The *qal* of *šābat* means "cease" in the intransitive sense; with that meaning, it does not take an object. Rather, as often in the Hebrew Bible, what we find in this verse is a cognate accusative: the noun is of the same root as the verb. The latter in this instance means simply to observe the Sabbath—in this case, the day of rest that is Yom Kippur.

Speaking of the sabbatical year (which draws its name from this passage), the same book uses similar language two chapters later: "When you enter the land that I assign to you, the land shall observe (*wəšābətâ*) a sabbath (*šabbāt*) of the LORD" (Lev 25:2). Almost the identical idiom appears in a covenant curse in the next chapter:

> [34]Then the land shall make up for its sabbath years (*šabbətōteyhā*) throughout the time that it is desolate and you are in the land of your enemies; then shall the land rest (*tišbat*) and make up for its sabbath years (*šabbətōteyhā*). [35]Throughout the time that [the land] is desolate, it shall observe the rest (*tišbōt*) that it did not observe (*lōʾ-šābətâ*) in your sabbath years (*bəšabbətōtêkem*) while you were dwelling on it. (Lev 26:35)

The NJPS translation of *tišbat*/*tišbōt* as "rest" / "observe the rest" requires comment. It is true that, in lying fallow in the seventh year, the land "rests." But, given the absence of a clear example in which the verb means to "rest" outside of a sabbatical context[16]—very much the context of its appearance here—the rest in question must be sabbatical in these verses, too. In other words, the *qal* of *šbt* here functions as a technical term for sabbatical observance, and the sin that must be expiated is that of failing to engage in such practice. The primary violation here is thus not of rest in general but of the Sabbath in particular.

The last three passages discussed all derive from what historical scholars of the Bible call the Holiness Code (Lev 17–26[27]), about the date of which opinion is sharply divided.[17] Further complicating the issue is the fact that this collection, like all biblical sources of any substantial length, seems to have undergone a process of growth of its own; to suggest a date for the finalization of the unit as whole (with allowances, of course, for text-critical issues) or its insertion into its present location in the Pentateuch does not necessarily point us toward the date of composition of any given passage within it. If, in line with what still seems to be the majority position, we accept a postexilic date for the Holiness Code (that is, one in, or a century or so after, the late sixth century BCE), we should see in this use of the word a late and limited repurposing of the old verb *šābat* from a meaning of "to stop, cease, desist" to one of "to observe the Sabbath." The instances in which the verb clearly conveys the latter meaning are, in fact, relatively few.[18] If *šābat* could carry such a denotation early on, it is strange that this sense does not seem to have diffused widely until rabbinic times. This alone can be taken as a point in favor of a later date for the Holiness Code itself, or at least the passages within it that have been our focus here. Alternatively—but with less likelihood, in my opinion— it could be argued that the verb *šābat* in the sense "to observe the Sabbath" (whether the weekly event, the yearly holy day of Yom Kippur, or the sabbatical year) was a term of art of a particular school already in the preexilic era that, for whatever socioreligious reasons, other sources simply did not adopt.

Let us now return to the question of the origin of the noun *šabbāt*, translated (or, more accurately, transliterated) as "Sabbath." If the noun comes from *šābat*, it surely is not derived from it in the second sense that we have examined, "to observe the Sabbath," for the latter—a rare, specialized, and likely late usage—is clearly dependent upon the much more widely attested noun.[19] Rather, if *šabbāt* derives from a verb, the verb in question must be *šābat* in the first sense, "to cease, stop, desist."[20] This has the obvious strength of reflecting a root that appears in the two verses that are pretty much universally regarded as preexilic references to the "seventh day," Exod 23:12 and 34:21, both of which contain the verb *tišbōt* (rendered above as "you shall cease from labor"). At first glance, the suggestion that *šabbāt* derives from *šābat* in the sense of to "cease" makes much sense. For the word seems to be of the same pattern as those of nouns like *gannāb*, "thief" (from the verb, *gānab*, "to steal") or *haṭṭāʾ*, "sinner" (from *hāṭāʾ*, "to sin")—forms, that is, in which the doubling of the second root consonant and the lengthening of the second vowel serve to designate, as an authoritative study of Hebrew syntax puts it, an "occupation, profession, or even repeated action."[21] In that case, *šabbāt* would mean something on the order of "stopper"—one who engages professionally or repeatedly in the act of stopping.

There are, alas, both semantic and formal problems with such a derivation. From the semantic vantage point, nouns of the same pattern as *šabbāt* refer to people—thieves, sinners, or, to give other examples, judges, charioteers, horsemen, hunters, butchers, and craftsmen.[22] But *šabbāt* is not a person and does not indicate an occupation or profession. Nor can it easily be taken to involve "repeated action," for the Sabbath is hardly a day of repeated stopping. Rather, stopping occurs only once, at the point in time at which the Sabbath begins, and it is its practitioners, not the day itself, who stop working. At the risk of over-fine reasoning, we can say that they are, or were, the "stoppers," and, even so, on the seventh day itself they have already, so to speak, ceased their stopping. If they are desisting from their work while the Sabbath is already underway, they have been violating it up to that point.

As for the formal considerations, it is imperative to note the suffixed forms in which *šabbāt* appears with gemination, or doubling, of the *t*—*šabbattô* (literally, "its Sabbath," Num 28:10; Isa 66:23), *šabbattəkem* ("your Sabbath," Lev 23:32), and *šabbattâ* ("her Sabbath," Hos 2:13). For technical reasons into which we need not delve here, this suggests that the historical pattern for the word is not *qattal* (where, in conformity to the convention among Semitists, *q*, *t*, and *l* represent the three root consonants), as is the case with nouns in the same category as *gannāb*, "thief," but rather *qattalt*.[23] Having exhaustively examined the instances of the latter pattern in Biblical Hebrew, Hans Rechenmacher concludes that, for the most part, it is employed to represent bodily, mental, or spiritual defects (for example, *qaddaḥat*, "fever"; *ʿaṣṣebet*, "sorrow"; *ḥaṭṭāʾt*, "sin").[24] This is, needless to say, not a category into which *šabbāt* comfortably falls.

Fortunately, there is another alternative.

Like an increasing number of scholars over recent decades,[25] Rechenmacher, driven by these technical linguistic considerations, turns to the Akkadian word *šabattu* (or *šapattu*) as the source of the Hebrew *šabbāt*.[26] *Šabattu* refers to the day of the full moon (that is, the fifteenth of the month).[27] If the Hebrew word derives from the Akkadian, we have a natural explanation of the doubled *t* and need no longer torture ourselves with attempts to relate *šabbāt* to nouns of the *qattalt* pattern. As for the doubled *b* in *šabbāt*, Rechenmacher attributes this, reasonably enough, to the tendency in Hebrew to close unstressed syllables that have short vowels. Hence, the attested word is *šab-bāt* rather than **ša-bāt*.[28]

Particularly attractive to some scholars has been the psychological or spiritual associations of the Mesopotamian *šabattu*, as they have understood them. Here, a lexicographic list found in the library of the seventh-century BCE Assyrian king Assurbanipal has proven especially suggestive, if not always reliably so.[29] The text glosses *šabattu* as "[the gods'] day of the heart's rest" (*ūm nûḥ libbi*) and thus suggests (or so it was thought) a strong parallel with the Israelite Sabbath, on which, in one famous text, God stops (*vayyišbōt, šābat*) his creative labors on the seventh day (Gen 2:2, 3), and in connection with which words having to do with rest or spiritual refreshment are prominent, including *nāḥ/yānûᵃḥ*, a Hebrew cognate of Akkadian *nûḥ*. Consider, for example, the Sabbath commandment in the version of the Decalogue in Exodus: "Remember the Sabbath day (*yôm haššabbāt*) and keep it holy.... For in six days the LORD made heaven and earth and sea and all that is in them, and He rested (*vayyānaḥ*) on the seventh day; therefore the LORD blessed the sabbath day (*yôm haššabbāt*) and hallowed it" (Exod 20:8, 11). Unfortunately for those who wish to make this happy connection, it was pointed out already at the end of the nineteenth century that *ūm nûḥ libbi* actually refers to the appeasement or pacification of the god's anger[30]—a rather different phenomenon that we shall explore at more length toward the end of this chapter.

This is not the only problem of a semantic nature with deriving "Sabbath" (*šabbāt*) from Akkadian *šabattu*. The Sabbath, as we were at pains to stress in the previous chapter, is a weekly event; it does not correlate with the lunar cycle, or any other visible astronomical phenomenon. *Šabattu*, by contrast, is purely lunar; it designates the day of the full moon and is thus both observable visually and independent of the key number seven. For these reasons, it might seem unlikely that the ancient Israelites borrowed the Akkadian term *šabattu* as a synonym for their own distinctive institution of "the seventh day."

But, as usual, the historical and textual picture is more complicated than first seems the case. For, in a number of texts that are likely preexilic and thus relatively early as biblical literature goes, it seems at least possible and to many—perhaps most—scholars overwhelmingly likely that "Sabbath" (*šabbāt*) actually refers not to the familiar weekly event but to a monthly one, the day of the full moon, exactly like Akkadian *šabattu*. And, if that is so, these texts argue that Hebrew did indeed borrow the word, except not at first in the sense it would come to have, "the seventh day of the week."

The first example comes from the lovely and moving tale of the childless Shunammite woman whom the miracle-working prophet Elisha rewards with a son in gratitude for the aid she and her husband have extended him (2 Kgs 4:8–37). The child, alas, dies, and his mother goes to seek the prophet's assistance, much to the bewilderment of her husband:

> ²²Then she called to her husband: "Please, send me one of the servants and one of the she-asses, so I can hurry to the man of God and back."
> ²³But he said, "Why are you going to him today? It is neither new moon nor sabbath (*lō'-ḥōdeš vəlō'-šabbāt*)." She answered, "It's all right."
> ²⁴She had the ass saddled, and said to her servant, "Urge [the beast] on; see that I don't slow down unless I tell you." (2 Kgs 4:22–24)

As this artfully crafted story, full of suggestive resonances with other biblical texts, develops, the Shunammite succeeds in persuading Elisha to return to her son and, most importantly, to resurrect him from the dead, proving at the same time his own faithfulness and the boundless power of his God.[31]

For our purposes, what is curious is her husband's assumption that on the new moon and the Sabbath, it would be appropriate to undertake a journey to visit a holy man and back. Were we to assume—anachronistically—that rabbinic law (*halakhah*) was in effect at this time, we should have to judge such a journey to be a serious violation of sabbatical law, for the halakhah fixes the limit of travel on the Sabbath at 2,000 cubits, or about 3,000 feet, from the settled area.[32] Was something along these lines also in effect in biblical times? In this connection, it is interesting to note that the rabbis find a prooftext for their norm in a verse from the story of the manna in Exodus: "Let everyone remain where he is: let no one leave his place on the seventh day" (Exod 16:29b). Although it is possible to read this prohibition as pertaining only to the gathering of manna, which is the immediate context, the etiological nature of Exodus 16—the first text in the biblical narrative specifically to mention human observance of the Sabbath or to use the noun[33]—speaks against this and recommends a more general practice. Even apart from the manna narrative and its particular focus, the passages about the seventh day in the Hebrew Bible do not give us the sense that the occasion generally involved travel to a holy man or anywhere else.

Even if that is not the case and in biblical times travel on the Sabbath was thought to violate no law, the Shunammite's saddling of the ass and, to boot, instructing her servant to urge it on—meaning to run behind it, poking it with a stick or striking it with a whip—would almost certainly constitute a double violation of the day that was made special "in order that your ox and your ass may rest, and that your bondman and the stranger may be refreshed" (Exod 23:12; cf. Deut 5:14). And yet the Shunammite's husband assumes that her journey would make perfect sense on the new moon or on the "Sabbath"— if that is indeed how we are to translate *šabbāt* in 2 Kgs 4:23.[34]

Jacob L. Wright notes another point pertinent to our text. The sequence of "new moon" and "sabbath" is odd, since "Biblical authors usually begin with what occurs more frequently." If "sabbath" here refers to the weekly event, we should expect it to precede the monthly occurrence of the new moon. But in this text—and, in fact, the next three that we shall discuss—the sequence is "new moon" followed by "sabbath." If both events are monthly, the problem disappears.[35] Neither is more frequent.

It is considerations such as these that have led many modern scholars to the view that, in this and a number of other preexilic texts that we shall examine anon, the word instead designates the *šabattu*, the day of the full moon.[36] If they are right, then both days the Shunammite's husband mentions, new moon and "Sabbath," are marked by lunar phenomena and are thus monthly, and not weekly, events. In that case, for a devout person to make a pilgrimage to visit a holy man would not be so unusual. It may well have been part of the observance of these two key ancient Israelite festivals, both of which, according to the theory, eventually fell into desuetude—along with the earliest meaning of *šabbāt* in Hebrew.

We again find the conjunction of new moon and "Sabbath" in Amos 8:4–7, though, as often, we cannot assume that the passage is authored by the eighth-century prophet of that name. In this case, the fact that the text seems to interrupt an account of a prophetic vision and prediction (8:1–3, 8–10) has suggested to many scholars that it is a secondary insertion, though by whom and when the putative interpolation was made remain unknown:[37]

> [4]Listen to this, you who devour the needy,
>   annihilating (*lašbît*) the poor of the land,

⁵saying, "If only the new moon (haḥōdeš) were over,
so that we could sell grain;
the sabbath (vahaššabbāt),
so that we could offer wheat for sale,
using an *ephah* that is too small,
and a shekel that is too big,
tilting a dishonest scale,
⁶and selling grain refuse as grain!
We will buy the poor for silver,
the needy for a pair of sandals."
⁷The LORD swears by the Pride of Jacob:
"I will never forget any of their doings." (Amos 8:4–7)³⁸

As in the story of the Shunammite woman, we again find the sequence ḥōdeš/šabbāt, though here divided into separate clauses in the familiar manner of biblical parallelism. The burden of the prophetic critique is that the unscrupulous rich value the opportunity for commercial exchange with the poor—and a fraudulent exchange at that—over proper observance of these two sacred occasions. Once again, we are left wondering whether both events are lunar or the second one, šabbāt, is instead the weekly Sabbath, as it indisputably is in most occurrences in the Hebrew Bible. To those familiar with the law of the Sabbath as it develops in Judaism, the prohibition on buying and selling will sound eminently familiar and seem to lend support to the latter understanding of the term. The likelihood of this interpretation grows in light of the clear evidence for the existence of such a prohibition at least as early as the fifth century BCE, when, in Nehemiah's renewal of the covenant, the returnees from exile pledge, "The peoples of the land who bring their wares and all sorts of foodstuff for sale on the sabbath day—we will not buy from them on the sabbath or a holy day" (Neh 10:32), and Nehemiah has to lock the gates of Jerusalem and threaten violence to enforce the norm (Neh 13:15–22). His speech on this occasion includes the claim that the hardship that had been visited upon Jerusalem was owing to just such desecration of the Sabbath (vv. 17–18). The passage may echo a preachment in the book of Jeremiah, given at a gate in the same city, that associates the well-being of Jerusalem with observance of the Sabbath and, in particular, with the prohibition on carrying loads through its gates (Jer 17:19–27). Unfortunately, the date of the text in Jeremiah is open to debate; it may be contemporaneous with Nehemiah and not an antecedent, even a distant one, of the latter's speech.³⁹

But do we have any grounds on which to assume that at the time of Amos 8:4–7, the day of the full moon (the ancient Israelite šabattu, as it were) did not entail the same prohibition on working or at least a custom of ceasing from labor? After all, vv. 5–6 assume that the day of the new moon (*ḥōdeš*) did. Why should the full moon be any different? Alternatively, it is possible that we are not dealing with a full-scale cessation of labor at all but only with a taboo against commercial transactions on days—those of the new and the full moons— when cultic activity was to take precedence over the marketplace.[40] In that case, the aspiration of the exploitative merchants in Amos 8:4–7 has nothing to do with rest on the seventh day, and the seventh day is not even mentioned. What bedevils us here—and, *pace* much scholarly opinion, prevents anything approaching certainty—is that we really know nothing about the norms governing the practice of the *šabbāt* when the Hebrew term referred to the day of the full moon (if it ever did). It may well be the case that the manner of observance of the day of the full moon overlapped with that of the weekly Sabbath, thus facilitating, not incidentally, the eventual transfer of meaning of the term *šabbāt* from the middle day of the month to the seventh day of the week. And so, if there really was an ancient Israelite *šabattu*, it may be within reason to suspect that it, too, entailed abstention from commerce among other labors, thus making efforts to identify the meaning of *šabbāt* in Amos 8:5 all the more difficult.[41]

Gnana Robinson, speaking of Amos 8:4–7 in his valuable study of the origin and development of the Sabbath in the time of the Hebrew Bible, acknowledges that "the new moon and the sabbath [that is, the day of the full moon] were at this stage days on which normal business life was somewhat affected," but he still writes, "*The prophet is concerned not with the observance of the sabbath as such but with the question of justice to the poor.*"[42] This would seem, alas, to be a distinction without a difference. If "the sabbath" in v. 5 was the weekly event, it was a day that, as we shall see at length in the next chapter, was conceived relatively early as working to the benefit of society's subordinates—the slave, the stranger, and the farm animals—very much like the sabbatical year, which was seen as benefiting the poor and the wild animals (Exod 23:10–12). It is true that what attracts the prophet's attention (whether he be Amos or someone else) is the social injustice of the situation he confronted rather than the violation of ritual law per se. But what made "the sabbath" under either definition relevant here was precisely its intrinsic involvement with justice for the vulnerable.

Does that tilt the scale in favor of interpreting *šabbāt* in Amos 8:5 as referring to the seventh day and not to the middle day of the lunar month? Only if we assume that the latter was not similarly associated with humanitarian concern for the less fortunate. And yet the pairing of that word with the day of the new moon (*ḥōdeš*), or first of the month, again renders such an assumption highly dubious and for the reason we have just seen—that conducting commerce on that day, too, seems at this period to have been thought, at least in some circles, illicit and quite possibly so at least in part because it violated the humanitarian associations of the festival itself.

Some might think that the verb *lašbît*, "annihilating," in Amos 8:4 speaks for an association with the weekly Sabbath rather than the monthly day of the new moon. After all, this is a form of the verb *šābat* ("to cease, stop"), which, as we have observed, is prominent in what are almost universally identified by scholars as early texts about the seventh day and hence speaks for an identification of the *šabbāt* in the next verse with that day. Alas, this reasoning, too, is based on a false premise—namely, that the wordplay that is ubiquitous in biblical poetry (and often narrative prose) is founded upon a solid philological base. In fact, it is instead founded on phonological similarity—on the ear, not the dictionary. My favorite example of this is found in the verse that narrates the beginning of the divine response to the desperate Hagar, whose son, she believes, is about to die:

> God heard (*vayyišmaʿ ʾĕlōhîm*) the cry of the boy, and an angel (*malʾāk*) of God called to Hagar from heaven (*haššāmayim*) and said to her, "What troubles you (*ma-llāk*), Hagar? Fear not, for God (*ʾĕlōhîm*) has heeded (*šāmaʿ*) the cry of the boy where he is (*baʾăšer hûʾ šām*)." (Gen 21:17)

The repeated report that God has heard or heeded the cry of the boy obviously plays on the latter's name, *yišmāʿē(ʾ)l*, Ishmael, meaning "God heard/heeded" or "May God hear/heed!"—a name that is striking for its absence anywhere in this chapter. In that case, the phonology draws attention to and reinforces the semantics. But in the very same verse, the paronomasia that involves the term for "angel" (*malʾāk*) and the first word the angel says, "What troubles you?" (*ma-llāk*) involves no semantic dimension. Rather, this is a play between two words that are similar only in sound and lack any etymological connection. The same sort of play can be detected in the etymologically unrelated words *šāmaʿ* and *šām* at the very end of the same verse, both of which also echo *haššāmayim* (also unrelated) in its middle.[43] There is no reason to think the paronomasia of *lašbît* and *šabbāt* in Amos 8:4–5 must be different in kind from this. Unfortunately, the wordplay tells us nothing about the day on which *šabbāt* here fell. The wordplay works equally well with either understanding of the noun *šabbāt*.

Some scholars think a verse in the book named for the eighth-century prophet Hosea provides an answer to the general problem of what the pair *ḥōdeš/šabbāt* means in these texts:

> And I will end (*vəhišbattî*) all her rejoicing:
> Her festival (*ḥaggāh*), new moon (*ḥodšāh*), and sabbath (*vəšabbattāh*)—
> Each festive seasons of hers (*môʿădāh*). (Hos 2:13)[44]

On the assumption that frequency and importance stand in an inverse relationship, Hans Walter Wolff finds a "descending order" in the sequence of
festivals, new moons, and sabbaths. Thus, he argues, the last item "can hardly
be understood as the day of the full moon." Instead, as a common—that is,
weekly—occurrence, it "is mentioned last before various other, not especially
important festivals." To Wolff, the term "festival" actually refers to "the week-
long main festival of the year in celebration of the vintage," the fall holiday
later known as Sukkot, or Booths.[45] So, the descending pattern would go from
annual ("festival"), to monthly ("new moon"), to weekly ("sabbath").

It is not at all clear, however, that the little list of special days in Hos 2:13
exhibits a pattern of increasing frequency or decreasing importance.[46] "Each
festive season of hers" (môʿădāh) may well refer to all the annual occasions,
including the supposedly most important one in the fall, and if it does, then
the verse ends, as it began, with the least frequent events. Note that môʿēd,
translated above as "festive season," appears in the two headings to the most
comprehensive liturgical calendar in the Hebrew Bible, Leviticus 23:

> [1]The LORD spoke to Moses, saying: [2]Speak to the Israelite people and
> say to them:
> These are My fixed times, the fixed times of the LORD, which you
> shall proclaim as sacred occasions.
> [3]On six days work may be done, but on the seventh day there shall
> be a sabbath of complete rest, a sacred occasion. You shall do no work;
> it shall be a sabbath of the LORD throughout your settlements.
> [4]These are the fixed times of the LORD, the sacred occasions which
> you shall celebrate each at its appointed time: [5]In the first month, on the
> fourteenth day of the month, at twilight, there shall be a Passover offer-
> ing to the LORD, and on the fifteenth day of that month the LORD's Feast
> of Unleavened Bread. You shall eat unleavened bread for seven days.
> (Lev 23:1–5)[47]

In the first of these, the word immediately introduces the Sabbath, which is
there explicitly said to be the weekly event (vv. 2–3), but the repetition of the
heading in v. 4 suggests that the Sabbath in the previous verse is the result of
interpolation, of which the goal is obvious: to include the Sabbath in that list
of festivals. That second heading (v. 4) prefaces a list of all the annual events,
"the set times (môʿădê) of the LORD." This suggests, in turn, the possibility
that "each festive season of hers (môʿădāh)" in Hos 2:13 might also refer to the
annual celebrations, possibly but not necessarily inclusive of a weekly sabbath.
In short, Wolff's assumption of an ascending order of frequency and descending order of importance in this verse is far from established, and the notion

that "sabbath" (*vəšabbattāh*) in this verse must of necessity be the familiar weekly event and not the day of the full moon cannot be sustained. The truth is once again that we simply do not know which it is. Nor, for reasons already given in our discussion of Amos 8:4, does the wordplay on the verb "to end" (*vəhišbattî*) with Sabbath (*šabbāt*) in Hos 2:13 resolve the issue.

In the case of a memorable oracle in the Book of Isaiah, however, there seems to be more basis for determining whether we are dealing with the monthly day of the full moon or the weekly Sabbath:

> [12]That you come to appear before Me—
> Who asked that of you?
> Trample my courts [13]no more;
> Bringing oblations is futile,
> Incense is offensive to Me.
> New moon (*hōdeš*) and sabbath (*vəšabbāt*),
> Proclaiming of solemnities,
> Assemblies with iniquity,
> I cannot abide. (Isa 1:12–13)

These verses convey one of Isaiah's main messages—that ritual observances in the absence of justice, especially justice for the less fortunate members of society, are worse than useless: far from pleasing the Deity, as they are supposed to, they offend him. In the case of pilgrimages to the Temple, an institution with which the prophet is closely associated (Isa 6), it would be better, given the dismal moral status of Israelite society, if these visits simply did not take place. What is potentially significant for our purposes in the excerpted passage is the apparent assumption that such events took place on the new moon and "sabbath," that on those days people made personal appearances in the LORD's temple, trampling His courts, as the prophet sarcastically puts it. But did such a practice actually exist?

The schedule of sacrifices in Numbers 28 includes special offerings the officiating priests were to make on the Sabbath and new moon (in that order; vv. 9–15) but nothing about personal appearances by the laity in the Temple (or, given the notion that this chapter is cast as announced to Moses, the Tabernacle) on either of these days is mentioned. If such an appearance is indeed assumed in Isa 1:12–13, the text recalls the question the Shunammite woman's husband posed when she was about to leave to visit the miracle-working prophet, Elisha: "Why are you going to him today? It is neither new moon nor sabbath (*lō'-hōdeš vəlō'-šabbāt*)" (2 Kgs 4:23). It might thus be argued that in the background of both passages there stands a custom or expectation of travel on the "sabbath." And that, as we saw in the case of the story of the

Shunammite and Elisha, appears to violate the norms of the Sabbath, at least as they were eventually to develop—if, that is, *šabbāt* here refers to the seventh day of the week and not to a monthly event, the day of the full moon. If such reasoning is sound—and we shall assess later whether it is—the latter possibility would thus actually seem the likelier. In that case, Isa 1:13 refers to a monthly, not a weekly, occasion.

The same notion of a pilgrimage to Jerusalem, but this time on a more universal scale, appears in the last chapter of the book of Isaiah in a section of the book that would seem to date from after the Babylonian Exile had come to an end (late sixth century BCE), perhaps even substantially later. On the assumption, long and widely (though not universally) held by critical scholars, that Isaiah consists, *grosso modo*, of three compositions (1–39; 40–55; 56–66), this last section has come to be called "Third Isaiah." Here are the relevant verses:

> 22For as the new heaven and the new earth
> Which I will make
> Shall endure by My will
> —declares the LORD—
> So shall your seed and your name endure.
> 23And new moon after new moon (*ḥōdeš baḥodšô*),
> And sabbath after sabbath (*šabbāt bašabbattô*),
> All flesh shall come to worship Me
> —said the LORD. (Isa 66:22–23)

The envisioning of a pilgrimage of this sort and this scale is characteristic of a number of passages from the early postexilic or later periods.[48] In visions of redemption from the travails of the Exile, passages in different parts of the book of Isaiah predict that the nations will personally return the exiled Israelites to their homeland in what seems like a ritual procession (e.g., Isa 11:11–12; 49:22–23).[49] A prophecy in the book of Zechariah (though in a section generally thought to date from the Persian or Hellenistic period) goes further. Instead of a one-time event, it speaks of yearly pilgrimage of all nations to celebrate the Feast of Booths (Zech 14:16–19). Though its relationship, if any, to the Zechariah passage is unclear, the passage above from Isaiah goes further still. It envisions not an annual but a monthly and even a weekly appearance of "all flesh" in the LORD's Temple—if, that is, "sabbath after sabbath" refers to the seventh day of the week.

Might "sabbath after sabbath" in Isa 66:23, however, instead refer again to the day of the full moon in the middle of the lunar month? Against this stands formidable evidence from elsewhere in Third Isaiah for the importance of the Sabbath in language that strongly suggests the weekly event—the language of "observing" (Isa 56:2; cf. Deut 5:12), for example, of "covenant" (Isa 56:4, 6; cf. Exod 31:16), of "holiness" (Isa 58:13; cf. Exod 16:23), or, finally, of the prohibition on "profaning" the day (Isa 56:2, 6; cf. Exod 31:14; Ezek 20:21). None of this language appears in connection with the four short texts above in which we have found reason to suspect—and no more than a reasonable suspicion is possible—that *šabbāt* denotes the monthly rather than the weekly event.[50] It would seem unlikely that the same source (Third Isaiah) would deploy the word in both senses.

To find a reference to *šabbāt* in the sense of the day of the full moon in a postexilic text also runs afoul of the assumption, now common in the scholarly literature, that such a usage was strictly preexilic, so that by the time of Third Isaiah, the word *šabbāt* had come to refer exclusively to the seventh day of the week, a sense that it supposedly lacked earlier.[51] It is incontestable that Hebrew *šabbāt* as a designation of the day of the full moon eventually fell out of the Hebrew language just as the observance of the day itself fell out of the religion of Israel (if, that is, either of these had ever been a reality). But the conclusion that the word came to designate the seventh day only at a historically late period assumes vastly more confidence in our ability to date biblical passages than the empirical evidence warrants. Hence, though the notion of a pilgrimage on the weekly Sabbath fits rather poorly with what we know of sabbatical practice in ancient Israel and early (or, for that matter, later) Judaism, it is probably preferable to conclude that Isa 66:22–23 refers to the weekly, not the old monthly, event. But certainty is again not possible.

Finally, another logical possibility, a mediating one that we shall discuss later in this chapter, bears mention here as well. It could be that not only the word for the day of the full moon (*šabbāt*, from *šabattu*) but also some of its observances came to apply to the seventh day, at least as imagined in prophetic visions of the coming redemption. In that case—necessarily a highly hypothetical one, given the scarcity of evidence—Isa 66:22–23 is speaking about the weekly event in colors drawn from its monthly namesake.

In this chapter, we have been seeking to understand the origins of the Hebrew word for "Sabbath" (*šabbāt*). On the reasonable conjecture that the earliest attestations of the weekly celebration use a different term, "the seventh day," which was largely (but not totally) replaced by "Sabbath," we have inquired into the original meaning of the latter term. We found that in the minds of many scholars, it seems unlikely for both formal and semantic reasons that the word is derived from the Hebrew verb *šābat*, to "stop, cease," despite the prominence of that word in early texts about the seventh day. It is, they argue, more probable that the noun *šabbāt* descended from the Akkadian *šabattu*/*šapattu*, the name of the day of the full moon, which fell on the fifteenth of the month.[52] This then led us to ask whether in some passages in the Hebrew Bible itself *šabbāt* has not been misunderstood as the weekly Sabbath rather than the monthly event that the noun, or at least its Akkadian etymon, originally denoted. We found four examples and conceivably a fifth in which a strong, but by no means overwhelming, case can be made that it did.

This, in turn, raises the larger question of how the term for the lunar event could have come to apply to the weekly one, to the last day, that is, of a regularly recurring seven-day calendrical unit. Here, although we are again reduced to speculation, as often when scholars seek to recover lost processes and practices, it is important to bear in mind that some speculations are better grounded than others.

In the case at hand, we should begin by recalling a point that we made earlier in this chapter, that nothing in the phrasing of the early texts we have mentioned (Exod 23:12 and 34:21) requires that "the seventh day" on which labor was to cease was as yet standardized throughout the society. In other words, the commandment was to cease from labor after six days; there was nothing that entailed that all communities, households, or individuals begin and cease their work on the same days. A seven-day unit (along with holidays) defined their work life, but there may not originally have been a nationally synchronized week. If an arrangement like this seems hard to imagine, it would be instructive to remember that the standardization of time is largely a product of modern transportation (especially the railroad) and communications. In the United States, for example, the establishment of different time zones dates to the late nineteenth century, and only in 1918 did Congress pass the Standard Time Act.[53] Even now, Jews observing the Sabbath in the United States, France, Israel, and Australia cannot be fully synchronized in their practice, even though, to be sure, none of them is celebrating the day on what is, say, Wednesday for another. The question of whether something happened on the Sabbath depends on where it happened and cannot be answered in the absolute, as it were. The analogy is far from perfect, of course, since the modern variation is owing to observable astronomical events and not merely social convention. I cite it simply to underscore the fact that the expectation of uniformity in the measurement of time is less natural than it might first appear today and would not have seemed at all inevitable in a subsistence agrarian economy like that of ancient Israel.

The same cannot be said for the days of the new moon (*ḥōdeš*) or full moon (*šabattu/šapattu/šabbāt*). These were fixed in the heavens, readily identified throughout ancient Israelite society by visible phenomena. As we saw in our discussion of Amos 8:4–7, however, if *šabbāt* there refers to the day of the full moon, there were probably substantial overlaps between the two holidays, the seventh day and the monthly *šabbāt* (and probably also between these two and the day of the new moon). Commerce seems to have been forbidden on each—on "the seventh day" because it involved work, not only for the house-holders but for their servants and pack animals as well, and on the lunar *šabbāt* perhaps for the same reason or perhaps because commerce, like farm work, prevented people from participating in the rites that characterized the day of the full moon. The latter was, after all, a holiday, according to this theory, and no holiday can retain its character and its social force very well or very long if it does not interrupt and supersede the workaday routine. So, some assimilation of the two regularly recurring events is to be expected, just as in biblical litera-ture the term *šabbātôn*, clearly related to *šabbāt* and translated as "complete rest" or the like, came to describe not only the weekly Sabbath but also the first day of the seventh month (later named Rosh ha-Shanah and understood as a new year's festival), the Day of Atonement, and the first and last days of the fall pilgrimage festival of Sukkot (Booths).[54] In other words, just as these festivals became, or always were, sabbatical in character, it is likely that the day of the full moon and the seventh day manifested similarities that grew over time, though without the two sacred occasions collapsing into each other. In other words, I can imagine—again, the nature of the evidence makes conjecture unavoidable—that, just as later on various holidays came to be described by the term *šabbātôn*, so did the term *šabbāt*, originally referring to the day of the full moon, come to apply to the seventh day of the week as well.

Also facilitating the process of semantic transfer in all likelihood was the longstanding use of the verb Hebrew *šābat*, "to stop, cease," in connection with what one is to do on "the seventh day," as in Exod 23:12 and 34:21.[55] The simi-larity of this word to *šabbāt* (<*šabattu*), the name of the day of the full moon according to the regnant theory, could have served as a catalyst in that transfer of meaning from the monthly to the weekly event, yielding the sense the term has in most of the Hebrew Bible and, of course, in subsequent Jewish tradition. The seventh day and the Sabbath thus became synonymous.

Whether that identification happened before or after the synchronization of the seventh day across households and communities is a question beyond reasonable speculation. As for the question of what factors brought about the synchronization itself, though, some answers readily suggest themselves. "It would not be surprising if the seven-day cycles from different individu-als and communities converged over time," notes Wright. "This convergence would have been driven in part by the need to agree on a common calendar to attend to mercantile, organizational, and cultic matters."[56] To this, one might add that the increasing consciousness of tribal and then national identity would naturally have aided such a process of standardization across the lines of local communities. In particular, the emergence of a united kingdom of Judah and Israel around 1000 BCE, with all the change this entailed for administration, taxation, and conscription, surely must have weakened local tradition to some extent, however uneven the process. The breakup of this arrangement into the separate kingdoms of Israel and Judah some two generations later (itself a powerful remanifestation of regional identity) resulted in two states but not a reversion to the premonarchical situation. Evidence that kings could be involved in setting the dates of holidays can be found in the account of King Jeroboam I of Israel, who "established a festival on the fifteenth day of the eighth month" (1 Kgs 12:32), a month later, that is, than one would expect based on the surviving (Judahite) calendars, though, interestingly, still on the full moon.[57] So, alongside the natural tendency of holidays to influence, and even to assimilate into, one another, we must also reckon with the real possibility that political factors played a role in synchronizing the various sequences of six days followed by the special seventh and perhaps also in bringing about the renaming of the special day as *šabbāt*, the Sabbath.

Before we assess the proposal that *šabbāt* ("Sabbath") in preexilic biblical texts refers not to the weekly event that the term has long denoted but rather to the day of the full moon on the fifteenth of the lunar month, it will be useful to explore tantalizing implications of this now old theory that have been unjustly forgotten.

One of the first scholars to explore the theory in any depth was Morris Jastrow Jr. (1861–1921). Like others before him, Jastrow drew attention to the last two words in the Akkadian term used to gloss *šabattu* as "[the gods'] day of the heart's rest" (*ūm nûḫ libbi*). We should not, he insisted, be misled by the fact that *nûḫ* is, as we have noted, cognate with the Hebrew verb *nāḥ/yānûªḥ*, "to rest," employed in one version of the Decalogue to describe what God did after six days of creation (Exod 20:11). For the idiom "did not at all convey the notion of cessation of labors" but actually "was a standing expression—almost a technical term—[for] the pacification of the deity's anger."[58] This then leads Jastrow to ask a bold question: "Can the Hebrew Sabbath have originally been an *ūm nûḫ libbî*, a day of propitiation or atonement, a day of rest for [the LORD] instead of a day of rest enjoined by [the LORD]?"[59]

The question may at first seem absurd. For the Sabbath in Judaism is far from a day associated with God's anger or even with the cessation of God's anger. As even a casual look at the traditional Sabbath liturgy (especially the table songs) readily shows, it is—at least ideally—a day of joy, celebration, tranquility, fellowship, and renewal. Nor, clearly, was this an innovation of the classical rabbis. Already in Third Isaiah, we see the Sabbath described in intensely positive terms, with no hint that it was associated with propitiation or atonement:

> [13]If you refrain from trampling the sabbath,
> From pursuing your affairs on My holy day;
> If you call the sabbath "delight,"
> The LORD's holy day "honored";
> And if you honor it and go not your ways
> Nor look to your affairs, nor strike bargains—
> [14]Then you can seek the favor of the LORD.
> I will set you astride the heights of the earth,
> And let you enjoy the heritage of your father Jacob—
> For the mouth of the LORD has spoken. (Isa 58:13–14)

In the background of these words there is, to be sure, an element of divine anger, whether that has anything to do with the Mesopotamian *šapattu*, as Jastrow thought or not. The anger was provoked by the community's failure to seek God and follow his ways, a failure manifested in their fasting "in strife and contention" rather than "fasting" as God desires—by performing acts of justice and compassion toward the oppressed, the vulnerable, and their own kinsmen (Isa 58:4–7). But in the verses quoted above, the Sabbath does not serve as reparation for those ethical failures; it is instead a thoroughly positive consequence of their having been remedied or a promise that will come into effect when they have at last been corrected. As the verses immediately preceding its mention make clear, the Sabbath is associated with victory, restoration, and the protective presence of the LORD (vv. 8–12)—all very positive things and as far in tone from propitiation and atonement as can be.

In Jastrow's thinking, however, Isaiah 58:13–14 indicates a new situation. It marks a transition from the Sabbath (originally, in his reconstruction, the fifteenth of the month) as a day of "the pacification of the deity's anger" to the one of delight and honor and the like familiar from subsequent Jewish tradition.[60] For the fast that the nameless prophet denounces a few verses earlier (vv. 1–7) was indeed intended, as biblical fasts are, to attract God's attention and favor by observing "a day when the LORD is favorable" (v. 5). Although it may at first seem that the point of the rebuke is to underscore the importance of social ethics to fast days, the wording suggests something more radical: a doing away with fasts altogether and a repurposing of the word to refer to deeds of lovingkindness instead:[61]

> [6]No, this is the fast I desire:
> To unlock the fetters of wickedness,
> And untie the cords of the yoke
> To let the oppressed go free;
> To break off every yoke.

⁷It is to share your bread with the hungry,
And to take the wretched poor into your home;
When you see the naked, to clothe him,
And not to ignore your own kin. (Isa 58:6–7)

Jastrow, the son of a rabbi, observes that "it has been customary to interpret [the prophet's] words as a sermon appropriate to the Day of Atonement."[62] The reason is not hard to find. In Jewish tradition, Isa 57:14–58:14 is the *haftarah*, or prophetic lection, for the morning of Yom Kippur (the Day of Atonement). The Torah portion with which it is paired is Leviticus 16, the passage about the rites of purification and expiation performed on that solemn day.[63] Given the traditional importance to Yom Kippur both of fasting and of repentance (neither of which is literally mentioned in Leviticus 16), it makes great sense to pair a description of the rituals of the day with a biting critique of those who reverently practice penitential rites while ignoring the ethical claims of the afflicted. In this way, the indispensability of both purification and expiation, on the one hand, and ethical responsibility and moral reform, on the other, is powerfully driven home, as beautifully befits Yom Kippur in its rabbinic formulation.

Jastrow goes on to note, however, that the prophetic author of Isaiah 58 "makes no mention of this day, whereas, after denouncing the futility of supposing mere abstention from food to be pleasing in the sight of the deity, he introduces, and evidently with intent, the Sabbath (vs. 13)."[64] In other words, as Jastrow understands the passage, the shift reflected here is not one from the Day of Atonement to the Sabbath but rather one from the Sabbath as a day of atonement to the Sabbath as a day of joy and celebration. "The so-called Puritanical Sabbath, solemn, austere, and devoid of all merry-making... represents the consistent result of the old Hebrew Sabbath viewed as a day of propitiation and atonement," he argues, whereas the newer situation, which endures in Judaism, is one in which the Sabbath is, as Isaiah 58 puts it, a "delight" (*ōneg*, v. 13).[65] In the Talmud, that very word from the same verse would be cited to authorize feasting on the Sabbath.[66] Indeed, the norm that develops in rabbinic tradition is for Jews to eat three meals on the Sabbath, one more than during the other six days of the week.[67]

The notion of the Sabbath as an occasion not only of propitiation and atonement but also of fasting will thus strike contemporary Jews, including those who are Sabbath-observant, as foreign in the extreme—perhaps a reality in distant antiquity but surely one that rabbinic Judaism, from which all modern forms of the religion descend, purged altogether. In a fascinating study, however, Yitzhak D. Gilat presents powerful evidence for the survival of fasting on the Sabbath into and even beyond the Talmudic period.[68] To understand just how tenacious this ascetic understanding of the Sabbath was—quite apart from Jastrow's derivation of it from the *šabattu*—we should take the time to examine some of the evidence.[69]

We begin with literature that dates from the Second Temple period but was composed later than Isaiah 58 and its polemic against fasting and in favor of a conception of the Sabbath as a day of "delight" (v. 13). In the last chapter of the book of Jubilees, an exceedingly important text from the second century BCE (though noncanonical in the ongoing Jewish tradition), we find a substantial listing of what is required and what is forbidden on the Sabbath. To anyone familiar with biblical and rabbinic texts, most of these items, and the denunciations of those who violate them, are unremarkable. An exception, however, is the mandate that anyone "who fasts . . . on the Sabbath day . . . is to die."[70] In another book from the same general period, Judith, we read this about the time after the eponymous heroine's husband had passed away:

> She fasted all the days of her widowhood, except the day before the sabbath and the sabbath itself, the day before the new moon and the day of the new moon, and the festivals and days of rejoicing of the house of Israel. (Jdt 8:6, NRSV)

Would Jubilees include the prohibition upon fasting among its short list of possible transgressions of the day if no one were inclined to violate its assumed norm? Would the author of Judith have mentioned that its heroine suspended her fasting on joyous holidays, including the Sabbath, if there were no one who did otherwise? Perhaps so, but the suspicion grows that there may have been a competing tradition in which fasting on the Sabbath was mandatory or at least commendable.

In point of fact, Gilat quotes a number of Gentile Greco-Roman authors from the first century BCE through the second CE, including Strabo, Petronius, Martial, and Suetonius, who describe the Jews as fasting on their Sabbath. He also points out ways in which scholars have sought to explain away this supposed misperception—by attributing it to an unjustified inference from the veridical fact that observant Jews do not light fires, cook, or bake on the Sabbath, for example, or to the classical authors' confusing the Sabbath with the Day of Atonement (*yôm hakkippûrîm*), the one fast day in the Jewish liturgical calendar on which sabbatical law applies.[71] But, as Gilat shows at length, there is also internal Jewish evidence—in fact, rabbinic evidence—for the practice of fasting on the Sabbath.

Consider as an illustration this report about a Babylonian sage of the fourth century CE:

Mar son of Ravina would fast the entire year, except for the Feast of Weeks, Purim, and the eve of Yom Kippur: the Feast of Weeks because it is the day the Torah was given; Purim [because] it is written [days of] "feasting and merrymaking" (Esth 9:22); and the eve of Yom Kippur because Ḥiyya son of Rav from Difti [said], "'you shall practice self-denial on the ninth of the month' (Lev 23:32)—Do people fast on the ninth of the month? Rather, this is to tell you that Scripture accounts anyone who eats and drinks on the ninth as if he had fasted on the ninth and the tenth." (b. Pesaḥ. 68b)

At first, the report of Mar son of Ravina's ascetic practice recalls that of Judith quoted above. Both make exceptions to their fasting on joyous festivals. ("Fasting" in such cases probably involved eating a bit in the evening, like the minor fast days of the Jewish calendar to this day or the Muslim Ramadan.) Unlike Judith, however, the Talmudic sage made no exception for the Sabbath.[72] Gilat rejects various traditionalist interpretations that seek to limit the scope of the ancient sage's fasting in order to bring it into harmony with normative practice. Instead, Gilat forcefully argues that Mar adhered to an alternative position, attested in the names of other rabbinic authorities as well, that allowed for, or even encouraged, fasting on the Sabbath in order to devote oneself to the study of the sacred sources.[73]

If so, it turns out that the putatively confused Greco-Roman authors were more in touch with the empirical reality than those Jewish scholars—ancient, medieval, or modern—who seek to deny that the Sabbath was ever an occasion for ascetic or penitential practice but was instead always the day of "delight" ('ōneg) that Isa 58:13 wanted it to be. The mistake, however, would not have occurred had the direction of historical development not been toward treating the day as one of joy and feasting rather than atonement and self-denial. Eventually, Gilat writes, Jewish sabbatical law reached a kind of compromise.[74] The Shulchan Arukh (1565 CE), the most authoritative code of Jewish law, stipulates that any fasting that takes place must conclude before the sixth hour of the halakhic day.[75] And in many traditional sources, it is clear beyond doubt that devotion to the study of the sacred sources, on the one hand, and liberal consumption of food and drink, on the other, are of the essence of the seventh day. As the creative exegesis of Isa 58:13 in a (probably) early medieval midrashic collection puts it:

"Remember the sabbath day and keep it holy" (Exod 20:8). By what means do you keep it holy? By means of scripture, Mishnah, food, drink, and rest. For everyone who treats the Sabbath as a delight (məʾannēg)—it is as if he brings delight (məʾannēg) to Him Who Spoke and the

Universe Came into Being, as it is said, "If you call the sabbath 'delight' (*ŏneg*), / The LORD's holy day 'honored' (*məkubbād*)" (Isa 58:13). In other words, if you call the Sabbath 'delight,' it is the Holy One, the LORD, whom you honor (*məkabbēd*). (S. Eli. Rab. 24)[76]

Whether the ascetic practices attested in Second Temple and rabbinic Judaism represent the survival of the Israelite version of the Mesopotamian *šabattu* that Morris Jastrow reconstructed is quite doubtful—for one thing, the text he quotes seems to be the only piece of evidence for it[77]—as is, we must add, the existence of the Israelite *šabattu* itself. It is surely conceivable (whether historically the case or not) that the weekly Sabbath, at least in some circles, was a day of self-denial that was eventually transformed into a day of joy and celebration, quite apart from the Mesopotamian *šabattu*. But Jastrow also connected the Sabbath in his hypothesized Babylonian and earlier Israelite understanding with the days of ill omen (Akkadian, *ūmū lemnutū*) attested in some Mesopotamian sources and sometimes said to fall on the seventh, fourteenth, and twenty-eighth days of the month and sometimes on the nineteenth and twenty-first as well, which will be discussed at more length in our next chapter.[78] The multiples of seven are indeed suggestive to anyone interested in the origins of the Israelite Sabbath, although the presence of the nineteenth in the sequence may be a warning not to make too close a connection between the two calendrical events.[79] Also critical to remember is the simple fact that more than seven days intervene between the twenty-eighth of any lunar month and the seventh of the next, as we shall have occasion to observe again. To these demurrals, some scholars might add another, that the Sabbath understood as the familiar weekly event of joy and celebration seems unlikely to have originated as an inauspicious day, Mesopotamian or other.

In reply to this last objection, however, Jastrow has already given a response. He is arguing not for total continuity between the Israelite/Jewish Sabbath and the Mesopotamian *šabattu* or the days of ill omen but rather for a revalorization of the older institution. On this reading, prohibitions originally intended as precautions against untoward events have been reinterpreted as positive manifestations of Godlike rest. "The emphasis laid at a later period upon cessation from labor, which was originally merely one feature of many," he wrote, "... permitted and suggested an interpretation of the precautionary rites prescribed for those occasions that obscured their original import."[80]

In point of fact, the divide between the sacred and the taboo is less than may at first seem the case, and the idea that something could fall into both categories at once is not unlikely. The same uncanny force that results in calamity for the one who violates an interdiction can also bestow good fortune for the one who obeys it. "An intimate connection between the holy and the repugnant,"

Robert North remarked, "is observable in the biblical ordinances; *reverence* in most languages is merely a derivative of *fear*; the Latin *sacer* means also 'accursed,' and the Arabic *ḥaram* is equally applied to shameful or venerable things."[81]

The biblical evidence amply supports North's application of this point to the matter at hand. The sanctity of the Sabbath in its classical and familiar sense as the seventh day of the week is something that must be guarded, as the wording in the Deuteronomic Decalogue makes clear: "Observe (*šāmôr*) the Sabbath day to keep it holy" (Deut 5:12). For those who fail to protect—another nuance of the same Hebrew verb—the sanctity of the seventh day, or, to use the biblical idiom, who "profane" it, the same strictures can spell ill fortune in the extreme. Exodus 31, for example, specifies death as their punishment (vv. 14–15). Is it surprising, then, that norms that protect from death should be deemed sacred, and the day defined by these norms viewed as set apart for the Deity? Or, to state the identical point in the reverse, is it surprising that to violate norms that define a day as sacred to the Deity would be seen as a taboo that results in the worst possible fortune? The covenantal monotheism that was increasingly prominent over the history of ancient Israelite religion makes the connection even likelier.[82] For surely if the negative consequences of violating a particular day were ascribed to the displeasure of the one God, then the positive consequences of upholding the day would be ascribed to the selfsame God—the sole author of the blessings and the curses of covenant alike.

Jastrow, thinking of the *šabattu*, writes, "An ûm nûḫ libbî, or day of propitiation and atonement, occupies an intermediate position between a 'favorable' and an 'unfavorable' day."[83] In the case of the Israelite and Jewish *šabbāt*, however, the day is, on Jastrow's reasoning, not—or at least long ago ceased to be—one of propitiation teetering between favor and disfavor. Instead, it was, or became, a favorable day, a "delight" in the words of Isa 58:13, but it retains that character only to the extent that the Israelite/Jewish community practices it, guarding it from the desecration that spoils it and threatens them at the same time. Whatever roots the Jewish Sabbath may have had in the *šabattu* and whatever ascetic characteristics it retained in some circles even in late antiquity, "the so-called Puritanical Sabbath" to which Jastrow referred is lightyears away from the day of joy, rest, and tranquility that the ongoing Jewish tradition continues to designate with the word *šabbāt*.[84]

We have devoted most of our attention in this chapter to the hypothesis that the Hebrew word for the Sabbath (*šabbāt*) derives from an Akkadian term (*šabattu*) for the fifteenth of the month, the day of the full moon. The hypothesis, as we have seen, involves far more than a point of etymology. For in its minimal form, the claim associated with this derivation is that only fairly late in the history of biblical Israel did the institution of the "seventh day" on which labor was forbidden come to be called *šabbāt*. In the most literal sense, the "Sabbath" is thus a postexilic phenomenon. But what about references to *šabbāt* in preexilic literature? Here, the hypothesis goes, we are dealing not with the weekly day of cessation of labor at all but rather with the *šabattu*, a monthly rather than a weekly holiday that, since the monthly event vanished from Jewish memory but the weekly one survives, has for millennia been mistranslated as "Sabbath."

In its more maximal form, the derivation of *šabbāt* from *šabattu* serves as a foundation for attributing much of the character of the Israelite weekly Sabbath to the influence of the older Babylonian day of the full moon. Here, the key point is that the *šabattu* was a day of propitiation and atonement in the face of the god's anger, an ill-starred occasion on which various ordinary activities should not be undertaken lest they fail and, worse, bring catastrophe upon those who perform them. The shift from such a negative occasion to the day of light and joy that Jews have long known as *šabbāt* occurred, in this reconstruction, only fairly late; traces of the older pattern, such as the now-defunct practice of fasting on the Sabbath, survived long after the profound shift in the general tone of the holiday had occurred.

I have been using the term "hypothesis" to refer to this derivation of Hebrew *šabbāt* from Akkadian *šabattu* and the closely related claim that, in preexilic texts, the Hebrew term, too, refers to the day of the full moon and not to the "seventh day," as becomes the case later. The fact is, however, that the consensus in favor of this claim is now so extensive that many scholars would doubtless balk at the use of the term "hypothesis" to characterize it. In a recent study, Reinhard Achenbach, for example, simply commences his discussion with the matter-of-fact statement that "in ancient Israel the new moon at the beginning of every new month and the *Shabbat* day at the full moon were regularly celebrated."[85] Still more recently, Julia Rhyder identifies the claim in question as one to which "the majority of scholars" would assent.[86] She is correct, and we should not be surprised that Achenbach is not alone in simply presenting the idea as if it is established fact.

Despite the strength of the consensus, however, there are dissenters, and it will be worthwhile to examine their arguments.[87]

Etymologically, it is not impossible that the noun *šabbāt* derives from the verb *šābat*, "to cease, stop" after all. The prominence of the verb in the two texts about "the seventh day" that the consensus dates to the preexilic period (Exod 23:12; 34:21) is striking. This is not to claim that *šābat* there has the specialized meaning "to celebrate the Sabbath / another holy day;" as we argued, it rather clearly does not. But the notion that it echoes an alternative name for "the seventh day" cannot be dismissed. There are, after all, other verbs in bibli-cal Hebrew that mean "to cease (from an activity), stop (doing something)," such as ʿāmad, ḥādal, and herpâ.[88] It seems unlikely to be coincidence that these verbs do not appear in Exod 23:12 and 34:21 but one that uses the same three consonants as the putatively postexilic name for the seventh day does. As often in the Hebrew Bible, we may be dealing with sophisticated wordplay here. If so, then minimally this attests to the existence of the noun šabbāt at the time those two verses were composed, regardless of the scientific etymology of the word. The fact that šabbāt is not attested as clearly and explicitly syn-onymous with "the seventh day" in what is generally accepted to be preexilic literature may be an accident of what has survived. "The seventh day" in this sense is itself sparsely attested.

As we have noted, the form šabbāt, with the doubling of the second con-sonant, corresponds to nouns that denote an "occupation, profession, or even repeated action,"[89] and the Sabbath does not fit comfortably into any of those three categories. Furthermore, the doubling of the final root consonant (t), which is apparent in suffixed forms, is another anomaly. Against this, it might be argued, nonetheless, that the Sabbath (šabbāt) does indeed cause the activity of stopping (šābat), just as a thief (gannāb) causes the activity of stealing (gānab). The analogy may not be perfect or the formation perfectly rule-governed, but language seldom is either of those things, and anyone who has even dabbled in word histories knows that the existence of unpredictable forms is not infrequent. As for the extra t, Ernst Haag, attributes this to the use of the feminine to provide an element of semantic abstraction.[90] Even so, the form is anomalous, but so is the claim that a monthly event, defined by the phase of the moon, came to denote a weekly event, defined independently of any astronomical phenomena. The word šabbāt, in other words, like the insti-tution it came to denote (or always did denote), is odd, and the oddity may be displaced, but is hardly eliminated, by the hypothesized derivation from Akkadian šabattu.

None of this is to deny that the day of the full moon may have had a signifi-cant meaning in biblical Israel that it eventually lost. According to the elabo-rate and mathematically precise liturgical calendar of Leviticus 23, the paschal offering is made at twilight on the fourteenth of the first month; the ensuing Feast of Unleavened Bread begins on the fifteenth; and, similarly, the Feast of Booths begins on the fifteenth of the seventh month (Lev 23:5–6, 34).[91] Inter-estingly, a later holiday, Purim, or the Festival of Lots, falls on the fourteenth of the twelfth month, except for Jews living in the Persian capital of Shushan, who celebrate it on the fifteenth (Esth 9:17–19).[92] As we shall see in the next chapter, in Second Temple and Rabbinic Judaism still other significant calen-drical occasions take place on the fifteenth of the month.[93] But even in the

Hebrew Bible, we find two references to an event known as the *kēseh* or *kēse'*, which seems to have been the day of the full moon. In Ps 81:4, the parallelism clearly indicates that this was a festive event: "Blow the horn on the new moon (*ḥōdeš*), / on the full moon (*kēseh*) for our feast day (*ḥaggēnû*)." Whether *kēseh* is a monthly event is unclear. Gerhard Hasel argues that it denotes instead an annual feast that falls on the new moon and refers his readers to the commentary of Mitchell Dahood, who suggested, in turn, that the feast in question is either Unleavened Bread or Booths.[94] For our purposes, what is significant is that in neither of its attestations (the other is Prov 7:20) is *kēseh/kēse'* identified with *šabbāt*. If the consensus among scholars is correct that the rare word denotes the day of the full moon, or the fifteenth of the month, then Biblical Hebrew had a term for that significant occasion, and it was not, or not only, *šabbāt*.

Does the sequence "new moon (*ḥōdeš*) and full moon (*kēseh*)" in Ps 81:4 provide, however, some evidence that *šabbāt* in the four preexilic texts that we discussed earlier also refers to the fifteenth of the month (Akkadian *šabattu*) and not, as has traditionally been thought, to the weekly Sabbath? If the full moon in question is a monthly event and not the day on which an annual festival occurs, it may. But, even so, Hasel argues that the Akkadian analogy is actually less precise than advocates of the *šabattu* thesis acknowledge. For, he observes, there is no known Akkadian text with a direct sequence of "new moon" (*arḥum*) and "full moon" (*šab/pattu*). Rather, a word for the seventh day of the month intervenes.[95] Noticing the same problem earlier, Emil Kraeling remarked that one could just as well "argue that the Sabbath was originally the seventh day after the new moon and marked the conclusion of the first quarter (the Babyl. *sibūtu*)."[96] The possibility that the Sabbath in the familiar sense originated in a scheme of counting off sequences of seven days will be considered in our next chapter. For our present purposes, the key point is that the Mesopotamian evidence does not cleanly endorse the consensus that, in the biblical sequence "new moon (*ḥōdeš*)" and "Sabbath (*šabbāt*)," the latter refers to the day of the full moon rather than to the seventh day of the week.

Now back to those four preexilic texts that speak of the "Sabbath (*šabbāt*)"—2 Kgs 4:22–24; Amos 8:4–7; Hos 2:13; and Isa 1:12–13. How strong is the case that the term here actually refers to something other than the weekly day of rest?

In the passage about the Shunammite couple in 2 Kgs 4:22–24, much has been made of the fact that the husband seems mystified as to why his bereaved wife sets out on a trip when "it is neither new moon nor sabbath (*lō'-ḥōdeš vəlō'-šabbāt*)." As we saw, the prospect of traveling on the weekly day of rest seems odd; one biblical text actually forbids a person to "leave his place on the seventh day" (Exod 16:29b), though it is unclear whether the prohibition is specific to the context of manna-gathering or more general. It is also incongruous that the wife takes along her servant and instructs him to "urge [the jenny ass] on," both actions arguably in violation of the injunctions against making one's slave or farm animal work on the Sabbath (e.g., Exod 23:12). And yet all her husband finds curious is that she is doing this on a day that is neither the new moon nor the *šabbāt*. Presumably, scholars have argued, to do so on *šabbāt* would be unexceptionable, and so the term here must be something other than the weekly day of rest. The translation "Sabbath" is therefore misleading.

It can be argued, however, that all these divergences show is development over time in the sabbatical law of ancient Israel and not the more radical claim that *šabbāt* in 2 Kgs 4:23 must denote a lunar event. It is interesting that the great sociologist Max Weber, who accepted a connection between the *šabattu* and the Sabbath, perceived no problem in the Shunammite lady's making such a trip on the weekly day of rest. "In Mesopotamia," he wrote, "the *shabattu* in historical times was a day of penance. In Israel, originally, the seventh day was obviously a happy day of rest from work; a day when people cared for other things than the usual occupational routine and especially visited the men of God (II. Ki. 4:23)."[97] If so, then the bereaved mother's identification of a visit to the "man of God" as the reason for her trip (v. 22) would be a point of more than incidental significance. Her riding on the donkey driven by her servant on the Sabbath would probably be a double violation of the relatively early sabbatical law attested in Exod 23:12, but whether that law was in effect in the time and place of this composition is unknown. At least equally unknown, however, is whether there existed in ancient Israel a mid-month festival called *šabbāt*. To assume that there did simply in order to avoid the contradictions with sabbatical law in this text is to propose one unknown to avoid another.

Does the pairing of "new moon (*ḥōdeš*)" and "sabbath (*šabbāt*)" in 2 Kgs 4:23 and elsewhere provide evidence that the latter term must, like the former, also refer to a lunar event? Perhaps, but if so, the evidence is slight. For the day of the full moon and the seventh day of the week were both regularly occurring events. There is no reason to believe that the pairing indicates that they occur with the identical frequency. The observation that biblical lists tend to proceed from the more to the less frequent also provides a bit of weight for the identification of *šabbāt* with the monthly day of the full moon rather than the weekly Sabbath. But note Isa 66:23, in which "new moon" (*ḥōdeš*) and "sabbath (*šabbāt*)" occur in that order in a late text in which, as I took pains to argue above, the latter term is almost certainly the weekly event.

In the case of Amos 8:4–7, our second mention of *šabbāt* in a preexilic text, we have already examined the argument that the stoppage of trade on the day in question had to do with communal celebration and not with a general cessation from labor. Since the prophet is concerned only with the abuse of the poor by unscrupulous merchants, we simply have no way of knowing whether that stoppage was part of a larger pattern or not. Even if there was a mid-month celebration called *šabbāt* when Amos preached in the eighth century BCE, we can say nothing about the extent of its practices. It stands to reason that if we do not know whether a given holiday existed, we also do not know what its observance entailed. The wiser course may be to assume—for it, too, is only an assumption—that the stoppage of trade on Amos's *šabbāt* is of a piece with the later biblical texts that unambiguously evidence a prohibition of buying and selling on the seventh day (Neh 10:32; 13:15–22; Jer 17:19–27).

We have already seen that our third example, Hos 2:13, offers no real criteria by which to ascertain the identity of the *šabbāt* that it references. An argument can be made that the word order in which "new moon" precedes "sabbath," as in all these instances, provides some evidence that the latter occasion is not more frequent than the former and thus cannot be the weekly Sabbath. But this is, again, hardly conclusive.

In the case of Isa 1:12–13, our last example, the appearance of throngs of people in the Temple courts can suggest, as we noted, a festival other than the weekly Sabbath, which is usually thought of as a quiet day spent at home, as Exod 16:29 conceivably stipulates. But apart from the case of the worldwide pilgrimage on the Sabbath envisioned in Isa 66:23, discussed above, one also must reckon with the law in the program of restoration in Ezekiel 40–48 that specifies that "the common people shall worship before the LORD on sabbaths and new moons at the entrance of the same gate [as that at which the prince waits as the priests offer his sacrifice]" (Ezek 46:3). In this case, unlike the passage in Isaiah, there is no room whatsoever for doubt that the "sabbaths" here are weekly events, and not monthly ones (v. 1).

In sum, none of those four texts that mention "new moon" (*ḥōdeš*) and "sabbath" (*šabbāt*) together requires us to interpret the second item as a monthly rather than a weekly occurrence. They do witness, as do many passages in the Hebrew Bible, to an early period in the history of the religion of Israel in which the day of the new moon was festive and the lunar character of the reckoning of time was more important than would be the case later. But that alone does not warrant our *assuming* that in the same period *šabbāt* must have denoted the day of the full moon or any other lunar event rather than the occasion of "the seventh day." The strongest piece of evidence for the contrary hypothesis is the word order in which one expects the more frequently occurring holiday to appear first, as indeed it does in Ezek 46:3, quoted above, which exhibits the inverse sequence, "on sabbaths (*baššabbātôt*) and new moons (*ûbeḥŏdāšîm*)," unmistakably intending the first term to refer to the weekly Sabbath (v. 1), as just noted.

Our conclusion must be that the claim that *šabbāt* in preexilic texts refers to the day of the full moon and not to the Sabbath remains a tantalizing speculation, one with some philological support but, as of yet, no conclusive evidence. Despite some unacceptable linguistic claims, Marcus Jastrow's elaborate reconstruction of the Israelite mid-month *šabbāt* as a grim day of propitiation or atonement, only later transmuted into a day of delight and feasting, may have support in the evidence for the practice of fasting on the Sabbath attested as late as the rabbinic period. Even on that point, however, we can hardly rule out another origin for the practice. It should not be forgotten that in the last analysis, Jastrow's reconstruction depended on but three Akkadian words (*ūm nûḫ libbi*) and the curious similarity of *šabattu* and *šabbāt*.

The hypothesis that the Hebrew word for the Sabbath derives from an Akkadian term for the fifteenth of the month, the day of the full moon, and at one point referred to it exclusively is stimulating and productive but remains just that—a hypothesis. Without disregarding the tantalizing hypothesis, we would be wiser to focus on the nature of the seventh day in the biblical sources themselves and to inquire about the origin of the practice of counting off six days and ceasing work on the seventh. That perplexing question we consider in the next chapter.

CHAPTER 3

Six Days and the Seventh

IF THE HISTORICAL ORIGINS of the Sabbath, in the sense of the special seventh day of the week, are unclear to us, it is not because historians have failed to search for them. And there are, it turns out, many tantalizing phenomena that suggest, to one degree or another, the cultural matrix out of which the Israelite institution may eventually have emerged.

One example lies in Atraḫasis, a fragmentary Mesopotamian account of creation and human origins from the eighteenth century BCE, best known for its resemblance to the much later biblical story of the flood in the time of Noah. At one point, the benevolent god Enki announces a plan to relieve the lesser gods of their burdensome labors by creating the human race:

> On the first, seventh, and fifteenth days of the month,
> Let me establish a purification, a bath.
> Let one god be slaughtered,
> Then let the gods be cleansed by immersion.
> Let Nintu mix clay with his flesh and blood.
> Let that same god and man be thoroughly mixed in the clay.
> Let us hear the drum for the rest of time,
> From the flesh of the god let a spirit remain,
> Let it make the living know its sign,
> Lest he be allowed to be forgotten, let the spirit remain.[1]

It would seem that human beings are here thought to be an amalgam of god and clay, brought most immediately into existence by the mother goddess here called Nintu (she has multiple names). A particular ritual of ablution is devised to address the impurity to which the slaying of the unfortunate god exposed the others. Occurring on the first, seventh, and fifteenth days, the ritual mentioned thus fell on the days of the new moon, the first quarter, and the midpoint of the lunar month (Akkadian, *arḫu sebūtu u šapattu*) and thus instantiates the religious significance of the phases of the moon that was already ancient in Mesopotamian culture by the time Atraḥasis was composed.[2] William W. Hallo notes that the institution of festivals or other special rites to mark the quarters of the moon endured long after the Old Babylonian period from which the earliest texts of Atraḥasis derive. He draws attention, for example, to the "ḫitpu offering," which, in certain much later (in fact, Persian-period) texts, typically fell on the seventh, fourteenth, twenty-first, and twenty-eighth days of the month—in other words, on those days of the month that are divisible by seven.[3]

Another antecedent for, and parallel to, the Israelite Sabbath that scholars have often adduced is that of those "inauspicious days" (Akkadian, *ūmū lemnutū*) attested in some Mesopotamian sources and falling on the seventh, fourteenth, and twenty-eighth of the month and sometimes on the nineteenth and twenty-first as well.[4] Indeed, the multiples of seven in this list, conjoined with the notion of abstention from various enterprises on these days, do suggest, at least at first glance, the familiar institution of the biblical and later Jewish Sabbath.[5] (They also recall the association of Saturn's Day with bad luck in the Greco-Roman and medieval European worlds that we explored in our first chapter.[6]) But a second glance uncovers more than one severe problem not only with viewing the *ūmū lemnutū* as the source of the Sabbath but also with interpreting them as general days of rest at all. For one, they are not, apparently, events that consistently occur in all months of the year. For another, it is not clear that the admonitions to abstain from one's characteristic activity were directed to all walks of life throughout society.[7] Thirdly, as in the case of the Greco-Roman authors who tried to connect Jewish rest on Saturday with the inauspicious nature of the planet governing that day, we must again face the difference between a day that is gloomy and ill-starred and one that is blessed and holy and should, in the words of a prophet, be regarded as a "delight" and "honored" (Isa 58:13). As we saw in the last chapter, a path of development can be imagined between these two ostensibly opposite phenomena, but the difference in the endpoints must still be acknowledged.[8] Finally, a fourth and the most severe problem with the analogy is that the multiples of seven may be less significant than meets the eye. Why is the twenty-first of the month sometimes left out, and why is the nineteenth there at all? To answer the latter question, it has been suggested that the nineteenth of the month is the forty-ninth day from the start of the previous month (if the length of the latter was thirty days) and thus represents 7×7, a kind of super-seven, as it were, and, strikingly, a calculation of noteworthy importance in biblical tradition as well (Lev 23:15; 25:8).[9] But, if so, then the interval on one side of the nineteenth day is actually five days (back to the fourteenth), and the interval on the other side is either two or nine days (to the twenty-first or twenty-eighth). In any case, the presence of the nineteenth poses a serious challenge to the notion of a seven-day sequence.

As troublesome as these obstacles are, the most formidable one is simply this: the seventh, fourteenth, twenty-first, and twenty-eighth of the month are not all seven days apart. For the length of the lunar month, as we saw in our first chapter, is 29.5 days; no lunar month ever comprises only twenty-eight days. If one assumes a month of twenty-nine days, then there are eight days from the twenty-eighth of one month to the seventh of the next. In a month of thirty days, the interval is nine days. In no case is there an interval of seven. In short, these various Mesopotamian parallels do not attest to a weekly event at all. They can reasonably be adduced in support of an early and longstanding Near Eastern fascination with the number seven, with a practice of counting out units of seven days for certain specialized ritual purposes, and with the days of the month that are multiples of seven (a phenomenon that also appears in the Bible[10]), but they fall far short of constituting a close parallel to the weekly event known as the Jewish Sabbath. At most, they constitute a precedent for counting off sets of seven days, though for a very different purpose from the observance of a Sabbath. As Hallo put it, "There is nothing in the biblical evidence to suggest that the sabbatical conception depended in any way on the luni-solar calendar; on the contrary, that calendar was progressively adjusted to the sabbatical."[11]

For Hallo, this independence of the Sabbath and, correlatively, of the week from the waxing and waning of the moon serves as the basis for an important contrast between ancient Israel and pre-Christian and pre-Islamic Mesopotamia:

> Finally, the importance of the Sabbath must be seen in the context of the continuing deemphasis of the lunar festivals. Moon worship flourished wherever Mesopotamian culture spread, and even after its demise it survived at places like Harran. But in Israel it failed to gain a foothold; the full moon was not worshipped, the quarters were not specially observed, and even the new moon was ultimately relegated to the status of a half holiday. We may sum up the contrast as follows: the ancient Mesopotamian year was based on the month, and the worship of the moon went hand in hand with it. The Israelite year was based on the week, and remained independent of the month even when the luni-solar calendar was borrowed from Babylonia.[12]

Whether "in Israel [moon worship] failed to gain a foothold" is, as a point of empirical fact, open to considerable doubt. Would so many biblical texts condemn the worship of the moon (among other astral bodies) if the practice were always weak? Consider this admonition:

> [19]And when you look up to the sky and behold the sun and the moon and the stars, the whole heavenly host, you must not be lured into bowing down to them or serving them. These the LORD your God allotted to other peoples everywhere under heaven; [20]but you the LORD took and brought out of Egypt, that iron blast furnace, to be His very own people, as is now the case. (Deut 4:19–20)

And would King Josiah in the late seventh century BCE, famously viewed by prominent biblical sources as a righteous reformer, have acted against the practitioners of what he and those sources saw as deviant cults if those cults lacked even a foothold among the populace? The account of Josiah's reign in the book of Kings suggests that the worship of astral bodies held far more currency than Hallo's sanguine generalization admits:

> He suppressed the idolatrous priests whom the kings of Judah had appointed to make offerings at the shrines in the towns of Judah and in the environs of Jerusalem, and those who made offerings to Baal, to the sun and moon and constellations—all the host of heaven. (2 Kgs 23:5)[13]

What the evidence, even the evidence internal to the Bible, suggests is a rather different and much more dynamic scenario. Here, the deemphasis of the moon—and of astral bodies and astrological calculations altogether—resulted from a fierce struggle, not only or at least primarily between Israelites and foreigners (in this case, the Neo-Assyrians), but also between different sets of Israelites presenting contrasting views of what proper worship was and where the governance of the universe truly lay.

The canonical shape of the scriptures, then, roundly condemns the worship of the heavenly bodies but also suggestively preserves, as Hallo remarks, vestiges of a different calendrical system—one in which the phases of the moon played a central role. "As for the full moon, the two principal 'seasonal festivals' were gradually related to it in some way," he observes. "To this day, the approaching full moon signals the coming of Pesach [Passover] in Nisan and Sukkoth [Booths] in Tishri and comes as close as a luni-solar calendar can to marking the vernal and autumnal equinox respectively."[14] Here, the reference is to the liturgical calendar of Leviticus 23, in which the paschal offering is to take place in the late afternoon of the fourteenth of the first month and the immediately ensuing festival of Unleavened Bread commences on the fifteenth (vv. 5–6) and in which, similarly, the week-long Feast of Booths begins on the fifteenth of the seventh month (v. 34).[15] As Hallo notes, H. L. Ginsberg argued persuasively that in other biblical calendars the festival of Unleavened Bread begins not on the full moon but on the new moon.[16] Why the shift occurred—Leviticus represents the later development, one familiar to Jews "to this day," as Hallo puts it—is unclear, but one cannot fail to note the significance of the midpoint of the month elsewhere in the developed Jewish calendar as well: for the Festival of Purim (Esth 9:17b–19), of later origin; for the Festival of Weeks in the solar calendar of the noncanonical book of Jubilees from the second century BCE (6:17–22; 44:1–6); for the New Year for Trees in the Mishnah (Roš Haš. 1:1);[17] and, finally, for the enigmatic fifteenth of Av, which is described in the Mishnah as one of the happiest days of the year, when young women went out in fine clothes in hopes of attracting their future husbands (m. Ta'an. 4:8).

Against Hallo, it can now be said that it is not at all clear that the only calendar in circulation until late in the Second Temple period was a lunar one (somehow adjusted, of course, so as to keep the festivals in their due seasons). A number of scholars have been developing arguments to the effect that the calendar of Leviticus 23, from which Hallo derives his dating of Passover and Booths to the fifteenth of the month (and thus the full moon), was actually solar.[18] If so, then there is no more reason to connect the fifteenth with the full moon there than there is in the Gregorian calendar that is used throughout the world today.

The idea that the calendar reflected in Leviticus 23 was indeed solar can, however, be taken to reinforce Hallo's major point—that ancient Israelite tradition exhibits a deemphasis on the moon, as indicated by the weekly festival of the Sabbath, which has no lunar associations. This is true even though rabbinic tradition upheld a lunar definition of the month, with every month beginning on the new moon. The overall picture that emerges is thus one of the new seven-day unit superimposed upon an older luni-solar arrangement, even though the complete loss of the lunar dimension in some biblical material did not ultimately pass into the rabbinic tradition, which is the only Jewish tradition to survive antiquity and endure into our own time. In the rabbinic system, the year always consists of purely lunar months but is adjusted in order to keep the annual festivals in their appropriate seasons. Thus, although a purely lunar year of twelve months, comprising only 354 days (=12 × 29.5), inevitably loses about 11¼ days relative to the solar cycle (roughly 365¼ days), Passover remained in the spring, for example, and Tabernacles in the fall.[19] The rabbinic solution was to adopt the Babylonian system in which seven years in a nineteen-year cycle conclude with an extra month, thus allowing the holidays to oscillate within a period of several weeks but never to lose their seasonality. Passover might begin at the end of March or in April, but it will not occur in July; Tabernacles might begin in early September or in October, but it will never fall in December, and so on.[20]

As for the weeks, they roll on, in sovereign independence of these astronomical issues, each one defined by and climaxing in its seventh day.

The notion that the seventh day in the sequence stands in contrast to the foregoing six and brings the series to a climax is older than ancient Israel and its Sabbath and is well attested even in the Hebrew Bible, as we shall see, in contexts that are not sabbatical.[21]

Striking Mesopotamian antecedents can be found in the famous account of the Flood as it appears in the eleventh tablet of the Epic of Gilgamesh:

> Six days and [seven] nights
> The wind continued, the deluge and the windstorm levelled the land
> When the seventh day arrived, the windstorm and deluge left off their
>   assault,
> Which they had launched, like a fight to the death.
> The sea grew calm, the tempest grew still, the deluge ceased.
> (Gilgamesh XI: 130–135)[22]

The pattern here is familiar: six days of intense activity, in this case a terrifying, world-engulfing storm, followed by a seventh in which all activity ceases, replaced by tranquility and quietude. A similar pattern can be detected a few lines later, when Utnapishtim (often dubbed "the Mesopotamian Noah") seeks to ascertain whether dry land has at last appeared.

> The boat rested on Mount Nimush,
> Mount Nimush held the ship fast, not allowing it to move.
> One day, a second day Mount Nimush held the boat fast, not allowing
>   it to move.
> A third day, a fourth day Mount Nimush held the boat fast, not allow-
>   ing it to move.
> A fifth day, a sixth day Mount Nimush held the boat fast, not allowing
>   it to move.
> When the seventh day arrived,
> I released a dove to go free,
> The dove went and returned,
> No landing place came to view, it turned back.
> The swallow went and returned,
> No landing place came to view, it turned back.

I sent a raven to go free,
The raven went forth, saw the ebbing of the waters,
It ate, circled, left droppings, and did not turn back. (Gilgamesh XI:
146–158)[23]

This passage, rightly compared with the much later Israelite account of
Noah's actions in Gen 8:6–12,[24] seems in one sense to represent the opposite
of the pattern represented in the biblical commands about the Sabbath and
in lines 127–33 above: here six days of inaction are followed by one of intense
activity, as Utnapishtim sends forth three birds, one after the other, to answer
the key question. On the other hand, the seventh day is still climactic here:
on this day, that to which the first six look forward is fulfilled. As in the Israelite
sabbatical week, those six days are identical and interchangeable; the seventh
alone represents the meaning of the entire series.[25]

Sequences of seven days—which, importantly, are plentiful in the Hebrew
Bible and not at all restricted to texts about the Sabbath—appear as well in the
parallel passage about the biblical Utnapishtim, Noah, at the end of the flood.
Noah sends out birds four times, the raven once and the dove thrice. Between
the second and third and the third and fourth dispatches of the dove, Noah
waits seven days (Gen 8:10, 12). It is not clear whether he then acts on the seventh day or on the eighth. If the former, then we have another example of the
seventh day as contrastive and climactic and possibly an echo of the passage
in Gilgamesh quoted above.

Closer to the world of the Hebrew Bible both geographically and culturally are the texts in alphabetic cuneiform discovered along the Syrian coast at
ancient Ugarit and dating to the Late Bronze Age, the period just before the
emergence of Israel. Written in a language whose features strikingly parallel
those of Biblical Hebrew (which it, in turn, illuminates), these Ugaritic texts
offer their own analogies to the pattern of six days of activity culminating in a
distinctive seventh.[26] Here, for example, is an account of the construction of
a palace for the god Baʿlu, the biblical "Baal":

[Hurriedly] they build his house,
    [hurriedly] they raise his palace.
(Some workers) [go] to Lebanon and its trees,
    To Siryon (and) its choicest cedars;
[They X] Lebanon and its trees,
    Siryon (and) its choicest cedars.
Fire is placed in the house,
    flames in the palace.

For a day, two (days),
 the fire consumes (fuel) in the house,
 the flames (consume fuel) in the palace;
For a third, a fourth day,
 the fire consumes (fuel) in the house,
 the flames (consume fuel) in the palace;
For a fifth, a sixth day,
 the fire consumes (fuel) in the house,
 the flames (consume fuel) in the palace;
Then on the seventh day,
 the fire is removed from the house,
 the flames from the palace.
(Voilà!) the silver has turned into plaques,
 The gold is turned into bricks.
(This) brings joy to Mighty Baʿlu:
You have built my house of silver,
 my palace of gold.
(Then) Baʿlu completes the furnishing of [his] house,
 Haddu completes the furnishing of his palace. (The Baʿlu Myth,
 6:16–39)[27]

In these lines, we read of what the translator rightly calls "a giant casting process,"[28] in which the palace of the victorious deity Baʿlu/Haddu emerges, as it were, on its own after the forging fires have done their work. Once again, the process takes six days, and, as the poet's repetitive style unmistakably conveys, there is no differentiation among the individual units in that period. It is only on the seventh day—unpaired, unparalleled, and consummative—that the work ends and the palace miraculously appears. It is tempting to connect Baʿlu's joy at this happy turn of events with the biblical report that after the six days of active creating, "God saw all that He had made and found it very good" and with his blessing and hallowing the seventh day immediately thereafter (Gen 1:31; 2:3). For the report that Baʿlu/Haddu completed the furnishing of his house/palace on the seventh day is reminiscent of the biblical report about the end of God's creation of the world:

> The heaven and the earth were finished, and all their array. ²On the seventh day God finished the work He had been doing, and He ceased (*vayyišbōt*) on the seventh day from all the work that He had done. (Gen 2:1–2)

More daringly, it might be suggested that the disappearance of the fire that casts Baʿlu's palace can be associated with a biblical law that precedes the detailed report in Exodus of the construction of the LORD's own palace in the wilderness, the Tabernacle:

> These are the things that the LORD has commanded you to do: ²On six days work may be done, but on the seventh day you shall have a sabbath of complete rest, holy to the LORD; whoever does work on it shall be put to death. ³You shall kindle no fire throughout your settlements on the sabbath day. (Exod 35:1–3)

It would be erroneous, however, to assume too direct a connection between the Ugaritic and the biblical texts. As we shall see at length in chapter 7, there is a clear homology between the building of temples and the act of cosmic creation in some ancient Near Eastern texts. That similar language of completion or expressions of contentment should appear in these two contexts is thus hardly surprising and should not be taken to imply specific influence. On the other side, that Baʿlu's palace and the LORD's world both come into existence over a period of seven days, with the seventh singled out and denoting finalization, probably does tell us something about the magical character, as it were, of the number seven in these two fairly closely related cultures.[29] (Note as well that 1 Kgs 6:38 reports that the LORD's earthly palace, the Temple in Jerusalem, took seven years to build.) As Arvid S. Kapelrud puts it, citing both biblical and Ugaritic passages, seven is "the number of completeness."[30] One can thus readily understand why a project with a cosmic resonance would take seven days or seven years to come to its final state. One can also understand why Kapelrud, this time speaking of the Ugaritic examples but with obvious pertinence to the biblical ones as well, would caution, "It might even be right to say that in most cases the number seven must *not* be interpreted literally."[31] As is often the case with numbers in the ancient Near East (and in folklore more generally), interpreters must reckon with the formulaic character and cultural resonance of the figures given.[32]

Mark S. Smith draws attention to another Ugaritic text relevant to the Israelite Sabbath in that it describes a "ritual that says the seventh day marks the end of obligations within the cultic realm."[33] To quote Dennis Pardee's translation, "On the seventh day (of the festival of the full moon), when the sun rises, the day will be free (of cultic obligations); when the sun sets, the king will [be free (of cultic obligations)]."[34] As Pardee understands these lines, "the point of the two commands seems to be that, though no specific cultic activity is required, the king must remain in his holy state ... until sunset, the end of the day of the festival."[35] It is the notion of a day in which holiness is mandated but "no specific cultic activity is required" that, Smith believes, "evokes the notion of the Sabbath day as 'free' from nonsacral obligations."[36]

As is the case with just about everything in Ugaritic, there is much about this text that is obscure. Smith's analogizing it to the Sabbath is surely suggestive. It is clear, however, that what the lines quoted above describe is neither a weekly event nor a community-wide observance. The text offers at best only a dim foreshadowing of Israel's day of light and joy.

What I have called "the magical character" of the number seven is attested far beyond the ritual, cosmogonic, and temple-building texts that are most relevant to the theology of the Sabbath in biblical texts like the opening creation story of Genesis.[37] To continue with the case of Ugarit, one could note as well the directions given to the army in the Kirta Epic:

> Go a day, a second,
>   a third, a fourth day,
>   a fifth, a sixth day.
> Then at sunset on the seventh (day)
>   you will arrive at 'Udmu the great (city),
>   at 'Udmu the well-watered (city).[38]

Here again, the members of the three sets of paired days are indistinguishable. The same thing happens on each of them: going. Only on the seventh does the army arrive at the city against which it is to commence operations. A few lines later, the pattern reappears, this time in the form of six paired days of siege, followed by the besieged king's sending messengers with an offer of capitulation "at sunset on the seventh." As was apparently the case with the construction of Baʿlu's palace, the consummation of the process occurs during the seventh day and not at its outset. The specification of "sunset" as the key moment adds to the suspense: the army reaches its destination and then accomplishes its mission in each instance only at the eleventh hour, as it were. Armies did not ordinarily travel by night.

I have been at pains to show that the organization of time into regular and uninterrupted sequences of seven days, with the last distinct from the first six and yet consummating the activity that took place in them, has some antecedents in the ancient Near Eastern conception of seven as a kind of "magic number." Seven has that same character in the Hebrew Bible as well, and the organization of creation into seven days in Gen 1:1–2:3 is but one of many dozens—in fact, probably hundreds—of such heptadic structures found in that collection.[39] It would be a capital error to view those other texts as intentionally echoing the organization of creation in the opening story of the Bible, just as it would be a mistake to assume that all references to the Sabbath in the same set of books presuppose the all-too-familiar image of creation in its opening chapter or at least did so when they were composed. As we shall see in our next chapter, the organization of creation into a week and the interpretation of the Sabbath as consummating creation is characteristic of a particular school or strain of thought in ancient Israel—namely, P or the "Priestly" source. It was not always there and is not universal in the Hebrew Bible.

It would also be a mistake to overemphasize the ancient Near Eastern texts in which the seventh day completes or fulfills the activity of the previous six. For one thing, these parallels, though illuminating of our topic, are rare. To see them as a defining element of their cultures or characteristic of their legacy to ancient Israel would be indefensible. For another, although seven is probably the most prominent among the formulaic numbers in the Hebrew Bible (and does not simply appear so to us because of the familiar opening of Genesis), others must also be mentioned, especially ten, twelve, and forty, not to mention two conspicuous multiples of seven: forty-nine and seventy. In this cultural context, it is conceivable that a week of ten or twelve days, and not seven, could have come into existence. Against that possibility, however, we should mention the fact that when sets of ten or twelve items are mentioned, the last item does not generally seem to be definitive or consummative, unlike the biblical Sabbath: the tenth item in the Decalogue (the prohibition on coveting in Exod 20:14 and Deut 5:18), for example, or the last in the lists of the twelve tribes of Israel (such as Naphtali in Gen 46:24) do not play a role in the sequence in any way analogous to the role of the seventh day.

We should also note that sometimes the defining action occurs not on the seventh day but just after it, on the eighth. Thus, for example, the male Israelites are to be circumcised on the eighth day—after completing their first week of life, that is, and not on its seventh day (Gen 17:12; Lev 12:3)—and, probably not coincidentally, the firstborn male animal is to stay with its mother for seven days, to be sacrificially offered only on the eighth (Exod 22:29). Here, too, we should mention the curious eighth day that, in some sources, follows the seven-day Festival of Tabernacles (Lev 23:33–36; Num 29:35–38; contrast Deut 16:13–15) and comes to be known in Jewish tradition as "Shemini Atzeret," or "Eighth Day of Assembly," and to be treated as a holiday in its own right. Other examples could be cited from ancient Israelite ritual legislation[40]—so many, in fact, that one can easily imagine that the week could also have been a unit longer by one day, with the Sabbath falling not on the seventh but on the eighth of the week. If such an institution ever existed, it has quite vanished from the record.

Although we have been referring to the seventh day of the week as the "Sabbath," as we saw in the previous chapter, texts that historians generally regard as the earliest mentions of the institution call it "the seventh day."[41] Consider again this paradigmatic passage:

Six days you shall do your work, but on the seventh day you shall cease from labor, in order that your ox and your ass may rest, and that your bondman and stranger may be refreshed. (Exod 23:12)

Here, the law of "the seventh day" follows a set of humanitarian norms that voice an unequivocal concern that the strong not oppress the weak.[42] Spreading "false rumors" and acting as "a malicious witness," for example, and thus distorting testimony "in favor of the mighty" are forbidden, although—and here we see the full extent of the famous passion for justice of the Hebrew Bible—so is "show[ing] deference to a poor man in his dispute" (Exod 23:1–3). False charges and bribes, "which blind the clearsighted and upset the pleas of those who are in the right," must be scrupulously avoided (vv. 6–8).[43] Similarly, the Israelite is not to "oppress a stranger"—meaning a resident alien— "for you know the feelings of the stranger, having yourselves been strangers in the land of Egypt" (v. 9).

This is then followed by another law with generosity toward the vulnerable again as its explicit goal:

[10]Six years you shall sow your land and gather in its yield; [11]but in the seventh you shall let it rest and lie fallow. Let the needy among your people eat of it, and what they leave let the wild beasts eat. You shall do the same with your vineyards and your olive groves. (Exod 23:10–11)

The phrasing alone demonstrates the close affinity of the seventh year—not yet termed "sabbatical"—with the seventh day of the next verse (v. 12, quoted above). In both, we see the pattern of six and seven, with the seventh item as distinctive. "Sow" and "gather" in v. 10 correspond to "do your work" in v. 12. "Let it rest and lie fallow" corresponds to "cease from labor."[44] Particularly suggestive is the arrangement of the beneficiaries of the two institutions, which forms a chiasm in the pattern of ABB'A' across vv. 11 and 12: "needy" (A); "wild beasts" (B); "ox and ass" (B'); "bondman and stranger" (A')—and thus underscores the humanitarian purpose of the two closely related institutions.[45]

The same point emerges with greater clarity when we compare the law of the seventh day in v. 12 with its parallel in the Deuteronomic version of the Decalogue (Deut 5:12–15), which also gives a humanitarian rationale for the institution, in striking contrast to the parallel and better-known text in Exod 20:8–11. In Deuteronomy, the householder's slaves (male and female), ox, ass, other beasts, and stranger are all again mentioned but only after the members of the household itself: "you, your son or your daughter" (Deut 5:14). In the briefer commandment in Exod 23:12, the addressee is not specified with a pronoun at all (like "you" in Deuteronomy) but only with the second-person forms of the verbs. As in the immediately preceding law of the seventh year, the emphasis lies neither on the addressee himself nor his family but on his subordinates, who are the beneficiaries of sabbatical rest. Note the subtle difference between "so that your male and female slave may rest as you do" in Deut 5:14 and "in order that your ox and your ass may rest, and that your bondman and stranger may be refreshed" in Exod 23:12. In Deuteronomy, the Sabbath is a ritual occasion in its own right and with its own name (yôm haššabbāt, 5:12), but still one with explicit humanitarian purposes. In Exod 23:12, "the seventh day"—not yet denoted with the noun "Sabbath" (šabbāt) but only as a day on which, using the cognate verb, "you shall cease" (tišbōt)— is more explicitly bound to the economic life of the farmer, and its humanitarian purpose is presented more exclusively.

It is not only that the law of the seventh day in Exod 23:12 harmonizes well with the law of the seventh year in the previous two verses. As Alexandra Grund points out in her thorough and learned study of the Israelite Sabbath, all three verses echo the humanitarian legislation that precedes them in Exod 23:1–9.[46] Thus, we find "ox" (šôr) and "ass" (ḥămôr) both occurring in vv. 4, 5, and 12; "needy" ('ebyôn) in vv. 6 and 11; and "stranger" (gēr) in vv. 9 and 12. What all these interconnections show is that in the laws of the seventh year and the seventh day in Exod 23:10–12, the text has not shifted from ethics to ritual (to utilize a common, perhaps unavoidable, yet misleading dichotomy). Rather, those last three verses present a regularly recurring and obligatory occasion for the application of the ethical norms specified in the first nine verses of the chapter. They have rightly been termed a "hinge" text between Exod 23:1–9 and vv. 13–19, which deal in the main with calendrical and other issues of a ritual nature.[47]

More distantly, the laws of the seventh year and of the seventh day in Exod 23:10–12 echo the ethical legislation with which the entire Covenant Collection opens, the law of the "Hebrew slave" ('ebed 'ibrî), the indentured servant whose years of labor are (unless he declines) capped at six, so that "in the seventh year he shall go free" (Exod 21:2). "Your bondman" (ben-'ămātəkā) in Exod 23:12, it would seem, is to experience every seventh day, albeit temporarily, something of the liberation that the "Hebrew slave" experiences when his seventh year of bondage finally arrives. If we may assume that this "bondman" falls into the category of a "Hebrew slave"—the original meaning of the latter term is much debated[48]—then we are within rights to observe that the seventh day functions here as a weekly earnest of his future manumission. As we shall see, the interpretation of the Sabbath as a foretaste of the coming redemption will become prominent in later Jewish thought (cf. Philo, Spec. Laws 67 [Colson, LCL]). Its earliest antecedent would appear to lie as far back as the laws of the Covenant Collection.

What does the law in Exod 23:12 forbid, and how does it envision that "the seventh day" should be observed?

As Grund sees it, the only labor that is forbidden in Exod 23:12 is agricultural. "A general prohibition on work is not yet given here," she writes, "but first [appears] in the two versions of the Sabbath-commandment of the Decalogue [Exod 20:8–11; Deut 5:12–15]."[49] This, however, assumes more knowledge of what "your work" (ma'áśeykā) and "you shall cease from labor" (tišbōt) meant at the time than that to which we can lay rightful claim. In part, Grund bases her judgment on the appearance of "your work (ma'áśeykā) from the field" in connection with the Feast of Ingathering (later termed Sukkot, or Tabernacles) a few verses later in Exod 23:16.[50] Although, as we have already seen, the command of the seventh day presupposes an agrarian society, the far-reaching assumption that other forms of productive labor did not fall under the prohibition of v. 12 seems quite unwarranted. Surely, the bondman and the stranger (who seems to have been an employee of the householder addressed) were also expected to perform work outside the field, especially in the admittedly brief periods when the planting or harvesting was completed. To imagine that at those times of year the law in question required nothing distinctive for the seventh day either of the bondman, the stranger, or, for that matter, the householder himself strains credulity. That "the field" should be mentioned in a law about a feast rightly termed "Ingathering" is hardly surprising and cannot be taken to mean that all "work" prohibited on the seventh day in v. 12 is assumed to be in the field.

In further support of the opposite view, however, Grund cites Exod 34:21, another verse widely and credibly taken as early:[51] "Six days you shall work, but on the seventh day you shall cease from labor; you shall cease from labor even at plowing time and harvest time." It is important to concede at the outset that the word "even" does not appear in the Hebrew to this verse. Its insertion by the NJPS, however, follows on a long Jewish tradition. For example, Saadia, an important Jewish authority in the Muslim world in the first half of the tenth century CE, glosses the verse exactly so: "even at the time of plowing and harvesting." Similarly, Rabbi Samuel ben Meir (Rashbam), active in northern France in the twelfth century, identifies the point of singling out these two activities, essential for the maintenance of life, as an indication that sabbatical rest is all the more obligatory in the cases of the other forbidden labors.

Clearly, such medieval rabbinic exegetes are indebted to the understanding of the Sabbath in the postbiblical Jewish tradition, in which a large variety of activities, and hardly agricultural ones alone, are classified as prohibited labor.[52] The structure and word order of the verse, however, suggest that the interpretation of these medieval authorities actually does reflect its immediate contextual meaning and is not simply a harmonization with rabbinic tradition.

Note that Exod 34:21 can be laid out as poetry, in fact, as a tricolon with each stich consisting of three words in Hebrew:[53]

šēšet	yāmîm	taʿăḇōd
ûḇayyôm	haššəḇîʿî	tišbōt
beḥārîš	ûḇaqqāṣîr	tišbōt
Six	days	you-shall-work,
but-on-the-day	seventh	you-shall-cease-from-labor;
at-plowing-time	and-at-harvest-time	you-shall-cease-from-labor.

Conceivably, one might argue that the parallel placement of "six days" in the first stich and "the seventh day" in the second with "plowing time and harvest time" in the last stich implies an equation, so that, as Grund thinks, the labor in question is limited to those two activities: six days you may plow and harvest, but on the seventh, you must cease from those specific forms of work and only those specific forms of work. It is more probable, in my opinion, that the placement of "at plowing time and harvest time" results from emphasis, as often happens when something other than the subject appears before the verb in Biblical Hebrew.[54] If everybody knew that "work" meant only agricultural labor (which, by the way, includes more than plowing and harvesting), there would be no reason to gloss the word at all and not much sense in putting the gloss in the first position in the clause. The likeliest interpretation, rather, is one that takes seriously the fact that each of the three three-word lines begins with an emphatic element: "*Six days* you shall work, *but on the seventh day* you shall cease from labor; *at plowing time and harvest time* you shall cease from labor." More than that, it would seem that the three emphasized elements are arranged in a ladder structure, moving from lowest to highest intensity. "Six days" are regular, as it were; they define the workaday life. "The seventh day" stands, as usual, in contradiction to the first six; it is special. Even more special are "plowing time and harvest time," periods essential for the sustenance of human life, when the same cessation from labor mentioned in the second stich is nonetheless in effect and thus reiterated. If this is right, then the NJPS translation "you shall cease from labor even at plowing time and harvest time," while prosaic, captures the sense of the verse accurately in English.

Given its literary context, Exod 34:21 has good reason to stress sabbatical observance during the periods of plowing and planting. As Shimon Gesundheit points out, it is significant that the verse appears in a liturgical calendar (vv. 18–26), one that, moreover, he argues is "but a midrashic revision of" the one that appeared in the festal calendar of Exod 23:14–19.[55] If that is so, then the sabbatical ordinance of Exod 23:12 has been incorporated into the calendar and no longer precedes it or functions as part of the textual hinge between social-ethical laws and the ritual material, as it did in chap. 23. Instead, as Gesundheit sees it, the appearance of the verse between the laws of the Feast of Unleavened Bread (34:18) and the Feast of Weeks (v. 22) relates to the fact that the latter is here explicitly said to take place at the time of the "wheat harvest" (*qaṣir ḥiṭṭîm*, v. 22); note the echoing of "harvest time" (*qāṣîr*) from v. 21. The point, then, was that the work of harvesting, which takes place in the period between these two holy occasions, "does not override the command to cease all labor on the seventh day"[56]—very much, it turns out, as those medieval commentators quoted above thought. "Even at plowing time and harvest time," the mandatory cessation from labor must be upheld.

To Gesundheit, the appearance of the sabbatical ordinance of Exod 23:12 (rephrased, of course) in the liturgical calendar of Exodus 34 represents another instance of "incorporating the mention of the weekly Sabbath in the listing of annual festivals," a practice that he sees as "uniquely Priestly" and thus indicative of a relatively late date of composition.[57] Given its poetic structure, it would seem likelier, though, that Exod 34:21 itself is not a recomposition of 23:12 in particular but rather an old ordinance of uncertain authorship that has been incorporated into its current location in the list of festivals in chapter 34 very much for the reason that Gesundheit gives. If he is right that Exod 34:18–26 is a midrashic revision of Exod 23:13–19, it may well be that the presence of a sabbatical ordinance just before the earlier text (23:12) provided the motivation for including the law of the seventh day of 34:21 in its present location. All this is, of course, at best extremely speculative, but, even if it be granted, it still remains doubtful that the highly symmetrical nine-word tricolon of 34:21 resulted from a deliberate revision of the specific text we have in 23:12. Literally, Gesundheit is right that "the law of weekly cessation from labor in Exodus 34 has omitted the humanistic, social rationale for the Sabbath found in Exod 23:12, just as the Priestly writers have done" (referring to "the Priestly calendars in Leviticus 23 and Numbers 28–29, at least in their final forms").[58] But how much intentionality lay behind this move is unknown; we cannot with any confidence invoke the argument from silence as evidence that the redactor did not share the humanistic rationale for the Sabbath. Even more unknown is the ultimate origin of Exod 34:21, in contradistinction to the likely process that resulted in our finding it in its current position.

What remains fairly clear, by contrast, is that the law of the seventh day in Exod 23:12 is quite early, predating the Deuteronomic and Priestly revisions of traditional material, and thus points to the antiquity of the connection of the seventh day with the seventh year and with the humanitarian concepts that motivated both in early Israel. Whether this connection constituted the sole understanding of the seventh day in that period is unknown, but, as we shall see later,[59] it is a connection with deep roots in the ancient Near East and a prominent place in the continuing biblical tradition as well.

How shall we move from these early texts about the Sabbath to the historical questions of how and to what extent it was observed in biblical Israel?

Initially, the two related questions, especially the second, seem easy, for material relating to the Sabbath is prominent in some of the most generally familiar texts. One thinks first, of course, of the account of God's creation of the world in six days and ceasing his work on the seventh, blessing and sanctifying that day (Gen 1:1–2:3), even though no injunction for any humans to do likewise appears there. The actual commandment to remember or to observe the Sabbath in order to protect its sanctity and to abstain from labor on it appears in both versions of the Decalogue as well (Exod 20:8–11; Deut 5:12–15). As the storyline of the Pentateuch would have it, the sabbatical commandment was announced even before Israel arrived at Sinai/Horeb, as part of the narrative about the manna, the miraculous food with which God sustained them during their wanderings in the wilderness (Exod 16:21–30). Indeed, given the number of passages in the Pentateuch that focus on the Sabbath—even explicitly classifying its violation as nothing less than a capital offense[60]—one can readily form the impression that the Sabbath was a well-known and carefully observed institution from the generation of the exodus from Egypt on.

But here the problem we discussed at the beginning of our last chapter confronts us anew. This is the problem of the difference between a traditionally religious and a historical approach to scriptural literature. For the religious traditionalist, the different biblical passages all speak to the same synchronous reality, and the divergences among them simply reflect different aspects of that one uniform truth. For the historian, by way of contrast, the same divergences are telltale signs of developments over time or of differences among social sectors. In the historical approach, therefore, the identification of the sources out of which the redacted whole (in this case, the Pentateuch) was assembled is essential. Otherwise, we shall inevitably fall prey to a historically illicit harmonization of passages and an equally irresponsible retrojection of later ideas and institutions into earlier periods. Although such harmonization and retrojection are defensible, and perhaps inevitable for religious practitioners and secular literary approaches, they are utterly devastating to the work of historical reconstruction. Where the latter is the goal, they must be rejected.

Even if we restrict ourselves to the historical method (or, as it is usually known in biblical studies, the historical-critical method), as we are doing here, another formidable problem presents itself: the problem of dating. It makes no sense to speak of developments over time if we cannot propound at least a defensible relative chronology and, ideally, a credible absolute chronology as well. Both of these, alas, are difficult, and absolute datings, even within broad limits, are especially so.

The Decalogue offers a good example. As recently as 1958, a highly and justly respected scholar, Roland de Vaux, could write that "the Ten Commandments, in their original form, go back to the time of Moses," and thus "the weekly sabbath goes back to the first origins [of the worship of the God of Israel]."[61] Speaking specifically of the difference between "Remember" and "Observe" in the two versions of the Decalogue (Exod 20:8; Deut 5:12), Alexandra Grund, writing in 2011, informs her readers, by contrast, that both versions are exilic at the earliest.[62] In each case, the position reflected the thinking of a large number of biblical scholars at the time the scholar wrote.[63] Grund's displays the preference for late datings and skepticism about the historicity of narratives that is regnant in the field today, especially in Europe. The assumption is that the literature tells us much more about the period of its composition than about the period it purports to describe, about which it likely has no information at all. The sea change in sentiment over the past several decades is not without its reasons. For the new thinking (which actually revives and reenergizes older currents of thought) builds upon the widespread consensus that we really have no compelling evidence about what de Vaux confidently calls "the time of Moses"—historians cannot reliably say even that Moses ever existed—and "the first origins [of the worship of the God of Israel]." Thus, we are reduced to speculation. Truth to tell, more than a small portion of shifts in thinking about such matters derives from fashions in scholarship and the practical incentives for scholars to appear innovative.

In support of his claim for the high antiquity of the Sabbath, de Vaux notes that "it is mentioned . . . in all the traditions of the Pentateuch," referencing the four sources of the classical Documentary Hypothesis (identified with the sigla J, E, D, and P), and he goes on to argue that "everywhere it is described in the same way, as a seventh day on which men rest after six days of work."[64] I think it is fair to say that this reasoning suffers from at least three formidable weaknesses—the difficulty with identifying the underlying sources, the assumption that each source is essentially a unity without significant interpolations, and the notion that something that is very widely attested in a variety of sources must be quite ancient. The fact is that the Documentary Hypothesis, although it still has its spirited defenders (albeit mostly in America and Israel),[65] has been largely abandoned in favor of something more like a fragmentary or supplementary hypothesis, in which the received text and its antecedent sources have grown by accretion and been shaped by redaction at multiple stages. The notion that the earliest source must accurately reflect the period it purports to describe has also, in the six decades since de Vaux wrote, suffered a drastic loss of credibility.

A better approach to answering our question about how and to what extent the Sabbath was observed in preexilic Israel would focus not on the explicit claims the texts make but on the unspoken realities they willy-nilly presume. A good case in point is the legal question of whether war may be conducted on the Sabbath. The issue comes to a head in the books of Maccabees:

> [29]At that time many who were seeking righteousness and justice went down to the wilderness to live there, [30]they, their sons, their wives, and their livestock, because troubles pressed heavily upon them. [31]And it was reported to the king's officers, and to the troops in Jerusalem the city of David, that those who had rejected the king's command had gone down to the hiding places in the wilderness. [32]Many pursued them, and overtook them; they encamped opposite them and prepared for battle against them on the sabbath day. [33]They said to them, "Enough of this! Come out and do what the king commands, and you will live." [34]But they said, "We will not come out, nor will we do what the king commands and so profane the sabbath day." [35]Then the enemy quickly attacked them. [36]But they did not answer them or hurl a stone at them or block up their hiding places, [37]for they said, "Let us all die in our innocence; heaven and earth testify for us that you are killing us unjustly." [38]So they attacked them on the sabbath, and they died, with their wives and children and livestock, to the number of a thousand persons.
>
> [39]When Mattathias and his friends learned of it, they mourned for them deeply. [40]And all said to their neighbors: "If we all do as our kindred have done and refuse to fight with the Gentiles for our lives and for our ordinances, they will quickly destroy us from the earth." [41]So they made this decision that day: "Let us fight against anyone who comes to attack us on the sabbath day; let us not all die as our kindred died in their hiding places." (1 Macc 2:29–41, NRSV)

Written roughly around 100 BCE (that is, well after all the Pentateuchal sources had been composed), this passage communicates considerable uncertainty about whether warfare on the Sabbath is allowed. The Jews who are the subjects of vv. 32–38 clearly believe that it is not; as a price for that unshakeable conviction they give their lives. Realizing, however, that the same conviction spelled certain defeat, the leadership of the traditionalist Jewish uprising resolved on purely practical grounds to fight nonetheless (vv. 39–41).[66] The absence of a textual precedent for this resolution, or even a nontextual tradition that might authorize it, is striking. Jubilees, a Jewish book mentioned in our previous chapter and written a generation or two earlier, explicitly prohibits warfare on the Sabbath (Jub. 50:12). As in the case of fasting on the seventh day, prohibited in the same verse (examined in our previous chapter), here, too, it would seem that the proscription presupposes that some elements of the society were inclined, like Mattathias and his associates in the passage above, to do exactly what the text forbids.

What is curious—but also revealing—is how late in the history of Israel this issue presents itself. For, according to the biblical narrative, war was exceedingly common throughout that history, from the period of the wanderings in the wilderness after the exodus through the fall of the Kingdom of Judah in 586 BCE. There were, for example, the wars that facilitated Israel's conquest of the land in the book of Joshua, the campaigns waged by the "judges" in the book that goes by that name, the Philistine wars in Samuel, and a host of other military operations of various sorts throughout that book and Kings as well. The issue here does not relate to the question of the historical reliability of these various narratives but rather to the oddity that the problem raised, according to 1 Maccabees, in the second century BCE never appears earlier. Is that because the position that Mattathias articulates was simply assumed in the earlier periods? If so, one wonders why the pious of his time and author(s) of the book of Jubilees, too, had forgotten it and why he is depicted as improvising on the spot out of sheer practical necessity when a time-honored tradition was at hand. Or should we assume, rather, that it was those who gave their lives rather than violate the Sabbath who continued the longstanding practice and that the position that Mattathias advocates was, correlatively, the innovation? If so, we must then wonder how the Israelites, incapacitated militarily every seventh day, ever won any wars at all. If it be replied that as reward for their sabbatical fidelity God granted them victory, why do the texts give no hint of such a homiletically useful interpretation? Why, to repeat the key question, does the question of warfare on the Sabbath never come up at all?

These questions, in turn, draw attention to another critical fact about the block of material that runs from Joshua through Kings. References to the Sabbath there are extremely exiguous. Apart from 2 Kgs 4:23—which, as we saw in the last chapter, most scholars currently think refers to a monthly "Sabbath," not the more familiar weekly one[67]—the only apparent references are in 2 Kgs 11:5, 7, and 9 and in 2 Kgs 16:18.[68] Those in 2 Kings 11 relate to the changing of the guard at the palace and the Temple, and the highly obscure reference in chapter 16 mentions some sort of architectural feature associated with those two buildings.[69] Whatever the word "Sabbath" means in them—the hypothetical Israelite full-moon festival cannot be ruled out here, either—these four verses tell us next to nothing about its observance or theology.

It is widely recognized that the block that runs from Joshua through Kings is, for the most part, heavily influenced by Deuteronomy and its characteristic theology. Given the presence of the Decalogue with its Sabbath command in Deuteronomy (5:12–15), it initially seems odd that the injunction to cease labor and engage in rest on the seventh day does not figure in that material. In point of fact, however, the Decalogue is the *only* place in Deuteronomy in which the Sabbath appears. What is odd, then, is not its absence in the block that some scholars call the "Deuteronomistic History" but rather its presence in only one place in Deuteronomy itself. And that occurrence, though quite possibly reflecting an earlier version of the command, now suggests that the Decalogue has already been revealed, as witnessed *inter alia* by the words "as the LORD your God has commanded you" (Deut 5:12).[70] This sole reference should not be understood as a weight-bearing beam in the edifice of the overall Deuteronomic theology. Thus, in the books of Kings Judahite monarchs are judged by their fidelity to the Deuteronomic insistence that sacrifices may be brought to only one site (e.g., Deut 12:2–28), interpreted there as the Temple in the Davidic royal capital of Jerusalem.[71] They are not judged by the degree to which they upheld the Sabbath or any other sacred occasion, in pronounced contrast with those Pentateuchal norms of Priestly origin that make violation of the Sabbath a capital offense or the text in Third Isaiah that, conversely, makes its observance a key to admission to the worshiping community.[72] None of this is to argue that the Sabbath was unknown to the Deuteronomic school and its various sources, only that it exhibited nothing like the central importance it displayed in Priestly materials or in sources dating from relatively early in the Persian period.

If the biblical texts offer us little by which to answer our question about the Sabbath in the preexilic period, perhaps inscriptions from the period can fill in the gap. Unfortunately, these, too, offer no evidence, or at least no good evidence—unless their silence be taken as itself telltale evidence.

The sources are two.[73] The first, which dates to the last three decades of the seventh century BCE, is known as the Meṣad Ḥashavyahu or Yavneh Yam Ostracon after the site located about nine miles south of modern Jaffa where its several fragments were found. The inscription is an appeal by a farm worker to the local military governor to have a garment restored to him that he claims was improperly confiscated ("The Meṣad Ḥashavyahu [Yavneh Yam] Ostracon," *COS* 3.41:77–78).[74] In support of the propriety of his own behavior (and thus the merit of his petition), the worker writes, "And your servant harvested and measured and stored, according to the schedule, before quitting (*lpny šbt*)."[75]

In a discussion published two years after the inscription was discovered, Frank Moore Cross initially translated the last two words "before Sabbath," attributing the idea to "a suggestion of Professor W. F. Albright," his teacher and a commanding figure in biblical archaeology of the time. Cross then adds this in brackets, "After completion of this paper, Professor Shemaryahu Talmon suggested to me a technical meaning of *šbt*, meaning 'time off,' or 'quitting time,' in colloquial language, citing Ex. 21:19 and Ruth 2:7. The proposal is most attractive."[76] The term "quitting" is based on vocalizing the word either as *šabōt* or as *šibt*. (The Masoretic forms would be *šabôt/šabōt* and *šebet*, respectively.) The former is the infinitive construct of the root meaning *šbt*, "to stop," whereas the latter and the one that corresponds with Talmon's suggestion is the same form of *yšb*, which has a wide range of meanings among which the most common is probably "to sit."[77]

If *lpny šbt* here means "before Sabbath," as Cross first thought, it is without parallel in the Hebrew Bible, the closest candidate being *lipnê haššabbāt* ("at the approach of the sabbath") in Neh 13:19. This phrase, however, displays the definite article, whereas our ostracon does not,[78] but that may be a distinction that makes no difference. As Alexandra Grund points out, there are a number of instances in which the noun *šabbāt* appears in the Hebrew Bible without the definite article.[79] If, on the other hand, we take *šbt* to represent a verbal form, there is still a grammatical anomaly: one would have expected, and the orthographic conventions of the inscription allow, *šbty*, literally "my quitting" (but better "I quit"—*šobtî* or *šibtî* in Masoretic Hebrew).[80] Note that both biblical parallels that Talmon cited display the possessive.

If *lpny šbt* in the Meṣad Ḥashavyahu Ostracon means "before Sabbath," the complainant's point is that since he had completed all his assigned labors and quit only as the seventh day approached, there was no warrant for his garment to be seized. In that case, the context presupposes the legitimacy, and perhaps even the necessity, of ceasing to work before the onset of the special day. If, however, the same phrase means "before quitting," his legal argument is identical, but any connection with the Sabbath vanishes. My own sense is that of the two grammatical anomalies involving *lpny šbt*, it is the absence of the pronominal suffix, not the definite article, that is the graver. If this objection is dispositive, then the Meṣad Ḥashavyahu Ostracon does indeed offer epigraphic evidence for the day in which labor must cease already in preexilic Israel. The weight of scholarly opinion, however, seems to be in support of translating the phrase as "before quitting."[81] This would leave us currently with no clear epigraphic evidence for the importance or even existence of the Sabbath in preexilic Israelite religion.

Our second extrabiblical source is the set of Aramaic inscriptions left by a settlement of Jewish soldiers on the island of Elephantine in Upper Egypt and dating from the fifth century BCE, although the origin of the community may conceivably lie centuries earlier.[82] Herein lies the most obvious problem with inferring anything about the Sabbath in preexilic Israel from these documents: they are postexilic and, since they come from a military outpost in the south of Egypt, their utility as information about Judaism as it was practiced in the much larger communities in the Land of Israel or Babylonia is less than ideal. What is beyond doubt, though, is that the Jews on that island unabashedly observed a religion quite different from the sort endorsed in biblical law and in the prophets alike. Karel van der Toorn puts it well when he writes, "The Elephantine Jews were polytheists and Aramean in their religious outlook."[83] Nonetheless, a few of the texts found there clearly mention the Sabbath, and the personal names *Šabbǝtay* and *Šabbǝtît*, which derive from *šabbāt* (Sabbath), are also in evidence.[84]

Some of the relevant Elephantine documents simply mention the existence of "the Sabbath day" or its eve,[85] without providing any information about the nature of the day or its observance. But the pertinent section of the most substantively informative document reads as follows:

> I am sending you vegetables tomorrow. Meet the boat tomorrow on Sabbath (*mḥr bšbh*) lest they get lost/spoiled. By the life of YHH, if not, I shall take your lif[e]! Do not rely upon Meshulemmeth or upon Shemaiah.[86]

Addressed to a woman named Islaḥ, who some scholars conjecture was the writer's wife,[87] the ostracon calls upon her to meet a boat with perishable foodstuffs on the morrow, which also happens to be the Sabbath. Now, as we saw in the last chapter, buying and selling on the Sabbath as well as bringing in goods to be traded are the objects of ire in several biblical texts.[88] To some scholars, this suggests either, minimally, that such prohibitions had not yet been formulated when the inscription was composed or, maximally, that the Sabbath was of no concern at all to its author and its recipient. In Gard Granerød's judgment, for example, "it appears that the Sabbath was but a point in time, a chronological fix [*sic*] point that all involved parties were familiar with. The inscription does not suggest that the Sabbath was accompanied by any religious rites."[89] More recently, Yonatan Adler cites this inscription as evidence "that Persian-period Judeans were regularly engaging in commerce on the Sabbath."[90] As we have observed, however, it is not so easy to generalize from the Elephantine community to contemporary Judeans/Jews. Nor is it clear that the document in question implies that conducting business on the Sabbath was unexceptionable even at Elephantine. As Bezalel Porten interprets the text, "concern for the preservation of the vegetables and the threat to take Islaḥ's life unless she met the boat on the Sabbath may imply some extraordinary situation and indirectly attest the regular observance of the Sabbath."[91]

Lutz Doering sees the matter of the vegetable shipment very differently. In his view, the ostensible threat on poor Islaḥ's life is a hyperbole motivated by the writer's intense eagerness to see his commercial transaction to a successful conclusion, and the ostracon that mentions "the day before the Sabbath" gives no indication that the reference alludes to any impending day of rest.[92] Like Adler, Doering believes the Elephantine corpus derives from a period in which a wide-ranging prohibition on work on the Sabbath was as yet unknown. In particular, the thinking that motivated Nehemiah's determined reaction to commerce on that day must not yet have come into existence.[93]

In a case like this, as often in the study of antiquity, the uncertainties are so overwhelming that scholars must carefully hedge any conclusions they draw (though, sadly, many do not). Even were we to grant that the threat on Islaḥ's life was only a hyperbole, there would still be room to imagine a motivation for the urgency other than the commercial one that Doering detects. Porten's alternative, that Islaḥ would not ordinarily unload a shipment of goods on the Sabbath and thus needed further incentive to do so, cannot be eliminated, even if the death threat is not to be taken literally. The explanatory clause "lest they get lost/spoiled" may indicate anxiety about a realistic monetary loss, but it may also and equally indicate an exceptional need for leniency in the application of customary sabbatical law because of that looming possibility.[94] As for Nehemiah's spirited prevention of trading on the Sabbath, there is no basis to assume that he was innovating rather than enforcing an established norm that had fallen into widespread, and in his mind indefensible, neglect. Here, an analogy with the denunciations of Israel for their wholesale desecration of the Sabbath in Ezekiel (whether original to the prophet of that name or not) suggests itself.[95] And if Amos 8:4–7 derives from the eighth-century prophet and concerns the seventh day of the week (rather than the fifteenth of the lunar month),[96] we have an even earlier, in fact preexilic, precedent to Nehemiah's actions some three centuries later.

In sum, in the best of cases, it is dangerous to extrapolate from the nonobservance of a law to its nonexistence—and the Jewish community at Elephantine, which in violation of Deuteronomic law maintained its own temple, after all, and venerated a goddess named Anat-Yahu, is not the best of cases. Rather than drawing sweeping conclusions about the history of sabbatical law from the scant evidence this community has left us, it would be better to assume considerable diversity in practice and in the underlying norms in the Judaism of the time.

As for the name *Šabbǝtay* and its feminine cognate *Šabbǝtît*, which indicate birth on the Sabbath (the former, usually spelled "Shabbetai" in English, is still in use), Doering concedes that their existence shows that the Sabbath was thought of as a distinctive day, though he concludes that they convey no indication of what laws defined the Sabbath or how widely it was observed.[97] More recently, however, Granerød disputes that these names have any relationship to the Jewish festival of the seventh day at all, noting that non-Jews also bear them. To him, "the name Shabbethai that appears in the vicinity of Elephantine should be explained as a Babylonian name, formed on the basis of the word *šapattu*, the Akkadian name of the day of the full moon," a position he reinforces by noting that "the name is attested in a Babylonian context, as well."[98] Given the emphasis on the weekly event in roughly contemporaneous Jewish sources and the absence therein of any indication that Jews were celebrating the Mesopotamian *šapattu*, however, this seems forced. Doering's view is less so. He expresses uncertainty about whether the name when used by non-Jews refers to anything more than the weekly calendrical occasion or, instead, alludes to some distinctly religious aspect of the day.[99]

As before, Porten is more decisive and again more religiously traditional. He thinks the distribution of the name *Šabbətay* constitutes evidence of an attraction by outsiders to Jewish Sabbath observance.[100] That may be so, but the degree to which either Jews or Gentiles were alert to the etymology of the name remains unclear. Consider the analogy of Anglophone Jews who name their sons "Peter" or "Paul" without knowing, or perhaps without caring about, the Christian resonance of those New Testament names. That Jews at Elephantine, on the other hand, named their own children *Šabbətay* or *Šabbətît* probably testifies to the importance of the Sabbath there, whatever the technical details or the actual extent of its observance may have been. The proposition that the use of such names at Elephantine and the religious importance of the holiday in Persian-period Jewish literature are unrelated phenomena strains credulity. But, as was the case regarding commerce on the Sabbath, the uncertainties surrounding these names are many, and the data are ambiguous.

Along with the Elephantine materials, we must also consider two other corpora of texts by or about Jews from very roughly the same period, but this time from Babylonia, not Egypt. The first is a set of about one hundred tablets dating from 572 to 447 BCE and produced in a town with the revealing name Āl-Yāḫūdu, "Judahtown" or "Jewtown." In this case, we find much more clarity about the actual Jewish practice of the Sabbath than we saw in Elephantine because, in a word, it would seem there was none. Whereas Yigal Bloch argues, based on sophisticated calendrical calculations, that Jews at Elephantine waited until nightfall (i.e., the end of the Sabbath) before signing contracts, thus apparently seeking to avoid violation of the sacred day, on the basis of the currently available data from Āl-Yāḫūdu, he discovers the reverse: Jews did indeed conclude transactions on the Sabbath.[101] At present, there seems to be no countervailing evidence to the impression that at that site the day was simply not observed.

Our second trove of texts about Babylonian Jewry comes from the next century. Known as the Murašu Documents, they are the business records of a family in the already ancient city of Nippur (now in southeastern Iraq), which was then part of the Persian Empire. The tablets date from the mid- to the late fifth century BCE and include records that involve individuals with identifiable Jewish names. Here, too, although the set of texts is smaller than what we have from Āl-Yāḫūdu, to quote Bloch, they "reveal no conscious effort on the part of ethnic Judeans in Babylonia to refrain from participating in transactions concluded on the Sabbath."[102]

We have now examined epigraphic evidence from sites in the Land of Israel, Egypt, and Babylonia, ranging in dates from seventh to the fifth century BCE. None of them affords any secure foundation upon which to base a very solid conclusion about the extent to which the Sabbath was observed or how it was conceived. The most we can say is that those inscriptions cannot be responsibly invoked to counter the curious absence of the Sabbath in the historical books. If anything, the paucity of inscriptional sources about the Sabbath reinforces the sense that it was not of great importance in all social sectors and may well even have been unknown in some.

This is, of course, in glaring contradiction to the high importance of the Sabbath in biblical literature from the exilic and postexilic periods, such as Ezekiel, Third Isaiah, Nehemiah, and, of course, the Priestly source of the Pentateuch if the latter dates from one of those periods.[103] An exceptionally long-lived position among scholars attributes the high status of the Sabbath in those texts precisely to the new situation that the exile brought about. To quote an exceedingly influential voice from the nineteenth century, Julius Wellhausen concluded that "it in fact gained in importance to an extraordinary degree during the exile, having severed itself completely, not merely from agriculture, but in particular also from the sacrificial system, and gained independence as a holy solemnity of rest."[104] To give a much more recent example, in Alexandra Grund's view the destruction of the Temple and the subsequent exile made it impossible for everybody to observe the festivals, including the old šab/pattu, and, as a result, "in this situation, it was natural that the seventh day assumed an elevated significance."[105] The Āl-Yāḫūdu and Murašu documents, however, indicate that the Sabbath may well have been widely disregarded in Babylonia, too, both during and after the exile, and this, in turn, can be taken to suggest that the widespread observance of the holiday may be later than Wellhausen and those who have followed his lead think. So, in fact, argues Yonatan Adler, who concludes that prior to the mid-second century BCE, "there is simply no reliable evidence that the notion of certain activities being forbidden on the Sabbath was widely observed—or even commonly known of—among the Judean masses."[106]

But can this be invoked as support for the proposition that much earlier, even before the exile, *no* sectors of Israelite society saw the Sabbath as a matter of utmost significance? In my judgment, the emphasis the day receives in Eze-kiel's oracles, which begin in 593 BCE[107] (some seven years before the fall of the Temple) might suggest a more complex picture, one in which certain perspectives and the schools that had been championing them all along came to the fore in the new circumstances of the exile. This is not to deny, of course, that in the case of Ezekiel one must be open to the possibility that the passages stressing the Sabbath are postexilic interpolations and reflect the high importance that institution assumed in the later period, as some scholars have argued.[108] Nonetheless, taken together, the textual and the currently available epigraphic data suggest that although the origins of the Sabbath are earlier than the exile, it came into literary prominence only during the exile or very soon before it and came to be widely practiced perhaps only several centuries later.

If Adler is right, and mass observance of the Sabbath came into existence only in the Hellenistic period, then surely what confronts us is one of the most astounding reversals in all of Jewish history: what had been the practice of small groups at various times became, in the Hellenistic period, a general practice and emblematic of the people at large. And so it was to remain for millennia.[109]

Whatever the human historical circumstances that brought about the heightened status of the Sabbath, the status itself has long survived them, and whereas many historians may think of the emphasis on the Sabbath that begins to predominate in exilic literature as compensation for a loss, many Jews over the centuries have thought of the Sabbath itself as quite the opposite—not as consolation for something missing but as a precious gift in its own right, one to be carefully protected and lovingly practiced.

Let us now summarize our discussion of the origin and early practice of the Sabbath and conclude with some reflections on the theological meaning of the institution in its earliest stages as far as we can reconstruct it.

The beginnings remain cloaked in a cloud of mystery, and, on the basis of our current information, efforts to pierce that cloud and identify a clear logic to its origin are unlikely to succeed. What we can do, and have attempted to do in this discussion, is to place the Sabbath in the larger cultural world out of which ancient Israel emerged and to explore what its earliest meaning may have been. We have found that the attribution of special significance to the number seven and the sequence of six items capped by a seventh and climactic one were widespread, predate the biblical sources, and continue and gain force in them. In particular, we have drawn attention to the way in which the seventh day in some ancient Near Eastern texts stands in contradiction to the previous six yet brings the activity that takes place in them to a successful conclusion. Seven was, to be sure, but one of several numbers with a special significance in those compositions and in the Hebrew Bible, and, even in the latter, a pattern of eight days—that is, seven plus a climactic one—can be found in more than one ritual context. Humanly speaking, what it was that caused some Israelites at some point to adopt the heptadic pattern and thus to invent the sabbatical week remains wrapped in that cloud of mystery.

In what seems be the earliest textual reference to the Sabbath, according to the reconstruction of many critical biblical historians, the occasion does not yet have that name but is simply denominated as "the seventh day" (Exod 23:12). That the verse in question immediately follows two about the seventh year as a time when the farmer must allow his fields to lie fallow and, moreover, do so explicitly for the benefit of the poor and the wild animals is highly suggestive. So is the obvious correlation of the immediately preceding verse (v. 11) with the point in the sabbatical ordinance itself that the seventh day must be free of labor so that the beasts of burden, the slave, and the stranger may be refreshed (v. 12). Like the seventh year, the seventh day held strong humanitarian associations and represented an effort to institutionalize and routinize the characteristic social ethic of the society.

It would be wrong, however, to interpret the seventh day (or, for that matter, the seventh year) exclusively on a horizontal axis, as if it were simply an ethical ordinance intended to realize an ideal of social justice. For—again, whatever the prehistory—it appears in Exod 23:12 on the lips of the Deity, who is, in fact, presented as the authority behind the special day and its guarantor and who in the same collection gives decrees that modern people would unreservedly classify as "ritual." There is, in other words, also a vertical axis to the early Sabbath, an axis that points to God's role in the institution and demands a theological interpretation and not merely a social one.[110]

Here, we can further develop an insight of Grund about the law of the seventh year (also not yet termed "sabbatical") in Exod 23:11. Drawing attention in particular to the mention there of the "wild beasts" that are free to eat of the growth in the fields lying fallow, she finds a kind of controlled reintroduction of the chaotic, uncultivated world into the domain of human culture.[111] Within the worldview of the Hebrew Bible—and even the structure of the Covenant Collection itself—this ritualized forbearance of claims to human proprietorship, however, cannot be disengaged from the affirmation of God's supervening ownership of the world. To this one might make an analogy to a wide variety of various biblical laws, such as that of the first fruits offering and the underlying idea that only after God's rights have been acknowledged may the farmer partake of what he has raised.[112] It is not simply that the farmer expresses gratitude to the divine source of his bounty through his offering. Rather, he also identifies himself as a kind of tenant on God's cosmic estate. In the words of a later text, the law of the Jubilee Year, "The land must not be sold beyond reclaim, for the land is Mine; you are but strangers resident

(*gērîm wətôšāḇîm*) with Me" (Lev 25:23). Human land tenure is but temporary and limited; it must be subordinate to God's permanent and absolute
ownership. Since, in this theological perspective, the farmer himself is, as it
were, a "stranger" (*gēr*) working on God's estate, it is not surprising that he
must allow his own stranger to be refreshed by ceasing to work his farm on
the seventh day. And since the farmer is himself a servant of God—whose
laws, after all, he is hearing in the Covenant Collection in which Exod 23:12 is
found—it is not surprising that he must allow his bondman to rest as well. The
wild animals, the beasts of burden, the stranger, the bondman, and, yes, the
householder himself—all must yield one day a week to the God whose laws
they are hearing. In Matitiahu Tsevat's words, "Every seventh day the Israelite
renounces his autonomy and affirms God's dominion over him. . . . Keeping
the sabbath is acceptance of the sovereignty of God."[113]

A productive comparison can also be made with the laws of the priestly
tithe in their differing versions, which the texts present as grounded in the key
idea that the priests have no territorial allotments because "the LORD is their
portion" (Deut 18:2).[114] The nonpriestly Israelite's ownership of the fruits of his
labors is legitimate—there is no denial of private property in these laws—but
it is not absolute. Theologically speaking, part of what he produces belongs
neither to himself nor to the community nor to the government but rather
to the ultimate proprietor. Socially speaking, an Israelite's acknowledgment of
the LORD's supervening claim works to the benefit of the landless and to the
ostensibly unproductive members of society as well.

Finally, the same can be said of those ordinances that forbid the farmer,
for example, to reap "all the way to the edges of your field, or gather the glean-
ings of the harvest," or "pick your vineyard bare, or gather the fallen fruit of
your vineyard." Instead, the same text goes on to instruct him, "you shall leave
them for the poor and the stranger: I the LORD am your God" (Lev 19:9–10).
Indeed, the image of the harvested field with its edges or corners left for the
poor by divine decree is an illuminating graphic analogy to the stipulated practice of sowing one's land and gathering its yield for six years, leaving the uncultivated growth of the seventh for the needy and wild animals (Exod 23:10–11).
More to our immediate point, it also illuminates the closely related practice
of working for six days and ceasing from labor on the seventh "in order that
your ox and your ass may rest, and that your bondman and stranger may be
refreshed" (v. 12). What is enjoined in all these instances is a human forbearance from making a claim to the totality: no fully harvested field, no set of
seven consecutive days of labor. And in all of them, the underlying theology
is one that affirms God's proprietary claim and sees it honored in donations
to the needy and vulnerable. This notion of the needy as the human stand-
ins for God is nowhere better stated than in the book of Proverbs: "He who

is generous to the poor makes a loan to the LORD; / He will replay him his due" (Prov 19:17).[115] What appears to be a gift turns out, by the logic of divine promise, to be a loan. It works to the benefit of the donor, the recipient, and the Deity alike. The dynamic in Exod 23:12 is not so specific, of course, but, as in that famous verse in Proverbs, here, too, the apparent gift to the poor and the vulnerable is rich with theological implications—ones that, in fact, remain with the Sabbath as it develops over the centuries.

From a historical-critical perspective, it would be an error to speak of the seventh day as it appears in Exod 23:12 and 34:21 as reflecting a doctrine of creation over the course of six days, consummated in the blessing and sanctification of the seventh that is so well-known from Gen 1:1–2:3 and the sabbatical commandment of the Decalogue in the version that appears in Exod 20:8–11. The reason is that the Exod 23:12 and 34:21 are generally taken to derive from an earlier period, so that reading them as presupposing these later texts (later, that is, in order of composition, not in order of their appearance in the redacted text) is based on mistaken chronology. If, on the other hand, we are deliberately interpreting the completed biblical text now in our possession rather than its antecedents as they were understood in their own time, such a move is not only warranted but, at some stage in the interpretive process, positively required. In that case, what I called the "ritualized forbearance of claims to human proprietorship [in the face of] God's supervening ownership of the world" must be connected to his authorship of the world in general and humankind in particular. But even within the parameters of historical interpretation—and without any commitment to canonical reading—one can see an affinity of the underlying theology of the seventh year and the seventh day with that of the creation story with which the Bible opens. Both attest to God's mastery of the world and its concomitant implications for human labor, Exod 23:12 and 34:21 attesting by implication and legal stipulation and Gen 1:1–2:3 attesting explicitly and narratively.

Finally, one can also see in the institution of the seventh day a kind of recurring calendrical enactment of the self-perception of the people Israel as understood in a wide swath of biblical sources. Consider as an example the LORD's dramatic and resonant offer of covenant in Exodus:

> [5]Now then, if you will obey Me faithfully and keep My covenant, you shall be My treasured possession among all the peoples. Indeed, all the earth is Mine, [6]but you shall be to Me a kingdom of priests and a holy nation. (Exod 19:5–6)

Although the whole world is God's, only Israel—whom, in a reworking of this text, Deuteronomy will significantly term "the smallest of peoples"

(7:7)—is his "treasured possession," set apart for him as a "holy nation." Similarly, the whole week falls under God's authority—"Six days you shall do your work" (Exod 23:12)—but the seventh alone is set apart as special, or as many other texts call it, "holy."[116] To understand the Sabbath even at an early period of ancient Israelite history, one must reckon with the fact that the operative identification is not only of Israel with the vulnerable slave and stranger; it is also of Israel with that which is holy—the holy day for the holy people, the holy people for the holy day.

CHAPTER 4

The Creation of the World or the Exodus from Egypt?

————————

FOR MOST PEOPLE, THE SABBATH is known primarily from its appearance as the fourth item in the Decalogue, or, as it is most often called in English, the Ten Commandments. In a Jewish context, the latter term is misleading, since rabbinic tradition enumerates the commandments of the Torah as 613, not ten (though it does give special prominence to the Decalogue). In that framework, the two sabbatical texts in Exodus on which we concentrated in the previous chapter (23:12 and 34:21) are thus no less obligatory than the Decalogue. Furthermore, the term "Ten Commandments" accurately renders neither the Hebrew of the biblical text itself, which is 'ăśeret haddəḇārîm, "The Ten Words/Utterances,"[1] nor the Rabbinic name, 'ăśeret haddibbərôt, "The Ten Acts of Speech/Revelations/Declarations." Nonetheless, since in English any term other than "commandment" to refer to the items in the Decalogue is awkward, we shall continue to use that less-than-ideal term here, at least with respect to its sabbatical norm. It should also be noted that over the centuries various communities, Jewish as well as Christian, have divided up the Decalogue in different ways, though always, of course, retaining the sum of ten specified in scripture. Even today, the Roman Catholic and Lutheran communions count the sabbatical commandment as the third, not the fourth.[2]

Less well-known among the general public than it should be is the fact that the Decalogue exists in two versions, one in Exodus and the other in Deuteronomy (Exod 20:2–14; Deut 5:6–18), and the two are not identical.[3] This has also occasioned some division of opinion over the centuries, as traditional scholars have debated how God could have issued both variants at once on Sinai (which Deuteronomy calls "Horeb"[4]). Referring to the difference in the first word of the fourth commandment (Exod 20:8 and Deut 5:12), an early midrash asserts that "'Remember' and 'observe' were spoken in one utterance—something that the mouth cannot utter and the ear cannot hear" (b. Šebu. 20b).[5] This is a solution that has become famous from its inclusion in *Lekhah Dodi*, the joyous hymn sung in synagogues on Friday evening to salute the arrival of the Sabbath:

"Observe" and "remember" in one utterance,
the one and unique God made us hear.
The LORD is one and his name is one,
for renown, for splendor, and for praise.

In this stanza, the author, Solomon Alkabetz, a sixteenth-century kabbalist living in the Galilean city of Safed, connects the miraculous oneness of the two variant openings of the fourth commandment to the at least equally miraculous—in fact, unparalleled—oneness of the God who issued the command. Combining the end of the famous first verse of the Shema ("the LORD is one," Deut 6:4[6]) with the wording of a prophecy about the coming of God's kingship that is dependent on it ("On that day, the LORD shall be one and his name one," Zech 14:9[7]), Alkabetz brilliantly deploys the textual variation in the two versions of the fourth commandment to underscore the eschatological dimension of the Sabbath: the oneness of the command is an earnest of the oneness of the divine name upon which all the world will someday obediently call. When, at the end of the hymn, the Jewish congregation rises to greet "the bride," as the song calls the Sabbath, they are preenacting the final redemption when they will greet God—there described (in a reworking of Isa 62:5) as her groom—and his promised messiah as well.[8]

Another mystery concerns the "two tablets" upon which many biblical texts report the Decalogue was incised.[9] Although a widespread assumption, rooted in antiquity, would have the ten utterances divided equally between the two tablets, the appearance of equality is, in one sense, a mirage. As Nahum Sarna points out, "such an arrangement would have resulted in a grave imbalance; one tablet would have contained 146 Hebrew words and the other only 26."[10] Another tradition, also of ancient origin, simply conceives of each tablet as inscribing the entire Decalogue, so that Moses is presented with two identical copies. Brilliantly bringing the two mysteries together, Saadia, a tenth-century Jewish authority in Egypt and Babylonia, asserts that each tablet was complete yet different from the other: one contained the version in Exodus 20 and the other the version in Deuteronomy 5.[11] God thus pronounced them both at once, "something that," as the midrash put it, "the mouth cannot utter and the ear cannot hear," and then, in a necessary concession to human finitude, wrote them in two versions, corresponding to the enigmatic "two tablets" mentioned repeatedly in the biblical text.

To historical-critical scholars, all these traditional efforts to harmonize the two variant Decalogues are not only unnecessary but actively dangerous, for they obscure both the historical process by which the text currently in our hands came into being and the diverse and developing religion of Israel that, to one degree or another, the redacted text conceals. As we have had occasion to observe, what traditional believers may see as an embarrassment to be explained away, historians see as a resource to be put to good use in their reconstructive labors.[12]

In the particular case of the Decalogue, the issue is not limited to the historical relationship of the two versions to each other; it also includes the process of growth within each of them and the hypothetical original version that predates both. Among those who seek to address the latter problem, the large measure of inconsistency internal to each text of the Decalogue is taken as a telltale sign of expansion. Most commandments are cast in the negative ("You shall not . . ."), for example, but two are phrased as positive obligations: "Remember/Observe" and "Honor" (Exod 20:8, 12; Deut 5:12, 16). Some are quite short—three of them consist of only two words in Hebrew (Exod 20:13a–c; Deut 5:17a–c)—while others, such as the prohibition on producing sculptures and other likenesses (Exod 20:4–6; Deut 5:8–10), are lengthy by the standards of biblical law and include theological reflections. (The two versions of the fourth commandment, to which we shall turn anon, fall into the latter category.) To historical critics, such expansions, like the motive clause at the end of the fifth commandment (Exod 20:12, itself slightly longer in Deut 5:16), serve as suggestive signs of growth in the period before either version underwent standardization. Something similar might be said about the fact that each Decalogue begins with God's speaking in the first person but then shifting into the third (at Exod 20:7 and Deut 5:11).[13] Finally, even the number ten appears in Exodus (though not Deuteronomy) only in connection with the second revelation of the Decalogue (Exod 34:28; Deut 4:13; 10:4). The possibility that the earliest version included fewer utterances cannot be discounted. In other words, the expansion may have involved more than additions or replacements within a given utterance; it may have involved the introduction of whole new commandments.

All this has led to a rich, creative, and unending series of conjectured reconstructions, some of them insightful and ingenious but none of them, given the nature of the evidence, able to command a consensus, at least for long.[14] Even on the particular issue of the relationship of the two versions, diametrically opposing opinions endure. In an impressively detailed study, Frank-Lothar Hossfeld, for instance, argues for the priority of some form of the Deuteronomic version over that in Exodus.[15] As he sees it, there was an original set of seven commandments that came to serve as the preface to the Deuteronomic law collection (Deut 12–26), and those seven were expanded by another hand, also in the Deuteronomic school, who added the commandments about false oaths (or, as it has often been rendered, taking the LORD's name "in vain"), the Sabbath, and the honoring of parents, thus eventually yielding the number ten.[16] In Hossfeld's thinking, as with others,' the fact that those three commandments refer to the LORD in the third person (Deut 5:11–16) is a telltale sign of their separate origin. Later, he argues, a Priestly source redacted the Deuteronomic Decalogue in accordance with Priestly theology and made it the headpiece to the whole account of Sinaitic revelation—hence, the version in Exodus 20. Hossfeld's position has won a considerable following but also an equally considerable set of critics, as one could predict, given the highly speculative nature of the whole enterprise and the correspondingly short longevity of its, or any other, guiding presuppositions on a topic like this.[17]

Norbert Lohfink is one scholar who subscribes to a sharply contrasting position. As he sees it, the version in Exodus 20 is historically prior, and however much internal growth can be detected either there or in Deuteronomy 5, the latter is still a deliberate, theologically driven recomposition of this or some other older version.[18] Certainly, in the Deuteronomic version as it now stands, the two appearances of the source citation formula, "as the LORD your God has commanded you" (Deut 5:12, 16), which are unparalleled in Exodus 20, speak for the historical priority of the latter (although we cannot know when those two clauses came into the text).[19] Richard D. Nelson makes the stimulating observation that in the Deuteronomic Decalogue, these formulae appear only in the commandments about the Sabbath and parents, "the two that positively 'command' (rather than forbid) behaviors. Moreover, since these two commandments are the only ones whose motivations differ from those of Exod 20," Nelson goes on to observe, "'as [the LORD] commanded' may stress that the imperatives themselves have been transmitted unchanged, even if the motivations have been expanded."[20] In other words, however innovative Deuteronomy may seem to us and however distinctive its theological orientation and characteristic vocabulary may be, it wants to be taken as restatement of the one Torah revealed to Moses on Horeb. The differences, that is, must all be understood to be in the service of the selfsame revelation that "the LORD your God has [already] commanded you."

Most of the differences between the two versions of the Decalogue—of which there are more than twenty[21]—are, to be sure, small. The largest and most consequential of them lies in the fourth commandment, as indicated below:

[8]Remember the Sabbath Day and keep it holy.	[12]Observe the sabbath day and keep it holy, <u>as the LORD your God has commanded you.</u> [13]Six days you
[9]Six days you shall labor and do all your work,	shall labor and do all your work,
[10]but the seventh day is a sabbath of the LORD your God: you shall not	[14]but the seventh day is a sabbath of the LORD your God; you shall not

do any work—you, your son or your daughter, your male or female slave,   or your cattle, or the stranger who is within your settlements.

¹¹For in six days the LORD made heaven and earth and sea, and all that is in them, and He rested on the seventh day; therefore the LORD blessed the sabbath day and hallowed it. (Exod 20:8–11)

do any work—you, your son or your daughter, your male or female slave, <u>your ox or your ass</u>, or <u>any of</u> your cattle, or the stranger who is within your settlements, <u>so that</u> <u>your male and female slave may</u> <u>rest as you do.</u>

¹⁵<u>Remember that you were a slave</u> <u>in the land of Egypt and the LORD</u> <u>your God freed you from there with</u> <u>a mighty hand and an outstretched</u> <u>arm;</u> therefore the LORD <u>your God</u> <u>has commanded you to practice the</u> <u>sabbath day.</u> (Deut 5:12–15)[22]

The divergences begin with the first word, "Remember" (*zākôr*) in Exod 20:8 in contradistinction to "Observe" (*šāmôr*) in Deut 5:12, as long ago noted in the traditional Jewish sources mentioned above. Within the biblical context, the difference is slight and may, conceivably, not even exist. As Moshe Weinfeld points out, both verbs "connote 'keep' as well as 'remember.'" Thus, when in the context of Joseph's report of his ostensibly megalomaniacal dreams and the resentment they provoked in his brothers, Gen 37:11 reports that "his father kept (*šāmar*) the matter in mind," the meaning is that he "remembered" it. In further support of the claim of synonymy, Weinfeld notes the use of the same two verbs in synonymous parallelism in Ps 103:18, where God's "steadfast love" and "beneficence" (v. 17) fall upon "Those who keep (*šōmərê*) His covenant / And remember (*zōkərê*) His precepts."[23]

Clearly, in such a context "keeping" or "observing" is something other than a mechanical act detached from thinking, and, conversely, "remembering" is no mere mental act detached from practice.[24] Indeed, as Weinfeld goes on to note, both verbs can be paired with the verb "to do" (*ʿāśâ*),[25] as indeed they are at the end of Ps 103:18 (above), whose last word is actually *laʿăśôtām*, literally, "to do them." In Deuteronomy in particular, the coupling of *šāmar* and *ʿāśâ* is quite common.[26] That Deuteronomy would employ *šāmar* where a parallel text used *zākar* is hardly surprising: *šāmar* is a characteristic Deuteronomic verb, appearing nearly thirty times in that book.

In the case of the variation in the initial words of the fourth commandment, Weinfeld goes on to note that the divergence may nonetheless be significant. The difference is not between a mental act and a practical observance. In Deuteronomy, rather, the question is whether the point is "observance of the law" (*šāmar*) or "historical remembrance" (*zākar*):

It should be noted, however, that *zkr* connotes commemoration, a concept so central to priestly theology (cf. the term *zkrwn*, characteristic of priestly literature). Indeed, the idea of commemoration comes up clearly in the motivation clause of the Sabbath commandment: the Israelites ought to rest because God rested on this day (Exod 20:11). Deuteronomy, which provides a different motivation for the Sabbath, distinguished between *šmr* "observe" and *zkr* "remember." The former is used for the observance of the law, while the latter is reserved for historical remembrance; thus for the observance of the Sabbath he uses *šmr*, whereas for its motivation he uses *wzkrt*: "*Remember* (*zkr*) that you were a slave in the land of Egypt ... therefore YHWH ... has commanded you to observe the Sabbath day" (v 15).[27]

In other words, although the semantic range of each verb includes both remembrance and practice, in the Decalogue of Exodus 20 the cessation of labor and the act of sanctification that are enjoined commemorate God's resting on the primordial seventh day. The human practice is thus in imitation of the divine act and a commemoration of the larger process—the creation of the universe—that it consummated. In Deuteronomy 5, by contrast, ceasing from work and sanctifying the Sabbath are in the nature of covenantal stipulations. What is to be "remembered" is not the Sabbath but rather God's taking the people Israel out of Egypt and the bondage they endured there, and it is this that is principally to motivate their practice of the sacred day.

In Weinfeld's thinking, it is instructive that the variant in Deuteronomy ends where the parallel in Exodus begins, with an injunction to remember (*vəzākartā* and *zākôr*, respectively). He sees the appearance of "remember" in Deut 5:15 as a purposeful reuse of the same verb in Exod 20:8 in order to shift the theological character of sabbatical practice from "sacred commemoration" to "historical remembrance." The wording thus offers another piece of evidence for both the priority of the formulation in Exodus and the Deuteronomic author's familiarity with it.[28] This is possible, but considering the prominence of historical memory, especially that of the exodus, in Deuteronomic preaching, the argument is unconvincing. In Deut 7:18, for example, Moses, concerned that the Israelites will quail before the populous Canaanite nations they will soon face, enjoins them to "bear in mind (*zākôr tizkōr*) what the LORD your God did to Pharaoh and all the Egyptians." Similarly, in Deut 9:7 he warns them to "remember" (*zəkōr*) the sorry history of their provocations and defiance of God "from the day that you left the land of Egypt until you reached this place." To cite a last instance, in exhorting his hearers to obey the priests in cases of skin diseases, the Deuteronomic Moses marshals the memory of Miriam: "Remember (*zākôr*) what the LORD your God did to Miriam on the journey after you left Egypt" (Deut 24:9).[29] In sum, the sentence "Remember that you were a slave in the land of Egypt and the LORD your God freed you from there with a mighty hand and an outstretched arm" at the end of the fourth commandment in Deut 5:15 is probably another instance of the same pattern and need not specifically reflect "Remember the Sabbath day and keep it holy" in Exod 20:8.

If the opening verse of the Exodus version of the fourth commandment and the closing verse of the Deuteronomic version resemble each other, the very last clause of each version does as well: "therefore (ʿal-kēn) the LORD blessed the sabbath day and hallowed it" (Exod 20:11b) and "therefore (ʿal-kēn) the LORD your God has commanded you to observe the sabbath day" (Deut 5:15b). There is, however, an unmistakable difference. Exodus 20:11b grounds the institution of the Sabbath in divine activity, the LORD's blessing and sanctifying the seventh day of the creation week. Deuteronomy 5:15b, by contrast, is not a statement about the origin or theological foundation of the Sabbath at all. Rather, it speaks to why "you"—that is, the people Israel, addressed in the person of the head of household—should observe it. It appeals to the manumitted and repatriated slave's experience of liberation from backbreaking bondage as a motivation for practicing the weekly day of cessation from labor. In that sense, the injunction upon Israel to remember slavery in Egypt and the LORD's intervention to deliver them from it follows naturally from the last clause of the previous verse, "so that your male and female slave may rest as you do" (Deut 5:14). "You"—the Israelite father to whom the Decalogue is addressed—are not so far from your slave after all. But for the grace of the God who commands you to practice the Sabbath, you would still be a slave yourself.

It can, in fact, be argued that the very structure of the Deuteronomic version of the fourth commandment attests to the centrality of slavery and the relief from it in the underlying theology. Here, the keen insight of Norbert Lohfink that the passage is structured as a fourfold chiasm, as indicated in the diagram below, is highly suggestive (Deut 5:12–15):

A Observe the sabbath day
  B the LORD your God has commanded you
    C the LORD your God
      D male and female slave
      D´ male and female slave
    C´ the LORD your God
  B´ the LORD your God has commanded you
A´ practice the sabbath day[30]

The actual injunctions to "observe/practice the Sabbath day" are thus positioned as bookends to the rationale that is developed within them in a structure that Nelson terms "concentric."[31] To be sure, not all the material in the commandment fits into the chiastic arrangement that he and Lohfink detect here. To give one example, Deut 5:13, "Six days you shall labor and do all your work," finds no counterpart later in the text. Nonetheless, if the overall structure, which is not paralleled in the Exodus variant (20:8–11), is intentional (as would appear to be the case), our eye is drawn most naturally to the central items in the chiasm, the repeating terms "male and female slave" (D and D′, above). It is they to whom the first three and last three elements of the fourth commandment point, thus reinforcing its concluding sentence. The Israelite householder's motivation for observing the Sabbath lies in his empathy with slaves and his recognition of why his own status changed: "Remember that you were a slave in the land of Egypt and the LORD your God freed you from there with a mighty hand and an outstretched arm" (Deut 5:15a). Note that whereas the entire household, including oxen, asses, cattle, and aliens resident in his community, are obligated in the prohibition on labor, it is the "male and female slave" alone who are said to "rest" along with the householder himself on the Sabbath day (v. 14). They are, as it were, his alter egos. Once again, but for the grace of the God who commands him to practice the Sabbath, his life and theirs would be the same—a dreary and monotonous one at that, utterly lacking respite.

Alexandra Grund is thus right to view the Deuteronomic Decalogue as making the Sabbath into a kind of weekly Passover.[32] Whereas the festival of Passover—or, in biblical parlance, the sacrifice of the Passover and the immediately ensuing seven-day Festival of Unleavened Bread—constitutes a yearly reminder of the exodus, the version of the fourth commandment in Deuteronomy makes the weekly Sabbath serve the same purpose. The rabbis of Talmudic times go further. Relying on Deut 16:3, "so that you may remember the day of your departure from the land of Egypt as long as you live"—or, more literally, "all the days of your life"—they make recollecting the exodus into a daily requirement, alongside the annual obligations associated with Passover and the weekly obligation to observe the Sabbath day. In halakhah (rabbinic law), one way by which the daily requirement can be fulfilled is through the recitation of the three-paragraph text known (after its first word) as the *Shemaʿ*, which Jews are obligated to recite in the morning and in the evening every day.[33] The last of those paragraphs (Num 15:37–41) focuses on the duty to affix ṣiṣīt, or fringes, to the corners of garments—an obligation that applies, as the rabbis understand the matter, only in the daytime. So why is that third paragraph recited in the evening? According to Simeon ben Zoma, a sage from the late first and early second centuries CE, the answer lies in the first word of the phrase "all the days of your life." "'The days of your life' [would mean] the days [only]," he taught; "'all the days of your life' [includes] the nights [as well]" (m. Ber. 1:5). On this understanding, remembering the exodus is for the Jew more than a daily obligation: it is also a nightly one.

If, as many (but not all) scholars believe, the version of the Decalogue in Deuteronomy is dependent on the one in Exodus, to which it appears to allude but from which it differs in significant ways, the grounding of the fourth commandment in the exodus was nonetheless already of venerable antiquity by the time Deuteronomy was promulgated in the late seventh century BCE.[34] As we have seen, an early Israelite collection of laws links the sabbatical ordinance to others that protect the vulnerable and, accordingly, places it directly after the law of the seventh year, in which the poor and the wild beasts may eat of what the fallow fields bring forth (Exod 23:10–11). The explanation for the Sabbath in that location is suspiciously similar: "in order that your ox and your ass may rest, and that your bondman and the stranger may be refreshed" (Exod 23:12).[35] In sum, if the actual wording of the fourth commandment in Exod 20:8–11 is older than that in Deut 5:12–15, the idea underlying the latter version is quite early—in fact, as we shall see, earlier than the casting of the Sabbath as a commemoration of creation.

It is possible to go further and to argue that the expression "your ox or your ass" in the fourth commandment in Deuteronomy (Deut 5:14) indicates a reformulation of Exod 23:12, which uses the same wording.[36] The version in Exodus, by contrast, simply reads "your cattle" (Exod 20:10) in accordance with the style of the Priestly source of the Pentateuch.[37] Against this, however, we should note that the linking of those two highly common farm animals is not unusual, especially in Deuteronomy,[38] and need not specifically reflect the sabbatical law of Exod 23:12.

More suggestive is Lohfink's observation that "your ox or your ass" in the Deuteronomic Sabbath commandment anticipates the phrasing "his ox, or his ass" in the very last commandment, the prohibition on coveting (Deut 5:21), just as its language about the exodus from Egypt echoes the first utterance of the ten, according to the traditional Jewish enumeration. Compare "I the LORD am your God who brought you out (*hôṣē'tîkā*) of the land of Egypt, the house of bondage" (Deut 5:6) in the opening of the Decalogue with "Remember that you were a slave in the land of Egypt and the LORD your God freed you (*vayyôṣî'ăkā*) from there with a mighty hand and an outstretched arm" (Deut 5:15) in the Deuteronomic version of its fourth commandment. To be sure, Lohfink thinks that the very use of the verb *hôṣî'* to describe God's moving Israel out of Egypt is evidence of a deliberate linkage between the foundational utterance of the Decalogue and the Deuteronomic rationale for the Sabbath. Elsewhere, he notes, Deuteronomy uses a different verb, *pādâ* (usually rendered "redeem") for this purpose, as in 15:15 and 24:18.[39] In point of fact, however, both verbs are commonly used in connection with the exodus from Egypt in Deuteronomy, and we cannot securely assume that the use of *vayyôṣî'ăkā* in Deut 5:15 constitutes a deliberate echo of *hôṣē'tîkā* in Deut 5:6.

But an echo it certainly is, whether intentional or not, just as the pairing of "ox" and "ass" is an adumbration, deliberate or other, of the ending of the Decalogue. As Lohfink goes on to point out, "This kind of key-word linking from the Sabbath commandment to the beginning and end of the decalogue does not exist in the Exodus version." The effect, he writes, is one of emphasizing "the center of the text."[40] Although no item in an even-numbered list can be literally labeled its "center," the fact remains that, whether by design or not, the wording of both the opening and the closing of the Decalogue in its Deuteronomic formulation points to the Sabbath commandment, spotlighting it in a way that is unparalleled in the Exodus version.

Lohfink has another strategy by which to define the fourth commandment as the center of the Deuteronomic Decalogue and, what is more, to support his interpretation of it as the "principal commandment" of the ten.[41] Whereas the version in Exodus presents the prohibitions on murder, adultery, theft, false witness, and coveting (20:13–14) as discrete commandments, unlinked to each other, in the Deuteronomic parallel they are connected by the coordinating conjunction *və*, meaning "and." A very literal rendering would thus be "You shall not murder, and you shall not commit adultery, and you shall not steal, and you shall not bear false witness against your neighbor, and you shall not covet" (Deut 5:17–18). If we take this linkage as indicating one unit of meaning, we must say that the sabbatical ordinance is followed by a short commandment (to honor parents, v. 16) and then a long one (the five conjoined prohibitions in vv. 17–18). As Lohfink would have it, this pattern represents the last panel in a chiastic triptych, as it were, whose first panel is the long unit in vv. 6–10, establishing the unique status of the LORD and the illegitimacy of graven images and other likenesses, and the short unit of v. 11, prohibiting false oaths.[42]

On such a reading, we have the chiastic pattern of a long unit–short unit on the first panel and short unit–long unit on the third. What constitutes the central panel of the triptych is none other than the long textual unit that is the Sabbath commandment (Deut 5:12–15). The overall pattern, then, is long (vv. 6–10)–short (v. 11)–Sabbath (vv. 12–15)–short (v. 16)–long (vv. 17–21).[43] As Norbert Lohfink would have it, then, the centrality of the sabbatical commandment within the Deuteronomic Decalogue is evidence for a reconception of the Sabbath as the principal norm of the whole series.

Lohfink's interpretation, alas, does not withstand scrutiny. Its outstanding weakness is the peculiarity of finding only five units in a list already numbered as ten in the Hebrew Bible itself, though admittedly not within either version of the Decalogue itself.[44] In order to arrive at the lower and odd number—and thus to identity the Sabbath commandment as the central item in the Deuteronomic text—Lohfink is forced to group as one long unit five verses that in the Jewish and most Protestant traditions are regarded as comprising two discrete utterances, and for good reason.[45] So much for the left panel of the triptych, as it were. On the right panel, Lohfink groups together five commandments—the prohibitions on murder, adultery, theft, false witness, and coveting—solely on the basis of the coordinating conjunction at the beginning of each of the last four. The claim that the word for "and," which is used much more widely in Biblical Hebrew than in English, authorizes us to regard these five injunctions as one unit surely strains credulity. In sum, the chiastic arrangement that Lohfink detects in the Deuteronomic Decalogue rests upon unlikely (if ingenious) divisions of the text.

Without this division into five units, with the long Sabbath commandment positioned in the center and flanked by two short ones, Lohfink's argument that this was the "principal commandment" in the Deuteronomic version largely collapses. He is, of course, correct to observe the points of diction that the fourth commandment shares with the opening and the closing of the Decalogue, but it is unlikely that so far-reaching a conclusion can be drawn on the basis of these overlaps. As we have seen, the evocation of the exodus is frequent and prominent in Deuteronomy, and the affinities of the Sabbath with a concern for slaves and animals was already established before Deuteronomy made the rather natural linkage between this general humanitarian concern and the exodus in particular. As for the conjunction of "ox" and "ass" in its version of the fourth commandment (Deut 5:14) and in the concluding prohibition upon coveting (v. 18), the conjoining of these animals is, as we have seen, well attested elsewhere in Deuteronomy as well.[46] It surely offers a thin reed upon which to lean for anyone seeking evidence that the Sabbath ordinance is positioned centrally in this version of the Decalogue.

Lohfink is therefore wise to label his notion of a "Sabbath-decalogue" only a "hypothesis."[47] The evidence would indeed seem to be against it. His dubious interpretation of the Deuteronomic version of the fourth commandment as the foremost norm in the Decalogue leads smoothly to his dating of the whole series to the exilic period at the earliest.[48] As we have had occasion to note, there is strong reason to believe that the Sabbath gained markedly in importance during and after the exile.[49] But once the argument for the centrality of the fourth commandment has evaporated, there is no evidence internal to the Deuteronomic Decalogue upon which to date it to that period.

Lohfink, of course, thinks otherwise and turns to the difference between the two wordings of the next commandment, the fifth, for additional support. Here are the variants:

Honor your father and your mother,
              that you may long endure
    on the land (*ădāmâ*) that the Lord your God is assigning to you. (Exod 20:12)
	Honor your father and your mother, <u>as the Lord your God has commanded you</u>, that you may long endure, <u>and that you may fare well</u>, on the land (*ădāmâ*) that the Lord your God is assigning to you. (Deut 5:16)[50]

As we have seen, the phrase "as the Lord your God has commanded you," which also appears in the Deuteronomic Sabbath commandment (Deut 5:12), can reasonably be taken as evidence for the historical priority of the version of the Decalogue in Exodus—or, at least, of some pre-Deuteronomic version of the Decalogue that the text regards as having already been given. But Lohfink sees in the other addition, "that you may fare well," another piece of evidence for exilic or postexilic dating, for it "detaches the promise of long life from the concept of the *ădāmâ*." "This is most easily understood," he writes, "if the promise had to be accommodated to the situation of exile in which, while it was perhaps regarded as temporary, one still had to take into account at least for the time being a loosening of the connection between blessing and *ădāmâ*."[51]

It would seem more reasonable, however, to see the expression "that you may fare well (*ləmaʿan yîṭab lāk*)," which occurs five terms in Deuteronomy,[52] as a typical Deuteronomic explication and expansion of the previous phrase, rather than as a furtive but historically momentous effort to acknowledge that Israel could be blessed outside its land. Note that three of those five occurrences do not mention the land and in one of the others (Deut 6:18), "faring well" seems to lead directly to the possession of the land.[53] There is, in short, no reason to think that the long life and the faring well to which Deut 5:16 refers are not occurring "on the land," and the notion that the addition is a telltale indication of an exilic situation is weak.

Despite the lack of internal evidence, a strong argument for a late dating of the Deuteronomic Decalogue, or at least for the entrance of the Decalogue into the Deuteronomic tradition, can still be mounted. Here, the principal evidence lies in the undeniable but perhaps surprising fact that the fourth commandment is the only reference to the Sabbath anywhere in Deuteronomy. Even in the liturgical calendar of chapter 16, it is totally absent—this in suggestive contrast to the calendar of Leviticus 23, in which the Sabbath is the first of the "fixed times" and "sacred occasions" listed and in which the related word *šabbātôn* (translated as ""complete rest") appears several times as a characterization of festal days.[54] As Grund notes, this suggests a later insertion.[55] To the same argument, one could add the almost total lack of concern for the Sabbath in the Deuteronomistic History (Joshua–Kings), as we have noted in the previous chapter.[56] In sum, it is unlikely that the earliest form of the Deuteronomic legal collection included any sabbatical material at all. And if, in accordance with the longstanding scholarly consensus, one dates the core of Deuteronomy to the late seventh century, the insertion of the Decalogue is, if not exilic, then surely very close to it.

Of course, nothing in this argument requires that the fourth commandment in its Deuteronomic version was composed (in contradistinction to "inserted") near or during the exile. As we have also seen, the humanitarian interpretation of the Sabbath was of venerable antiquity in Israel, and the Deuteronomic casting of it in terms of the exodus is not a huge leap. One could imagine that some version of the Decalogue that now appears in Deut 5:6–18 was produced long before that passage was inserted into its present location and coordinated with the version in Exod 20:2–14. It may even have existed with a connection of Sabbath and exodus even before it was retouched in the characteristically Deuteronomic idiom. We just do not know and should not claim otherwise.[57]

The better-known Sabbath commandment in Exod 20:8–11 clearly exhibits an affinity with the opening, and thus most familiar, creation story of the Bible (Gen 1:1–2:3). Indeed, the verbal resonance between the Exodus version of the fourth commandment and the description of the seventh day in Gen 2:1–3 is patent. Most obviously, God "blessed the seventh day and hallowed it" (Gen 2:3; Exod 20:11)[58]—language that is totally unparalleled in the Deuteronomic variant. The exceedingly broad consensus among critical scholars that the fourth commandment in the Exodus Decalogue is of Priestly (P) origin is well founded.

This should not blind us, however, to some significant divergences between the seventh day of creation in Genesis and the commandment to observe the Sabbath in Exodus 20. For one, the noun "Sabbath" never occurs in Genesis 2:1–3 (or anywhere in the Bible before the episode of the manna in Exodus 16). Instead, we hear only that God "stopped" (*šābat, vayyišbōt*) on the seventh day, using verbal forms of the same root, which we explored at some length in chapter 2.[59] The second difference is also easily missed: God is never said to "rest" in Genesis, as he is in Exodus 20 (*vayyānaḥ*, v. 11). The verb *šābat* means to "stop," not to "rest." Although one may reasonably infer the latter activity from the former, the extant lexical evidence still matters in a context like this.

Third, the phrase "heaven and earth and sea" in the Decalogue of Exodus does not appear in the opening creation story of Genesis or, for that matter, anywhere else in the Hebrew Bible. In Gen 2:1–3, finally, the operative term is məla'ḵtô, literally "his work," which occurs fully three times in that paragraph of a mere thirty-five words. In Exod 20:8–11, forms of the same noun occur twice, but only in reference to what the humans addressed are forbidden to do on the Sabbath and never in reference to what God had finished on or before the seventh day.

The likelihood, then, is that although the fourth commandment in the version of Exod 20:8–11 ultimately derives from circles that may broadly be termed "Priestly," to attribute it specifically to the P source of the Pentateuch is more than the evidence can sustain. We simply do not know whether the organization of creation into a schema of seven days and the corollary etiology of the Sabbath as a memorial to creation originated with P or was ever unique to that source. Conceivably, Gen 1:1–2:3 and Exod 20:8–11 derive from a common antecedent that has been adapted to the respective contexts and functions.

If we wanted to engage in the sort of necessarily insecure speculation about the compositional history of the two Decalogues that we mentioned earlier and to conjecture about that hypothetical common antecedent, we could easily imagine that the Sabbath commandment was originally much shorter, as are most of the utterances in either list of ten. Perhaps it began with neither the zāḵôr of Exod 20:8 nor the šāmôr of Deut 5:12 but with another term, such as 'āśô, as in the closing phrase of its Deuteronomic version, "to practice (la'ăśôt) the sabbath day" (Deut 5:15; cf. Exod 31:16).[60] In circles that we have broadly characterized as Priestly, the hypothetical earliest form, "Practice the Sabbath day to keep it holy," would then have been reworded and expanded so as to make sabbatical observance into an act of sacred commemoration. In Deuteronomic circles, the same commandment was instead put into the idiom of covenantal observance and its longstanding humanitarian dimension stressed but now explicitly connected with the Israelites' liberation from slavery at the exodus, thus echoing the opening of the Decalogue itself.

Whether such a process of expansion and reinterpretation took place or not—and, on the basis of the available evidence, there is no way to move beyond rank speculation—in its present form, the Torah presents us with the two Decalogues with two ostensibly very different understandings of the Sabbath. Whatever the compositional history that lay behind the two versions, they are now contemporary with each other, existing within the same Torah and ascribed to the same divine author through his chosen prophet, Moses, though articulated at different moments in the latter's career. They are thus possessed of what I have elsewhere termed "literary simultaneity," as distinguished from historical contemporaneity.[61] No amount of historical speculation, however plausible, could ever invalidate one of them as nonnormative in favor of the other or set both aside in favor of a conjectured, and thus somehow authoritative, antecedent. It was the equal worth of the two versions of the fourth commandment that underlies the famous midrash that "'Remember' and 'observe' were spoken in one utterance—something that the mouth cannot utter and the ear cannot hear" (b. Šeḇu. 20b), mentioned at the outset of this discussion. In the wording of the Friday night Kiddush, the rabbinic liturgical fulfillment of the command recited over a glass of wine, the affirmation of the equality and joint authority of the two utterances appears in a near-identity of phrasing: the Sabbath is both "a commemoration of the act of creation" (*zikkārôn ləmaʿăśēh ḇərēʾšît*) and "a remembrance of the exodus from Egypt" (*zēḵer lîṣîʾat miṣrāyim*).

Even without the involvement of a humanly incomprehensible occasion of supernatural revelation, however, the two understandings of Sabbath may not be so far apart as they first seem. To explain why, we must explore the etiology of the Sabbath as a testimony to God's creation of the world. To that momentous topic we turn in our next chapter.

CHAPTER 5

Sharing His Majesty's Repose

APART FROM THE FOURTH COMMANDMENT in the Decalogue, the biblical Sabbath is best known from the creation story that opens the Torah and thus the entire Bible, Gen 1:1–2:3, of which the last paragraph speaks of God's ceasing his labors on the seventh day of the primordial week, blessing and hallowing it. As on the seventh day, so throughout the previous six, God appears as serenely and sovereignly in charge. He encounters no resistance or opposition and benefits from no assistance as he announces his intentions and orders the earth or the waters to bring forth the creatures he wants. Whoever it may be that he addresses with the famous words, "Let us make man in our image" (Gen 1:26), even those addressees neither answer him nor contribute in any way to the creative act. The universe that emerges over the primordial workweek is solely his creation. Here, nature has neither a will of its own nor even a personality, and the created order, far from being the result of a collaboration or a conflict among transcendent forces, is instead the perfectly executed handiwork of the lone divine actor. What some may see as divinized nature has been demythologized. It is now creation; only its creator is divine.

In its account of the last day of the primordial week (Gen 2:1–3), this overture to the Torah never uses the noun *šabbāt* ("Sabbath") but rather calls the occasion "the seventh day," a phrase it uses thrice in its three verses, along with two attestations of the telltale verb *šābat* (to "cease"). God stops his active labors on that day, having finished them and pronounced all that he had made "very good" the day before (Gen 1:31). Now the unopposed creator God sanctifies and blesses the day itself. With that, he sets it apart from the created world for himself alone; no one else observes it. In fact, no human is told to practice the Sabbath, or even told the Sabbath exists, until the episode of the manna when Israel (*not* all humanity) is instructed to observe "a holy sabbath of the LORD" (Exod 16:23). In our own time, practicing Jews still recall the first revelation of the Sabbath by having two loaves of bread on the Sabbath table in commemoration of the doubled amount of manna (*leḥem mišneh*) their ancestors in the wilderness are reported to have gathered on the sixth day (Exod

16:22) in obedient preparation for the seventh. As for God, however, nothing in the Bible tells us whether he somehow practiced the Sabbath at all between creation and his gift of the manna, apart from his acts of cessation, sanctification, and benediction on that primordial seventh day.

The depiction of creation over the seven days of Gen 1:1–2:3 can be, and often has been, productively contrasted with the "combat myth," a very different model and one that is well attested not only in the ancient Near East long before the emergence of Israel but also in the Hebrew Bible itself.[1] In the biblical texts that reflect this model of creation, there is neither a seven-day sequence nor a picture of a world tranquilly emerging at the command of its unopposed creator. To the contrary, the picture is one of conflict, and the world is truly and securely established only when the creator has won his victory and, not incidentally, validated his now incontestable claim to cosmic kingship. Here is a fine example:

> [12]O God, my King from of old,
> who brings deliverance throughout the land;
> [13]it was You who drove back the sea with Your might,
> who smashed the heads of the monsters in the waters;
> [14]it was You who crushed the heads of Leviathan,
> who left him as food for the denizens of the desert;
> [15]it was You who released springs and torrents,
> who made mighty rivers run dry;
> [16]the day is Yours, the night also;
> it was You who set in place the orb of the sun;
> [17]You fixed all the boundaries of the earth;
> summer and winter—You made them. (Ps 74:12–17)

To be sure, if we think of creation as the production of something out of nothing, a passage like this cannot qualify, for the waters (among other things) exist already at the outset. The same, however, is true of Gen 1:1–2:3, where the waters exist at the beginning, even before God has begun to speak (Gen 1:2), only to be divided on the second day of creation and drained into the "seas" on the third (Gen 1:6–13). Does that disqualify even the opening passage of the Torah as an account of creation? Only, it seems to me, for those who subscribe, usually inadvertently, to a very different understanding of the term from that presupposed in antiquity. For the ancients generally adhered to a more capacious and more ecological notion of creation, one in which the term would be better understood as referring to the events through which malevolent chaos was made to yield to a stable, humane, and life-sustaining order, with that last word understood (in our categories) as social, political, and natural alike.[2]

In the passage above, chaos appears in the form of an aquatic monster, Leviathan (v. 14), who cannot be rigidly distinguished from the "monsters" (*tannînîm*) or, for that matter, from "the sea" in the previous verse. Note that the latter term (*yām*) appears without the definite article and most likely refers to the figure known as Yamm, the ferocious oceanic enemy, and ultimately the victim, of the god Ba'al in Canaanite mythology.[3] However distant from Gen 1:1–2:3 this excerpt from Psalm 74 may be, it, too, ends with a sense of the now unopposed creator God in his unchallenged mastery. Perhaps it is the same situation that the psalmist has in mind when, looking back upon those events from the very troubled circumstances in which he now finds himself, he describes God as "my King from of old" (*malkî miqqedem*, v. 12), that is, the figure who demonstrated his incomparable and unassailable claim to kingship in the primordial events that established what is—or, to be precise, what should be—the present world order.

The qualification is essential, for bracketing Ps 74:12–17 are passages that describe an empirical reality that is quite the reverse of the ideal world of the unopposed God who stands behind a humane order of things. Here are the two verses that appear just before our passage:

> [10]Till when, O God, will the foe blaspheme (*yəḥārep̄*),
> will the enemy forever revile (*yənā'ēṣ*) Your name?
> [11]Why do You hold back Your hand, Your right hand?
> Draw it out of Your bosom! (Ps 74:10–11)

The blaspheming enemy appears on the other side of the passage as well, and the painful absence of the rightly acclaimed divine victor-creator in the current hideous situation occupies the rest of the poem:

> [18]Be mindful of how the enemy blasphemes (*ḥērēp̄*) the LORD,
> how base people revile (*ni'ăṣû*) Your name.
> [19]Do not deliver Your dove to the wild beast;
> do not ignore forever the band of Your lowly ones.
> [20]Look to the covenant!
> For the dark places of the land are full of the haunts of lawlessness.
> [21]Let not the downtrodden turn away disappointed;
> let the poor and needy praise Your name.
> [22]Rise, O God, champion Your cause;
> be mindful that You are blasphemed by base men all day long.

[23]Do not ignore the shouts of Your foes,
  the din of Your adversaries that ascends all the time. (Ps 74:18–23)

The close resemblance of the verses on each side of the evocation of God's cosmogonic victory (especially vv. 10 and 18) may suggest that the present location of the latter passage results from interpolation. Whether that be historically so or not, the discordance between God's glorious world-ordering activity in vv. 12–17 and his inactivity—nay, his failure to act in accordance with his demonstrated power and longstanding reputation—in the rest of the psalm is striking.[4] The reality made present in the acts of creation is still available, or so the psalmist hopes, for otherwise why does he recall them at all and goad his God to rise up and champion his own cause? We are not, in short, dealing with some sort of limited deity, lacking omnipotence.[5] But neither are we dealing with a creator God whose resounding cosmogonic victory characterizes the present world order without qualification or interruption, all opponents to his reign having been utterly dispatched at creation and all violent assault on him and his people having irreversibly ceased. The good world that emerged at creation is not false, and it bears upon the present reality—but present reality it is not.

The hope of the speaker in Psalm 74 is that God will act to close the gap between the foundational disclosure of his insuperability at creation and the current reality in which he is insulted ceaselessly and with impunity and his faithful covenant partners mortally assaulted. Leviathan (under whatever name) has returned with a vengeance, as it were, and the LORD must defeat him anew if the just and life-sustaining order established at creation is to be restored. A passage in the book of Isaiah predicts that the day will come when exactly that happens:

> In that day the LORD will punish,
> With His great, cruel, mighty sword
> Leviathan the Elusive Serpent—
> Leviathan the Twisting Serpent;
> He will slay the Dragon (*tannîn*) of the sea. (Isa 27:1)

In fact, this expectation of an encore to the cosmogonic victory is still alive and well much later, attested in both Jewish apocalyptic literature and its Christian appropriation. In the Similitudes of Enoch, a Jewish text from around the turn of the era, the day is envisioned when two great monsters, a female named Leviathan (a masculine name in the Hebrew Bible) and a male named Behemoth, have been parted, so that "[t]hese two monsters, prepared according to the greatness of the Lord, will provide food for the chosen and righteous" (1 En. 60:7–8, 24).[6] These two beasts had already appeared together in the book of Job, a much earlier text, where they represent the fearsome monsters only God can subdue (Job 40:6–41:26).

Although the rich corpus of Enoch literature produced in Second Temple Judaism is not canonical in the ongoing Jewish tradition (rabbinic Judaism), the notion that God would in the end slay Leviathan and reward those faithful to him carried over into the Talmud and subsequent Jewish folklore as well. Thus, Rabbi Yoḥanan, active in the Land of Israel in the third century CE, is reported to have taught that "the Holy One (blessed be He!) will in the future make a banquet for the righteous from the meat of Leviathan." He is similarly quoted as teaching that "the Holy One (blessed be He!) will in the future make a booth (*sukkâ*) for the righteous from the skin of Leviathan." In the same Talmudic passage, it is said that "the Holy One (blessed be He!) will spread out the rest [of Leviathan's skin, presumably] over the walls of Jerusalem, and its radiance will shine from one end of the world to the other, as it is said, 'And nations shall walk by your light, / Kings by your shining radiance' (Isa 60:3)" (b. B. Bat. 75a). This ancient expectation of an eschatological slaying of the aquatic monster still finds expression in a text found in traditional prayer books and recited upon leaving the sukkah at the end of the Festival of Booths: "May it be Your will, LORD our God and God of our fathers, that as I have fulfilled [Your commandment] and sat in this sukkah, so next year may I have the privilege of sitting in the sukkah made from the skin of Leviathan."[7]

In the rabbinic case, it is hard to know how much of the urgency of the old combat myth and its apocalyptic recontextualization remains alive and how much we are instead seeing set pieces of folklore about the end-time largely bled of the old conflict and the theology that generated it. In the early Christian case, the matter is quite different. Given the prominence of acute apocalyptic expectation in nascent Christian communities, we find the visions of a forceful intervention by God to punish the wicked and vindicate the faithful in plentiful evidence, and in the book of Revelation in particular, we hear much about the gruesome fate of the dragon—also identified with the "serpent," "the Devil," and "Satan"—in the imminent conflict.[8] In the depiction of the end, when the dead are resurrected and judged, we again hear of the sea:

> [1]Then I saw a new heaven and a new earth; for the first heaven and the first earth had passed away, and the sea was no more. [2]And I saw the holy city, the new Jerusalem, coming down out of heaven from God, prepared as a bride adorned for her husband. (Rev 21:1–2, NRSV)

Here, the echoes from the Hebrew Bible are patent. "A new heaven and a new earth," for example, derives from a prophecy of redemption and restoration in Isaiah:

[17]For behold! I am creating
A new heaven and a new earth;
The former things shall not be remembered,
They shall never come to mind.
[18]Be glad, then, and rejoice forever
In what I am creating.
For I shall create Jerusalem as a joy,
And her people as a delight;
[19]And I will rejoice in Jerusalem
And delight in her people.
Never again shall be heard there
The sounds of weeping and wailing. (Isa 65:17–19)[9]

Isaiah 65:17, in turn, is itself a transparent adaptation of Gen 1:1—but one that, importantly, acknowledges by implication that the first creation was not perfect; it included elements that will justly be forgotten once the creator finally and irreversibly vanquishes his old death-dealing foe. In all these examples— from Isaiah, Revelation, and the Talmud alike—we find in the glorification of Jerusalem a key indication that God's dramatic end-time intervention reverses not only the ravages of nature (the next verse in Isaiah goes on to say that he who dies at one hundred will be deemed a youth) but also the sad fate of the community of God's faithful, at last restored to their proper condition. And, as we shall soon see at length, the restoration of the temple city is key to the prophesied new creation in part because the building of a temple and the creation of the world are, in a deep sense, homologous. They are not ultimately detachable. And this, as we shall further observe, is highly relevant to the Sabbath in the opening creation story of Genesis.

The contradiction between the two models of creation is patent. Genesis 1:1–2:3 displays the unopposed God's pronouncement on the sixth day that he "saw all that He had made, and found it very good" (1:31). By contrast, our sample of texts that speak of the survival of the chaos monster (or the evil he embodies) hope for, and look forward to, the latter's elimination and, in some cases, a new and better creation.

How shall we put these two visions together?

As the philosopher Paul Ricoeur would have it, the opening passage in Genesis evidences a "new system in which creation is good from the first" and thus "neither Evil nor History can any longer be referred to some primordial disorder." That being the case, the evocations of the combat myth elsewhere in the Bible must be seen as "cut flowers,"[10] literary allusions without theological or moral force behind them, rather like, say, the pagan deities in the work of the staunchly Puritan poet John Milton.

To be sure, there is much to be said for such a view. For one thing, the placement of Gen 1:1–2:3 at the outset of the entire Bible subordinates all subsequent models of creation to a substantial degree. That those other models appear in highly poetic and usually fragmentary passages rather than in the tightly controlled and sequential prose of the Genesis text is another justification for taking the latter as self-consciously normative in a way the others are not. Finally, we must also take note of the fact that not far beneath the evocations of the chaos monster in some of those poetic texts lies the predicted demise of an all-too-human historical enemy and not a primordial beast. Ezekiel, for example, delivers an oracle in which the LORD proclaims his intention to destroy the "[m]ighty monster (*tannîm haggādôl*), sprawling in its channels," who dared boast, "My Nile is my own; / I made it for myself," thus denying the LORD's unique status as creator and as a result dooming the self-deifying boaster himself to become "food / To the beasts of the earth / And the birds of the sky" (Ezek 29:3, 5).[11] Yet the preface to the same oracle and its first verse explicitly identify its target as "Pharaoh king of Egypt" (vv. 2–3)—clearly a lesser figure than the fearsome beast slain in the primordial combat. In the case of Psalm 74, discussed above, such a precise identification of the blaspheming adversaries is not provided, but the context makes clear that these figures play a role closely analogous to that of the "sea," the "monsters," and Leviathan in vv. 12–17. They are, that is, the current embodiment of evil and, as such, a standing challenge to the once triumphant creator God.

Although each of these points in support of Ricoeur's interpretation has its force, the actual relationship between the two models of creation is more complicated than he acknowledges. The placement of Gen 1:1–2:3 at the outset of the Torah is a datum of great moment, to be sure, but so is the sheer historical fact that the combat myth, far from being a vestige of antique mythology now altogether replaced by the "new system," survived in Israel and grew in force and focus in Second Temple Judaism. This leaves us with no choice but to reckon with the coexistence of the two models. The combat myth would never be the same after Gen 1:1–2:3 appeared and attained wide circulation, but Gen 1:1–2:3, whatever its intention, did not altogether displace the combat myth or do away with the sense that the goodness of primordial creation still allows monstrous evil to work its will—until, that is, evil is at long last vanquished. Indeed, the very expectation of "a new heaven and a new earth" betrays the simultaneous reality of the two models, the one speaking of God's creation of heaven and earth and the other of the coming of a dramatically better world order than the sadly flawed and vulnerable one now in existence.

Similarly, we can readily acknowledge that some passages paint contemporary historical foes of God and his people in the colors of the old myth. This does not imply, however, that the aquatic enemy was not thought, at least in some circles, to be also a real—and continuing—danger. The passage about Behemoth and Leviathan mentioned earlier (Job 40:6–41:26) does not refer to historical figures at all but rather to menacing mythical beasts for which no person could ever be a match. That they do not menace human life now is owing solely to God's continuing mastery over them; even the gods are afraid of Leviathan (41:17). And, even if one says that the primordial enemies were indeed definitively eliminated in the process that resulted in creation, this does not at all entail that the evil they embody cannot reappear and acquire a foothold in the created order. There is, for example, no reason to think that Psalm 74 regards the chaos monster as still extant, but neither is there reason to think that the challenge the latter presents to God's reputation is unreal.

Now let us imagine ancient Israelites who subscribe to both models of creation at the same time. That is, they believe that a lone, unopposed God effortlessly created a world that he pronounced to be "very good" (Gen 1:31), on the one hand, but also and on the other hand, that God defeated a ferocious, malevolent, and superhuman beast at the time of creation—a beast that in the fuller form of the combat myth can come back (whether literally or embodied in some new eruption of overpowering evil) and wreak havoc.[12]

How can these Israelites subscribe to both of these beliefs at once? Are they not, as Ricoeur assumes, mutually exclusive?

To answer, we turn to some highly productive theoretical work on the nature of ritual, bearing in mind that biblical passages about creation often exhibit strong signs of connection to ritual practices. This is obviously the case with Gen 1:1–2:3, which came to serve as an etiology of sabbatical observance,[13] but it is very likely also true of the combat myth in texts like Psalm 74, which takes the form of a community lament and doubtless reflects the ritual practices associated with that genre.

In *Ritual and Its Consequences: An Essay on the Limits of Sincerity*, Adam B. Seligman, Robert P. Weller, Michael J. Puett, and Bennett Simon (henceforth "Seligman"), drawing on a number of other recent studies, present a cogent argument that "ritual creates a subjunctive, an 'as if' or 'could be,' universe," as distinguished from "an 'as is' vision of what often becomes a totalistic, unambiguous vision of reality 'as it *really* is.'"[14] In this, ritual is to be contrasted with what the authors call "sincerity," which "imagines a world 'as is' instead of ritual's multiple worlds of 'as if.'"[15] Needless to say, in a cultural climate in which sincerity commands high prestige and the only alternative to it is reflexively thought to be mendacity, it takes a special effort to appreciate the vision underlying ritual as Seligman conceives it. Yet I am convinced that a question like the one we are pursuing here renders that effort eminently worthwhile.

The famous anthropologist, Stanley J. Tambiah, states well the way in which our instinctive modern Western categories lead us astray when we seek to understand such ritualized speech and action: "Rituals as conventionalized behaviour are not designed or meant to express the intentions, emotions, and states of mind of individuals in a direct, spontaneous, and 'natural' way. Cultural elaboration of codes consists in distancing from such spontaneous and intentional expressions because spontaneity and intentionality are, or can be, contingent, labile, circumstantial, even incoherent or disordered."[16] So understood, ritual is not an insincere or mendacious rendering of empirical reality, but, to be sure, in some sense it does create an illusion. Seligman gives the example of the ritual of saying "please," which "creates an illusion of equality by recognizing the other's power to decline"—an illusion, to be sure, "but with no attempt to deceive" and thus one that must be sharply distinguished from a lie.[17] "Illusions," importantly, "are a form of the subjunctive. Illusion is what can be, as indeed so many symbolic worlds can."[18] Like verbs in the subjunctive mood, this ritual subjunctive expresses a wish, a hope, a possibility, in contradistinction to those in the indicative, which express a plain, empirical fact. That the liturgical and mythic texts that serve as librettos to rituals, or at least as literary counterparts to the ritual performances, can be cast in the indicative mode should not be taken to mean that they peddle false descriptions of immediately experienced reality. Rather, as Seligman puts it, "[p]articipants practicing ritual act as if the world produced in ritual were in fact a real one. And they do so fully conscious that such a subjunctive world exists in endless tension with an alternate world of daily experience."[19] It is not the case, that is, that those who participate in ritual action need be under any illusion that what they do or say in the ritual context describes quotidian reality. Quite the contrary, "the meaning produced through ritual action always exists in problematic tension with the nonritual world."[20] I would simply add that, while the tension may be problematic in some respects, one must not exclude the possibility that in others it is spiritually productive.

Consciousness of the tension between the world ritual creates and ordinary, or secular, experience can be found among those who subscribe to mythology as well ("mythology" in this usage obviously being very different from a designation of mistaken belief). In his highly stimulating study, *Did the Greeks Believe in Their Myths?*, the French classicist Paul Veyne puts the point memorably:

Mythological time and space were secretly different from our own. A Greek put the gods "in heaven," but he would have been astounded to see them in the sky. He would have been no less astounded if someone, using time in its literal sense, told him that Hephaestus had just remarried or that Athena had aged a great deal lately. Then he would have realized that in his own eyes mythic time had only a vague analogy with daily temporality; he would also have thought that a kind of lethargy had always kept him from recognizing the difference.[21]

The difference between the subjunctive reality of ritual, liturgy, and myth and the indicative reality that secular modernity tends to identify with the way things really are has wide application to biblical studies. Minimally, it suggests that the speaking voice in liturgical passages need not be taken as always and uncomplicatedly expressing literal autobiography. Bearing the difference in mind may explain, for example, how more than a few psalmists can claim to be fully innocent, to "walk without blame," "wash their hands in innocence," and the like.[22] There is surely a large element of exaggeration for rhetorical effect in such passages, but I submit something else is at work here as well: in the liturgical-ritual context of such compositions, the speaker is assuming an idealized identity, pledging his allegiance to the behavior that his God loves and inducing God to act accordingly in return. A similar point can be made, I suspect, about a verse that has caused controversy among some Jews:

I have been young and am now old,
but I have never seen a righteous man abandoned,
or his children seeking bread. (Ps 37:25)

Sung in the grace after meals in the Jewish liturgy, the verse understandably leaves some people incredulous. No righteous person has ever been abandoned? No children of a righteous father have ever been reduced to begging for food? On what planet is that the case? It is hardly a surprise that the psalmist's mind-boggling affirmation offends some who otherwise would be reciting the prayer in which the verse appears.

Yet a closer look at the whole psalm is alone enough to complicate such a summary judgment. For the same speaking voice acknowledges that the righteous can be impoverished and (repeatedly) that evil persons can prosper (for example, Ps 37:16), even becoming "powerful, / well-rooted like a robust native tree" (v. 35). This makes it highly unlikely that the offending verse is to be taken as describing empirical reality. And, in fact, a major point of the whole poem is to assert that the idealized situation affirmed in such verses is the only one that can last; what is called for is faith in God's justice and patience until it arrives—until, that is, the ideal becomes real, the subjunctive becomes the indicative.[23] Hence, just after that simile of the well-rooted tree, we read this about the wicked man to whom it applies: "Suddenly he vanished and was gone; / I sought him, but he was not to be found" (Ps 37:36).

Here, too, there is room to doubt that the ostensibly autobiographical language is to be understood as reflecting the speaker's ordinary experience. Surely, God's justice is not so swift! Rather, it would be wiser to assume, to recall Seligman's words, that the speaker is "fully conscious that such a subjunctive world exists in endless tension with an alternate world of daily experience."[24] Indeed, in his repeated references to the triumph of the unjust and the affliction of the righteous, the psalmist keeps that alternate world very much in view, even as he urges his readers to remember that it, unlike the justice of God, is not ultimate.

All this enables us to answer our question about how it might have been possible for the same mind to believe in both models of creation that we have discussed—one in which God, magisterial and unopposed, creates a world that he pronounces "very good" (Gen 1:31) and one in which God defeats a monstrous enemy who—or the evil he embodies—is nonetheless still extant, yet to be vanquished, and in continual danger of reappearing. The very good world of Gen 1:1–2:3 in which God reigns supreme is in the subjunctive; it does not describe the current observable reality. Neither does the world in which God definitively eliminated the chaos monster in primordial times, as those texts powerfully attest that speak of the monster as an uncontrolled current reality; it, too, is in the subjunctive. But when Seligman writes that "such a subjunctive world exists in endless tension with an alternate world of daily experience,"[25] his word "endless" would trigger resistance at least from those ancients who foresaw God's victory over the chaos monster at the end-time and, for that matter, from the author of Psalm 37 as well. For such texts affirm that God will, one way or another, indeed close the painful disjunction between the world of ritual or myth and that of quotidian experience.

The same disjunction is different from, but suggestively reminiscent of, the disjunction between the enchanted world of the Sabbath and the workaday reality of the other six days of the week. The difference is obvious: work is not evil or in any way negative in the Hebrew Bible, nor is the need to work unjust or contrary to God's intentions. Indeed, even Adam in the Garden of Eden has been placed there "to till it and tend it" (*ləʿobdāh ûləšomrāh*, Gen 2:15): the need to earn a living is not the consequence of sin, original or other. Nonetheless, the alleviation of labor and, even more so, its absence for a day are much to be desired. Even now, people who generally enjoy their work still look forward to holidays and weekends; few look forward to Monday morning. In the case of the three "pilgrim festivals" of biblical Israel, the holiday entails (for men) coming into the very presence of the LORD[26]—a dramatic disjunction, to use Seligman's word, from quotidian experience.

When, as in the Decalogue of Exodus 20, the Sabbath is understood as deriving from God's own cessation of labor on the primordial seventh day, the sense of a disjunction from empirical reality is all the more striking. For by then God had completed his creative labors: "The heaven and the earth were finished, and all their array" (Gen 2:1).[27] To be sure, it is not certain that the verb *šāḇat* ("to cease"), which occurs twice in the paragraph about the special day (Gen 2:2, 3), implies that he *rested* then. But it is highly unlikely that the verb in this passage, attributed to the relatively late Priestly source, is unrelated to the prominence of the same word in texts that explicitly connect "ceasing" with "resting" and "being refreshed."[28] Indeed, as we have seen, in some circles the verb *šāḇat* became a term for observing the Sabbath.[29]

The notion of a regularly repeating interruption by the higher reality represented by sabbatical rest is what makes this contrast reminiscent of the disjunction between the world of ritual or myth, as Seligman and Veyne understand it, and ordinary experience. For one day out of seven, the people Israel are in something akin to what Veyne calls "mythological time and space." They were not, to be sure, "in heaven," where the Greeks imagined their gods to dwell, but rather on earth imitating their own sole and incomparable God in their own homes and villages. Still, on that day the Sabbath-observers' experience has what Veyne calls "only a vague analogy with daily temporality."[30] A passage in early rabbinic midrash illustrates this disjunction nicely:

"Six days you shall labor and do all your work" (Exod 20:9).
Is it possible for a human being to do all his work in six days? Rather,
   rest (*šaḇôt*) as if all your work has been done.
Another interpretation: Rest (*šaḇôt*) from the very thought of labor.
   As it says,
[13]If you refrain from trampling the sabbath,
From pursuing your affairs on My holy day;
If you call the sabbath "delight,"
The LORD's holy day "honored";
And if you honor it and go not your ways
Nor look to your affairs nor strike bargains—
[14]Then you can seek the favor of the LORD.
I will set you astride the heights of the earth,
And let you enjoy the heritage of your father Jacob—
For the mouth of the LORD has spoken" (Isa 58:13–14).
(Mek. de Rabbi Ishmael, *baḥōdeš* 7)[31]

The generating question in the midrash derives from a particular reading of "all your work" (*kol-məla'ḵteḵā*), in which the first word can mean either "any" or "all." In Exod 20:9, its most natural reading would be the former, yielding the phrase "any work of yours" or, better, "any work you have." In short, the verse simply means that its addressee is to do all his work in the six days of the week and none on the seventh.

But the potential meaning of *kol* as "all" provides midrashic license to make a point that Seligman's and Veyne's thinking helps us appreciate: observance of the Sabbath must be conducted as if the observers lived in a world in which they have no foreseeable tasks, a world of total and unending sufficiency. A greater disjunction from ordinary experience is hard to imagine. Perhaps it is one that cannot be imagined; perhaps it can only be embedded in actual practice and intimated rather than grasped. As such, the Sabbath is, in Chaim N. Saiman's felicitous words, "an aspirational time that peers into the messianic future."[32]

The second point in the midrash, by contrast, assumes that work does indeed confront the Sabbath observers. The point of the commandment in Exod 20:9, then, is that they must train their minds to exclude all thoughts of the workaday reality and live only in the sabbatical moment, as it were, without the distraction, the anxiety, or even, on a positive note, the resolve that the thought of tasks to be accomplished can arouse. Without such mindfulness, even those who refrain from forbidden activities on the seventh day will inevitably fail to attain the high spiritual state associated with sabbatical practice. The deeds will be there; the spirit will not.

There is, in fact, empirical evidence to support the claim that genuine rest necessarily has a mental component and cannot be brought about merely by ceasing to labor. As one study summarizes the research, "people may physically detach themselves from a stressful work situation, but unless they redirect mentally, emotionally, or spiritually, they will not necessarily experience respite. In other words, leisure can be as taxing as work."[33] Bearing this in mind, we can come to a greater appreciation of the rabbinic norms that prohibit reviewing, planning, or discussing work on the Sabbath. Such activities are, in the Yiddish parlance, *vokhedik*, not *shabesdik*: they belong in the reality of the week, not in the enchanted but fragile day that is the Sabbath. Unchecked, they eat away at the spiritual core of the seventh day.

The midrash we have been discussing is exactly that—a midrash and not the plain sense of the biblical verse it expounds. It does, however, point to a deeper theological reality in the appropriation of Gen 2:1–3 by Exod 20:8–11. The people Israel's cessation from labor on the Sabbath must imitate the cessation of God on the seventh day of his primal work. It must, in other words, be performed as if everything had been completed and found to be "very good," with no tasks remaining. It must be a blessed and hallowed day, a day of God-like sufficiency.

In the history of Jewish and Christian theology, the unopposed and self-sufficient nature of the creator God in Gen 1:1–2:3 has traditionally come to expression in the doctrine of what in Latin is called *creatio ex nihilo*, "creation out of nothing," of which the Hebrew counterpart is *yēš mēʾayin*, "existence out of nothing." As we have already had occasion to note, this formulation does not reckon sufficiently with the waters that already exist in Gen 1:2, before God's first act of creation in the next verse; it also does not reckon with what appears to be—and even some rabbinic sources took to be[34]—a kind of primal matter here called *tōhû vābōhû* ("unformed and void," v. 2). As J. Richard Middleton points out, however, the text presents a more complicated picture, one that cannot be generalized into either the traditional doctrine, on the one hand, or the notion that God's creative power was somehow limited, on the other: "While the majority of God's creative acts in Genesis 1 presuppose the existence of the *tohû wabohû* (the earth in its initial watery or chaotic state) and represent God shaping or developing the primordial 'stuff' into more complex creatures, three exceptions seem to be light (on day 1), the firmament (on day 2), and humanity (on day 6). These three creative acts are all portrayed rhetorically as ex nihilo or de novo, without the mention of any prior matter used in their construction."[35] It is essential to note, though, that however we picture that "primordial 'stuff,'" it represents not an ordered world but a state of chaos effortlessly organized by God the creator according to his own wishes. As in the case of the combat-myth model of creation, God is very much in command here. Unlike the aquatic opponent of the combat myth, this primal material presents no challenge to him. In both cases, God emerges unambiguously in control, having triumphed over the chaotic monster in violent conflict or organized the primal matter into an ordered reality utterly subordinated to its creator's will and in undeviating conformity with his intentions.

As all this suggests, the model of creation represented in Gen 1:1–2:3 is not, in fact, so distant from the combat myth as first seems the case. Consider God's creating an "expanse" (*rāqîaʿ*) to divide the waters below from those above, calling the divider "Sky"(Gen 1:6, 8). As often noticed, this recalls the victorious creator god Marduk's splitting his oceanic opponent Tiamat in half toward the end of the Babylonian epic, Enuma Elish, forming the sky from one of her halves.[36] Another and more momentous reverberation of the Enuma Elish (or some other version of the same basic story) will appear when God enables Moses to split the death-dealing sea so that the Israelites escaping Egypt may cross safely on dry land (Exod 14:16, 21).[37] Finally, the singling out of the "great sea monsters" (*hattannînîm haggədōlîm*) in Gen 1:21 recalls the use of the same word to parallel or even denote "Leviathan" in evocations of the combat myth, as we have seen (Ps 74:13–14; Isa 27:1). Since the account of the fifth and sixth days of creation in Gen 1:20–25 otherwise relates the creation of animals in broad generic categories ("birds that fly," "living creatures of every kind that creep," "wild beasts of every kind," and the like), the specificity of this word is striking. The author seems to have singled out those aquatic monsters to let us know they are not primordial and creation did not require their dismemberment: they were created on the fifth day of the hexameron, along with all the other birds and sea-life, effortlessly. As I have noted elsewhere, this recalls a psalmist's comforting words that the LORD created Leviathan "to sport with."[38] To the creator God, the great monster, fearsome to everybody else, is but a toy.

In the thinking of some scholars, Gen 1:1–2:3, having done away with the combat myth altogether, presents us with a worldview that has little or no place for the evil that the primal enemy symbolized. Mark S. Smith states that position well: "Genesis 1 does not deny evil (certainly not in any explicit way), but it simply ignores it and instead elevates a vision of the good, perhaps in response to Israel's experience of trauma and evil during the sixth century BCE. We might say that Genesis 1 offers a decidedly hopeful vision, perhaps even a wildly optimistic one."[39] As for the uncreated waters in Gen 1:2, he writes, they "are simply there. There is no hint in the text that they are evil." In words he quotes from Ronald S. Hendel, the text thus presents us with "the image of the calm, passive, and purely material ocean."[40] To be sure, Smith qualifies his view in an important way on the next page, when he writes, "The waters in Genesis 1 are not 'evil,' but express both a lack of order on the margins of creation and a part of the divine order within that creation. The waters evoke the potential threat of destruction from the periphery and its positive life-giving capacity within creation."[41] The issue here seems to turn on the perhaps over-fine point of distinguishing "a lack of order on the margins of creation" and "the potential threat of destruction" from "evil." In any event, the undifferentiated primordial waters of Gen 1:2 seem to disappear through transformation, first turning into the water above and the water below with the creation of the sky and then being drained into the seas and bracketed by dry land (Gen 1:6–10). If they survive "on the margins of creation," they are not, in fact, part of the order God establishes with his creative act but a continuing negation of it. To me, this implies the persistence of evil.

That the image in Gen 1:2 is of "the calm, passive, and purely material ocean" is also open to much doubt. What we call the oceans and the text calls "seas" (*yammîm*, 1:10) do not come into existence until the third day. By contrast, the waters of Gen 1:2 are mentioned as part of an apposition to a term we have already mentioned, *tōhû vābōhû* ("unformed and void"), which here designates the nature of things before creation began. The first term in this two-part phrase refers to a wilderness or wasteland and often serves to underscore the severe inhospitality of a locale, as in this description of the LORD's first encounter with the people Israel/Jacob: "He found him in a desert region, /

In an empty howling waste (*tōhû*)" (Deut 32:10). In other instances, the same term designates something worthless and insubstantial but in a way that is anything but innocent or neutral, as in Samuel's warning about the danger of turning to false gods: "Do not turn away to follow worthless things (*haṭṭōhû*), which can neither profit nor save but are worthless (*tōhû*)" (1 Sam 12:21)

The second term in Gen 1:2, *bōhû*, is more obscure, appearing only in conjunction with the first, and may have been coined solely to rhyme with it. Other than in Gen 1:2, *tōhû* and *bōhû* occur in tandem only twice, and in both cases the context suggests something far from calm; it unambiguously suggests, instead, a life-threatening scenario. One of these cases, an oracle in Jeremiah, foresees the undoing of creation because of the LORD's fiery rage against his disobedient people:

> I look at the earth,
> It is unformed and void (*tōhû vāḇōhû*);
> At the skies,
> And their light is gone. (Jer 4:23)[42]

All this argues that the primal waters of Gen 1:2 are not "simply there," as Smith would have it, and that there is compelling textual reason that they do indeed represent "evil," if the term is equated to a life-endangering destructiveness. And, in fact, a few chapters later, at the onset of the flood, the life-sustaining order established at the cost of the primal chaos is reversed when "all the fountains of the great deep burst apart, / And the floodgates of the sky broke open" (Gen 7:11).[43] To be sure, *tōhû vāḇōhû* does not recur in the story of the flood, but the all-important creative acts of separating the waters below from those above and of draining the former into the seas are dramatically undone. Although the picture is quite different from that of the combat myth—we are, it must be stressed, dealing with creation without opposition—the underlying theology is again one in which only the mercy of the omnipotent God preserves the life-sustaining order established through creation. But for that, chaos would return, and in all its death-dealing devastation.

Smith may, then, be right that "Genesis 1 offers a decidedly hopeful vision," but it is not "a wildly optimistic one."[44] Rather, its hopefulness is a corollary of its subjunctive nature, as Seligman might put it, of its existing in an "'as if' or 'could be,' universe," as distinguished from "an 'as is' vision of what often becomes a totalistic, unambiguous vision of reality 'as it *really* is.'"[45] Like the Sabbath, which is not only its conclusion but also its consummation, the creation of the "very good" world in Gen 1:1–2:3 stands in hopeful opposition to ordinary reality.

In grounding the observance of a particular *day* in creation itself, biblical texts like Exod 20:8–11 and (by implication) Gen 2:1–3 are, so far as we now know, unique within the ancient Near East. There, the ritual conclusion and culminating event of the process of creation is more likely to take the form of a temple. Such structures, in fact, were often understood to have a cosmic dimension, so that the erection of the sanctuary was itself homologous with the creation of the world, and its reconstruction or renovation could be understood as an act of renewal of cosmic scope.⁴⁶ The very names of some ancient Near Eastern temples testify loudly to the connection. Bernd Janowski points out, for example, that the ziggurat completed under the Babylonian king Nebuchadnezzar II (reigned 605–562 BCE) bore the name "Etemenanki," Sumerian for "The House [i.e., Temple] That Is the Foundation of Heaven and Earth." As he points out, such names are common in Mesopotamia and include among their variants "The House That Is the Site of Heaven and Earth" (in Dilbat) and "The Bond of Heaven and Earth" (in Larsa).⁴⁷ It thus comes as no surprise to find cosmic symbolism used not only in the nomenclature but also in the structures and decorations of temples.⁴⁸ In the rabbinic tradition, the interpretation of the Temple as a microcosm, a mini-cosmos, as it were, continued long after the Mesopotamian or Egyptian antecedents had fallen into disuse or been destroyed and is amply attested in classical midrash and in later mysticism as well.⁴⁹

In the case of the model of creation represented by the combat myth, we sometimes find the victor crowning his triumph and demonstrating his incontestable claim to kingship through the construction of a temple, that is to say, a palace for a god. Thus, in the Enuma Elish, after the Babylonian god Marduk has overcome his aquatic enemy Tiamat and her minions, the gods known as the "Anunnaki" address their savior thus:

> Now, Lord, you have liberated us,
> What courtesy may we do you?
> We will make a shrine, whose name will be a byword,
> Your chamber that shall be our stopping place, we shall find rest
>   therein. (Enuma Elish VI:49–54)⁵⁰

What they build, much to their lord's pleasure, is Babylon and, more specifically, Esagila, the temple of Marduk, the counterpart or replica of the abodes of the gods Ea and Enlil.⁵¹ The temple is thus a visually imposing token of the triumphant god's creation of the world, his liberation of his loyal underlings, and also—and inseparably from these two—his universal kingship. No wonder its construction and his enthronement within it lead immediately to a festive banquet and much merriment.⁵²

The Hebrew Bible is no exception to this ancient Near Eastern conception of temples as cosmic in nature, as I have argued at length in earlier studies.[53] Here, it will suffice to draw attention to only a few of the passages that imply the connection, for example:

> [68]He did choose the tribe of Judah,
> Mount Zion, which He loved.
> [69]He built His Sanctuary like the heavens (*rāmîm*),
> like the earth that He established forever. (Ps 78:68–69)

To the attentive reader, the simile used to describe the royal shrine in Jerusalem (the next verse will tell of the election of David), "like the heavens, / like the earth," may suggest not only creation in general but perhaps even a connection with Gen 1:1. In my judgment, the use of *rāmîm* for "heavens," rather than *šāmayim*, as in the latter verse, by itself casts this notion of an echo or other reuse of that specific text into doubt. But the notion that the Temple is like heaven and earth—that is, like the cosmos—is significant, as is the fact that Psalm 78 attributes its construction to the LORD himself with no reference to any human agent. That, too, is something the Temple and the world have in common.

The same homology appears in texts reflecting the hopes and fears evoked by the construction of the Second Temple late in the sixth century. In one such instance, the very notion of building an abode for the LORD is disparaged on the grounds that he already has one—the one he built himself:

> [1]Thus said the LORD:
> The heaven is My throne
> And the earth is My footstool:
> Where could you build a house for Me,
> What place could serve as My abode?
> [2]All this was made by My hand,
> And thus it all came into being
>   —declares the LORD.
> Yet to such a one I look:
> To the poor and brokenhearted,
> Who is concerned about My word. (Isa 66:1–2)[54]

On the other side of the controversy but reflecting the same homology are those oracles that speak of the reconstruction of the ruined sanctuary as the renovation of the whole world, indeed as God's creation of "a new heaven and a new earth" and the corresponding institution of paradisiacal conditions for humans and animals alike. As we saw above, these are words that are applied to an imminent future in postexilic Jewish literature but later adapted to the eschatological consummation in apocalyptic literature, including early Christian apocalyptic.[55] The Temple restored and the world renewed are not, at least in origin, two separate visions of the ultimate future. They are, rather, inextricably linked and founded in the same idea: the Temple is a microcosm, and the world is—in its ideal state—a Temple.

In the reflexes of the combat myth in the Hebrew Bible, too, one finds a connection of creation with temple-building.

Consider, first, the famous and influential Song at the Sea in Exod 15:1–18. To be sure, this ancient poem speaks neither of the origination of the cosmos nor of a divine victory over the sea. Instead, it celebrates the Lord's astounding defeat of a historical foe, "Pharaoh's chariots and his army" (v. 4), at and by means of raging waters. This characteristically Israelite shift is not to be underestimated, but neither does it set aside the multiple resonances of the combat myth within the poem.[56] As usual, there is in this instance both continuity and discontinuity between ancient Israel and its antecedents or contemporaries. For it is precisely the Lord's victory at the sea that demonstrates beyond all doubt his incomparability among the gods and, most directly to our point, leads to his acclamation as king in the shrine that his own hands establish (vv. 11, 17–18). Whatever the actual identity of the structure to which the poem refers (a matter of dispute), once again a very particular temple caps the universal God's victory—an event with international reverberation (vv. 14–16) and of incalculable significance. It establishes a new order in the world.

The nexus of creation, kingship, and Temple (attested in far more biblical passages than we need examine here)[57] appears in marvelous concision in this poem of a mere five verses:

> [1]The Lord is king,
> He is robed in grandeur;
> the Lord is robed,
> He is girded with strength.
> The world stands firm;
> it cannot be shaken.
> [2]Your throne stands firm from of old;
> from eternity You have existed.
> [3]The ocean sounds, O Lord,
> the ocean sounds its thunder,
> the ocean sounds its pounding.
> [4]Above the thunder of the mighty waters,
> more majestic than the breakers of the sea

is the LORD, majestic on high.
⁵Your decrees are indeed enduring;
holiness befits Your house,
O LORD, for all times. (Ps 93)

The first four lines (v. 1a–d) portray the God of Israel as he assumes his royal office, donning the purple, we might say. The next two lines (v. 1e–f) may seem to shift the focus suddenly to something very different, the establishment of an unchallengeable world order, but the abruptness of the transition immediately disappears if we remember the nexus of divine kingship with creation. In v. 2, the basis of the LORD's reign in primordial reality is explicit: his kingship dates back to the very beginning. If v. 3 sounds like another unexpected shift, here, too, awareness of the combat-myth model of creation dispels the misimpression; the LORD's kingship and its corollary, his right to a temple, are rooted in his mastery of the threatening deep. "Majestic on high," he looks down in unshakeable tranquility upon the thundering, pounding waters (v. 4). Despite the uncertainties of translation in v. 5, what is clear there is his right to rule and to possess a temple eternally.

The superscription to Psalm 93 in an ancient translation of Psalm 93 by Greek-speaking Jews designates the poem "For the day before the Sabbath."[58] Similarly, the Mishnah, an early rabbinic collection of (mostly) law, identifies the same poem as the one that the Levites (the Temple singers) chanted on the sixth day of the week, with the previous psalm as the one for the Sabbath itself, as its biblical superscription, in fact, requires (Ps 92:1; m. Tamid 7:4). Although it should not be presupposed that the author of Psalm 93 knew of the seven-day creation schema of Gen 1:1–2:3, the notion that God's kingship was established when he finished his creative labors—in this case, presumably his vanquishment of the threatening waters—makes eminent midrashic sense. There is, to put it differently, a palpable affinity between the LORD's looking down, "majestic on high," upon the crashing waves in the psalm and God's pronouncement at the end of the last day of the hexameron that he found everything he had made to be "very good" (Gen 1:31). Reflecting the same complex of ideas, a statement in the Talmud, quoted in the name of Rabbi Akiva (d. ca. 135 CE, Land of Israel), attributes the recitation of Psalm 93 on Friday to the fact that on that day "he completed his work and assumed kingship over them" (b. Roš Haš. 31a). In some contrast with this, though, a blessing in the traditional Jewish liturgy for the Sabbath morning relates that it was then that God "ascended and took his seat on his glorious throne"; the prayer seems to go so far as to report that the seventh day itself recites Psalm 92, the song "for the sabbath day."[59]

Such passages build upon the strong association in the Hebrew Bible itself between God's assuming his throne and his attainment of "rest." Speaking about the Ark, which is central to understanding the divine presence in much of the Hebrew Bible and comes, appropriately, to be housed in sacred structures, a psalmist writes as follows:

> [6]We heard it was in Ephrath;
> we came upon it in the region of Jaar.
> [7]Let us enter His abode,
> bow at His footstool.
> [8]Advance, O LORD, to Your resting-place (*mənûḥāteḵā*),
> You and Your mighty Ark!
> [9]Your priests are clothed in triumph;
> Your loyal ones sing for joy. (Ps 132:6–9)

The key point for our purposes is that the enthronement of the victorious God is associated with "rest." "Resting-place," in fact, reappears a few verses later, this time on God's own lips and with an explicit reference to Zion, the Temple Mount, where he is eternally enthroned:

> [13]For the LORD has chosen Zion;
> He has desired it for His seat (*môšāḇ*).
> [14]"This is my resting-place (*mənûḥātî*) for all time;
> here I will dwell (*'ēšēḇ*), for I desire it." (Ps 132:13–14)[60]

The translation "dwell" in v. 14 is not inaccurate, but it obscures the connection with God's enthronement, his "sitting" (which the verb *yāšaḇ* can also denote) on his regal chair (*môšāḇ*). The divine repose is the final and consummative moment in the ritual process and represents the security and finality of the LORD's kingship. Later, the Chronicler will quote this psalm to conclude his version of Solomon's great speech at the dedication of *the* Temple—that is, the shrine atop Zion in Jerusalem that had by then become (as the Chronicler saw it) the sole licit shrine (2 Chr 6:41–42). In this conception, the Temple is not merely a place of worship; it is also the place in which the victorious God attains the rest that is his due and that manifests his unassailability.[61]

This notion of a god's reposing in his temple is, in fact, well-attested elsewhere in the ancient Near East.[62] More relevant to our subject, the temple affords rest to others, as in the case of the Anunnaki in the Enuma Elish, who, as we have seen, resolve to build a sanctuary for their triumphant deliverer Marduk in which they can find repose as well.[63] Underlying this is the widespread, cross-cultural conception of temples as places of refuge and safety, to which the derivations of English words like "sanctuary" and "asylum" still attest. In the biblical case, the same conception appears in passages in which the speaker expresses the wish to live his whole life in the Temple, where even in the full view of his enemies he will be secure.[64]

A number of passages in the Hebrew Bible describe the God of Israel as giving rest to his people collectively, as he does as well to select individuals among them. In particular, this gift of rest is associated with the people Israel's finally becoming secure against all enemies in the land he promised them, as in the conclusion to the long account of Israel's conquest in the book of Joshua:[65]

> [41]The LORD gave to Israel the whole country which He had sworn to their fathers that He would assign to them; they took possession of it and settled in it. [42]The LORD gave them rest (*vayyānaḥ*) on all sides, just as He had promised to their fathers on oath. Not one man of all their enemies withstood them; the LORD delivered all their enemies into their hands. [43]Not one of the good things which the LORD had promised to the House of Israel was lacking. Everything was fulfilled. (Josh 21:41–43)[66]

In these words, it is not hard to detect a strong echo of the old combat myth. Joshua's victories correspond to God's hard-won triumph over the chaos monster; Israel's rest in the promised land reworks God's regal repose on his throne after the battles; the holy land echoes the holy Temple.

The same joining of the themes of God's demonstrable reliability and Israel's total security appears in the beautiful prayer with which Solomon concludes his speech at the dedication of his Temple:

> [56]Praised be the LORD who has granted rest (*mənûḥâ*) to His people Israel, just as He promised; not a single word has failed of all the gracious promises that He made through His servant Moses. [57]May the LORD our God be with us, as He was with our fathers. May He never abandon or forsake us. [58]May He incline our hearts to Him, that we may walk in all His ways and keep the commandments, the laws, and the rules, which He enjoined upon our fathers. [59]And may these words of mine, which I have offered in supplication before the LORD, be close to the LORD our God day and night, that He may provide for His servant and for His people Israel, according to each day's needs—[60]to the end that all the peoples of the earth may know that the LORD alone is God, there is no other. [61]And may you be wholehearted with the LORD our God, to walk in His ways and keep His commandments, even as now. (1 Kgs 8:56–61)[67]

The word for "rest" here (*mənûḥâ*) is identical to the one translated as "resting-place" in connection with the LORD's own abode in Psalm 132 above (twice).

In the land that the singular and universal God has granted his unique people and enabled them to secure against all odds—thirty-one kings west of the Jordan, according to Josh 12:24—their flesh-and-blood king has now, as he tells him, built "a stately House, / a place where You / May be enthroned (*ləšibtəkā*) forever" (1 Kgs 8:13).[68]

It bears reiteration that in all these cases we are once again encountering literature that is in the subjunctive mood. Whatever taste of security from enemies and evildoers the psalmists may have had in the Temple, it did not, after all, last their whole lifetime. They may possibly have experienced a moment of asylum and tranquility—but only a moment. The same point can be made about the rest that the LORD is reported to have granted Israel in Joshua's time. Whatever historical value the report may have had, one can see even from the canonical scriptures that the situation did not last: Israel is again at war in the very next book (Judges) and sometimes losing. And as for Solomon's prayer, it is exactly that—a prayer and thus cast in the volitive ("May he ... and may you"). One needn't read much further in Kings itself to see that the situation of continual divine favor and human faithfulness for which it petitions, if ever it was the empirical reality, did not long remain so.

According to the canonical Hebrew Bible, the Temple of Solomon was preceded by a portable shrine, the "Tabernacle" (*miškān*) or "Tent of Meeting" (*ʾōhel môʿēd*) erected in the wilderness under Moses's direction, implementing the LORD's detailed instructions. Some scholars have noted, with considerable interest, that the latter are delivered in seven discrete speeches.[69] Given the other evidence for a homology of temple and world, the suspicion arises that the structural similarity of the process of temple-building in the wilderness and that of world-construction in Gen 1:1–2:3 is not coincidental.[70] Peter Kearney goes so far as to argue that the contents of each of those seven speeches mirror the acts of creation in the corresponding days of the hexameron.[71] Thus, the "laver of copper ... for washing" (Exod 30:18) specified in the third speech is parallel to the "Seas" that God created on the third day of creation (Gen 1:9–10). In fact, he points out, the corresponding "tank" in Solomon's Temple bears the name *yām*, "sea" (1 Kgs 7:23). Similarly, as Kearney would have it, the incense specified in the fifth speech about the construction of the Tabernacle and its paraphernalia corresponds to the fifth day of creation. For on that day God brought into being "all the living creatures that creep" in the seas (Gen 1:21), and the onycha used in the incense (Exod 30:34) was derived from mollusks. And so on.

Kearney's effort to match the first six sets of directives for the construction of the Tabernacle in Exodus with the corresponding acts of creation in Genesis 1 ultimately fails to convince. The copper laver mandated in the third

divine address on the subject (Exod 30:17–21) is there never called "sea" at all;
Kearney's notion that the author intended us to think of the intertext of 1 Kgs
7:23, where the analogous (but not identical) item in Solomon's Temple bears
that name, is far-fetched. As for the incense Moses is instructed to prepare in
the fifth speech (Exod 30:34–38), onycha is but one of its four ingredients. The
other three are, in fact, derived from plants, not sea creatures, and the identification of Hebrew *šəḥēlet* with onycha is itself less than secure; an argument
has been made that it, too, is plant-based.[72] Moreover, unlike the days of the
primordial week in Genesis, the speeches to Moses about the Tabernacle in
Exodus are not numbered; even attentive readers can understandably miss the
fact that there are seven of them. And even if they note it, there is, as we saw
at some length in chapter 3, no strong reason to assume that a series of seven
items need recall the week of creation in particular. For there is a multitude
of sequences of seven in the Bible, some labeled as such and others not, that
have nothing to do with creation.[73] A good, nicely redundant example is the
fall of Jericho on the seventh day after seven priests carrying seven ram's horns
have led a procession that circled the city seven times (Josh 6:2–20). As we
saw in chapter 3, the notion that a six-day sequence attains its goal on the seventh is found outside Israel as well.[74] The Israelite Sabbath may have developed
(in part) out of that idea, but that idea surely did not develop out of the Sabbath. The "seventh day" in Joshua 6 is not a Sabbath.

Apart from the general homology of world-building and temple-building
in the ancient Near East, there is, however, still one compelling datum to connect the instructions about the construction of the Tabernacle in Exod 25:1–
31:17 to the creation of the world in Gen 1:1–2:3. Whereas Kearney's attempt
to correlate each of the first six speeches to Moses with the corresponding day
of the hexameron does not succeed, it is much harder to dismiss the fact that
the seventh speech not only enjoins the Sabbath but speaks of it in terms
that overlap strikingly with the account of the seventh day in Gen 2:1–3:

> [12]And the LORD said to Moses: [13]Speak to the Israelite people and say:
> Nevertheless, you must keep My sabbaths, for this is a sign between
> Me and you throughout the ages, that you may know that I the LORD
> have consecrated you. [14]You shall keep the sabbath, for it is holy for you.
> He who profanes it shall be put to death: whoever does work on it, that
> person shall be cut off from among his kin. [15]Six days may work be done,
> but on the seventh day there shall be a sabbath of complete rest, holy
> to the LORD; whoever does work on the sabbath day shall be put to
> death. [16]The Israelite people shall keep the sabbath, observing the sab-
> bath throughout the ages as a covenant for all time: [17]it shall be a sign for
> all time between Me and the people of Israel. For in six days the LORD

made heaven and earth, and on the seventh day He ceased from work and was refreshed. (Exod 31:12–17)

The passage combines a number of notes that we have heard in various others along the way. The idea that the Sabbath must be "kept" (or "observed"), using the verb *šāmar*, which appears in fully three of these six verses (vv. 13, 14, and 16), recalls the beginning of the fourth commandment in the Deuteronomic Decalogue: "Observe (*šāmôr*) the sabbath day and keep it holy" (Deut 5:12). The opening of Exod 31:14—"You shall keep (*ûšəmartem*) the sabbath, for it is holy for you"—is especially close, closer than the parallel in Exod 20:8, which begins with "Remember" (*zākôr*). By contrast, the language of six days of work followed by a seventh, which is the Sabbath, in the passage above (Exod 31:15) is also present in both versions of the Decalogue (Exod 20:9–10; Deut 5:13–14), though, of course, in slightly different form. The report that "on the seventh day [the LORD] ceased from work" (Exod 31:17) recalls both the seventh day of creation (Gen 2:2b, 3b) and the related wording in the Exodus version of the fourth commandment (20:11). Interestingly, though, whereas Exod 20:11, unlike Gen 2:1–3, tells us that God "rested (*vayyānaḥ*) on the seventh day," the passage above uses a different verb altogether (*vayyinnāp̄aš*), rendered above as "was refreshed" (Exod 31:17). But this word, too, we have already seen. It appears in an early legal collection, where it commands the householder to cease from labor on the seventh day "in order that your ox and your ass may rest (*yānûªḥ*), and that your bondman and the stranger may be refreshed (*yinnāp̄ēš*)" (Exod 23:12).[75]

The several echoes in Exod 31:12–17 of earlier texts or oral traditions correlates well with the scholarly consensus that the passage derives from a late stratum, which source critics usually identify as the Holiness source (H), a further extension and significant reformulation of the P (for "Priestly") document.[76] As the name implies, this source is especially concerned with matters of sanctity—the sanctity of God, the sanctity of the people Israel, the sanctity of the Tabernacle and its appurtenances and rites, the sanctity of the Aaronic priesthood (the *kōhănîm*), and the sanctity of the festivals, including, as here, the sanctity of the Sabbath.

In this last of the seven sets of instructions to Moses about the Tabernacle, then, the holiness of the people Israel and that of the Sabbath come together neatly: Israel's upholding the sanctity of the seventh day is the sign that the LORD has sanctified them. They become holy (in part) by protecting the day God has consecrated. Here, the Sabbath is not, as in some other sources, a humanitarian institution decreed for the benefit of human and animal underlings, or at least that etiology (which we have explored in our previous two chapters) does not appear in this passage; whether it is presupposed is unknown. Nor is the Sabbath only a human imitation and implementation of God's rest on the primordial seventh day, as in Exod 20:11. It is again that, but now it is also a community-defining norm; desecrating the Sabbath, like other violations of cultic sancta, is now explicitly labeled a capital offense (Exod 31:15). But in the larger theological perspective, the Sabbath is more than a legal obligation: the special day is an everlasting sign of Israel's own specialness (vv. 16–17). Another verse ascribed to H puts it memorably: "You shall be holy to Me, for I the LORD am holy, and I have set you apart from other peoples to be Mine" (Lev 20:26).

The directives to Moses about the construction of the Tabernacle end precisely where the Priestly account of creation also comes to its conclusion, with God at rest after his six days of labor. The seventh day and the seventh speech thus correspond at a deep level. The Sabbath crowns the Tabernacle, just as it crowns creation and defines the deepest rhythm of the cosmos itself. For the Holiness school, this collocation of Sabbath and shrine was a natural one, and, given the profound connections of world-building and temple-building, it comes as no surprise that a source with a significant investment in priesthood and temple would so focus on Sabbath as well. Indeed, twice in a collection of laws ascribed to that same circle, we find a verse in which the linkage could not be clearer: "You shall keep My sabbaths and venerate My sanctuary: I am the LORD." (Lev 19:30; 26:2).

In a less explicit way, the narrative about the erection of the Tabernacle at the very end of Exodus also recalls the Priestly creation story, as a number of scholars over recent decades have noted.[77] Here, the principal connection lies in the overlap of language between the end of the primal week and the conclusion of the construction of the shrine under the direction of Moses, as seen in the pairings:

1. And God saw all that He had made (*kol-ʾăšer ʿāśâ*), and found it (*vəhinnēh*) very good. And there was evening and there was morning, the sixth day. (Gen 1:31)	And when Moses saw that they had performed all the tasks (*kol-hamməlāʾkā*)—as the LORD had commanded, so they had done (*vəhinnēh ʿāśû ʾōtāh*)—Moses blessed them. (Exod 39:43)
2. The heaven and the earth were finished (*vaykullû*), and all (*vəkol*) their array. (Gen 2:1)	Thus was completed all (*vattēkel kol*) the work of the Tabernacle of the Tent of Meeting. (Exod 39:32)
3. On the seventh day God finished (*vaykal*) the work (*mələ'ktô*) that He had been doing (*ʾăšer ʿāśâ*). (Gen 2:2)	So Moses finished (*vaykal*) the work (*hamməlā 'kā*). (Exod 40:33)[78]

4. And God blessed (*vayḇārek̠*) the seventh day (Gen 2:3)	Moses blessed (*vayḇārek̠*) them. (Exod 39:43)
5. and declared it holy (*vayqaddēš*). (Gen 2:3)	to consecrate (*vəqiddaštā*) it and all its furnishings (Exod 40:9)[79]

Like the correspondence between the seventh day of the primordial week and the seventh set of instructions for constructing the wilderness sanctuary (both of which exhibit, in turn, overlaps in wording with this list as well), the correspondences above again underscore the homology of world-building and temple-building. This time, however, the Exodus passages make no reference to the Sabbath. Rather, and more subtly, they intimate a homology between the states of completion and sanctification present temporally on the seventh day and spatially in the Tabernacle. The former represents holiness in time; the latter, holiness in space. But, as the verbal correspondences imply, both Sabbath and sanctuary gesture toward and bring to earth, however fleetingly, the same elevated state of being.

Israel's story in the Torah does not end with the Priestly account of the construction of the Tabernacle at Sinai and the inauguration of divine service within it, however. Rather, the Pentateuchal story comes to its ultimate fulfillment when, in the sixth book of the Bible, Israel under Joshua has at last assumed possession of the promised land and set up the tent-shrine for the LORD's presence at Shiloh. Only then have God's interlocking covenantal assurances to Abraham come to completion: his descendants are a populous nation living in the promised land and in his presence:

> These are the portions assigned by lot to the tribes of Israel by the priest Eleazar, Joshua son of Nun, and the heads of the ancestral houses, before the LORD at Shiloh, at the entrance of the Tent of Meeting. And they finished (*vayk̠allû*) dividing the land. (Josh 19:51)[80]

In manifold ways, great and small, the Priestly creation account (Gen 1:1–2:3) is oriented toward the divine repose attained in its seventh and last section. There is evidence, however, that this sabbatical focus has been imposed on a text that did not originally have it. An early rabbinic text already observed that "By ten acts of speech (*ma'ămārôt*) the world was created (m. Avot 5:1), referring to the ten times the verb *vayyō'mer* ("and [God/He] said") appears in the passage. Similarly, modern scholars have noted that, with two acts of creation on its third and its sixth days (and none, of course, on the seventh), there is a total of eight such works, not seven, during the primordial week.[81]

Whatever the prehistory of the passage, however, the significance of the number seven is threaded into its current form in many ways, some obvious and some subtle, as several scholars have by now noted.[82] To start literally at the beginning, the first verse of Gen 1:1–2:3 consists of seven Hebrew words; the second, of fourteen.[83] It is, of course, true that the assignment of verse numbers is of medieval origin; terms like "Gen 1:1"or "2:2" would have been mystifying to the ancients. It is, however, also the case that the traditional Hebrew (or Masoretic) text marks the end of verses with a distinctive cantillation note, and in this case the note appears first after seven words and then after another fourteen. How far back such a practice goes is not really known, but it seems likely that the ancient chanting of the text included a way of indicating the ends of semantic units, as the tradition understood them. If so, beginning the creation account with a verse of seven words and ending it with a little paragraph about the seventh day (in which that ordinal number appears three times) is unlikely to be coincidental. Add to this the fact that the number of Hebrew words in the entire passage comes to a multiple of seven (469),[84] and the likelihood grows that a very deliberate compositional intention is at work.

More evidence for the same conclusion lies in the fact that, of the three significant Hebrew nouns in Gen 1:1—those for "God," "heaven," and "earth"— the first occurs thirty-five times in Gen 1:1–2:3, and the third, twenty-one times. Both of these figures are, obviously, multiples of seven. Umberto Cassuto claimed that the sum of the occurrences for the two words for heaven, "heaven/sky" (*šāmayim*) and "expanse" (*rāqiaʿ*), which are identified as synonyms in 1:8, is also twenty-one times.[85] In fact, in the Masoretic text the first appears eleven times, and the second, nine, thus actually leaving the sum in this case one short. If the word *mabdîl* in 1:6 can be taken as a substantive ("divider") rather than a verb ("may separate"), then there would be a third synonym and Cassuto would have his twenty-one instances after all. The resultant structure would thus be parallelistic, "Let there be an expanse (*yəhî rāqiaʿ*) in the midst of the water and let there be a divider (*vîhî mabdîl*) between water and water." But, since the word is unique to this verse, this possibility is at best a conjecture. A more credible way to reach the figure of twenty-one words for "heaven"/"sky"/"expanse" in Gen 1:1–2:3 would be to use the Hebrew that underlies the Septuagint version of the same passage.[86] For Gen 1:9 in that witness displays a clause not present in the Masoretic Text: "and the waters that were under the sky (*ouranós*) were gathered to their gathering places, and the dry land appeared." The Hebrew noun that the Greek *ouranós* renders throughout the passage is *šāmayim*, which seems therefore to have appeared twelve times, not eleven, in the version the Septuagint was translating.

In other cases, however, Cassuto's calculations fail to convince. For example, he finds seven instances of the words *ʾôr* ("light") and *yôm* ("day") in the first paragraph of this creation story (Gen 1:1–5); they are defined as synonyms in v. 5. When, however, he writes that there are seven instances of the term for "light" (*'ôr*) in the account of the fourth day, in which the sun, moon, and stars are created (Gen 1:14–19), he cannot be including *yôm* ("day") but must instead be limiting himself to the total occurrences of the three words of the root *'wr* in this paragraph.[87] For, were he to take seriously the synonymy of *'ôr* ("light") and *yôm* ("day") this time, his count would be off. Similar weaknesses attend some of his other claims for strings of seven in Gen 1:1–2:3.

The fact remains, though, that most of Cassuto's heptads are valid and the probability that they represent coincidences, low. For example, the expression "God saw that . . . was good" (or "very good") appears seven times, but not, as one might first think, because it is said every day. Rather, it is missing on the second and seventh days and, as if in compensation, occurs twice on the adjacent third and sixth days.[88] In other words, the division of Gen 1:1–2:3 into seven paragraphs, one for each day of the primordial week, does not account for the sevenfold appearance of the expression—as if to suggest that the number seven has an independent significance and that it is this that accounts for the organization of time into repeating units of seven days culminating in a radically different one at the end of the series.

But what is probably the most impressive of the heptads is the one that characterizes the last of those seven paragraphs:

> ¹The heaven and the earth were finished, and all their array. ²On the seventh day God finished the work that He had been doing, and He ceased on the seventh day from all the work that He had done. ³And God blessed the seventh day and declared it holy, because on it God ceased from all the work of creation that He had done. (Gen 2:1–3)

The heptadic structure appears when we divide these three verses into their natural semantic subsections and indicate the number of Hebrew words in each:

> ¹The heaven and the earth were finished, and all their array. (5)
> ²On the seventh day God finished the work that He had been doing, (7)
> and He ceased on the seventh day from all the work that He had done. (7)
> ³And God blessed the seventh day and declared it holy, (7)
> because on it God ceased from all the work of creation that He had done. (9)

This yields a total of five clauses in thirty-five words—the same count as we found for the word "God" (*'ĕlōhîm*) in the full text of Gen 1:1–2:3. But again, this does not break down into the expected, and monotonous, pattern of seven Hebrew words per clause. Rather, the deficiency of the first clause, which displays only five words, is rectified in the last, with nine.[89] More than that: the three intermediate clauses, the only ones with seven words, all display the ordinal number "seventh." As Cassuto concludes, "It is impossible to believe that all this is nothing but coincidence."[90]

For Cassuto, a critic of the Documentary Hypothesis and kindred fragmenting methods of textual interpretation, the multiple and subtle heptadic patterns are proof positive that Gen 1:1–2:3 is a coherent integer and not a text cobbled together from preexistent sources.[91] He may be right, but one cannot discount the possibility that an energetic redactional artist has recomposed a previous document, perhaps one that lacked the focus on the number seven or the Sabbath, in order to root the seventh day in primordial times, endowing it with what the historian of religion Mircea Eliade calls "the prestige of origins."[92] What is certain, however, is that in its current shape the account of the primordial week exhibits a pattern in which the seventh day stands alone. For, as the chart below shows, what is created in each of the first three days correlates with what is created in the corresponding day of the last three.[93] The generality or habitat is created on the first three days and the particularities or what fills the habitat is created on the last three. The seventh is thus the day nonpareil:

	7—Sabbath
Earth and Sea—3	6—Land, Animals, and Humans
Sky—2	5—Birds and Sea Animals
Light—1	4—Lights

A midrash in the name of a mid-second-century CE sage from the Land of Israel captures the point beautifully:

> Rabbi Simeon bar Yochai taught:
> The Sabbath said before the Holy One (blessed be He!): "Master of the Worlds, all of them have a partner, and am I to have no partner?"
> The Holy One (blessed be He!) said to her, "The Community of Israel—that is your partner!" And when Israel stood before Mount Sinai, the Holy One (blessed be He) said to them, "Remember what I said to the Sabbath: 'The Community of Israel—that is your partner!'"
> (Hence,) "Remember the Sabbath day and keep it holy." (Exod 20:8)
> (Gen. Rab. 11:8)

The midrash begins with a complaint by the Sabbath precisely about her having no partner. Is she doomed to be a permanently unmarried woman, a state that rabbinic culture, with its high estimation of marriage and child-rearing, regarded as most unfortunate? God responds, not surprisingly, with a firm denial. The people Israel will be the Sabbath's mate, and Sinai will be, as it were, the site of the wedding.[94] God is, the midrash avers, reminding Israel of what he promised the Sabbath at the time of creation—that she would have a husband to protect and care for her. Hence, the choice of the verb "Remember" in the Exodus version of the Decalogue (in contradistinction to "Observe" in the Deuteronomic version, as we saw in the last chapter). Here yet again, creation, Sabbath, and Sinai are inextricably connected.

We have observed that the opening creation story of Genesis comes to its conclusion with the account of God's ceasing his creative labors on the seventh day—heaven, earth, and all their array having been finished—and blessing and sanctifying that day. In that sense, the seventh is not only the last but also, and more importantly, the climactic day of the series, adumbrating the way the people Israel is to organize time and the sacred occasion that will be a sign of its own consecrated status. In fact, however, such an interpretation is too simple. For there is another climactic moment in the series—namely, the last act of creation in the hexameron, the creation and commissioning of humankind:

> [26]And God said, "Let us make man in our image, after our likeness. They shall rule the fish of the sea, the birds of the sky, the cattle, the whole earth, and all the creeping things that creep on earth." [27]And God created man in His image, in the image of God He created him; male and female He created them. [28]God blessed them and God said to them, "Be fertile and increase, fill the earth and master it; and rule the fish of the sea, the birds of the sky, and all the living things that creep on earth." (Gen 1:26–28)

This passage is as riddled with uncertainties as it is famous. The most obvious of the problems involves those first-person plurals in the first verse: "Let us . . . our image . . . our likeness." In all the rest of Gen 1:1–2:3, God speaks only in the third person (for example, "Let there be" in 1:3 or "Let the water" in 1:9) or, rarely, the second ("Be fertile and increase," 1:22) but never in the first, and he gives no indication whatsoever that anyone else is involved in his originating acts. Other entities—the waters, for instance, or the earth—are commanded in the third person but not invited to share in the deed; God is the singular creator. The creatures of the seas and the air are given that command to "Be fertile and increase," but God alone creates them, conferring with no one else beforehand. Indeed, complicating the problem is the fact that 1:27–28 follows that same pattern: God acts alone. If those God addresses in the previous verse ever responded to the invitation, we never hear about it. Nothing suggests that they participated in the creation of humankind. The next time God speaks, it is not to the addressees of v. 26 but to the new creatures themselves (vv. 29–30). An ancient solution to the conundrum of the first-person plurals remains the likeliest: as is the case in other passages in the Hebrew Bible, God is here depicted as a king addressing his cabinet—the other, but fully subordinate, members of the divine council.[95] One memorable midrash takes the proposal of Gen 1:26 as a question ("Shall we make man?") and relates this:

> While the ministering angels were arguing back and forth, engaged with each other, the Holy One (blessed be He!) created him. He said, "What good can you do now? Man has already been made (*ne'ĕśâ*)." (Gen. Rab. 8:5)

This midrash draws strength from the orthographic identity of *na'ăśeh*, "let us make" / "shall we make," with *ne'ĕśâ*, "he has been made." The consonants of the two words (in antiquity, only consonants were written) are the same. Midrashically, this helps make sense of the shift from the plurals of Gen 1:26 to the singulars of v. 27: God proposed the creation of humankind to his council, and while they debated the proposition—after all, it is not obvious whether the existence of humans is good or bad for the world or, for that matter, for the lesser divinities themselves—he acted alone. The human race exists because of his decisiveness; it owes nothing to the subordinate deities.

The likelihood that Gen 1:26 is addressed to the lesser divinities raises the possibility that humans were created not only in his image, as v. 27 makes explicit, but also in the image of the other deities—in other words, that *baṣelem 'ĕlōhîm* in that verse means "in the image of the gods" rather than, as rendered above, "in the image of God." Middleton points to Gen 9:6 as possibly adding support to this hypothesis:

> Whoever sheds the blood of man,
> By man shall his blood be shed;
> For *baṣelem 'ĕlōhîm*
> Did He make man. (Gen 9:6)[96]

"The occurrence of the phrase *ṣelem 'ĕlōhîm* in Genesis 9:6 is somewhat jarring," he writes, "if the phrase means 'image of God,' since 'his image' would have been the more natural construction. It may have both God and angels in its purview. And 1:27 uses both 'his image' and 'image of *'ĕlōhîm*' in parallel lines, which on the surface sounds redundant, unless *'ĕlōhîm* includes both

God and the heavenly court."⁹⁷ If so, humans are created in the image not only of their creator but also of his heavenly courtiers as well.

Middleton makes the same suggestion about a passage that is often, and rightly, compared with Gen 1:26–28 and on which, in fact, it sheds considerable light:

> ⁴When I behold Your heavens, the work of Your fingers,
> the moon and stars that You set in place,
> ⁵what is man that You have been mindful of him,
> mortal man that You have taken note of him,
> ⁶that You have made him little less than divine (*ʾĕlōhîm*),
> and adorned him with glory and majesty;
> ⁷You have made him master over Your handiwork,
> laying the world at his feet,
> ⁸sheep and oxen, all of them,
> and wild beasts, too;
> ⁹the birds of the heavens, the fish of the sea,
> whatever travels the paths of the seas. (Ps 8:4–9)

"That *ʾĕlōhîm* [in v. 6] is likely a reference to the heavenly court (or is intentionally ambiguous, referring to both God and the heavenly host)," Middleton observes, "is indicated by the somewhat clumsy use of *ʾĕlōhîm* in a sentence that would more naturally read 'little lower than *yourself* [or here, and more accurately, 'little less than *yourself*], since the psalm otherwise consists in direct second-person address to God."⁹⁸

In fact, this interpretation of *ʾĕlōhîm* in Ps 8:6 as referring to the angels has a long and rich pedigree in Jewish exegesis. It appears as early as the Targum and is well-attested among the classical medieval commentators. Rabbi David Qimchi (Provence, 1160–1235), for example, explains that in having a soul, which is not bodily in nature, human beings are like angels. What makes them less than angels, however, is that they also have bodies.⁹⁹

The precise relationship between the terms applied to humankind in these two texts—"image of God/gods" (Gen 1:27) and "little less than divine/God/gods" (Ps 8:6)—is unclear. Functionally, though, they seem synonymous, for both of them preface accounts of humankind's regal majesty over the other creatures. In the case of Genesis 1, the commands to "master" the earth and to "rule" over the other animals (v. 28) denote authority and control; the latter verb (*rādâ*), as Middleton notes, "is often linked with kingship." In fact, the very syntax of Gen 1:26 "points to 'rule' as the *purpose*, not simply the consequence or result of the *imago Dei*," or image of God.¹⁰⁰ As for Psalm 8, the royal role there is signaled by the words "adorned him with glory and majesty" in

v. 6; the verb (*tə'aṭṭərēhû*) is more literally rendered "crowned." Human governance over the rest of creation is more explicitly affirmed in the next verse, "You have made him master (*tamšîlēhû*) over Your handiwork" (v. 7). So, whether the specific language is that of "the image" or that of "little less than," the connection of humanity to kingship is clear.

This is, it turns out, a connection deeply rooted in ancient Near Eastern cultures. As many scholars have now documented, Egyptian and Mesopotamian kings alike could be described as the "image" of their gods.[101] In the biblical case, however, the metaphor has generated considerable ethical reflection—and not simply because the Bible serves as a continuing source of authoritative guidance for many, as is not the case with the literary remains of those other, and long vanished, civilizations. The association between the creation of humanity in God's image and the way they should treat each other—in contrast with how they treat animal life—is already explicit in the Bible itself. It appears memorably in the address of God to Noah and his sons, the last verse of which we have just examined:

> [3]Every creature that lives shall be yours to eat; as with the green grasses, I give you all these. [4]You must not, however, eat flesh with its life-blood in it. [5]But for your own life-blood I will require a reckoning: I will require it of every beast; of man, too, will I require a reckoning for human life, of every man for that of his fellow man!
> [6]Whoever sheds the blood of man,
> By man shall his blood be shed;
> For in His image
> Did God make man. (Gen 9:3–6)

Here, the rationale for the prohibition of murder is precisely God's creation of humankind in his own image. Bloodshed is thus akin to deicide. Perhaps, recalling the use of the use of the word "image" (*ṣelem*) as a term for the icons of deities,[102] the ancient audience was meant to interpret the act forbidden in Gen 9:6 as analogous to the smashing of idols—a furious act, that is, of uncompromising opposition. But this time, rather than a sign of wholehearted faithfulness to the true God, it is a heinous renunciation of him.

In applying the language of royalty to the entire human race (male and female), the Priestly source is reflecting a democratization of sorts. This move will seem less revolutionary if we remember the large role that covenant plays in so much of the Hebrew Bible. For the partners to a covenant are themselves kings, and when the whole people Israel are granted the status of covenanters with the divine suzerain, they all can be said, to some degree, to be assuming a regal role.[103]

In recent years, however, some scholars have gone further, claiming that the creation of humankind in the image of God establishes equality within human society as well. "It is significant, in this connection," writes Middleton, "that while humans are granted rule over the earth and the animals, there is no mandate in Genesis 1 for humans to rule each other. The democratization of the image in this text thus suggests an egalitarian conception of the exercise of power." To him, this indicates "an implicit delegitimization of the entire ruling and priestly structure of Mesopotamian society (and especially the absolute power of the king)."[104] Elsewhere, he goes so far as to claim to find here "the root of the later Christian notion of the priesthood of every believer."[105] The justly influential Jewish scholar Shai Held advances the same interpretation, though without Middleton's Protestant *Tendenz*. "The Torah's assertion that every human being is created in the image of God is," he argues, "a repudiation of the idea, so common in the ancient world, that some people are simply meant to rule over others. If everyone is royalty, then on some level, when it comes to the interpersonal and political spheres, no one is."[106]

Whatever the contemporary political utility of this position, as exegesis of the creation of humankind in Gen 1:26–28, it is, in my judgment, indefensible. One reason is that the passage says nothing whatsoever about the organization of society. It does not mandate human equality, only the God-given authority of the human race over the animal world. Even if the passage says that all humans (male and female) hold a lofty commission in the manner of kings, the text in no way implies that there should be no kings among them or that no one should rightly defer to monarchs, priests, or other officials. The idiom of covenant derives most immediately from the language of kings' deferring to other kings,[107] and the Priestly source itself explicitly makes the future emergence of kings a part of its covenantal promise of progeny to Abraham and Sarah (Gen 17:6, 16). And if the narrative sections ascribed to that source are indeed of a piece with the Priestly cultic legislation, then the notion that Gen 1:26–28 opposes priesthood in the name of the full equality of an undifferentiated humanity is exceptionally far-fetched. For nothing is more central to the laws that have come to be called "Priestly" than God's singling out of men of Aaronic lineage (the *kōhănîm*) for special duties, restrictions, privileges, and benefices.[108] If an ancient Israelite precedent for the Protestant notion of the priesthood of all believers exists, the Priestly source of the Pentateuch is an exceptionally unpromising place to look for it.[109]

More apt is a comparison between the lofty commission of God's last creation (the human race) at the end of the hexameron, on the one hand, and Mesopotamian compositions that attribute the creation of humankind to the gods' desire to free themselves of labor, on the other.[110] In the Enuma Elish, for example, the victorious creator-god Marduk, speaking of the creature he is about to form, makes the rationale for doing so unmistakable: "I shall create humankind, / "They shall bear the gods' burden that those may rest."[111] Here, the repose of the deities is at the expense of human work; the imposition of forced labor upon humankind liberates the gods and grants them rest. The same is true in a Babylonian poem about the great flood, Atraḫasis, where Mami, the divine midwife, is asked to:

> Create a human being that he bear the yoke,
> Let him bear the yoke, the task of [the god] Enlil,
> Let man assume the drudgery of god.

And that she does, announcing to her grateful fellow gods: "I have done away with your heavy forced labor, / I have imposed your drudgery on man."[112]

In the transition between God's last act of creation in the hexameron and his repose on the seventh day in Gen 1:1–2:3, Samuel A. Meier finds an illuminating parallel to this well-attested Mesopotamian motif:

> God's rest is made possible because there is a substitute in his image delegated to maintain the world order and ensure the fruitfulness of the earth. The day on which God rests in the Bible—as in other ancient Near Eastern traditions—is therefore the first day of humanity's labor. The seventh day is God's rest and the day on which humanity begins to work. God can cease from his activity because humanity is now bearing the burden....
>
> It is for this reason that the writer of Genesis 1 studiously avoids using the noun "sabbath" anywhere in this text. This is not a rest for creation, much less for humanity; this is a rest for God.[113]

Meier is certainly right that in Gen 2:1–3 only God rests, or, more minimally and perhaps more literally, ceases from labor—a point that is often missed. As has already been observed, we hear nothing about any human observance of the seventh day until the episode of the manna in Exodus 16, and there is no reason to believe that any ancient Israelites saw the Sabbath as applying to other groups than their own; in that sense, it is not universal. Meier is also correct that the noun šabbāt ("Sabbath") appears nowhere in Gen 1:1–2:3 or, for that matter, anywhere else in the biblical narrative until the manna falls (Exod 16:23).

But does the writer "studiously avoid" the term? If such was his intent, he failed miserably. For, as we saw above, in his account of that last day of the week of creation (Gen 2:1–3), he uses the nearly homophonous verb šābat ("ceased") twice in a three-verse paragraph that includes three semantic units of seven words, all of which include the phrase "the seventh day." Surely to denote "the day on which God rests," a writer seeking to avoid a connection with the Sabbath would have chosen a different verb (such as *nāḥ*, "to rest," which does not appear in the passage).[114] The lexical data suggests, rather, that the author regards the Sabbath as rooted in the very structure of creation—and the sabbatical week as a divine ordinance, not a human convention—but also as hidden away until it could be revealed to the people Israel after the exodus. The ancient audience would have instantaneously recognized the identity of the seventh day of creation as the Sabbath and looked forward to the moment in the narrative when God explicitly declared it to be such.[115]

There is also room to doubt Meier's notion that "the seventh day is God's rest and the day on which humanity begins to work." Gen 2:1–3 never mentions human work, or human beings at all; its focus is exclusively on God. Nor does the lofty commission to the newly created human race in Gen 1:28 include any words for work, toil, burden, drudgery, or the like, notions for which the lexicon of Biblical Hebrew is by no means poor. Even the assignment of plants and trees as the sources of human food in the next verse makes no allusion to agriculture. It would seem that in the Priestly vision, primeval humanity were frugivores and gatherers—and hardly delegated to perform hard work of the sort from which the Mesopotamian gods were so happy to be liberated by the creation of human beings.

The majestic repose of God the creator on the seventh day is not, then, at the expense of his last creatures, the human race. The latter are not commanded to toil but just the opposite—to master the earth and rule the creatures in the sea and sky and on earth in the manner of kings. This is not to say, however, that the Mesopotamian notion of creation as an act of liberation has no parallel in the Hebrew Bible. Meier's connecting the two remains a very productive insight, even if his conclusion is rejected. For when the Sabbath is rooted in creation, then the humans who practice it are experiencing something analogous to the repose of the creator—and, more distantly, the relief of the liberated lesser Mesopotamian gods. The same point can by extension be made of the text that explicitly describes the fallow year in the language of the Sabbath, thus yielding the term "sabbatical year" (Lev 25:2–7). In the same chapter of Leviticus, the radical (and radically conservative) provisions for the fiftieth, or Jubilee, year after seven sabbaticals strongly recall the benevolent proclamations of Mesopotamian and other kings (Lev 25:8–55). Creation is thus itself an act of social benevolence.[116] That the same institution can be described as rooted in creation or in the exodus, as in the two versions of the Sabbath commandment in the Decalogue, is thus hardly surprising (Exod 20:8–11; Deut 5:12–15). What is perhaps surprising is that it is human beings rather than gods who are liberated at creation.

In his lovely and inspiring little book, *The Sabbath*, Abraham Joshua Heschel speaks of the Sabbath as "a palace in time."[117] Whereas other cultures, he claims, sanctify land and buildings, "Judaism is a *religion of time* aiming at the *sanctification of time*": "Judaism teaches us to be attached to holiness in time, to be attached to sacred events, to learn how to consecrate sanctuaries that emerge from the magnificent stream of the year. The Sabbaths are our great cathedrals; and our Holy of Holies is a shrine that neither the Romans nor the Germans were able to burn."[118] Alexandra Grund objects to Heschel's phrase "a palace in time" and recommends substituting "a sanctuary in time."[119] To be sure, if the proprietor of the palace were a flesh-and-blood king, Heschel's metaphor would indeed be weak. But, as his contrast with the "great cathedrals" suggests, the imagined palace is not a secular but a sacred one, the kingly abode of the lord of space and time alike. The Sabbath is indeed a sanctuary in time, but, as I hope to have now shown, it is one that mediates the spiritual reality that is (ideally) characteristic of God's palace in space as well. In some profound sense, the sacred day and the sacred place point to the same transcendent experience—the precious moment of human access to the repose of the victorious Creator enthroned in his cosmic temple.

CHAPTER 6

What Is "Work"? or, the Indispensability of Law

IT IS OFTEN THOUGHT that what the Fourth Commandment of the Decalogue prohibits on the seventh day is limited to labor.[1] The wording itself, however, suggests a more complicated situation, one that has, in fact, contributed enormously to the development of the Jewish Sabbath over the centuries. Much of the discussion has necessarily focused on one key word:

> [9]Six days you shall labor (taʿăḇōd) and do all your work (məlaʾktekā), [10]but the seventh day is a sabbath of the LORD your God: you shall not do any work (məlāʾkâ)—you, your son or daughter, your male or female slave, or your cattle, or the stranger who is within your settlements. (Exod 20:9–10; cf. Deut 5:13–14)

What, precisely, constitutes məlāʾkâ?[2] If we read the two clauses of v. 9 as standing in synonymous parallelism, then we have a simple answer: "do all your work (məlaʾktekā)" is synonymous with "to labor." Alternatively, we could wonder whether even in such a construction, the two clauses mean precisely the same thing. Could it not be, as some have argued, that the second specifies or amplifies the first rather than merely echoing it in the interest of stylistic variation? As James L. Kugel puts it, to say that the two halves of a parallelistic poetic colon express the same idea is to evade the key question: "what is that same idea that is being repeated?"[3] Perhaps the same question applies here as well.

Applied to the text above, the question becomes, what is "that same idea" that is conveyed conjointly and inseparably by the verb labor (taʿăḇōd) and the verb "do" with məlāʾkâ as its object? What is labor/work? Might it be that not all labor qualifies as work, or that not all of what is commonly classified as work in a given culture falls into the category of labor forbidden on the Sabbath?

Some might argue that "work" refers to one's occupation, that which a person does to earn a livelihood. On that interpretation, the disabled, the unemployed, and all other persons not in the workforce are incapable of violating the Sabbath—surely a most unlikely conclusion. One reason to judge it so is that the Fourth Commandment does not begin with the prohibition of work at all but rather with a positive injunction: "Remember/Observe the sabbath day and keep it holy" (Exod 20:8; Deut 5:12). The Israelite is to sanctify the seventh day of the week, and in the Bible (as elsewhere) sanctifying entails sharply separating the holy from the nonholy. Whatever the məlā'ḳâ of the Fourth Commandment originally included, it was characteristic of the first six days of the week, in which it was permitted (perhaps even commanded), but it turned into an act of desecration—desacralization—on the Sabbath. The Israelite householder is warned not to lose sight of that key difference and to guard against the profanation of the sacred day brought about by doing məlāḳâ.

Within the Hebrew Bible itself, we find a few activities that are explicitly forbidden on the seventh day and must thus reflect the thinking on our question of various communities in the course of the millennium or so over which that very diverse set of books was composed. Probably the chronologically earliest is a verse we have already examined at some length: "Six days you shall work, but on the seventh day you shall cease from labor; you shall cease from labor even at plowing time and harvest time" (Exod 34:21). As we have argued, although no word for "even" occurs in the Hebrew, the structure of this short verse of three clauses of three words each suggests that the phrase "at plowing time and harvest time" stands in the climactic position and describes the sort of "work" and "labor" from which the Israelite must cease on the seventh day.[4] Even in those crucial seasons, that is, the prohibition on labor and the commandment to "cease" are to remain fully in effect. The verse does not tell us whether plowing and harvesting are the only activities forbidden then, but it is highly unlikely that they were. Not all farm work falls into those two categories, and even in highly agricultural societies like ancient Israel, some people labored in occupations other than farming. It is hard to imagine that they were deemed exempt from the prohibition of labor on the seventh day. It may be that "plowing and harvesting" here constitute a merism and thus encompass all varieties of agricultural labor.[5]

One narrative is especially suggestive about what activities were thought to be forbidden on the Sabbath in biblical times. Exodus 16 begins with the newly freed Israelites complaining about the their lack of food in the wilderness, then describes the LORD's abundantly meeting their needs with the gift of manna. At the same time, he tests their obedience and their faith in him: Will they rely upon him to provide or will they try to squirrel away some of the miraculously supplied food for the next day? This, in turn, leads to a discussion of the difference between the Sabbath and the other days of the week, with particular attention to the need to prepare for the Sabbath on the sixth day:

[4]And the LORD said to Moses, "I will rain down bread for you from the sky, and the people shall go out and gather each day that day's portion—that I may thus test them, to see whether they will follow My instructions or not. [5]But on the sixth day, when they apportion what they have brought in, it shall prove to be double the amount they gather each day."
…
[21]So they gathered it every morning, each as much as he needed to eat; for when the sun grew hot, it would melt. [22]On the sixth day they gathered double the amount of food, two *omers* for each; and when all the chieftains of the community came and told Moses, [23]he said to them, "This is what the LORD meant: Tomorrow is a day of rest, a holy sabbath (*šabbātôn šabbat-qōdeš*) of the LORD. Bake what you would bake and boil what you would boil; and all that is left put aside to be kept until morning." [24]So they put it aside until morning, as Moses had ordered; and it did not turn foul, and there were no maggots in it. [25]Then Moses said, "Eat it today, for today is a sabbath of the LORD; you will not find it today on the plain. [26]Six days you shall gather it; on the seventh day, the sabbath, there will be none."
[27]Yet some of the people went out on the seventh day to gather, but they found nothing. [28]And the LORD said to Moses, "How long will you refuse to obey My commandments and My teachings? [29]Mark that the LORD has given you the sabbath; therefore He gives you two days' food on the sixth day. Let everyone remain where he is: let no one leave his place on the seventh day." [30]So the people remained inactive (*vayyišbətû*) on the seventh day. (Exod 16:4–5, 21–30)[6]

Here, the act of "gathering" is seen as appropriate to the first six days of the week but not to the seventh. God therefore provides a double portion on the sixth day to allow for the sabbatical inactivity of the people. So, alongside the prohibition on gathering the miraculously supplied food on the Sabbath, there is a positive commandment to do extra work on the sixth day to prepare for the special one to follow. This is reminiscent of the pattern in the description of the sixth and seventh days of creation in Genesis. There are two acts of creation on the sixth day and, correspondingly, two statements that God found what he made to be good, but there is neither an act of creation nor a statement of approval on the seventh (Gen 1:24–2:3). The doubling on the sixth day makes up for the ostensible deficiency of the seventh. In the case of the manna, Israel's great test is to trust in God's promise that the extra manna gathered on the sixth day, unlike that gathered on the first five (Exod 16:19–20), will not spoil but will instead provide sustenance without human effort. The narrative in Exodus 16 thus brilliantly links the gift of the manna to the gift of the Sabbath and, at the deeper theological level, dramatizes the common element of the two phenomena—radical trust in God's provision.

Unfortunately, not everyone passes the test: "Yet some of the people went out on the seventh day to gather, but they found nothing" (Exod 16:27). The happiness and abundance of the Sabbath is inextricably associated with the norms that define the day and thus necessarily restrict what may be done on it. On this, Brevard S. Childs, an especially astute biblical scholar and Protestant theologian, makes a profound observation: "Christian commentators have traditionally stressed the joy of the early concept of the sabbath which is surely correct. But the restrictive side of the day set aside to God belongs to the same tradition and cannot be dismissed. Not all the people were enjoying the sabbath. Some were out hunting for manna. Once again, the theme of God's testing the obedience of the people recurs. 'How long will you refuse to keep my commandments?' God gives them a double portion of bread, but he demands a different way of life."[7]

I might add that the trust called for in the story of the manna does not at all equate to quietism, a reliance on God that altogether excludes human effort. To the contrary, the narrative pairs the prohibition to gather manna on the Sabbath with an implied injunction to gather twice as much on the previous day (Exod 16:29). Preparing for the Sabbath, we thus learn, is part of the proper practice of the Sabbath. Here, faith is not disjoined from the doing of deeds. Rather, the key disjunction is between the first six days of the week and the seventh, with the sixth as a day of active preparation for the holy occasion to follow.

Although it could conceivably be argued that the sabbatical provisions in the story of the manna in Exodus 16 are specific to the immediate narrative and its theological point about the LORD's test of a doubting Israel in the wilderness, it would seem more reasonable to regard those elements of practice as essential to the ongoing observance of the Sabbath, at least as understood in the source from which that passage is drawn. They are, in other words, laws presented narratively rather than abstractly. If so, in addition to the prohibition on gathering on the seventh day, we also find one on cooking, at least by implication: "Bake what you would bake and boil what you would boil; and all that is left put aside to be kept until morning" (v. 23). To be sure, the verse does not explicitly forbid baking and boiling on the next day (the Sabbath); theoretically, it could be instructing its hearers only to process the food for the sixth day then and leave the surplus until the seventh, when no new provisions would appear but the previously collected manna could legitimately be baked or boiled.

gainst such a literalistic reading, we must consider a law regarding the k-long holiday of Unleavened Bread, now usually called "Passover":[8]

You shall celebrate a sacred occasion on the first day, and a sacred occasion on the seventh day; no work at all shall be done on them; only what every person is to eat, that alone may be prepared for you. (Exod 12:16)

The similarity of the first and last days of Passover to the Sabbath is clear. All three days are holy, and work is strictly forbidden on them. But in the case of Passover, an explicit exception is made for "what every person is to eat" and for that alone. Were such an exception standard—that is, if it applied to the weekly celebration of the Sabbath—it would be hard to understand why it is stated in connection with Passover at all. The more reasonable conclusion is that here and in Exodus 16 alike, baking, boiling, and the like on the Sabbath were assumed to be prohibited; Exod 12:16 reinforces the point by explicitly distinguishing the paschal from the sabbatical norm. Not coincidentally, this difference between festal and sabbatical law becomes the explicit norm of rabbinic Judaism and the continuing halakhic tradition. With certain limitations, cooking on holidays is permitted; on the Sabbath, it is forbidden.

It is also worthwhile to note that a traditional Jewish practice in effect to this day is based on the message of faith in God's miraculous sustenance conveyed in the story of the manna in Exodus 16. In the words of the Talmud, "On the Sabbath a person is obligated to break bread over two loaves, as it is written, 'double the amount of food' (Exod 16:22)" (b. Šabb. 117b). The Hebrew phrase rendered here as "double the amount of food" (*leḥem mišneh*) becomes the term for the two whole loaves that must be present at every Sabbath and festival meal.

Finally, before leaving the passage about the manna, we must consider the possible import of one last injunction in Exod 16:29b, "Let everyone remain where he is: let no one leave his place on the seventh day." Taken literally and again assumed to be a continuing norm rather than one restricted to the narrative at hand, these words forbid leaving one's quarters on the Sabbath. More likely, such literalism is ill-advised, and the half-verse simply enjoins the Israelites in the immediate story not to venture forth in search of manna on the seventh day (for which God has already provided them with a double portion on the sixth), as some of them indeed have, much to God's consternation (Exod 16:27–29a). Certainly, in rabbinic Judaism, as it has developed over the centuries, social gathering for purposes of study, prayer, and feasting became characteristic of the day and have remained very much so into our time. Sabbath-observant Jews do not just sit at home all day.

This is not to say, however, that Jewish law over the centuries has ignored the words of Exod 16:29b. Far from it.

Consider, for example, the book of Jubilees, an important work of the mid-second century BCE, which, though not canonical or in any way authoritative in the ongoing rabbinic tradition, is a treasure trove of information about Jewish practice and biblical interpretation in its own time, at least as conducted by whatever sect it reflects. Here are the verses that are key to our present discussion:

> [12]Any person who does work: who goes on a trip; who works farmland whether at his home or in any (other) place; who lights a fire; who rides any animal; who travels the sea by ship; any person who beats or kills anything; who slits the throat of an animal or bird; who catches either a wild animal, a bird, or a fish; who fasts and makes war on the Sabbath day—[13]a person who does any of these things on the Sabbath day is to die, so that the Israelites may continue observing the Sabbath in accord with the commandments for the Sabbaths of the land as it was written in the tablets that he placed in my hands so that I could write for you the laws of each specific time in each division of its times. (Jub. 50:12–13)[9]

The prohibitions on working or plowing should now be familiar to us; some of the others, such as those on kindling, fasting, or making war, we shall soon examine. But what about those on making a journey and, relatedly, traveling by boat?[10] If any biblical injunction lies in the background of these two prohibitions, it must be that which commands the Israelites to stay in their places rather than collecting manna on the seventh day.[11] On the information currently available, however, it is impossible to say just how much earlier than Jubilees such an interpretation had existed.[12]

What we do know is that in antiquity (and beyond) some did interpret the verse to mean that one had to stay in one's house throughout the Sabbath. The Samaritans, for example, understand it to forbid leaving home except to go to the synagogue, and a similar aversion to walking about on the Sabbath has been (or was) attested among Ethiopian Jews. Among the Qaraites, an anti-rabbinic group that took shape in the eighth century CE (and, like the Samaritans, survives, though in drastically reduced numbers, to this day), a number of variant practices have been attested; one of them is that a person generally should not leave home on the Sabbath.[13]

Apart from these particular groups, the notion that travel on the Sabbath is restricted remained alive and well in Jewish law, though the exact limitation was long a matter of dispute. One of the Dead Sea Scrolls forbids a person to go more than a thousand cubits, or roughly 1,500 feet, outside his city.[14] Rabbinic tradition allows twice that distance, a figure derived from the dimensions of the pasture lands outside the cities assigned to the Levites in Num 35:5.[15]

arding that injunction at the end of the manna narrative in Exod 16:29b
et everyone remain where he is: let no one leave his place on the seventh

day"), it bears mention that the rabbis also pressed this verse into service to support the prohibition on carrying in the public domain on the Sabbath (a distinctive rabbinic twist on the biblical interdiction on carrying loads on the seventh day.)[16] In the New Testament, finally, the Mount of Olives, which is just east of Jerusalem across the Kidron Valley, is said to be "a Sabbath's trip" away (Acts 1:12), thus showing a limitation on travel on the seventh day—and probably like the rabbinic figure of 2,000 cubits—to be very much in effect in the author's world.[17]

As familiar as these practices are to Sabbath-observant Jews today, a related practice from Jewish antiquity must surely seem surprising in the same degree. The Jewish historian Josephus, writing around 75 CE about the sect known as the Essenes, tells us that they are "stricter than all Jews in abstaining from work on the seventh day; for not only do they prepare their food on the day before, to avoid kindling a fire on that one, but they do not venture to remove any vessel or even to go to stool" (Josephus, *J.W.* 2.148 [Thackeray, LCL]).[18] It is tempting to connect this abstention from defecation during the Sabbath with a provision in the Temple Scroll, a key document among the Dead Sea (or Qumran) finds, that the latrines must be set at a distance of 3,000 cubits outside the holy city,[19] a figure that exceeds both the 1,000-cubit limit of travel on the Sabbath cited above from another such scroll and the more lenient rabbinic norm of 2,000 cubits.

Whether Josephus and the Qumran evidence speak to the same reality is a question riddled with uncertainties. As the former presents the issue, the Essene abstention from defecation is of a piece with their general sabbatical rigorism. The Scrolls, however, do not speak directly to the issue of defecation on the Sabbath at all; their concern lies with protecting the sanctity of the idealized Temple city, which would be severely damaged by the presence of human solid waste.[20] The prohibition at Qumran, then, must be inferred from a correlation of the limits of travel with the placement of the latrines— a correlation further bedeviled by the appearance of these two key distances in different documents that cannot be simply assumed to be speaking to the same community or the identical situation. If one adds the archaeological evidence from Qumran to this messy mix, the uncertainties multiply, and no far-reaching conclusions are secure enough to pass the smell test.[21]

The complications and uncertainties that come from efforts to correlate Josephus's comments about Essene sabbatical practice with the Qumran documents do not, however, cast into doubt his report that in honor of the Sabbath, the Essenes abstained from defecation on the sacred day. This, as mentioned, is not a rigorism that carried into rabbinic Judaism. Josephus, in fact, clearly regards it as peculiar to the sect in question. (In my own judgment, it just as surely stands in glaring contradiction to words of Moses in Exod 5:1 that have resounded over the centuries, "Let My people go.") But, like much else in Second Temple Judaism, this unusual practice, too, attests to the seriousness with which the Sabbath was taken at the time and the lengths to which devoted Jews would go to protect its sanctity.

Still within the book of Exodus, we find an additional law about how the Sabbath is to be practiced, one that has proven to be more ambiguous than it may at first seem:

> These are the things that the LORD has commanded you to do: ²On six days work may be done, but on the seventh day you shall have a sabbath of complete rest, holy to the LORD; whoever does any work on it shall be put to death. ³You shall kindle no fire throughout your settlements on the sabbath day. (Exod 35:1–3)

What is new here, in comparison with other passages we have examined, is the prohibition on fire in v. 3, and what is less than ideally clear is the meaning of the verb (*təba'ărû*), rendered here as "kindle." Does it refer, as that translation assumes, to igniting a fire, or does it mean instead simply to allow a fire to burn? If the former, then there is no problem with enjoying a fire on the Sabbath, so long as it has been kindled beforehand and no new combustibles are added to it in the course of the special day. If the latter is the case, however, then all fires must be extinguished before the Sabbath begins.

In the piel stem, which is the one that appears here, the verb in question can have either meaning,²² and among the successor communities to biblical Israel the ambiguity has contributed to considerable sectarian tension over the millennia. The Samaritans and the Qaraites understand the prohibition of Exod 35:3 to fall upon combustion in general and not only ignition.²³ Vered Noam and Elisha Qimron have mounted a strong case that a law reflected in the Dead Sea Scrolls, too, forbids "the transfer, before the Sabbath, of coals intended to continue burning on the Sabbath."²⁴ If so, then in the Second Temple period, the prohibition on allowing a fire to burn on the seventh day appeared among Jews and not only Samaritans, and the Qaraite practice centuries later may, conceivably, have marked the reappearance of an older norm that, like the ideal fire in a rabbinic Jewish household on the Sabbath, had never quite died out.

What seems clear is that the rabbis knew of the alternative construction and actively sought to refute it. "On the Sabbath you don't light a fire," reads the conclusion to the discussion of our verse in an early midrashic work, "but you [li]ght a fire from the eve of the Sabbath [that is, late Friday afternoon] for [the S]abbath" (Mek., Šabbata² 2). Even more striking is a mishnah that speaks of the lighting of lamps on Friday evening as nightfall approaches not as an option but as a necessity: "Three things a man must say inside his house on the eve of the Sabbath when darkness is falling: Have you tithed? Have you prepared the *'erub*? Light the lamp!" (m. Šabb. 2:7). The first question derives from the fact that the Mishnah presupposes that one cannot tithe on the Sabbath itself and so the tithes for food eaten on the sacred day must have been set aside beforehand. The second question has to do with setting up various boundaries within which it is permissible to walk or to carry on the Sabbath. Unlike the first two, the third thing the Jewish father is to say to his household is not a question but an imperative: the Sabbath lamp must be lit! As this mishnah goes on, it notes that if there is doubt as to whether night has fallen, the lamp may not be lit. The lighting of the Sabbath lamp (or, today, the Sabbath candles, traditionally lit by the woman of the house) marks the onset of the special day and demarcates it from Friday and the latter's preparations. According to the rabbinic construction of Exod 35:3, not only is it permissible to have a prelit fire on the Sabbath; it would seem to be obligatory to do so.[25]

In traditional Jewish liturgy, the second chapter of the Mishnah, in which the text excerpted above appears, is generally recited on Friday evening just before the formal service of the Sabbath begins, evidently in order to delay the latter for the benefit of latecomers. (In some traditions it is said after the service, and in others not at all.) It has been plausibly suggested that the origin of this post-Talmudic custom lies in the controversy between the Rabbanite and Qaraite communities late in the first millennium CE.[26] The recitation of a chapter of the Oral Law—whose authority the Qaraites disputed—on a matter that sharply differentiated the experience of the Sabbath in the two Jewish communities served to underscore the importance of lighting a fire late in the daytime on Friday for the benefit of the Sabbath, rather than sitting in a dark and perhaps cold home. As one scholar aptly puts it, "The Rabbinic Sabbath is a day of luxuriation; for the other sects, it is, at least in part, an ascetic discipline."[27]

Today, as mentioned, the traditional practice is for the women of the house to light the Sabbath candles (men must do so if the women do not), thus accepting the sacred day and its obligations upon themselves. Today, before that essential (and quietly joyous) moment, in the more traditionally observant households men and women alike are often busy setting electric timers or turning lights on and electric devices off in preparation for the advent of the holy day—in this respect, too, so different from the other six.[28]

But why the prohibition on starting a fire on the Sabbath in the first place? Why does Exod 35:3 single out this activity at all?

Here, as usual, the biblical text lacks the hoped-for explanation; all it gives is the norm itself.[29] In my view, the most reasonable suggestion involves the connection of fire to cooking, forbidden (as we have seen) on the Sabbath in contrast with festivals, or at least the festival of Passover.[30] In a deeper sense, cooking—transforming raw foodstuffs into edibles—contradicts the ethos of sufficiency on the Sabbath, the need to act and think "as if all your work has been done," in the words of a midrash we examined in our previous chapter.[31] As in the case of those who tried to collect manna on the seventh day (Exod 16:27–29), cooking evidences a lack of trust in the divine provider and betrays an anxiety at odds with the deepest spiritual meaning of the Sabbath, at least as conceived in the Priestly tradition responsible for both of these passages. But even if the fire is not started or maintained for this purpose—even if the purpose is simply the provision of heat—it will nonetheless require tending throughout the day, with new fuel added or the original fuel rearranged, and this, too, is quite the opposite of the quiet confidence and radical acceptance of the given that is characteristic of the special day.

In Abraham Joshua Heschel's influential thinking, the relevant point is that the Sabbath puts a limitation on technology and the world of space—the world of things—to which technology speaks. "Life goes wrong," he writes, "when the control of space, the acquisition of things of space, becomes our sole concern." In contrast to the modern passion to subdue space and acquire things, "Judaism is a *religion of time* aiming at *the sanctification of time*," and its great achievement lies not in physical structures or visible images, which Heschel sees as characteristic of civilization as usually conceived, but rather in the sanctification of time through the traditional observance of the holy days.[32] "The Sabbath," he memorably writes, "is the day on which we learn the art of *surpassing* civilization."[33]

It is important to remember, though, that surpassing civilization is not the same as living in independence of civilization or distancing oneself from it—at least not in the rabbinic understanding of the Sabbath, to which enjoying fire and cooking are all very central so long as the preparations have been completed before the sacred day begins. If the Sabbath signified freedom from technology, all that setting of timers and the like late on Friday afternoon would hardly take place, and Jewish observance would be more like that of the Samaritans and Qaraites. As it turns out, rabbinic tradition is explicit that Jews are not responsible for the sabbatical rest of their utensils (*šaḇîtat kēlîm*), in contrast to their own and that of their animals.[34]

Technology, then, and the world of space and things are not renounced or deprecated on the Sabbath. They are not, as Heschel seems to think, the opposite of the things of spirit or redolent of idolatry. They have, in fact, their own role in its observance—and sometimes it is a prominent role indeed. Consider prescription from the Shulchan Arukh, the most influential compendium wish law (Galilee, 1565):

One should put on beautiful clothes and rejoice as the Sabbath is coming in, like one who is going out to meet the king or one who is going out to meet a bride and groom. For "Rabbi Ḥanina would robe himself and stand at sunset as the Sabbath was coming in. 'Come,' he said, 'let us go forth to greet the Sabbath Queen.' Rabbi Yannai put on his clothes as the Sabbath was coming in and said, 'Come, O Bride, come, O Bride.'" (Shulchan Arukh, 'Ôraḥ Ḥayyîm 262:3, quoting b. Šabb. 119a)[35]

Whether one grounds the practice in the conception of the Sabbath as royalty in the manner of the first rabbi or as a bride, following the second, the norm is to honor the day with one's finery: as these classic sources conceive it, the Sabbath is not an occasion of casual rest and relaxation. Its entry is an event of high formality, and not one on which Jews should choose to dress down if they can possibly avoid it. The Sabbath is fundamentally misconceived if it is treated as simply a day off. Rather, as the liturgy would have it, it is in the nature of a queen or a bride on her wedding day, and those greeting her must show themselves cognizant of the elevated nature of the occasion and eager to accord the special visitor the dignity she deserves.

One could make a similar point about the beautiful accoutrements for the rituals and meals of the day that have long characterized the practice of the Sabbath as well as the bounty and high quality of the food served at its three mandatory meals. But in all these cases, the material things must not be the "sole concern" of the Sabbath-observer, as Heschel rightly points out. Instead, they—and the workaday activities of production and acquisition that account for them—are to be subordinated to the sanctity of the day and to the reliance on God that the occasion seeks to realize in practice. We are not, then, dealing with Heschel's priority of time in general over space but of space in the service of one very special time—space, like time, reordered and restricted in deference to its master and creator.[36] Civilization (to use Heschel's term) is not left behind or stopped: it is redirected for the day dedicated to the service of the generous God who ordains that incomparable occasion. In the rabbinic understanding of Exod 35:3, fire is to be mobilized for the enjoyment of the Sabbath—but neither ignited nor tended on the Sabbath itself.

But with one striking exception.

In Numbers 28–29, there is a comprehensive list of sacrificial offerings specific to each calendrical event, whether weekday, Sabbath, New Moon, or festival. After the daily offering of two yearling lambs, one in the morning and one in the evening, and their specified meal offerings and libations, we read this:

⁹On the sabbath day: two yearling lambs without blemish, together with two-tenths of a measure of choice flour with oil mixed in as a meal

offering, and with the proper libation—[10]a burnt offering for every sabbath, in addition to the regular burnt offering and its libation. (Num 28:9–10)

In other words, after the sacrifice made every day of the year, another one is made specifically on the Sabbath (hence, the essentially two-part rabbinic Sabbath service on Saturday morning, with the second part termed, not coincidentally, *mûsāp̄*, "additional").

But how could the officiants make a burnt offering without fire, and is the placing of the meat of the animal and the accompanying flour upon the altar not a clear violation of Exod 35:3? If we seek to correlate that verse with the sacrificial laws of Numbers 28, the conclusion to which we must arrive is that the required practice inside the Tabernacle (and, later, the Jerusalem Temple) must have been thought to be exempt from the prohibition on tending and adding to fires on the Sabbath, and indeed that very point is explicitly made as early as the book of Jubilees:

> [10]For great is the honor that the Lord has given Israel to eat, drink, and be filled on this festal day; and to rest on it from any work that belongs to the work of humanity except to burn incense and to bring before the Lord offerings and sacrifices for the days and Sabbaths. [11]Only this (kind of) work is to be done on the Sabbath days in the sanctuary of the Lord your God in order that they may atone continuously for Israel with offerings from day to day as a memorial that is acceptable before the Lord; and in order that he may receive them forever, day by day, as you were ordered. (Jub. 50:10–11)[37]

Hundreds of years later, rabbinic sources will address the same point. One way they do so is by concentrating on the words "throughout your settlements" in Exod 35:3: "'throughout your settlements' you do not make a fire, but you do make a fire in the Temple" (Mek. de Rabbi Ishmael, *Šabbattāʾ* 2). In Talmudic discourse, after some precise analogical reasoning typical of the genre, they come to the identical conclusion: "The Temple service overrides the Sabbath" (e.g., b. Šabb. 132a-b).

If the Sabbath represented the unqualified triumph of time over space and of the intangible and invisible over the material, such an exception would be incomprehensible. In fact, however, in classical rabbinic sources time and space are made, ideally, to work conjointly to glorify the God who ordains that special day. A sharp binary of the two, in sum, does not do justice to the ~~wish~~ Sabbath.

We have already dealt with the prohibitions on buying and selling on the Sabbath as well as with those passages that reflect a related interdiction on carrying loads.[38] Another passage we have examined in a different context arguably includes not only prohibitions on various activities but also allusions to some positive sabbatical behaviors:

> [13]If you refrain from trampling the Sabbath,
> From pursuing your affairs on My holy day;
> If you call the sabbath "delight,"
> The LORD's holy day "honored";
> And if you honor it and go not your ways
> Nor look to your affairs nor strike bargains—
> [14]Then you can seek the favor of the LORD.
> I will set you astride the heights of the earth,
> And let you enjoy the heritage of your father Jacob—
> For the mouth of the LORD has spoken. (Isa 58:13–14)

Thus, Rabbi David Qimchi (1160–1235, Provence) identifies "trampling the Sabbath" as "walking beyond the Sabbath boundary" and refraining from doing so as turning back "in honor of the Sabbath." He understands "pursuing your affairs" as a blanket term for all violations for which rabbinic law could legitimately have prescribed capital punishment. On the positive side, Qimchi, following Talmudic precedents,[39] interprets "if you call the Sabbath 'delight'" to be a commandment upon the Jew "to give the body delight on the Sabbath day with good, pleasant foods, so that, by differentiating it from the other days of the week for the better, he will remember the act of creation and that God brought a new thing out of nothing and that the Sabbath is on the seventh day of the week and, as a result of that, he will offer praise and glory to God with his mouth and his heart, and his soul will find delight in it." As for "go not your ways," Qimchi understands this as meaning that one's "way of acting on the Sabbath should not be like one's way of acting during the weekdays." Similarly, "honor it" he interprets to mean, on the basis of a Talmudic text, that one's clothing, gait, and food and drink (including the timing of meals) must be special to the occasion. The warning against "look[ing] to your affairs" he sees as directing one's speech away from mundane concerns and toward heavenly matters, including those in the service of practical religious duties, such as arranging marriages, teaching Torah, and even, perhaps surprisingly, teaching one's children a trade so that they do not end up as thieves or robbers. Finally, and in accordance with his own understanding of the parallel expression, "look to your affairs," and again in accordance with Talmudic tradition,

Qimchi identifies "nor strike bargains" with the imperative to speak little and in a pleasant tone on the Sabbath, once again differentiating the one sacred day of the week from the other six.[40]

Whether Qimchi and the classical rabbinic sources on which he depends are correct in finding allusions to such specific rules already in the language of the prophetic oracle excerpted above, it would appear beyond dispute that more sabbatical norms existed in ancient Israelite culture than we find in the surviving collections of biblical law. The condemnations of carrying loads (presumably of merchandise) and of buying and selling on the Sabbath, as well as the norm that burnt offerings must be made on that day, all speak to a larger understanding of sabbatical observance than the codes themselves make explicit. Furthermore, whether Qimchi is right about the positive commandments he and his sources think they hear in Isa 58:13–14, it stands to reason that the day must have involved some practices other than the negative ones of not working, lighting a fire, carrying loads, and the like, and the positive one of the priests' executing the statutorily required sacrifices. In other words, there must have been some activities that realized the expectation that the Sabbath be regarded as a "delight." It is unlikely that the holiness of the day was thought to be honored by doing absolutely nothing.

As usual with the Bible, we can confidently assume that much more was going on than the text explicitly reports.[41] How much later tradition, rabbinic and other, preserves ancient practices unattested (at least explicitly) in the Bible is unknown, but it would not be reasonable to think that all those older traditions and practices simply disappeared in the intervening centuries.

Some sabbatical norms that surfaced in the Second Temple period (whenever they originated) caused considerable controversy. A parade example is a law in Jub. 50:8 that specifies capital punishment for "any man ... who sleeps with a woman."[42] Here again, the modern Sabbath-observant Jew will surely be surprised. For the Talmud, like the modern tradition deriving from it, takes quite the opposing position. In discussing how frequently men in various occupations must perform their marital duty, it rules that rabbinical scholars (talmîdê ḥăkāmîm) themselves are obligated to satisfy their wives "from the eve of the Sabbath to the eve of the Sabbath"—that is, every Friday night. The same text then goes on to mention the practice of a particularly assiduous scholar who spent most of his time in the rabbinic academy but would always come home as the Sabbath was approaching. From the context, it is clear that he did so in order to fulfill what was expected of him sexually and that the text approves of his practice (b. Ketub. 62b).[43] Needless to say, Jubilees would not.

It is tempting to regard the prohibition on marital intimacy on the Sabbath attested in Jubilees as an innovation of the particular sect that authored and revered the book itself. But, as we have already considered at some length,[44] some scholars have long sought to reconstruct the origins of the Sabbath as lying not in a day of joy and pleasure but in one of ill omen and of self-denial and thus viewed the prophetic text excerpted above (Isa 58:13–14) as marking a moment of transvaluation: now the day is to be called instead a "delight" (v. 13). But, if this reconstruction is correct—and it remains, as we saw, in the realm of speculation—do we have any reason to imagine that all Jews immediately accepted the new position? The more realistic approach is to assume that, as usual in the history of religion, change was not uniform, linear, or unidirectional, and older and newer practices and beliefs coexisted for long periods. Applied to the question of conjugal relations on the Sabbath, this approach would suggest that the prohibition we find in Jubilees is likely not an innovation of the sect associated with that book but rather the preservation of an older practice.

In addition to the possibility that the Sabbath originated in a day of self-denial, we should also consider that the prohibition on sex may have had a more precise ritual source. Lutz Doering suggests that a driving motive here is again one of protecting the sanctity of the day. Utilizing insights of Jacob Milgrom,[45] he draws attention to the process by which "desecration," rendered in Hebrew by the verb *ḥillēl*, came to overlap with the related notion of "pollution" (in the ritual sense), marked by the verb *ṭimmē'*. In the case of Jubilees, protecting the Sabbath from desecration or profanation comes to mean protecting it from ritual contamination as well. "When the sanctification of the sabbath consists, among others, of avoiding pollution," Doering writes, "the sabbath regulations become open for purity rules."[46] As an analogy, he rightly adduces the process for the sanctification of the people at Sinai in Exod 19:10–15, in which we find instructions both to launder clothes and (for men) to avoid contact with women; soiled clothing and sexual intimacy both impair the sanctity of the people, just as, in the same text, touching the mountain impairs its special state of being.[47] In a case like this, it would be pedantic to distinguish holiness from purity, or desecration from ritual pollution. If sexual contact pollutes the purity on the mountain, it can also—so reasoned Jubilees and kindred sources according to this analogy—desecrate the Sabbath.

The prohibition in Jub. 50:12 on fasting on the Sabbath and the corollary expectation that Jews will "eat, drink, and bless the Creator of all" (2:21) on that day comprise another law that requires explanation, and in this case the matter is more complicated.[48] Discussing the ample rabbinic emphasis on the exceptionally high quality of the foods Jews supposedly consume on that day, Sarit Kattan Gribetz detects an effort to deflect two common critiques found in Gentile sources in late antiquity. The first is that "the Jewish prohibition against cooking on the Sabbath resulted in cold or even revolting food."

The second is "the common (mis)conception in antiquity that Jews fasted on the Sabbath." The cause of the "(mis)conception," she speculates, is that "the prohibition against purchasing and cooking food on the Sabbath might have contributed to the belief that Jews fast on that day, or, alternatively, abstaining from freshly cooked food might have been considered a form of fasting—i.e., a form of abstention, as the term is applied in Christian contexts."[49] These are highly compelling speculations; it would seem eminently feasible that one or both of them played a role in the evident rabbinic eagerness to emphasize the tastiness of Sabbath dishes in the texts Gribetz discusses. But do they go so far as to justify removing the parentheses from her term "(mis)conception" even in Jewish contexts? Were there, in other words, Jews for whom fasting was indeed an accepted, or even mandatory, sabbatical practice?

There is good reason to think there were. If fasting was always and universally understood among Jews to be incompatible with Sabbath observance, it is passing strange that Jubilees would include the practice in its short list of activities prohibited on that day—and one for which the specified punishment is capital.[50] Why prohibit something that no one does and that contradicts the whole cast of the day, to boot? As we have pointed out in chapter 2, the book of Judith, which is roughly contemporary with Jubilees, similarly goes out of its way to note that its eponymous heroine's fasting did not take place on Sabbaths and New Moons (and the days before them) or on holidays.[51] The passage, in fact, reads like a list of days on which fasting is forbidden, so that even a paragon of devotion like Judith would be careful to eat then. Is this the case so that no one would be misled into a deviant but unattested practice, or is it, rather, to underscore the illicit nature of an attested practice of fasting on the Sabbath? The case for the latter interpretation seems the stronger.

As we have seen, Yitzhak D. Gilat draws attention to a curious omission in a Talmudic account of a fourth-century CE Babylonian authority who "would fast the entire year, except for the Feast of Weeks, Purim, and the eve of Yom Kippur."[52] Why is the Sabbath (along with some holidays) missing? Rejecting convenient harmonizations with what has become normative practice, Gilat argues that fasting on the Sabbath for the purpose of sacred study was permitted and, in some circles, perhaps encouraged.[53] If he is right, we again see the survival of an older understanding of the Sabbath as a day of self-denial. Here, we must once more recall Morris Jastrow's proposal long ago that the origins of the Israelite Sabbath lay in a monthly occasion of propitiation and his suggestion that the denunciation of fasting in Isa 58:2–7 is of a piece with the insistence in v. 13 that the Sabbath should be understood as a "delight."[54] In sum, a day of ascetic renunciation has become a day of religiously directed and regulated celebration. Fasting has become feasting, except the evidence suggests that in some circles the older pattern—sternly forbidden as early as Jubilees (mid-second century BCE)—survived for centuries.

In antiquity, then, some Jews seem to have honored the sanctity of the seventh day by abstaining from food, just as some did so by abstaining from sex. Jubilees, which forbids both sexual intimacy and fasting on that day, shows just how complicated the actual historical picture was. Even in the rabbinic tradition, from which all modern forms of Judaism are derived, some vestige of the practice of fasting on the Sabbath survives. In chapter 2, we saw that the normative Talmudic ruling comes to be that a Jew is not to fast beyond the sixth hour of the halakhic day. In other words, the compromise is that at most, half of the daytime can be spent without eating.[55] The general tenor of rabbinic discussion, however, is very much on the other side on this issue, extolling the importance of feasting on the Sabbath and requiring an extra meal on that day, for a total of three (that is, dinner on Friday night, lunch on Saturday, and a third meal in the late afternoon or early evening on Saturday, before the Sabbath is out).[56] The Talmud even includes statements so extravagant as to promise that one who observes the three-meal norm will be spared the fearsome sufferings associated with the period just before the messianic advent or with postmortem punishment.[57] Here again, it seems unlikely that such inducements would come to mind were that norm also the preponderant social reality at the time. And here again, the key prooftext to authorize such ostensible indulgence is the word "delight" ('ōneg) in Isa 58:13.

Apart from that influential verse and its arguable opposition to fasting on the Sabbath, there is evidence that the converse practice of feasting on that day was not an innovation of rabbinic Judaism but something the rabbis inherited from their Second Temple forebears. Erwin Goodenough, for example, draws attention to the term paraskeuē ("preparation"), which Greek-speaking Jews employed to refer to the day before the Sabbath (pronounced paraskevi, it is still the Greek word for "Friday"). That the preparation in question was culinary is highly probable and, in fact, made more so by the ancient translation of the phrase into Latin as cena pura, "pure supper." "The term," Goodenough observes, "was generally used but came to mean especially the Sabbath-evening (Friday evening) meal, the most important single meal of the week."[58]

But what if one cannot afford the culinary delicacies associated with the special meals on the special day? According to a pronouncement in the name of Rav (early third century CE), "even something of little account, if it is for the honor (kabôd) of the Sabbath that one prepared it, qualifies as a 'delight' ('ōneg)" (b. Šabb. 118b). This refined ethical statement once more plays artfully on the key biblical passage that connects honoring the sacred day with delighting in it:

[13]If you call the sabbath "delight" (*'ôneg*),
The LORD's holy day "honored" (*məkubbād*);
And if you honor it (*vəkibbadtô*) and go not your ways
Nor look to your affairs nor strike bargains—
[14]Then you can seek the favor (*tit'annag*) of the LORD.
I will set you astride the heights of the earth,
And let you enjoy the heritage of your father Jacob—
For the mouth of the LORD has spoken. (Isa 58:13–14)

The honor of the day and the joyous celebration that is a key part of its observance are inextricable from each other and from the generosity of the God who ordained the Sabbath as his holy day—a day of feasting and not fasting.

By the time of the Seleucid decrees in 167 BCE—the events that resulted in the victory of the Maccabees and the establishment of the new holiday of Chanukkah—practice of the Sabbath had clearly become a major distinguishing feature of the Jews. Hence, its prominent position amidst the list of rites that, according to 1 Maccabees, King Antiochus IV forbad:

> [41]Then the king wrote to his whole kingdom that all should be one people, [42]and that all should give up their particular customs. [43]All the Gentiles accepted the command of the king. Many even from Israel gladly adopted his religion; they sacrificed to idols and profaned the sabbath. [44]And the king sent letters by messengers to Jerusalem and the towns of Judah; he directed them to follow customs strange to the land, [45]to forbid burnt offerings and sacrifices and drink offerings in the sanctuary, to profane sabbaths and festivals, [46]to defile the sanctuary and the priests, [47]to build altars and sacred precincts and shrines for idols, to sacrifice swine and other unclean animals, [48]and to leave their sons uncircumcised. They were to make themselves abominable by everything unclean and profane, [49]so that they would forget the law and change all the ordinances. [50]He added, "And whoever does not obey the command of the king shall die." (1 Macc 1:41–50, NRSV)

However one reconstructs the complex dynamics of the historical situation, it remains clear that to the author of 1 Maccabees (probably late second century BCE), the desecration of the Sabbath has the same symbolic resonance as the biblically better-attested atrocities listed, such as offering sacrifices to false gods: it manifests and publicly signals the Jews' departure from their traditional Torah and its laws, as v. 49 explicitly claims.[59] What is more, the failure to obey the king's decree—which is to say, observance of the traditional rites—will result in nothing less than capital punishment.

The very name "Maccabees" recalls the leaders of the Jewish armed resistance to this decree (not that all Jews were inclined to resist it), but the very act of taking up arms in defense of such institutions as the Sabbath posed again the question with which we began this chapter: What qualifies as "work" prohibited on that day? Only this time, life and death hung in the balance.

And, as a passage we have had occasion to examine in a different context attests,[60] some chose death:

> [29]At that time many who were seeking righteousness and justice went down to the wilderness to live there, [30]they, their sons, their wives, and their livestock, because troubles pressed heavily upon them. [31]And it was reported to the king's officers, and to the troops in Jerusalem the city of David, that those who had rejected the king's command had gone down to the hiding places in the wilderness. [32]Many pursued them, and overtook them; they encamped opposite them and prepared for battle against them on the sabbath day. [33]They said to them, "Enough of this! Come out and do what the king commands, and you will live." [34]But they said, "We will not come out, nor will we do what the king commands and so profane the sabbath day." [35]Then the enemy quickly attacked them. [36]But they did not answer them or hurl a stone at them or block up their hiding places, [37]for they said, "Let us all die in our innocence; heaven and earth testify for us that you are killing us unjustly." [38]So they attacked them on the sabbath, and they died, with their wives and children and livestock, to the number of a thousand persons. (1 Macc 2:29–38, NRSV)

Rather than living in guilt, having profaned the sacred day (whose desecration, as we have seen, the Torah defines as a capital offense[61]), these faithful Jews died in innocence. They valued the sanctity of the day above their very lives.

What is curious, and perhaps historically revealing, is that the permissibility of waging war on the Sabbath does not seem to have arisen previously. In the multitude of accounts of warfare found in the Hebrew Bible, the question of whether it may be conducted on God's holy day (and, if so, under what limitations) is never broached. We see nary a report of Israelites' ceasing military operations for that reason, nor do we see a single narrative in which it is decided or presupposed that their own lives take precedence over this traditional practice. The firm impression with which 1 Maccabees leaves us, then— that the issue was a new one in the second century BCE—seems historically likely.

Against this conclusion, one might argue instead that in earlier Israelite religion the Sabbath was so central that the biblical narrators simply assumed all Jews observed it, even in warfare and thus at the cost of their lives. Needless to say, were that the case, however, one would expect to find few accounts of victories by such Sabbath-observant armies but many of defeat at the hands of their enemies on the seventh day or perhaps, conversely, some reporting that God miraculously rescued his faithful in reward for their unqualified refusal to desecrate his holy day. We find, in fact, nothing of the kind.

Alternatively, it could be argued that in earlier times it was universally known that saving a life, including one's own, overrode the other sabbatical norms. But, here again, one wonders why no text in the Hebrew Bible ever announces that all-important proviso or even alludes to it, and, what is worse, why the issue seemed so new and so undecided as late as the second century BCE, when the events recorded in 1 Maccabees are supposed to have happened and when, a generation or two later, the author of that book wrote of them.

In fact, reports of an event from much earlier suggest that the issue was indeed unresolved at the time it so horrifically confronted the Maccabees. Writing in his *Jewish Antiquities* about the Hellenistic general Ptolemy I Soter's conquest of Jerusalem around 320 BCE, the Jewish historian Josephus attributes the victory to essentially the same cause:

> And this king seized Jerusalem by resorting to cunning and deceit. For he entered the city on the Sabbath as if to sacrifice, and, as the Jews did not oppose him—for they did not suspect any hostile act—and, because of their lack of suspicion and the nature of the day, were enjoying idleness (*argia*) and ease (*rathumia*), he became master of the city without difficulty and ruled it harshly. This account is attested by Agatharchides of Cnidus, the historian of the Diodochi, who reproaches us for our superstition (*deisidaimonian*), on account of which we lost our liberty, in these words. "There is a nation called Jews, who have a strong and great city called Jerusalem, which they allowed to fall into the hands of Ptolemy by refusing to take up arms and, instead, through their untimely superstition (*deisidaimonian*) submitted to having a hard master." (Josephus, *Ant.* 12.4–6 [Marcus, LCL])[62]

On the basis of the Greek terms in parentheses above, one might conceivably infer that Josephus shares the highly negative view of Jewish Sabbath-observance of his source, a pagan historian who flourished in the second century BCE. But in *Against Apion*, a later work than the *Jewish Antiquities* and one specifically focused on refuting anti-Jewish calumnies, Josephus renders the contrary judgment:

Agatharchides finds such conduct ridiculous; dispassionate critics will consider it a grand and highly meritorious fact that there are men who consistently care more for the observance of their laws and for their religion (*eusebeian*) than for their own lives and their country's fate. (Josephus, *Ag. Ap.* 1.212 [Thackeray, LCL])

Where the pagan Agatharchides sees laziness and religious gullibility, the Jewish historian finds a variant of martyrdom, as the Jews prefer defeat and death to disobedience to their traditional laws and the abandonment of genuine devotion. In sum, the refusal of Jews to violate the Sabbath even at the cost of their very lives, initially so baffling to Josephus's pagan readers, turns out to exemplify a key virtue of Greco-Roman culture: indomitable resolution in the face of the most horrendous adversity.

From this account of the refusal of the Jews of Jerusalem to wage war on the Sabbath late in the fourth century BCE, one might in principle argue that the normative practice was exactly so: one must not fight on the Sabbath. But, given the many historical uncertainties surrounding the report of Agatharchides, it would be unwise to advance such a far-reaching conclusion. The more likely answer to our question of making war on the Sabbath is to be found elsewhere—in the view, widely shared among scholars, that sabbatical observance as a nearly universal or at least very widespread practice among the Jews was a late developing reality.[63] Despite the ancient roots of the practice, it rose to prominence only in the time of the Babylonian exile (586–538 BCE) and the ensuing Second Temple period, when, not coincidentally, the Jews lacked national sovereignty. Things changed, of course, when the family that came to be known as the Maccabees rose up to fight for the old ways, as the continuation of our passage in 1 Maccabees reports:

> [39]When Mattathias and his friends learned of it, they mourned for them deeply. [40]And all said to their neighbors: "If we all do as our kindred have done and refuse to fight with the Gentiles for our lives and for our ordinances, they will quickly destroy us from the earth." [41]So they made this decision that day: "Let us fight against anyone who comes to attack us on the sabbath day; let us not all die as our kindred died in their hiding places." (1 Macc 2:39–41, NRSV)[64]

This decision to wage war during the Sabbath is here presented as an ad hoc response to the threat of annihilation; in support of it, strikingly, Mattathias and his friends cite neither scripture nor tradition. Rather than giving their lives in obedience to their ordinances, these Jews decide to risk their lives by fighting in support of them.

As Josephus would have it, "these words persuaded them, and to this day we continue the practice of fighting even on the Sabbath whenever it becomes necessary" (*Ant.* 12.277). It would be an error, however, to believe that 1 Maccabees settled the issue. For, as we have seen, Jubilees, which is generally taken to date from some time after the war recorded in that book, lists one who "makes war on the Sabbath day" among those meriting capital punishment (50:12). It would also seem that unlike 1 Maccabees, 2 Maccabees knows nothing of a dispensation from sabbatical observance in order to engage in warfare.[65] Finally, as we have also had occasion to note, the Roman general Pompey's capture of the Temple in 63 CE is explicitly ascribed by a pagan intellectual to the Jews' observance of the Sabbath. "Thus the defenders were captured on the day of Saturn," writes the Roman historian Dio Cassius (ca. 155–ca. 235 CE), "without making any defence, and all the wealth was plundered" (Dio Cassius, *Hist. rom.* 37.18 [Cary and Foster, LCL]).[66] If this is so—and as we saw in chapter 1, there is some reason to think the defeat actually occurred on the Day of Atonement, not on a regular Sabbath[67]—then even a century after the decision of the Maccabees, some Jews still regarded warfare as forbidden on the Sabbath.

It bears mention in this regard that even though Josephus speaks highly of those who gave their lives rather than take up arms against Ptolemy I on the Sabbath, he also at times limits the scope of warfare that is licit on the Sabbath. "The Law permits us to defend ourselves against those who begin a battle and strike us," he writes concerning the attack of the Roman general Pompey's conquest of Jerusalem in 63 BCE, "but it does not allow us to fight against an enemy that does anything else" (Josephus, *Ant.* 14.63 [Marcus, LCL]).[68] This is, obviously, not a terribly realistic *modus operandi* for winning wars nor even for defending against an adversary preparing an assault. It does, nonetheless, evidence again the seriousness with which Jews of his time took the Sabbath and the correlative gravity with which they contemplated its violation.

The lack of unanimity on the issue of warfare on the Sabbath among Jews in late Second Temple times is hardly surprising, for that was a time of great sectarian division and little or no practical chance of standardizing belief and practice. That we are dealing with an issue on which the scriptures themselves are silent placed the prospect of such standardization even farther out of reach. With the mounting ascent of rabbinic Judaism after defeat by the Romans in the First Jewish War (66–73 CE), however, things began to coalesce and a concern for systematization of practice and even belief (as well as of the biblical text itself) becomes increasingly evident. As for conducting warfare during the Sabbath, the Tosefta, a rabbinic collection of law from around the third century CE, addresses the question directly:

Gentiles who come against Israelite towns: they go out against them with weapons, and they violate the Sabbath on their account. When? When they come to take lives. But if they do not come to take lives, they do not go out against them with weapons, and they do not violate the Sabbath on their account. (t. ʿEruḇ. 3:5)[69]

In the background of this formulation lie two sabbatical prohibitions that we have already encountered, one on carrying in the public domain and, most likely, another on traveling a certain distance beyond the city limits. If the objective of the military action is to prevent the aggressor from committing a massacre in the Jewish community—even if the enemy has not yet begun the actual battle—those rules are suspended. Otherwise, they remain in force.

Conceptually, the teaching in the Tosefta exemplifies another widely attested and highly consequential principle in rabbinic law: "Saving a life over-rides the Sabbath."[70] Where life is immediately at stake, as with a serious illness or a medical emergency, sabbatical laws that prevent an effective response can be superseded; in fact, according to halakhah, they must be. Moreover, the Mishnah is explicit that they must still be set aside even when it is uncertain whether life itself is in danger.[71] Rav Judah in the name of Samuel, a Babylonian sage of the third century CE, put it memorably in commenting on a verse in the Torah, "You shall keep My laws and My rules, by the pursuit of which man shall live: I am the LORD" (Lev 18:5). "He shall live by them," said Samuel pointedly, "but not die because of them" (b. Yoma 85b).

On the same page in the Talmud, there is a midrash by Rabbi Jonathan ben Joseph on the words "for it [i.e., the Sabbath] is holy to you" in Exod 31:14. "It is handed over to you;" reads his comment, "you are not handed over to it" (b. Yoma 85b). The textual basis for this interpretation lies in the use of the pronoun, "to you" (lāḵem), which might seem superfluous. Why couldn't the verse simply say, "for it is holy," surely an unobjectionable assertion? The answer is that the wording is chosen to underscore a key point: the Sabbath is holy for you, but you are not holy for it. Its holiness, that is, depends on "your" existence. In context, the practical takeaway is unmistakable: the life of the Sabbath-observant Jew supersedes the Sabbath itself. To say it again, one must not give up one's life because of sabbatical law—unlike other commandments that rabbinic law requires a Jew to fulfill even on pain of death.[72]

In the New Testament, a variant of this saying appears in the mouth of Jesus, though with a very different meaning and a very different message:

²³One sabbath he was going through the grainfields; and as they made their way his disciples began to pluck heads of grain. ²⁴The Pharisees said

to him, "Look, why are they doing what is not lawful on the sabbath?"
[25]And he said to them, "Have you never read what David did when he
and his companions were hungry and in need of food? [26]He entered the
house of God, when Abiathar was high priest, and ate the bread of
the Presence, which it is not lawful for any but the priests to eat, and
he gave some to his companions." [27]Then he said to them, "The sabbath
was made on account of humankind, and not humankind on account
of the sabbath; [28]so the Son of Man is lord even of the sabbath." (Mark
2:23–28, NRSV)[73]

It would seem likely that the two sayings stand in some sort of historical
relationship, though the problems in specifying that relationship are well-nigh
insurmountable. Note, for example, that in both the Talmudic passage and this
story about Jesus and his disciples, the question of Temple practice is brought
into relationship with the issue of sabbatical observance. In the larger Talmudic passage in which Rabbi Jonathan ben Joseph's comment appears, a verse
(Exod 21:14) is adduced to authorize that even the Temple service may be
interrupted to take away a murderer, thus proving that a concern for human
life is paramount. Since, as we have seen above, the Temple service overrides
the Sabbath, the concern for human life must, by this logic, also supersede the
Sabbath.[74] To be sure, Rabbi Jonathan ben Joseph's midrash appears a few lines
below that discussion and is not immediately a part of it, but the similarity
to the New Testament passage quoted above remains striking. There, David's
having taken from a temple food that only priests may eat is cited as precedent
for suspending sabbatical law as understood by the Pharisees, and the adage
that "The sabbath was made on account of humankind, and not humankind
on account of the sabbath" is offered as authorization for this move.

But what precisely is the relationship of these two passages? Given the
highly traditional character of rabbinic literature, on the one hand, and
the long-contentious questions surrounding the compositional history of the
gospels, on the other, one cannot be sure even of the relative chronology. Most
likely, Rabbi Jonathan ben Joseph dates to the early to mid-second century CE,
a century or so, that is, after Jesus died.[75] But is the midrash he spins his own
innovation or simply the restatement of a longstanding interpretation of the
words in Exod 31:14 on which he comments? Or, alternatively, is he creatively
finding a prooftext in that verse for a principle of Jewish law long accepted and
well-known, at least in early rabbinic circles or its prerabbinic antecedents?
Note that almost the identical statement, again offered as a midrash on the
same verse in Exodus, is ascribed to Rabbi Simeon ben Menasyah, who lived,
however, toward the end of the second century CE; nothing there indicates
that a previous source is being quoted.[76] And as for the parallel statement in

Mark 2:27, is there any sound reason to think it was said by the historical Jesus and not placed in his mouth by a later source, perhaps one who wrote from a context of conflict with some Jewish group about a detail of Sabbath law? And if Jesus did articulate the principle, do we have good grounds to think that he was its originator and was not simply citing a well-known teaching—as a matter of fact, one that, in a slightly variant form, happened to appear in the mouth of a rabbinic authority a century later?[77]

Despite the evident similarities, however, our New Testament passage takes the issue of sabbatical law in a radically new direction, one that is not paralleled in the rabbinic text. Jesus does not, to be sure, abolish the Sabbath, demean it, disparage those who observe it, or transfer it to another day than Saturday (this last change does not, by the way, occur anywhere in the New Testament). Nor is the scriptural basis for the statement that "the sabbath was made on account of humankind, and not humankind on account of the sabbath" (Mark 2:27) revolutionary. It would seem to lie in the order of events in Gen 1:26–2:3, in which God follows the creation of humankind with his own repose and the blessing and sanctification of the seventh day, thus apparently suggesting that the Sabbath was a gift to humanity, not humanity a gift to the Sabbath. But, by invoking a key Christological title, Jesus goes much further: he lays claim to sole authority over the Sabbath. As the "Son of Man (*huios tou anthrōpou*)," he asserts his own personal lordship over the day that "was made for man (*dia ton anthrōpon*)" (v. 28). And—though by implication only—as the "Son of David" as well (another key Christological title in the New Testament), he can rightly claim the authority that, in this particular interpretation of 1 Sam 21:2–7, his royal forebear exercised over religious practice. Just as David's needs took precedence over the holy bread (*leḥem qōdeš*), so does Jesus's authority extend to the day known in the Hebrew Bible as the "holy sabbath" (*šabbat qōdeš*).[78]

So, whereas in rabbinic tradition, sabbatical law is a matter of customary practice collegially debated and gradually standardized by a group of authorities, in the gospels it is determined by one figure's unparalleled status. Jesus, not the Pharisees, establishes what is and what is not a violation of the Sabbath.

Another difference between the two passages brings us back to the question with which we began the comparison, whether the duty to save a life overrides the Sabbath. Rabbi Jonathan ben Joseph's comment implies that it does, and that is how the Talmudic discussion in which it is embedded takes it. In the case of the parallel comment ascribed to Jesus in Mark 2:23–28, by contrast, saving a life is not at issue. There is no indication that Jesus's disciples pluck the grain on the Sabbath day in order to avoid starving, nor in the passage in 1 Sam 21:2–7, to which Jesus alludes, is there any reason to believe that David asks for five loaves of bread to save his life—or even, for that matter, that the episode has any relevance to the Sabbath. The point of the New Testament passage as it now stands, rather, is to establish Jesus's own personal authority over the Sabbath and, by implication, to vindicate his disciples at the expense of the Pharisees, who are depicted as challenging the Jesus-followers' sabbatical practice or lack thereof. The main subject is thus not the Sabbath at all; it is the authority of Jesus and, correlatively, the status of his disciples over against a rival Jewish group.

In times of war, the principle that saving a life takes precedence over the Sabbath articulated by Rabbi Jonathan ben Joseph may be less useful than it first appears. If conducting warfare on the Sabbath depended only on that principle, the Jews would not be in much better condition than that in which the Maccabean warriors found themselves in 1 Macc 2:29–38. For in that case it would only be when life itself was in imminent danger that they could legitimately defend themselves. It is not surprising, then, that rabbinic law also came to allow for offensive actions in wartime:

> They do not besiege Gentile cities in less than three days before the Sabbath, but if they have begun [the siege], they do not stop. And thus would Shammai say: "until it has been reduced" (Deut 20:20)—even on the Sabbath. (b. Šabb. 19a)

The law in Deut 20:19–20, which the early rabbinic (or proto-rabbinic) authority Shammai quotes, does not, in fact, mention the Sabbath. Its point, rather, is to forbid cutting down fruit trees to provide wood for siegeworks. "Only trees that you know do not yield food may be destroyed," it stipulates; "you may cut them down for constructing siegeworks against the city that is waging war on you, until it has been reduced." But in that last clause, Shammai finds an intimation of a more general principle: once hostilities have commenced, Jews are allowed to proceed until the threat has been altogether eliminated. They do not have to break for the Sabbath. For those who accept the authority of the rabbis, the painful question raised in 1 Maccabees had at long last been resolved.

In one instance in the Torah, no less a figure than Moses himself is uncertain about just what qualifies as "work" forbidden on the seventh day:

> [32]Once, when the Israelites were in the wilderness, they came upon a man gathering wood on the sabbath day. [33]Those who found him as he was gathering wood brought him before Moses, Aaron, and the whole community. [34]He was placed in custody, for it had not been specified what should be done to him. [35]Then the LORD said to Moses, "The man shall be put to death: the whole community shall pelt him with stones outside the camp." [36]So the whole community took him outside the

camp and stoned him to death—as the LORD had commanded Moses.
(Num 15:32–36)

Moses's perplexity here is itself perplexing. Do we not already know from the
episode of the manna in Exodus that gathering is forbidden on the Sabbath?[79]
To this question, several answers suggest themselves.

One concentrates on the difference in the activities forbidden in the two
stories. The verbs for "gathering" manna in Exodus 16 and for "gathering"
wood in Numbers 15 (*lāqaṭ* and *qōšēš*, respectively) are altogether distinct.
The assumption that either text can easily be understood as prohibiting all
activities covered by that English verb is less than compelling. It could also
be that the story of the manna is intended to underscore the already attested
prohibition on cooking with fire on the Sabbath[80] but does not exclude gathering sticks with which a fire might be built after the Sabbath. It is also possible
that the prohibition on gathering wood derives precisely from that on lighting
a fire, presumably the objective of the man's gathering wood in the first place.[81]
In that case, we are dealing with something on the order of what the rabbis
will later call *səyāg laṭṭôrâ*, "a fence around the Torah": an act that may in and
of itself seem innocuous is prohibited because of a forbidden act to which it
can reasonably lead. If it seems odd to prescribe capital punishment for a violation of this principle, it must be remembered that other Pentateuchal texts
make Sabbath violation a capital offense without gradation or consideration
of intention—this very unlike the rabbinic system.[82]

Another proposed contribution of Num 15:32–36 to biblical sabbatical
law, one suggested already in early rabbinic literature, lies in its specification
of stoning as the means of execution.[83] What is missing in the passages that
prescribe capital punishment for Sabbath violators is "the manner of death,"
Simeon Chavel observes. "On the assumption that this detail matters, the
story in Num 15:32–36 fills in this gap."[84] This is an attractive solution, though
the assumption that the text in question knows of predecessors that classify the violation as a capital offense (like the assumption, for that matter, that
it knows of the episode of the manna) is not incontestable.

Jacob Milgrom, too, focuses on the manner by which the capital punishment specified in Num 15:35 is carried out in the next verse, but detects a different innovation in the passage. For him, the main point is that the execution
is carried out by the community. "Sins against God are generally punished by
God," he writes, that is, presumably without human involvement. In this case,
Milgrom therefore maintains, "the surprising element is that the violation of the
Sabbath calls for death at the hands of man." In v. 35, God explicitly authorizes
"the whole community" to administer the punishment; Sabbath violation thus
becomes, so Milgrom claims, a matter for human adjudication. But why the

change? "The reason," he argues, "seems to be that the public violation of the Sabbath and the public worship of idolatry (e.g., the Molech) would demoralize the entire community if not immediately punished."[85] And, in fact, the way the passage begins suggests the centrality of the community to the issue at hand. The violator is alone when a group of his fellow Israelites happen upon him red-handed: "Once, when the Israelites were in the wilderness, they came upon a man gathering wood on the sabbath day" (Num 15:32). The group then arrest him, as it were, and bring him not only before Moses and Aaron, as one might expect, but also before "the whole community" (v. 33). For Moses and Aaron merely to wait for God to take the violator's life as he lingered in custody would surely not have been adequate to the challenge posed by those who, having taken great offense at his action, arrested him and by "the whole community," who here are empowered as judges in their own right, alongside the two leaders who have had much experience hearing instructions directly from God's mouth. In fact, the expression "the whole community" (*kol-hā'ēdâ*) occurs fully three times in this little story of just five verses, further underscoring their key role in protecting the sanctity of the Sabbath. The passage thus begins with a group's posing a question about a deviant individual and ends with the community's putting into effect the answer that the LORD's oracle to Moses provides.

What is less than ideally convincing in Milgrom's interpretation is his claim that violation of the Sabbath had fallen, in ordinary practice, solely into a category of "sins against God [that] are generally punished by God" so that Num 15:32–36 constituted a decisive innovation. In chapters 3 and 4, we developed at length the notion that in some currents of ancient Israelite thinking, the Sabbath was very much a humanitarian institution, with profound implications for society. On a rigid application of source-critical method, one might, of course, claim that the societal dimension was recognized only by those sources that explicitly refer to it and the others assumed, like Milgrom, that violation of the Sabbath was a sin against God alone. Though logically possible, such a view is unrealistic. Surely, the community of Israelites, charged collectively with guarding the holiness of the day, could not have allowed its desecrators to go unpunished until God eventually wreaked his retribution. In fact, pragmatically speaking, one who performed labors generally regarded as forbidden on the Sabbath would have a large advantage over those who heeded the prohibition. In the case at hand, for example, would there be enough sticks left after the holy day to meet the needs of those who refrained from collecting them out of religious scruples that the violator lacked? More than just the demoralization of the larger community is at stake here.

In sum, whereas Milgrom proposes "that the case of the wood gatherer, which was decided by oracle, provided the precedent for the principle that all work on the Sabbath would be punishable by death and *karet*" (referring to the mysterious punishment by which its desecrators would be "cut off"),[86] there is good reason to doubt that Num 15:32–36 is the *source* of the idea that human agents must carry out the sentence. More likely, that had long been the practice, and the little story turns either on the issue of whether gathering wood is itself a violation of the Sabbath or on "the manner of death," as Chavel termed it. In its present form, the story also rather clearly underscores the obligation of the collective to adjudicate the case and administer the sentence. Perhaps it is a mistake to insist that only one issue is at stake in the story. It seems to speak to all of these.

The notion that those who sought to uphold the sanctity of the Sabbath ever regarded its violation as strictly a private matter between God and the human agent seems scholastic and legalistic. I suspect the Israelites who came upon the wood-gatherer in the wilderness would not disagree.

Whatever the issue (or issues) behind the tale of the wood-gatherer in Numbers 15, the way in which it was resolved—with a divine oracle—was inherently unreliable and could not survive the end of prophecy as a source of authoritative knowledge. In rabbinic tradition, for which authority resides in the teachings of the sages themselves and in their interpretations of scripture, an effort is attested early on to systematize the violations of the Sabbath:

> The primary categories of prohibited labors are forty minus one:
> (1) sowing, (2) plowing, (3) harvesting, (4) binding sheaves, (5) threshing, (6) winnowing, (7) selecting, (8) grinding, (9) sifting, (10) kneading, (11) baking; (12) shearing wool, (13) bleaching it, (14) hackling it, (15) dyeing it, (16) spinning, (17) stretching the threads, (18) making two meshes, (19) weaving two threads, (20) dividing two threads, (21) tying, (22) untying, (23) sewing two stitches, (24) tearing in order to sew two stitches; (25) hunting a deer, (26) slaughtering it, (27) flaying it, (28) salting it, (29) curing its hide, (30) scraping it, (31) slicing it; (32) writing two letters, (33) erasing in order to write two letters; (34) building, (35) pulling down; (36) extinguishing, (37) kindling; (38) striking with a hammer; (39) taking out from one domain to another. (m. Šabb. 7:2)[87]

The language of "forty minus one" in place of the expected "thirty-nine" would appear to derive from a law in the Torah about the administration of lashes to a person found guilty:

> He may be given up to forty lashes, but not more, lest being flogged further, to excess, your brother be degraded before your eyes. (Deut 25:3)

Lest the lasher miscount or be carried away and the guilty person (the law in Deuteronomy has nothing to do with the Sabbath) indeed be "flogged ... to excess" and thus suffer the public humiliation against which this verse warns, the Mishnah rules that Deuteronomy's "forty" be understood as "a count that is near forty" but less—hence, the rendering of thirty-nine as "forty minus one" (m. Mak. 3:10). This, it turns out, is also the number of "primary categories of prohibited labors" on the Sabbath. In rabbinic law, these thirty-nine primary categories—literally, "fathers of work" (*ăḇôt məlāʾḵôt*)—are then subdivided into various "descendants" (*tôlādôt*). Among other things, this subdivision has bearing on the degree of culpability involved. For example, to quote Judith Hauptman, the last two clauses of m. Šabb. 7:1, the Mishnah that appears just before the list of the thirty-nine primary categories, "together stipulate one sin-offering for each primary labor violation, but not for each and every labor performed."[88] In other words, multiple violations that fall under the same primary category on the same Sabbath would result in only one such offering.

Hauptman points out, however, that the list of the "primary categories" is problematic. Why, for example, are these thirty-nine the only such categories? "The list omits some key labors, like cooking, which is forbidden on the Sabbath, as is evident from chapters 3 and 4 [of the Mishnah], and doing laundry, also forbidden on the Sabbath, as is evident from chapter 1 (m. Šabb. 1:8, 9)," she writes. "Chapters 12 and 13 speak of many other forbidden Sabbath labors, also not on the list of thirty-nine, and treat them in exactly the same way as the labors on the list."[89] All this strongly suggests that the list in m. Šabb. 7:2 is compositionally secondary and did not originally serve as the comprehensive inventory that subsequent generations took it to be. Hauptman constructs an impressive argument that it was, in fact, composed to clarify and expand upon the statement in the previous Mishnah about the limited liability of one who performs many individual acts of labor that all fall into the same category.

Questions of origin and compositional history aside, the list of the thirty-nine categories of labor forbidden on the Sabbath has indeed proven enormously influential on the development of Jewish sabbatical law over the centuries. Its normative status is reflected in a passage in the Talmud in which the rabbis seek a scriptural warrant for it. Surely, they reasoned, it is not the arbitrary creation of earlier sages without any basis in the written Torah:

> Again they sat and it was asked of them: Regarding what we have learned in the Mishnah, "The primary categories of prohibited labors are forty minus one"—to what do they correspond? Rabbi Ḥanina bar Ḥama said to them: To the acts of labor in the Tabernacle. (b. Šabb. 49b)

The discussion breaks off to examine an alternative explanation, one that depends on a rather puzzling enumeration of the various forms of the word for "work" or "labor" (*məlāʾḵâ*) in the Torah. When it resumes, however, the preference for the connection to the Tabernacle is evident:

> It was taught [by the Tannaitic sages] that it corresponds to the acts of labor in the Tabernacle. For it was taught: They do not incur liability except for labor of the sort that existed in connection with the Tabernacle. They sowed; you must not sow. They reaped; you must not reap. They lifted boards from the ground to the wagon; you must not bring anything in from the public domain to the private domain. They lowered boards from the wagon to the ground; you must not take anything from the private domain to the public domain. 'From one private domain to another private domain'—what work is he doing? Abbaye and Rava both said (and some say it was Rav Adda bar Ahavah): It means from one private domain to another private domain via a public domain. (b. Šabb. 49b)

The sowing and reaping in question probably relate to the vegetal sacrifices offered in the Mosaic Tabernacle and to the spices used in the incense.[90] The statements about the two domains take the wagon in which the boards used for the construction of the Tabernacle were carried and the ground from which or to which they were placed as representative of private domains and public domains, respectively. It is worthy of note that here again we see the connection between Sabbath and shrine that we explored at length in our previous chapter.[91]

It is, nonetheless, far from self-evident that observance of the Sabbath should override the construction of the Tabernacle. After all, as we learned above, the priestly service in the Tabernacle (and, afterward, in the Temple) overrode the strict sabbatical prohibition on lighting and maintaining a fire.[92] If the sacrifices performed in the Tabernacle suspend the holy day, shouldn't the very construction of the sacred space in which they were offered do likewise?

At one level, the rabbinic identification of the thirty-nine forbidden labors with those involved in the construction and inauguration of the Tabernacle stands outside the plain sense of either scripture or the Mishnah that the rabbis in the text above are probing. But it is not without some suggestion in the written Torah itself. Exodus 31:12-17, which reiterates the importance of sabbatical practice and specifies its violation as a capital offense, happens to be the last of seven speeches in which God instructs Moses on the details of the construction of the Tabernacle and its appurtenances, as we have observed.[93] The sense of a conclusion is further underscored by the next unit, a single verse reporting that God presented Moses with "the two tablets of the Pact, stone tablets inscribed with the finger of God" (Exod 31:18). What follows in chapters 32–34 is the story of the tablets egregiously violated, the covenant broken but then amazingly and mercifully restored, new law revealed, and Moses's special status publicly and vividly demonstrated. Throughout those three chapters, the construction of the Tabernacle, the very locus of God's presence amidst his people, stands in abeyance, interrupted by the story of Israel's sin, God's gracious openness to Moses's urgent importuning, and the restoration of the broken covenant by the actions of these figures.

When the Tabernacle narrative resumes, it does so by reiterating once more the last point it made before it broke off: the importance of the Sabbath and the capital status of its violation, adding only the prohibition on fire that we have already examined (Exod 35:1–3). Nahum M. Sarna states the implication well: "This structural pattern is intended to make an emphatic statement about the hierarchy of values that informs the Torah: The Tabernacle enshrines the concept of the holiness of space; the Sabbath embodies the concept of the holiness of time. The latter takes precedence over the former, and the work of the Tabernacle must yield each week to the Sabbath rest."[94] The diction adds further weight to the argument. The phrasing of "Nevertheless (’ak), you must keep My sabbaths" in Exod 31:13 begins with a word that has been recognized since antiquity as having what Sarna terms "restrictive force."[95] As Rashi, the great eleventh-century French commentator, explained the verse, "As for you [i.e., Moses], even though I have charged you with commanding them in regard to the work (məlā’ḵâ) of the Tabernacle, let it not be a light thing to override the Sabbath because of that same work (məlā’ḵâ).... Although you (pl.) are anxious and eager to do the work (hamməlā’ḵâ), the Sabbath you must not override because of it."[96]

By identifying the "fathers of work," the primary categories of labor forbidden on the Sabbath, with the activities associated with constructing the Tabernacle, the Talmudic rabbis converted a subtle message arguably latent in the compositional structure of Exodus into explicit, publicly available law. And by so doing, they further ensured that the holiness of the seventh day would survive the loss of Tabernacle and Temple and define the Jewish people in whatever space it found itself. The thirty-nine prohibited labors came to structure the elaborate halakhah of the Sabbath as it grew over the centuries and as it continues to grow into our own time, as new situations present new challenges to the Israel's ancient day of light and joy—as well as new opportunities to ensure it continues to be observed in the future.[97]

Without the rabbinic elaboration of the sabbatical law, what would the practice of the Sabbath look like?

Before we can answer that question, we must first take proper note of a much-neglected aspect of the Sabbath as it appears in biblical and rabbinic sources—the exclusive relationship between it and the people Israel.

Both sets of texts underscore the distinctive bond between the two. Even the Decalogue—despite what one often hears—does not claim universal validity. It is not presented as natural law or a necessary underpinning of a religiously plural polity. Rather, it is addressed to those whom the LORD brought "out of Egypt, the house of bondage" (Exod 20:2). Similarly but more explicitly, Exodus 31 presents the same God as stating that the Sabbath is "a sign between Me and you throughout the ages, that you may know that I the LORD have consecrated you," the "you" here being unmistakably identified as "the Israelite people" and not, it must be stressed, universal humanity (v. 13). An early rabbinic midrash makes the point crystal-clear: "'A sign between Me and you,'" it reads, "'and not between Me and the nations of the world'" (Mek., Šabbata' 1). The Israelites are to sanctify the Sabbaths as a sign that the unique and unparalleled God who is known by the four-letter proper name conventionally rendered "the LORD" sanctifies them, a unique and unparalleled people, whose separation from the rest of humanity is signaled by the unique and unparalleled day they observe. The holiness of the Sabbath corresponds to the holiness of the nation to whom it has been given, and the holy nation, correlatively, protects the holiness of the Sabbath. A sage in the Talmud offers a midrash of his own in order to make a juridical point:

> Resh Laqish said: A gentile who has observed the Sabbath deserves the death penalty, for it is written, "A day and a night they shall not observe a Sabbath" (Gen 8:22). A master has said: Their forewarning is their death sentence. (b. Sanh. 58b)[98]

Needless to say, the plain sense of the verse quoted does not suggest anything remotely like the midrash proposed by Resh Laqish (Rabbi Simeon ben Laqish), who lived in the Land of Israel under Roman occupation in the third century CE. The verse, rather, speaks of a gracious resolution that God makes in response to the "pleasing odor" (Gen 8:21) from the sacrifice that Noah offers just after he leaves the ark:

> So long as the earth endures,
> Seedtime and harvest,
> Cold and heat,
> Summer and winter,
> Day and night
> Shall not cease (*yišbōtû*). (Gen 8:22)

In the logic of Resh Laqish's midrash, however, the Noahide context implies that the little poem is speaking about universal humanity, the "descendants of Noah" in rabbinic parlance, in contradistinction to the Jews, who are known as "Israel." In a similarly midrashic move, the rabbi plays on the literal ambiguity of the concluding verb, "Shall not cease" (*lōʾ yišbōtû*), which, as we have seen, could in principle also mean "shall not observe the Sabbath"—however unlikely such a meaning is in the immediate scriptural context.[99] Every Sabbath, of course, includes "Day and night" (though in rabbinic law, the order is the reverse). When we put these three midrashic moves together, the result is a divine decree against non-Israelites who observe the Sabbath, one that in the words of the unnamed master quoted at the end results in no less a punishment than the death penalty.

It is hard not to be surprised or even shocked by the harshness of this ruling. The historical context, though, provides some noteworthy extenuation. In the wake of the bloody defeats of the Jews in their homeland by Rome and under the burden of the latter's imperial administration, some resentment of outsiders is both to be expected and is, in fact, amply attested in rabbinic literature. Correlatively, the Jews in Resh Laqish's time were in no position to administer capital punishment; the ruling about a Gentile who observes the Sabbath has a theoretical feel to it and did not reflect actual practice. In fact, as the halakhah comes to be fleshed out over the centuries, even in theory the death penalty was not to be administered to the violator. As Maimonides, the great codifier, philosopher, and communal leader of twelfth-century Egypt, put it in his own code of Jewish law, such a Gentile should be punished but not executed: "they inform him that he deserves the death penalty for this, but he is not to be killed" (Mishneh Torah, *hilkôt məlākîm* 10:9).[100]

Nor does the Talmudic statement reflect the range of Jewish thinking about what the Sabbath means for the world at large that appears in more recent expressions of the tradition, including those by very traditional figures. Consider this quotation:

> The Sabbath was something quite new, which had never existed in any nation or in any religion—a standing reminder that man can emancipate himself from the slavery of his worldly cares; that man was made for spiritual freedom, peace and joy (Ewald). "The Sabbath is one of the glories of our humanity. For if to labour is noble, of our own free will to pause in that labour which may lead to success, to money, to fame is nobler still. To dedicate one day a week to rest and to God, this is the prerogative and the privilege of man alone." (C. G. Montefiore).[101]

The author is none other than J. H. Hertz, the Chief Rabbi of the British Empire from 1913 to 1946, a figure of impeccable Orthodoxy, writing here in a work that was, to boot, used in Orthodox (and other) synagogues for decades. Nonetheless, he approvingly cites an observation of Heinrich Ewald, a nineteenth-century Protestant Old Testament scholar, about the meaning of the Sabbath not simply for Israel but for "man." The same term then appears in Rabbi Hertz's quotation from a British liberal Jewish scholar a bit senior to him, Claude Montefiore, who goes so far as to call the Sabbath "one of the glories of our humanity"—where the antecedent of the possessive adjective is similarly universal. To be sure, Hertz does not contradict the Talmudic passage and call for Gentiles to practice the Jewish Sabbath, but he clearly feels no compunction on finding in the institution a message that readily transcends Jewish particularity. It is reasonable to infer, in fact, that the Chief Rabbi intended his comment in part to underscore that the Christian Sunday is a valuable extension of, and reasonable analogue to, the Jewish Sabbath—quite the reverse of the view of Resh Laqish in the Talmudic passage quoted above. In Rabbi Hertz's estimation, for all their other differences, the two observances convey the same universal message.

In Roman Palestine in the third century CE, when Resh Laqish lived, things were very different. The lines between the Jewish and Christian communities were not so clear, and the possibility that Gentiles would accept aspects of Jewish practice without converting to Judaism could only further muddy the picture and, importantly, weaken the exclusive claim to authority over Jewish practice that the rabbis advanced. For in that case people not committed to the full range of halakhah as they defined it—individuals who had never formally accepted the obligations of being Jewish and been officially accepted as converts—would be observing Israel's special day as if they were Jews, impersonating members of a community to which they could belong but had chosen not to. In fact, as the discussion in the Talmud continues, the odd scenario of a Gentile's observance of Monday as the Sabbath is also included in the prohibition.[102] Apparently, in this particular strain of Talmudic thought, the non-Jew was expected to work constantly, never taking a day off—not on the Jewish Sabbath, not on the Christian Sunday, nor on any of the other five days of the week, a position that Maimonides, significantly, rejects explicitly.[103] After centuries of living as a minority in societies that have taken Sunday and, more recently, the "weekend" off from work, it is no wonder that today most Jews are more likely to think like Rabbi Hertz than like Rabbi Simeon ben Laqish.[104]

As strange as the Talmudic evocation of a Gentile who for some reason observes the Sabbath on a day other than Saturday or Sunday may seem, this happens to be precisely what the author of a recent and thoughtful book advocating the observance of the Sabbath does. "Our family Sabbaths each Wednesday," A. J. Swoboda, who pastors a church in Oregon, teaches Bible, theology, and World Christianity at Bushnell University, and heads a Doctor of Ministry program around the Holy Spirit and Leadership at Fuller Seminary, writes. As in Judaism, in which the holy day begins on the evening before, the festivities for the Swoboda's Sabbath start earlier:

> On Tuesday evenings, after preparing for the Sabbath, we sing a song together.... Our family sings a song called *Shabbat Shalom*, or "Sabbath Peace." Each person in the family is named.... We have six chickens, and we usually name them in this song too. Then we eat a big meal, read books together, and go to bed. In the morning, we wake up. We have two rules on the morning of the Sabbath. First, nobody makes their bed. Second, pancakes. Pancakes are essential to our Sabbath.... It is a pancake feast—slappy cakes, bacon, eggs, coffee with extra honey in it.[105]

Like the seventh day in Jewish tradition, Swoboda's Tuesday-Wednesday Sabbath is a time of rest, relaxation, family time, celebration, and joyous feasting, and, as the book from which this quote is drawn amply attests, it also, like the Jewish practice, involves a keen awareness of the spiritual hazards of defining oneself by one's work, status, and degree of control over the environment, natural or social. This is hardly coincidence. As the name of the song his family sings each Tuesday evening indicates, this Christian pastor's concept of the Sabbath is in many particulars indebted to its Jewish forerunner, a fact its author generously acknowledges.

Nonetheless, echoes of an ancient and prominent strain of Christian anti-Judaism are also unmistakable in Swoboda's exposition, as in this attack upon the growth of sabbatical law:

> So even if we do remember the Sabbath, we often add or subtract from it. On the one side, moralists and legalists add precept upon precept to the Sabbath, as the Pharisees and Sadducees did during the times of Christ, a tendency that time and again infuriates Jesus in the Gospels. Others have subtracted from the Sabbath commandment or ignored it altogether as though it did not matter to God or the well-being of creation. Both of these extremes grieve our Creator. Addition and subtraction are simply different ways of forgetting what God has said.[106]

Unfortunately, Swoboda gives no source to support his claim that the Sadducees added to sabbatical law, but his inclusion of the Pharisees in the same indictment doubtless reflects a passage we have already examined, Mark 2:23–28, and its parallels.[107] But does Jesus's allowing his disciples there to pick grain on the Sabbath, much to the disapproval of the Pharisees, imply that he is opposed to "add[ing] precept upon precept to the Sabbath"?[108] Or does it instead, as we suggested above, underscore his own personal authority over sabbatical law and perhaps also the special and superior status of his disciples relative to their Pharisaic rivals within the world of first-century CE Judaism? Swoboda's words seem to suggest that with regard to the Sabbath, Jesus adhered instead to something like what will much later become the Protestant doctrine of *sola scriptura*, the authority of the Bible alone, whereas his Pharisaic critics added norms of sabbatical practice that were needless and, what is worse, without divine authorization. While in the New Testament there are indeed passages that pointedly present Jesus as undermining and deauthorizing Jewish traditions,[109] the assumption that he did so in order to limit sabbatical law to the tiny amount found in the Hebrew Bible is unwarranted.

There is a more fundamental problem here: Is Swoboda talking about the historical Jesus of Nazareth or, instead, about the interpretations of him in the New Testament documents, which present, of course, Christologies that differ among themselves? We need not untangle the complex and nettlesome historical and hermeneutical issues in a claim like Swoboda's that Jesus opposed the growth of sabbatical law relative to the small amount of it that appears in the Hebrew Bible and, in fact, was infuriated by it. But it should not go unremarked that in another gospel, Jesus, for all his contempt for the Pharisees as self-serving hypocrites, is quoted as instructing his disciples that "The scribes and the Pharisees sit on Moses' seat; therefore, do whatever they teach you and follow it; but do not do as they do, for they do not practice what they teach" (Matt 23:2–3, NRSV). It is hard to square this with Swoboda's generalization that Jesus is depicted as opposed to "add[ing] precept upon precept to the Sabbath" or any other subject of Jewish law. It is also hard not to relate these words of the Matthean Jesus to the later rabbinic claim that the rabbis teach authoritatively on the basis of an "Oral Torah" analogous to, or even of the same origin as, the written Torah of Moses. Indeed, there is room to wonder just how much of what Pastor Swoboda has appropriated from Judaism would exist were it not for the normative claims of such postbiblical authorities.

Although Swoboda echoes New Testament attacks upon Jewish groups for "add[ing] precept upon precept to the Sabbath," his own family's practice departs markedly from the more minimal norms that appear in the Hebrew Bible. This does not bother him: "I remember spending one Sabbath day picking up piles of wood that lay around our house. Such an activity, I agree, may seem ironic given the Old Testament admonition against picking up sticks on the Sabbath day. But that, for me, was the most restful thing I could do that day."[110] The reason is not hard to find. For Swoboda, the norms have little or no value of their own. What validates them is the spiritual state to which they lead, and whether that spiritual state has been reached depends purely upon the private subjective judgment of the individual. If the Sabbath is truly in effect only to the extent that it results in "rest," and if picking up piles of wood results in that sense of "rest," then the Sabbath really has been observed, no matter what the Old Testament has to say on the matter.

Referring to the incident about Jesus's disciples' plucking heads of grain on the Sabbath, Swoboda explains the theological rationale: "First, it is not the work of the Spirit to stand and critique other people's activity on the Sabbath. If we ever spend our day of rest judging everyone else's activity, we have improperly understood the heart of the Sabbath. And second, what looked like work for some was actually rest and nourishment for others. Only Jesus is the judge. Jesus defended the disciples' activity on the Sabbath. Again, defining work and defining the Sabbath rest is challenging and can only be discerned by listening to the Holy Spirit." And, commenting on the story in Luke 13:10–17 in which a synagogue-leader faults Jesus for healing a demon-afflicted woman on the Sabbath, Swoboda draws the same conclusion: "This is true: what is work for one is not work for another. What was work for the Pharisees was not work for Jesus."[111]

In sum, the precedent of Jesus's dismissal of the objections of Jewish leaders serves Swoboda as a limitless warrant for replacing public norms with private intuitions, "listening to the Holy Spirit," even when this involves violations of explicit Old Testament law. There is not, and presumably never can be, a stable, communal definition of the Sabbath. If it seems strange that Pastor Swoboda's family "Sabbaths each Wednesday," since the Decalogue identifies the occasion with the seventh and final day of the week[112] and much postbiblical Christian writing identifies it with the first or "Lord's Day," the explanation is simple: an individual's discernment of the Holy Spirit trumps scripture and tradition alike.

My point here is not to fault the pastor for failing to observe the sabbatical norms of the Old Testament. As we have just seen at length, there is no expectation in classical Jewish sources that Gentiles should observe the Jewish Sabbath; quite the opposite, there are sources that caution harshly against their doing so. In this, ironically, Judaism and Christianity are generally in agreement. Nor is the point that Pastor Swoboda should adhere to one version or another of traditional Christian sabbatical practice. I have no basis on which to make such a judgment and no desire to render one. My point, rather, is to illustrate the major differences between the Sabbath as it is defined in the elaborate corpus of Jewish law, on the one hand, and as it exists where law is eschewed and replaced by private judgment, spiritual intuition, or the like, on the other.

An obvious difference concerns what is meant by the very term "Sabbath." As noted, whatever the original meaning of the Hebrew word, in biblical law the term is consistently identified with the seventh and climactic day of the week, sharply contrasting with the previous six days by its prohibition on the activity that characterizes them: "work." In Swoboda's understanding, by contrast, one can "Sabbath" any day. "My approach to our commitment is what I call the *one-in-seven principle*," he writes. "That is, I don't believe the Sabbath must be observed on one specific day. I do not think Saturday *or* Sunday has to be the day of worship. Rather, we must find one day out of seven as a day of rest."[113] Thus, Swoboda critiques the Seventh-Day Adventists (who, like the Jews, observe Saturday as the Sabbath) for "rigidity" and accuses their approach of being "excessive and unrealistic," unsuited for "real people in a real world."[114]

One effect of this is to sever the ties between the Sabbath and the calendrical system. The biblical pattern of uninterrupted seven-day sequences is retained, but without any necessary sense that the Sabbath stands in a distinctive relationship with the other six days. Needless to say, this contrasts sharply with both the traditional Jewish and the traditional Christian understandings of the institution—and the commandment in the Decalogue to observe it.

A corollary to this is that the Sabbath ceases to be a communal occasion and becomes instead a private event, limited, if not to discrete individuals, then at least to family units. The Smiths may keep Wednesday as their one day in seven, but the Joneses may keep Thursday, and the Johnsons, Monday. Here, too, the point is not to render a value judgment but simply to note the marked divergence between Sabbath as it is understood in this intensely individualistic thinking and as it is presented in the Hebrew Bible and as well as Judaism and Christianity, where the communal dimension is essential. Exodus 31:12–17, it will be recalled, interpreted observance of the seventh day as a sign of Israel's special and unparalleled status, and that passage, in turn, informed Talmudic worries about members of other communities who seek to practice the Sabbath or to devise a simulacrum of it.[115] When sabbatical practice characterizes only individuals or disconnected family units, an enormous change has taken place, however one assesses the results.

As we saw in some detail in chapter 3, the ancient Sabbath was not only a social phenomenon itself but also part and parcel of a wider set of institutions and practices based on common conceptions on which it drew but which it also, in turn, reinforced; the Sabbath was interwoven with, and surely affected, the way indebtedness, slavery, agriculture, and the treatment of the resident alien, for example, were practiced, or at least were supposed to be. For this to be the case, however, not only must the day be stipulated; the activities proper to the day and antithetical to it as well must be particularized, at least broadly speaking, and they must become commonly known. If the definition of Sabbath is infinitely elastic—a function, that is, of nothing more than personal or familial preference accountable to no external norms—then continuity with the ancient institution has, again whether for good or for ill, shrunk strikingly.

Without a fairly comprehensive body of sabbatical law, then, there is no Sabbath in the sense the term holds in the Hebrew Bible and rabbinic Judaism. This is not to deny that there are valid and valuable spiritual insights and practices that have spun off from the Jewish Sabbath in various directions, including the Christian Sabbath. But the ancient Jewish institution has survived in large part precisely because it is more than a set of spiritual insights and practices. It is also a matter of law and obligation, individual and communal.

Given the amount of law that defines and protects the Sabbath in classical Judaism, another concern may come readily to mind: How in such a circumstance is it possible to find in the day the spiritual refreshment and enrichment that is, or is supposed to be, characteristic of it? Are those who observe the Sabbath not constantly preoccupied with the restrictions—the thirty-nine categories of forbidden activities and the multitude of subcategories—and with the fear of sinning by violating them?

To be sure, the personality type vulnerable to such preoccupations may well be found in all cultures, and there is no reason to think the traditional Jewish culture is any exception. Unfortunately, this image of law-observant Jews as oppressed by their Torah ("the law") and ridden with anxiety lest they violate it is also part of an ancient and phenomenally durable Christian caricature of Judaism. It is of a piece with notions of the Jewish God as distant, implacable, judgmental, and lacking compassion, mercy, grace, and love, and with a view of his Torah as yielding only condemnation and never reconciliation. The advantage of this reading to Christianity is obvious: the Old Testament thus poses the problem to which the New Testament offers the answer. In Jesus and the events surrounding his life, death, and postmortal action, the distant God has at last come close, the implacable God has granted grace, the God of condemnation has offered love and justification to the sinner, and the God of law has offered salvation through faith. In such a theology, Torah remains essential to Gospel, but Gospel inverts and supersedes Torah. Gospel and gospel alone establishes the highest and final truth.

This particular Christian theology has a number of sources, but its advocates have traditionally found the letters of the apostle Paul to be especially rich and productive. Over the last half-century or so, however, Paul has been subject of a wide-ranging and revolutionary reinterpretation, one that has many currents and, of course, points of continuing contention.[116] Suffice it to say that far fewer critical scholars of the New Testament are inclined to regard the theology briefly outlined above as a helpful summary of the apostle's actual thinking.

For our purposes, the key question is not whether this more recent view of Paul (and other early New Testament sources) is correct but rather whether the more traditional Christian theology it aims to replace does justice to the image of the theologies of the Hebrew Bible and rabbinic Judaism. And on this question the consensus is broader and compelling: the description of Israelite religion (or at least its more law-centered versions) and postbiblical Judaism at issue is a tendentious caricature. It neglects or minimizes, among other things, the many affirmations in both the Hebrew Bible and postbiblical Jewish literature (especially the collections most relevant to our topic, namely, rabbinic literature) of God's graciousness, compassion, mercy, enduring love, and openness to repentance. It also neglects the nature of the Torah and its commandments as sites of intimacy with God and signs of his superlative and unbreakable love for those to whom he has graciously given it.[117]

Within a proper understanding of the relevant Jewish theology, those who violate the Sabbath, then, need not, and should not, feel overwhelmed with guilt, immobilized by fear of punishment, or convinced that their relationship with God has been dealt a lasting blow. All such affects are indeed in contradiction with Israel's day of light and joy as it appears in traditional rabbinic thought—a day on which, revealingly, liturgies of confession and repentance are omitted and public signs of mourning are forbidden. Instead, those who find themselves in violation of a sabbatical norm should become informed about the issue, resolve to correct their behavior in the future, and repent of it, secure in the ubiquitous rabbinic affirmation that the God of Israel treasures repentance and accepts sincere penitents.[118] Neither an apocalyptic sense of sin as a dark cosmic force nor grandiose acts of reparation are in order here.

Out of the same reality of a large and detailed corpus of laws governing the practice of the Sabbath, another common misunderstanding arises very naturally. Even if one is not nervously and dangerously preoccupied with the possibility of violation, how is it humanly possible to remember all those laws and observe the Sabbath appropriately?

To answer this, an analogy with language learning is in order. Consider the following English sentence:

1. "I saw three large split-level houses."

Theoretically, there are a number of alternative ways to say essentially the same thing, such as:

2. "I saw large three split-level houses."
3. "I saw houses, three large split-level."
4. "Saw I three large split-level houses."
5. "I saw three split-level large houses."

The rule that excludes number 2 is simple: where there is a series of adjectives one of which is a number, it is the number that must come first. Number 3 is also easily excluded. In English, the adjectives ordinarily precede the nouns they modify. A similar rule excludes number 4: the subject ordinarily precedes the verb. (Where the reverse is the case, the speaker is probably aiming for a higher register, such as a poetic one.) But what about number 5? Here, although the rule is less obvious, native speakers and those who have acquired fluency will know the correct order of adjectives and will place the one indicating size before the one indicating shape.

How many native speakers of English are aware of the four rules given above? The truth is obvious: exceedingly few, unless they have a professional or avocational interest in grammar. And yet equally few are those who would naturally say numbers 2–5. Instead, doing so marks the speakers as having an insecure grasp of English, either because they are children or native speakers of another language with a still inadequate command of spoken English. But even in the latter case, increasing experience with the language will usually remedy the situation, at least if the will to improve is present. Study, especially if combined with the desire to put what is learned into practice, works wonders.

The situation is similar with regard to observing the Sabbath. The right behavior is usually picked up through mimesis rather than the conscious application of rules. Children unself-consciously imitate observant adults and older siblings in the family and community, or newcomers experience the day in the context of those who have long practiced it and thus gradually acquire a sense of what is and what is not appropriate to it, often without knowing the rule, at least at first.[119] But given the high importance of the study of Torah, including practical halakhah, in Jewish tradition, a large proportion of those involved in the practice of the Sabbath inevitably come to acquire the equivalent of that "professional or avocational interest in grammar" and, if they so desire, gradually refine and adjust their practice accordingly.

Much can be learned from books, but as the great Jewish theologian Franz Rosenzweig wrote a century ago, "We know it only when—we *do*."[120] And in order for there to be a "we" in the first place—a community in the biblical sense, that is, one extending through the generations, not a collection of disconnected contemporary individuals—law is indispensable. It is not the entirety of the Sabbath, but without it, there is no Sabbath as classical Judaism conceived it.

CHAPTER 7

Paradise Pre-Enacted

IN THE PREVIOUS CHAPTER, WE EXPLORED the key category of sabbatical law—what, according to the biblical and rabbinic corpora, must be done and what must not be done if the commandment to practice the Sabbath is to be fulfilled. What we found in both cases is that the latter category is clearer and more specific than the former. The Bible, in addition to its famous and famously vague prohibition on "work," forbids such activities as plowing and harvesting, starting a fire (arguably, even allowing a fire to burn at all), gathering wood, and, by traditional law but, apparently, not written ordinance, making deals, carrying loads—presumably of merchandise—into the public square, treading winepresses, or engaging in commerce altogether.[1] In the case of rabbinic law, we discussed the larger body of prohibitions catalogued in the Mishnah as the thirty-nine categories of forbidden labors, although, as we noted, not all prohibited activities fell into that handy list.

As for the positive activities—what must be done on the Sabbath—here the various biblical texts are vaguer. Their addressees are instructed to "remember" and "observe" the day, to "cease" on it, to "keep it holy" and thus protected from desecration, and to call it a "delight" and "honored."[2] All of these leave it unclear precisely what the good-faith Sabbath observer is supposed to do, and, in some cases, it is not even certain that casting the instructions without an adverb of negation means they involve some positive action. Does remembering the Sabbath day to keep it holy mean more than just not forgetting to avert its desecration through illicit activity? Is such ceasing an action or an avoidance of action? Does terming the day "a delight" and honoring it involve some positive action, or can the injunction be fulfilled simply by abstaining from the deal-making and other activities forbidden in the same verse from the prophet (Isa 58:13)?

Understandably, the dominance of prohibitions over positive ordinances might give the impression that the experience of the day was a negative one, of a time of hardship and denial, and it would be foolhardy to gainsay that some people's experience of the Sabbath has validated that impression. In 1836, writing under a pseudonym to protest a proposed law to impose restrictions on the Christian Sabbath, Charles Dickens described the likely results this way:

> Sunday comes, and brings with it a day of general gloom and austerity. The man who has been toiling hard all the week, has been looking toward the Sabbath, not as to a day of rest from labour, and healthy recreation, but as one of grievous tyranny and grinding oppression. The day which his Maker intended as a blessing, man has converted into a curse. Instead of being hailed by him as his period of relaxation, he finds it remarkable only as depriving him of every comfort and enjoyment. He has many children about him, all sent into the world at an early age, to struggle for a livelihood; one is kept in a warehouse all day, with an interval of rest too short to enable him to reach home, another walks four or five miles to his employment at the docks, a third earns a few shillings weekly, as an errand boy, or office messenger; and the employment of the man himself, detains him at some distance from his home from morning till night. Sunday is the only day on which they could all meet together, and enjoy a homely meal in social comfort; and now they sit down to a cold and cheerless dinner: the pious guardians of the man's salvation having, in their regard for the welfare of his precious soul, shut up the bakers' shops. The fire blazes high in the kitchen chimney of these well-fed hypocrites, and the rich steams of the savoury dinner scent the air. What care they to be told that this class of men have neither a place to cook in—nor means to bear the expense, if they had?[3]

It would, of course, be irresponsible to extrapolate from the baleful effects of Sabbatarianism, the Christian movement that inspired the proposed legislation, as the youthful Dickens envisaged them (the bill did not pass), to the ancient or modern Jewish Sabbath. Despite the obvious genetic connections and commonalities (for example, both traditions have historically accorded high importance to the Decalogue and thus, at least in principle, to its fourth commandment), the vast differences between the Jewish Sabbath and the Christian Sunday—or Saturday for those Christians who seek to hallow the seventh, not the first day of the week—must not be neglected. And even were we to restrict our examination to Christian sources, it would still be inappropriate to generalize from the particular social and economic situation that called forth Dickens's powerful protest to the observance of the Christian Sabbath *tout court*.

Even with those necessary historical qualifications duly noted, it remains the case that, as Dickens's polemic makes unmistakably clear, the conscientious practice of the Sabbath in either tradition entails considerable inconvenience and even sacrifice. This, in turn, poses the key question: What is the positive experience purchased at the expense of the many and thoroughgoing abstentions that the day entails and thought to outweigh them by far?

The question reminds me of an exchange I had with a landlady many years ago. An immigrant from a country with no Jewish population and mystified by my family's practice, she asked about some aspect or another of it (which one I cannot recall). When I explained that we were acting in accordance with the laws of the Sabbath, she somewhat angrily blurted out, "That's too strict!" "Relative to what?" I wanted to respond (I wisely held my tongue). "Suppose," I thought of saying, "I told you that observing that law would result in a million dollars appearing in our bank account the next night. Would it still be too strict? What about a thousand dollars? Worth it then? Might a hundred make you withdraw your objection?" The point is simple: as in the case of all forms of what can broadly be termed asceticism—that is, renunciation of conveniences or indulgences for religious reasons—a tabulation of what is renounced is meaningless or at least cripplingly superficial in the absence of an account of what is gained. The larger conceptual framework cannot be indefinitely ignored in the name of immediate practicality.

But how should we discover what Sabbath-observant Jews think they are gaining by keeping the seventh day in the manner that they believe their Torah instructs them? From one vantage point, the answer is obvious. What they are gaining is nothing so crude or material as money but something that is actually priceless: fidelity to the covenant with their God enacted by obedience to his sovereign will that the seventh day be kept sacred. In the process, they come to know, or make it possible for others to know, that he has consecrated them along with the day that the Torah defines as a sign of this unparalleled relationship.[4] Neglect those key theological claims, reduce the Sabbath behavioristically to nothing more than an observable set of actions performed or avoided, and you have impoverished your understanding of Israel's day of light and joy. Some Jews may, of course, still practice it out of sheer force of habit or commitment to ethnic or cultural identity, but it is hard to imagine that they will long do so with the full rigor of the ancient institution and accept the attendant inconveniences and sacrifices with as much joy as the traditional theological rationale has historically elicited. As we shall see in our final chapter, there is much reason to doubt that a secularized Sabbath is on a continuum with the sacred seventh day of ancient Israelite and Jewish tradition—or will have proven to possess the same astonishing longevity.

From another vantage point, however, it is much harder to specify what Sabbath-observers think they are gaining. For, just as lists of activities thereon engaged in or disengaged from cannot convey the inner spirit of the day, neither can a set of theological claims, however foundational and indispensable they be. There is, in other words, something ineffable about the day, something in its very atmosphere that evades ordinary discourse because it transcends the scope of ordinary things and the terms that can communicate them. Abraham Joshua Heschel connects this ineffability with that very preponderance of prohibitions over positive commandments that we mentioned above:

> Indeed, the splendor of the day is expressed in terms of *abstentions*, just as the mystery of God is more adequately conveyed *via negationis*, in the categories of *negative theology* which claims that we can never say what He is, we can only say what He is not. We often feel how poor the edifice would be were it built exclusively of our rituals and deeds which are so awkward and often so obtrusive. How else express glory in the presence of eternity, if not by the silence of abstaining from noisy acts? These restrictions utter songs to those who know how to stay at a palace with a queen.[5]

As Heschel sees it, "our ritual and deeds" must be protected by the "abstentions" that quiet the otherwise unavoidable distractions of quotidian life and allow a supra-temporal reality—invisible, intangible, and yet not insensible—to take up residence among us, or to be more precise, that allow *us* to take up residence with that reality, the Sabbath Queen. That "the splendor of the day is expressed in terms of *abstentions*" befits the "holy sabbath of the LORD" (Exod 16:23), who, according to the apophatic theology of Maimonides (among others) that Heschel here echoes, is not only beyond speech but also beyond all positive affirmation. Doctrines alone cannot convey the splendor of the Sabbath or the nature of the God to whom the day is special.

In rabbinic midrash, this likeness, as it were, of God and the Sabbath is especially evident in the correspondences rabbinic interpreters sometimes draw between language about God's actions on the seventh day of the creation week, on the one hand, and mandatory or customary sabbatical practices, on the other.

Thus, when Genesis reports that "God blessed the seventh day and declared it holy" (2:3), one sage reports that he did this "by robing (*baʿăṭîpâ*)," an odd interpretation, to be sure—until, that is, one reads the very next comment: "one must change [one's garments for the Sabbath]." This, in turn, is followed by the qualification that "one must mix them up," presumably meaning that if he lacks a complete wardrobe dedicated to sabbatical use, he should at least incorporate something different in that special day's attire. Finally, another rabbi suggests that "one must let it drape down," in all likelihood to contrast the Sabbath with workdays, on which it is more practical to tuck one's clothing up while laboring (Gen. Rab. 11:2).[6]

If the statement that "God blessed the seventh day" by "robing" is less than ideally clear, the matter can perhaps be clarified by noting the beginning of the Psalter's great chapter about creation:

> [1]Bless the LORD, O my soul;
> O LORD, my God, You are very great;
> You are clothed in glory and majesty,
> [2]wrapped in a robe of light. (Ps 104:1–2a)

A similar image appears at the beginning of another psalm that we have already discussed, one dealing with divine kingship and the closely related theme of the temple as a cosmic institution.[7] For our purposes here, the key point is that the poem also, and not at all coincidentally, treats of creation:

> [1]The LORD is king,
> He is robed in grandeur;
> the LORD is robed,
> He is girded with strength.
> The world stands firm;
> it cannot be shaken. (Ps 93:1)

Both texts begin with a scene in which God dons the purple, as it were, visibly and without challenge demonstrating his right to kingship over the universe. The Mishnah, interestingly, identifies Psalm 93 as the song the Levites sang in the Temple on Friday, or in the language of its superscription in the Septuagint, "For the day before the Sabbath" or "the pre-Sabbath."[8] It remains in the traditional Jewish liturgy for both Friday morning and for the service of ushering in the Sabbath that evening. Whether the scene of divine robing with which the little poem opens takes place before or after creation is unclear; in context, the question may be misconceived. For our purposes, the key point is that the LORD enacts his enthronement in his temple—itself inextricably connected to the unshakeability of the world order the Creator establishes—through robing himself "in grandeur" and girding himself with a belt of "strength." Rabbi Akiva, as we had occasion to note in chapter 5, is quoted in the Talmud as attributing the recitation of Psalm 93 on Friday to the fact that on that day "[God] completed his work and assumed kingship over them" (b. Roš Haš. 31a). Only then is he at liberty to assume the majestic repose of the seventh day. In the slightly different account in the traditional Sabbath morning liturgy, it is on the seventh day itself that he "ascended and took his seat on his glorious throne."[9] Either way, in Psalm 93 the connection of robing and the unchallengeable royal status of the Creator is vivid.

In Psalm 104, the connection with creation is more explicit and detailed. Although this long poem evidences knowledge neither of a seven-day process nor of a Sabbath, some connection, however indirect, with Gen 1:1–2:3 has long been mooted. More distantly, the "Hymn to the Aten," associated with the putatively monotheistic reform of Pharaoh Amenhotep IV, or Akhenaten, in the mid-fourteenth century BCE has long been suggested as a plausible antecedent to both texts.[10] To be sure, although these two psalms use a different root to describe the divine robing (*lbš* in Ps 93, *'ṭh* in Ps 104) from the one that the midrash will use (*'ṭp*),[11] the fact that God the Creator is donning his royal attire here makes it all the more likely that his blessing the seventh day with "robing" in the midrash is of a piece with these poems. If, to complete the loop, we put these psalms together with the midrash in Gen. Rab. 11:2, the result is an image in which God, having finished his six days of work, now robes himself in his kingly garb as he assumes his throne on the consummative seventh day. And, by blessing the day itself "by robing," he again enables his chosen votaries to participate in his lordly rest. By wearing fine clothes and doing so in a way that enacts their noble leisure, they participate in his majestic repose. They do not become mini-gods, of course, but by imitating God for one day out of every seven, they lift themselves out of the familiar workaday world and participate in something higher for that precious period. And that one special day each week is, as we shall soon see, an earnest of a higher and unending reality to come.

After the discussion of "robing," the same chapter of midrash goes on to say that "he blessed it with the lamp." That is, when "God blessed the seventh day" in Gen 2:3, he did so in connection with the commandment to light a lamp at its onset, which is specified in the Mishnah and was discussed in our previous chapter.[12] (Today, the obligation is usually discharged when the woman of the house lights the Sabbath candles.) The ostensibly burdensome prohibition upon lighting or tending a fire on the Sabbath, then, turns out not to be a source of hardship or an indication that God acts sadistically after all. To the contrary, it is a manifestation of blessing and divine generosity. In fact, the sage in question witnesses personally to the supernatural properties of the Sabbath lamp, or, to put it differently, to the heavenly connections of the mitzvah centered on it. "In my case this actually happened," he reports. "One time I lit the lamp for the Sabbath night, and when I came after the Sabbath, I found it burning and not diminished at all" (Gen. Rab. 11:2). The miraculous event, reminiscent of the biblical stories of Moses at the burning bush or Elijah's and Elisha's miracles to benefit impoverished widows,[13] is a sign of the divinely guaranteed sufficiency of the day on which, paradoxically, acts of production are strictly forbidden. As in the case of miracles more generally, the odd and improbable happenstance points to a higher reality, one that in this world is hidden ordinarily—but not invariably.

The key theme of provision or sufficiency appears in yet another interpretation of God's blessing the seventh day: "he blessed it with an additional expenditure." To illustrate this, the explanation observes out that, using the same verb, God blessed (*vayḇāreḵ*) the sea creatures and the birds that he created on the fifth day of primordial week: "Be fertile and increase, fill the waters in the seas, and let the birds increase on the earth" (Gen 1:22). Consequently today, the midrash rather optimistically goes on:

> People slaughter fowl and catch fish and eat them, but since "blessing" is written in connection with it, the supply is not at all diminished. Then what can you say about the seventh day? Rabbi Levi said in the name of Rabbi Ḥama son of Rabbi Ḥanina: Because of the expenditure. (Gen. Rab. 11:3)

The assumption is that divine blessing on the fifth day confers fertility and thus counteracts the losses incurred through human consumption of fowl and fish. But how does one confer fertility on a *day*, as when "God blessed the seventh day" (Gen 2:3)?[14] The answer is that Sabbath-observers incur no loss for the outlays the day entails, such as for the special clothing, foods, wine or, for that matter, the earnings forfeited though their cessation of labor.

Although a Roman intellectual like the historian Tacitus could see nothing better in the Jewish Sabbath than "laziness,"[15] the midrash counters by pointing to the generous nature of the God who, in the Torah's telling, commanded the curious institution in the first place. The likely objective was to defend this characteristic Jewish practice not only from its cultured Gentile despisers but also from practical Jewish doubts about the wisdom of adhering to it. To some wavering Jews, the message must have been comforting: the mysterious action of divine blessing makes good what would otherwise be a significant monetary loss.[16]

A number of stories on one page of the Babylonian Talmud convey the identical message with great effectiveness. Probably the most memorable is this one:

> In the neighborhood of Joseph-Who-Honors-Sabbaths lived a certain Gentile whose wealth was very great. Astrologers said to him, "All your property—Joseph-Who-Honors-Sabbaths is going to devour it!" So he went and sold all his property and with its proceeds bought a pearl and

put it in his head-covering. When he was crossing at a ford, the wind blew it off and cast it into the water, and a fish swallowed the pearl. They pulled the fish up and brought it in toward sunset on the Sabbath. They said, "Who will buy it at a time like this?" They answered, "Go and take it to Joseph-Who-Honors-Sabbaths; he has a routine of buying [as the Sabbath is approaching]." They took it to him, he bought it, cut it open, and found the pearl in it! He sold it for thirteen roomfuls of gold dinars. A certain old man ran into him and said, "Whoever lends to the Sabbath, the Sabbath repays." (b. Šabb. 119a)

Quite apart from its unlikely content, the story betrays its parable-like nature in its very language. Surely, its hero was not really named, but at most nicknamed, "Joseph-Who-Honors-Sabbaths." In any event, the name perfectly reflects his status in the story as a paradigm for its message—that a Jew should "treat the Sabbath as costly" (perhaps in context a more accurate, if less fluent, rendering of *môqîr* than "Honors"), despite the putative danger of incurring a financial loss for so doing. The name itself tacitly suggests that others were not inclined to treat the Sabbath so generously. That the pearl, or possibly jewel, with which the hero's piety was rewarded fetched "thirteen roomfuls of gold dinars" is even more outlandish if taken as realistic narration, as obviously it should not be. Was it perhaps the Hope Diamond that the wealthy Gentile in Joseph's neighborhood happened to buy? No wonder Rabbi Jacob ben Meir (the twelfth-century French authority known to traditional Talmudists as "Rabbeinu Tam") interprets the less-than-ideally clear Aramaic term *'ylyt'* as "vessels."[17] Even if he is right, thirteen vessels filled with gold coins are no small reward!

It is hard to know how seriously the author of this little talmudic tale expects its readers to take it. On the one hand, its fable-like genre is obvious. The pious man's very name not only alludes to his extraordinary devotion but perhaps also expresses other people's misguided mockery of it. But, if so, the joke is on them. Rather than resulting in loss, his commitment to honoring the Sabbath wins him an unimaginable fortune. As if the didactic point were not already pellucid, the old man who runs into him at the end states it unequivocally. On the other hand, the very unlikelihood of the tale raises the question of its relationship to empirical reality. Surely, not everyone who richly honors the Sabbath is similarly compensated! Are we to view the tale as simply a kind of children's story, pleasing in its simplicity and useful for its moral edification but without any larger conceptual significance?

My sense, rather, is that the fairy-tale character of the little story was readily obvious to its original hearers or readers. The name of the protagonist, the unlikelihood of the denouement, the explicit moral lesson that an elder just happens to deliver at the end—all of these bespeak awareness of the difference between the world in which the tale takes place and the world outside it, in which piety is not always rewarded nor clear moral lessons immediately and easily derived from experience. In other words, the tale belongs to a world more characteristic of ritual, one that, it will be recalled, Seligman and his coauthors characterize as "a subjunctive, an 'as if' or 'could be,' universe," as distinguished from "an 'as is' vision of what often becomes a totalistic, unambiguous vision of reality 'as it *really* is.'"[18] Although the narrative is quite serious about the practical need to make the expenditures necessary to treat the Sabbath with the special honor it requires, it also (though much more subtly) underscores the disjunction between the Sabbath and ordinary, empirical reality. Once again, it is the extremely improbable happenstance that points to a higher (and better) reality. The Sabbath is in this world but not entirely of it.

After dealing with the issue of expenditures, the midrashic collection in Genesis Rabbah 11 offers yet another interpretation of "God blessed the seventh day" (Gen 2:3): "he blessed it with tasty foods." We have already discussed the likely historical resonance of the rabbinic stress on having a special menu for the Sabbath as a rebuttal to the charge that the Jews fasted or ate only low-quality foods on that day.[19] But, apart from its role in a particular polemic taking place in late antiquity, what was the underlying theology of this midrash? Here again a brief anecdote conveys the message pointedly:

> Our Teacher prepared a meal for Antoninus on the Sabbath. He served him cold dishes, of which he ate, and he found them delicious. He prepared a meal for him on a weekday consisting of hot dishes. He said, "I found the others better tasting than these." He replied, "These are lacking a certain spice." He said, "Does the king's pantry lack anything?" "The Sabbath," he replied. "Do you have the Sabbath?" (Gen. Rab. 11:4)

"Our Teacher" (*rabbēnû*) refers to Rabbi Yehudah ha-Nasi, or Judah the Patriarch, the leading rabbinic authority in the Land of Israel in the late second and early third centuries CE, when it was, of course, under Roman domination. "Antoninus" can refer to several Roman emperors; for our purposes it does not matter which one. The assumption in this little anecdote, an eminently reasonable one at that, is that hot foods are preferable to cold and certainly more befitting a royal guest. Although rabbinic halakhah allows foods to be kept warm (but not cooked) on the Sabbath, the rabbi serves his honored guest cold foods, which the latter, amazingly, finds superior. The magic ingredient, it turns out, is something even the emperor's storehouses lack—the Sabbath.

The parallel in the Babylonian Talmud, told of a rabbi who lived about three generations earlier and thus about a different emperor (unnamed), focuses not on the taste of the food but on its aroma, produced, it turns out, by a spice "whose name is Sabbath." When the emperor asks for some of this exotic ingredient, the rabbi replies, "It works for someone who observes (*məšammēr*) the Sabbath, and it doesn't work for someone who does not observe (*məšammēr*) the Sabbath" (b. Šabb. 119a). Here again, we encounter the notion that there is something uncanny and otherworldly about the Sabbath. It mediates what I termed above "a supra-temporal reality—invisible, intangible, and yet not insensible." In this talmudic midrash, the sense that makes the reality available is that of smell, but what produces the exceptionally pleasing aroma is immaterial in the philosophical sense of the word. There is thus no bottle that can contain it, no shelf on which it can be stored. Rather, it is an atmosphere, an ambience, and one brought about, revealingly, by the human activity of "observing" the Sabbath or, as the Hebrew *məšammēr* might imply, "protecting" or "guarding" it. The calendrical occasion, the inexorable arrival of the seventh day of the week, makes the exotic ingredient possible; the human action of observance makes it available. No less than his rabbinic host, the Roman emperor lives through Friday nights and Saturdays, but he lacks the Sabbath and cannot even recognize it because he does not practice it. To quote Rosenzweig again, speaking of the Torah in general, "For we know it only when—we *do*."[20]

Another interpretation of "God blessed the seventh day" (Gen 2:3) in Genesis Rabbah 11 focuses again on light, only this time the light is not the mandatory Sabbath lamp. It is, rather, "the light of a person's face," for, the midrashic text goes on to explain, "the light of a person's face is not the same during all the other days of the week as it is on the Sabbath" (Gen. Rab. 11:2). In this case, the reference is probably not to a literal glow, like a halo, enveloping the Sabbath-observing Jew's countenance, but instead to the visible manifestation of the underlying preternatural peace that, ideally, suffuses the atmosphere of the day and transfigures it. In this, it is analogous to the exotic ingredient that imparts a delightful aroma even to cold dishes in the midrash just discussed. If so, what the interpretation mandates is not a tangible mitzvah on the order of lighting the Sabbath lamp; it is, rather, the cultivation of an attitude, one of inner tranquility outwardly evident to all viewers. That, in this interpretation, is the gift with which "God blessed the seventh day" in Gen 2:3.

The next midrash also focuses on light, but here the reference is to the heavenly bodies that, according to Gen 1:14–19, God created on the fourth day. Since these are equally available every day of the week, it can be wondered what the connection with the Sabbath is. If the answer given, which centers on the figure of Adam, seems odd, it should be recalled that in Genesis the paragraph about the seventh day falls between the creation of the human race on the sixth day (Gen 1:26–28) and the story of Adam and Eve in Gen 2:4b–3:24.

"Even though the lights were spoiled on the day before the Sabbath [i.e., Friday]," the interpreter explains, "they were not smitten until after the Sabbath was over." Here, we must remember that in the underlying rabbinic interpretation, Adam sinned the very day he was created, on the Friday of the primordial week.[21] (As for Eve's sinning, these texts, for better or for worse, often leave her out altogether.) In other words, although the Torah does not narrate the misdeed in the Garden of Eden until after the paragraph about the Sabbath, the rabbis understand the event itself to have taken place beforehand—and, it turns out, to have cosmic consequences. The cryptic text at hand assumes that one consequence of this primal transgression was a dimming of the heavenly luminaries. Hence, the statement that they were "spoiled" (*nitqalqəlû*)— or perhaps "cursed" (*nitqalləlû*)—before the Sabbath.[22] But, lest the primordial Sabbath appear inferior to the other days of the week, "God blessed the seventh day" by delaying the diminution of the heavenly light until it was over. In short, the Sabbath is—or at least the primordial Sabbath was—an exception to the sad but now ordinary state of things brought about by the primal transgression. It gestures toward an alternative reality, a paradisiacal world in which the consequences of human sinfulness are not in effect.

In rabbinic literature, the associations of the primordial human with light are abundant, and it strains credulity to think they are unrelated to the midrash that God blessed the primordial Sabbath, too, "with the light of a person's face" (Gen. Rab. 11:2). One memorable example is attributed to Rabbi Meir, a sage living in the Land of Israel in the mid-second century CE. The text of Gen 3:21, it will be recalled, tells that, just before the expulsion from Eden, "the LORD God made garments of skins ('*ôr*) for Adam and his wife, and clothed them." The midrash, though, reports that "in Rabbi Meir's Torah, they found it written 'garments of light ('*ôr*).' This refers to Adam's garments, which were like a torch—wide at the bottom and narrow at the top" (Gen. Rab. 20:12). Vexing though the problem of a rabbinic sage's apparently having a variant version of the written Torah be, the underlying difference is clear. It is the difference between the Hebrew word for "light," which begins with the letter '*aleph* and that for "skin," which starts with an '*ayin*. (Scholars conventionally transliterate these letters with different sigla, ' and ', respectively.) Today, most Hebrew-speakers, especially if they are Ashkenazic, articulate neither of these gutturals, but already in antiquity there is evidence for their interchangeability after a certain point.[23] Hence, the ease with which they might be confused or, put more charitably, productively pressed into service to create a theologically charged midrash.[24]

Lest this interpretation of Adam's divinely given and luminescent clothing be taken as a peculiarity of "Rabbi Meir's Torah" (however those words be understood), it should be noted that several ancient Aramaic translations render the key words in Gen 3:21 as "garments of glory," an interpretation reflected in various ways in a number of other ancient Jewish and Christian texts.[25] What remains clear, despite all the permutations and variations of the idea as it appears in these sources, is a strong association of Adam with some sort of preternatural radiance.

Another memorable illustration involves the curious talmudic report of a visit by Rabbi Bena'ah (Land of Israel, late second–early third centuries CE) to the cave in which Adam was supposedly buried, after having visited that of Abraham and Sarah:

> Rabbi Bena'ah said: I looked at his two heels, and they resembled the two orbs of the sun. Compared to Sarah, everybody else is like a monkey compared to a human being. Compared to Eve, Sarah is like a monkey compared to a human being. Compared to Adam, Eve is like a monkey compared to a human being. Compared to the *Shekhina* [i.e., the immanent manifestation of God], Adam is like a monkey compared to a human being. (b. B. Bat. 58a)

This curious passage is excerpted from a larger narrative about Rabbi Bena'ah's marking out caves in which human remains are found in order that passers-by not incur impurity. Since the first grave he finds is that of Abraham, it is obvious that the cave in question is that of Machpelah in Hebron, also known as "Kiriath-arba," where Genesis reports that the patriarch buried his wife Sarah and was himself buried two chapters later, as would be two other patriarchal couples, Isaac and Rebecca and Jacob and Leah.[26] Given that "Kiriath-arba" can be understood to mean "the City of the Four," rabbinic interpreters naturally wondered who the fourth couple interred there was. They answered the question by identifying the couple as Adam and Eve.[27]

The passage quoted above sets up something analogous to a great chain of being, reasoning backward from a monkey to Sarah, from Sarah to Eve, from Eve to Adam, and, finally, from Adam to the visually perceivable manifestation of God himself. There is a visible likeness among all members of this chain, but there are also key qualitative differences among them. As the rabbis understand the divine proposal, "Let us make man (*'ādām*) in our image, after our likeness" (Gen 1:26), the referent is the individual named Adam and not, as the plain sense of the verse would suggest, humankind in general, male and female.[28] Adam being thus the closest person or thing to God, it is not surprising that the lowest part of his body, his heels, are comparable to the glow of the sun itself. The primal human is, in short, not only a being of cosmic dimensions and import: like God, who began his creation by wrapping himself "in a robe of light" (Ps 104:2), Adam is also luminous.[29]

In both Second Temple Jewish literature and early Christian texts, this language of luminous human beings becomes plentiful. A case in point appears in the text that serves as the clearest account in the Hebrew Bible of an expectation of the resurrection of the dead. At the time of redemption, it is predicted in Daniel 12, "the knowledgeable (or, "the teachers," *hammaśkîlîm*) will be radiant (*yazhîrû*) like the bright expanse of sky, and those who lead the many to righteousness will be like the stars forever and ever" (v. 3). A similar vision of the eschatological glorification of the righteous appears in the Similitudes (or Parables) of Enoch, a noncanonical composition from around the turn of the era:

> In those days a change will occur for the holy and chosen,
> and the light of (many) days will dwell upon them,
> and glory and honor will return to the holy. (1 En. 50:1)

Also noteworthy is 1 En. 62:15–16, which envisions that the "righteous and chosen" will "put on the garment of glory" (v. 15).[30] In early Christian literature, perhaps the most striking appearance of this already ancient motif appears in the account of Jesus's transfiguration in Matthew:

> [1]Six days later, Jesus took with him Peter and James and his brother John and led them up a high mountain, by themselves. [2]And he was transfigured before them, and his face shone like the sun, and his clothes became dazzling white. (Matt 17:1–2, NRSV)

Given the early Christian interpretation of Jesus as the new Adam,[31] it is tempting to connect the report of Jesus's facing shining "like the sun" and the sudden radiance of his clothing with the midrash about Adam's incandescent body and luminescent clothing discussed above. Caution, however, is indicated. On the one hand, the sages whose names are associated with those midrashim date from a period after these New Testament texts, not before. On the other hand, the expectation of such radiance and luminosity is much older than the specific midrashim attributing the phenomena to Adam. Minimally, as is so often the case, we should see both the Christian and the rabbinic texts as reworkings of older Jewish notions.

The glowing body and/or clothing of Adam, of "the holy and chosen," and of Jesus alike are characteristic of the existence of the redeemed as understood in at least some circles in Second Temple and rabbinic Judaism and early Christianity. They parallel the notion that "God blessed the seventh day" (Gen 2:3) "with the light of a person's face," which, the midrash goes on to observe, "is not the same during all the other days of the week as it is on the Sabbath"

(Gen. Rab. 11:2). This, in turn, suggests that among its many other key aspects, the rabbinic Sabbath is itself a kind of preenactment or proleptic experience of ultimate redemption, a restoration to the state of Adamic innocence. If that suggestion is valid, then we should not be surprised to find texts in which it is the Sabbath that saves Adam from condemnation to Gehinnom (roughly, the rabbinic "hell") after his transgression in the Garden of Eden or even works to secure his acquittal altogether. To such texts we now turn.

Those inclined to read Genesis 2–3 through the prism of Christian notions of "the Fall" and "Original Sin" will be understandably taken aback by the very notion of Adam's being spared the torments of hell and, all the more so, by that of his being acquitted of his grievous misdeed. To be sure, the idea that Adam, or Adam and Eve together, suffered the consequences of their sin and passed them down to their descendants—that is, all humankind—is clearly attested in ancient Jewish interpretation, including rabbinic midrash.[32] It is not an innovation of Christianity.

One such consequence is death. Although it would be overgeneralizing to say that the ancient rabbis understood all human death to be punitive—and, even more so, as caused by Adam's transgression—we must be equally alert to the stream in rabbinic thought that sees human mortality as punishment for humankind's first disobedience.[33] On the words, "The grapes for them are poison (rôš)" (Deut 32:32), for example, an early rabbinic midrash thus comments, "You are the descendants of the primeval (rî'šôn) Adam, upon whom and upon all of whose descendants until the end of all the generations I decreed the punishment of death" (Sifre Deut 323).

But death is not the only consequence. On the clause, "Your earliest ancestor ('ăbîkā hārî'šôn) sinned" (Isa 43:27), Rabbi David Qimchi (Provence, 1160–1235), following a long tradition, commented, "How could you not have sinned, since 'your earliest ancestor sinned,' and that is Adam ('ādām hārî'šôn)? For man (hā'ādām) is stamped with sin."[34] In this stream of Jewish understanding, sin, too, is part of humankind's inheritance from their primal father and mother. To be sure, at the risk of theological hair-splitting, one might want to argue that it is not sin itself but only the strong human inclination to sin (which the rabbis called the yēṣer or yēṣer hāraʿ, the "Evil Inclination") that is hereditary, though in the case just cited, the phrasing strongly suggests otherwise. In a fuller discussion, moreover, we would have to consider various countervailing rabbinic statements, such as one to the effect that Israel nullified the effects of Adam's misdeed by accepting the Torah on Sinai. But, then again, we would also have to consider sources that speak of Israel as promptly renewing their guilt through their worship of the Golden Calf.[35] In short, as so often in dealing with rabbinic theology, one can speak of tendencies and emphases but not of a single forcefully articulated and normative position. A strong unitive, standardizing impulse is, rather, typical not of aggadah but of halakhah.

In Christianity, the matter is quite different. Indeed, as early as the apostle Paul (whose writings predate much of the Gospel literature), we find an unqualified and emphatically negative evaluation of Adam. The prominence of Adam himself and the narrative that Christians tend to term "the Fall" is quite at odds with what one finds in the Hebrew Bible, where the story is rarely, if ever, referred to and where neither human sinfulness nor the universality of death is ever attributed to the misdeed in the Garden of Eden outside of Genesis 3 itself.

Why, then, the change? Part of the answer lies in the increasing emphasis in Second Temple Judaism on Genesis in general, on Adam and Eve in particular, and on the baleful consequences of their sin as an explanation for the human condition.[36] It is a capital mistake (though, sadly, a common and tenacious one) to read the New Testament solely in relation to the Hebrew Bible without regard for the intervening, contemporary, and immediately subsequent Jewish literatures.[37] The larger part of the answer, however, lies in the fact that the apostle Paul used the figure of Adam as a foil for Jesus in making some of his most central affirmations about the latter's life, death, and resurrection. The last of these three is especially germane to our question. A strong expectation of the resurrection of the dead at the end-time was characteristic of some (but not all) streams of Judaism at the time.[38] For Paul, the report that Jesus had been resurrected served, among other things, as a sign that the end-time had already begun and the dismal human condition, dominated by sin and death, was about to be reversed:

> [20]But in fact Christ has been raised from the dead, the first fruits of those who have died. [21]For since death came through a human being, the resurrection of the dead has also come through a human being; [22]for as all die in Adam, so all will be made alive in Christ. [23]But each in his own order: Christ the first fruits, then at his coming those who belong to Christ (*hoi tou christou*). (1 Cor 15:20–23, NRSV)

Contrary to what many modern Christians too easily assume, the positive effects that Jesus, the new Adam—or perhaps more accurately, the anti-Adam—here brings about for humanity are not universal. They benefit only those who, as Paul puts it here, "belong to Christ," or as he often phrases the point, those who are "in Christ." As he proclaims in his Letter to the Romans:

> [1]There is therefore now no condemnation for those who are in Christ Jesus. [2]For the law of the Spirit of life in Christ Jesus has set you free from the law of sin and of death. (Rom 8:1–2, NRSV)

The story of Adam as Paul understood it markedly aided him in developing his stark differentiation between universal humankind and that unique sub-set—actually, quite a miniscule one in Paul's own lifetime—who "belong to Christ." In his longest meditation on Adam (Rom 5:12–21), Paul structures his claim around these two men, "Adam" and "Jesus Christ," one at each end of history, as it were. The first, the father of universal humankind, represents disobedience, justified condemnation, and death, which are taken as the universal and inescapable human lot. Until, that is, the coming of Jesus, who represents—more than that, who brings about—the diametric opposite of these. Through his obedience and his acceptance of an unjust death sentence, the Pauline Christ effectuates acquittal from sin and enables humanity to attain eternal life.

Adam, then, represents the old order of sin and the death sentence in which it rightly results, and Jesus represents righteousness, the free gift of exoneration (or "justification"), and eternal life, which is purchased for the many by the action of the new Adam, who more than undoes the evil of the old, as the Torah ("law") cannot:

> [18]Therefore just as one man's trespass led to condemnation for all, so one man's act of righteousness leads to justification and life for all. [19]For just as by the one man's disobedience the many were made sinners, so by the one man's obedience the many will be made righteous. [20]But law came in, with the result that the trespass multiplied; but where sin increased, grace abounded all the more, [21]so that, just as sin exercised dominion in death, so grace might also exercise dominion through justification leading to eternal life through Jesus Christ our Lord. (Rom 5:18–21, NRSV)

In rabbinic literature, this notion of the unqualified condemnation of Adam is also in evidence. A particularly striking example lists "six things that were taken away from Adam: his radiance, his life, his height, the fruit of the earth, the fruit of the tree, and the heavenly luminaries" (Gen. Rab. 12:6). The primal man, whom another rabbinic text describes as the "the world's candle" (y. Šabb. 2:6),[39] has now lost not only the preternatural radiance that we have discussed but also "his life," which, as the same midrash goes on to make clear, means his immortality. The Godlike Adam is now literally cut down to human size. And not only he but nature itself, "the fruit of the earth, the fruit of the tree, and the heavenly luminaries," are all affected.

As we have observed, a number of rabbinic texts evidence a desire to assign not only Adam's creation but also the trial for his misdeed to the sixth day of creation, thus also dating the events of Gen 2:5–3:24 to that very busy day in the life of the primordial human. In one such text, for example, in the very first hour of the day (which, in the rabbinic understanding, always consists of twelve hours, as does the night), the dust out of which he was to be created was gathered into a lump; in the second a form or model of the future human was created, and so on. Where this account intersects with our discussion is in the last three hours of that fateful day:

> In the ninth, He brought him into the Garden of Eden. In the tenth, He gave him the commandment. In the eleventh, he sinned. In the twelfth, he was banished and left, in order to fulfill the scripture, "Man (*'ādām*) does not abide in honor [/ he is like the beasts that perish]" (Ps 49:13). ('Aḇot R. Nat. A 1)

The biblical verse at the end beautifully expresses the brevity of human bliss and, in the context of the midrash, the fragility of humanity in the face of temptation. And as this text comes to a close, there would seem, as in Paul's thinking, to be no hope for the primeval human himself. Adam, the symbol of universal humanity, is condemned and banished. He faces a bleak life and eventual death.

So far, so Pauline. But things become very different in another version of the same midrash. In this variant, the sixth day of creation falls on the fall New Year's festival, Rosh ha-Shanah (in rabbinic Judaism there are actually four New Year's days, each for a different purpose).[40] This festival, which occurs on the first day of the seventh month, is also known in rabbinic tradition as the "Day of Judgment," that is, the occasion when, as in the words of the Mishnah, "'all creatures pass before Him like a body of troops,' as Scripture states, 'He who fashions the hearts of them all, / who discerns all their doings'" (m. Roš Haš. 1:2, citing Ps 33:15).[41] It is thus hardly surprising that the narrative now assumes a forensic cast. The guilty Adam is on trial, the hours are growing short:

> In the eighth, He brought him into the Garden of Eden. In the ninth, He gave him the commandment. In the tenth, he violated the commandment given to him. In the eleventh, he was brought into judgment. In the twelfth, he went out from the presence of the Holy One (blessed be He!) a free man. He said to him, "You are a sign for your descendants. Just as you came into My presence for judgment on this day and went forth a free man, so are your descendants destined to come into My presence for judgment on this day and to go forth free. When? "In the seventh month, on the first day of the month" (Lev 23:24). (Pesiq. Raḇ Kah. 23:1)

Why in this telling is Adam not condemned, as he is in Paul's extended meditation in Romans and in the other rabbinic account of his first day that we have examined?

The answer clearly lies in the dynamics of Rosh ha-Shanah, the autumnal New Year's day on which, in this version, all the action takes place. Some might argue that God has graciously endowed the day in and of itself with the capacity to exonerate sinners, quite apart from anything the latter may do. A more likely answer, however, centers on repentance (*təšûḇâ*), which, though not explicitly mentioned in this passage, is central to the rabbinic theology not only of Rosh ha-Shanah but of the ten days from it until Yom Kippur, inclusive. It would be odd were repentance not at work in this midrashic etiology of Rosh ha-Shanah as well. If so, then the theology in question asserts that by undertaking repentance, sinners may become, in effect, new people, free of the guilt of their transgression and at least the heavenly consequences of the occasioning sin. Thus, Adam here goes forth a free man not because he is somehow innocent of the charge or copped a plea but because he has, as the verbal root of the Hebrew word for "repentance" (*šûḇ*) suggests, "turned around" or "returned." As in the case of Rom 5:12–21, condemnation has given way to exoneration (Paul's "justification"). In both the Jewish and the Christian texts, because of God's amazing grace, the burden of guilt has been lifted from the sinner's shoulders.

We cannot know whether the account of Adam's paradigmatic first day in Pesiq. Rab Kah. 23:1 was, in fact, composed as an answer to Paul's use of the Garden of Eden story to promote Jesus as the answer to sin. On the available evidence, that must remain a tempting speculation. What is more secure, though, is the productive contrast between the two passages, productive precisely because of the substantial overlap between them. In both cases, for example, a negative, sinful Adam yields to a positive, righteous one. Expulsion from the Garden is not the last word in God's interactions with humankind. But in the rabbinic case, God's gracious pardon does not come at the cost of suffering and death and is not part of an eschatological inversion of the order of things. It is not a messianic exception to the way the God of Israel has characteristically been acting. Rather, he is forbearing by nature and has always been so. And he is so forbearing that he does not have to see blood to forgive—neither the blood of an animal sacrifice nor that of a righteous human being offering himself up to convert divine wrath into mercy for sinners. The absence of any mention of expiation through the sacrificial cultus, elsewhere a major focus of rabbinic attention, is striking here. It stands in stark contrast to the Pauline and other early Christian interpretations of Jesus's crucifixion as expiatory.

In Pesiq. Rab Kah. 23:1, all that matters about the sixth day of creation is that it coincides with Rosh ha-Shanah. That it also falls on Friday and thus precedes the primordial Sabbath is of no importance here. Elsewhere, however, we find midrashim that present a parallel emphasis on the Sabbath as God's gracious mechanism for securing exoneration for the guilty Adam. One relatively late midrash, for example, again narrates Adam's first day by the hours, this time concluding that in the twelfth "he received an acquittal," but with no reference to Rosh ha-Shanah. So why the acquittal? As often in midrash, this one answers with a narrative:

> The Sabbath interceded on his behalf and redeemed him from the verdict, and he received an exoneration. He began to praise the Sabbath, as it is said, "A psalm. A Song; to the sabbath day" (Ps 92:1). The Sabbath said to him, "Let us—me and you—praise the Holy One (blessed be He!) that He endowed me with the power [to intercede on your behalf], as it is said, 'It is good to praise the LORD" (Ps 92:2), etc.
>
> Until [the Sabbath] came to intercede, the King, as it were, was sitting on His throne and having regrets about His world, saying, "Everything I created I created for man. Now he is about to receive a verdict that will nullify all the work I have done, and the world will revert to being 'unformed and void' (Gen 1:2)." But even as the King was feeling regret about His world, the Sabbath entered and he [i.e., Adam] received an acquittal. Then the Holy One (blessed be He!) said, "Everything I have made the Sabbath has brought to completion (*šiḵlalâ*)," as it is said, "And God (*vayḵal*) finished by means of the seventh day [the work that he had been doing]" (Gen 2:2). (Pesiq. Rab. 46:2)[42]

Here, the approaching Sabbath is personified as a woman (not surprisingly, since generally, in postbiblical Hebrew the noun is grammatically feminine) and acts as a kind of heavenly advocate, securing an acquittal for the obviously guilty Adam. The grateful defendant, in turn, begins to sing a psalm to the Sabbath herself. Hence, the superscription to Psalm 92, understood here not as "for the sabbath day" but rather as "*to* the sabbath day." In response to this theologically problematic move, however, the Sabbath gently redirects the misguided psalmist to the one who truly deserves the honor. Hence, the next verse, sung by the Sabbath and Adam together, "It is good to praise the LORD, [/ to sing hymns to Your name, O Most High]" (Ps 92:2). If the Sabbath has the power to advocate a pardon, it is only because God has so endowed her.

It turns out, however, that things are more complicated than such an interpretation of Ps 92:1–2 alone would suggest. For, although the Sabbath redirects the primordial human's praise toward God, God then credits her with nothing less than saving creation itself, bringing to completion (or, as the verb *šiḵlalâ* can also suggest, "perfecting") his work in the hexameron. Adam here is not only the last of God's creations and the one commissioned to rule over the other animals; he is also the consummation of the creative process, its *telos*, the one being for whom all else has been fashioned. If he is found to be unworthy, then the world itself might as well have been left in its chaotic state, and the transgression in the Garden of Eden would prove to be what Christians tend to call it, "the Fall," not just of humankind but of all nature. What prevents that catastrophic state of affairs, what redeems humankind in their guilt and saves creation itself in this text, is none other than the Sabbath. The seventh day enables God's pure and lofty intentions for creation to endure in the world despite the perennial reality of human vulnerability to transgression. It symbolizes and manifests an ideal world bracketed by the sorry reality of the empirical world in which fallible humans dwell. It represents once again, in Seligman's words, "a subjunctive, an 'as if' or 'could be,' universe," as distinguished from "an 'as is' vision of what often becomes a totalistic, unambiguous vision of reality 'as it *really* is.'"[43] The Sabbath enables its observers to glimpse a perfect world, however limited its duration. Even in the face of the undeniable reality of human transgression, it helps preserve the innocence of Eden.

Given the uncertainties of dating rabbinic traditions (all the more challenging when dealing with late midrashic collections) and the famously unsystematic character of rabbinic theology, it is dangerous to overgeneralize from examples such as the one just discussed. But it would also be dangerous to overlook the existence of other texts, some of an earlier date, that similarly connect the Sabbath with exoneration or pardon. Consider, for example, this teaching quoted in the Talmud in the name of Rabbi Yochanan, a sage in the Land of Israel in the third century CE:

> Anyone who observes the Sabbath according to its law, even if he engages in idolatry like the generation of Enosh, is forgiven, as it is said,
>   Happy is the man (ʾĕnôš) who does this
>   [The man who holds fast to it;
>   Who keeps the sabbath and] does not profane it. (Isa 56:2)
> Don't read "does not profane it" (mēḥalləlô) but rather "it is forgiven to him (māḥûl lô)." (b. Šabb. 118b)

This midrash presupposes another, which asserts on the basis of a particular reading of Gen 4:26, that idolatry—in the rabbinic mind the worst of sins—began in the generation of Adam's grandson, Enosh, whose name can mean "humanity" in general; hence, the "anyone" of Rabbi Yochanan's midrash. If any Jew, even one guilty of idolatry, observes the Sabbath, his sin is forgiven.

This extravagant statement should not be taken as practical juridical advice, as if the idealized Jewish court would acquit defendants of the charge of idolatry so long as they were Sabbath-observers. Rather, it is of the same order as the statement that the Sabbath "is equal to all the other commandments together" (e.g., y. Ber. 1:5). The provocation for such rhetorical excess would seem to be a social situation in which not only the niceties of sabbatical law but perhaps basic observance of the Sabbath itself are being neglected. Even so, the connection between the Sabbath and forgiveness in Rabbi Yochanan's comment is striking and reflects an important current in the rabbinic theology of the Sabbath. His statement is of a piece with the midrashic narrative in which the seventh day procures Adam's surprising acquittal that we examined above. The Sabbath restores its practitioner to a kind of Edenic innocence.

Another rabbinic narrative throws further light on the same idea. This one is not cast as an exegesis of a biblical verse but rather as an interaction between Rabbi Akiva, the great sage martyred by the Romans about 135 CE, and Tineus Rufus, a Roman governor from the same period.[44] When the latter demanded proof for the characteristic Jewish claim that God distinguished the seventh day for special honor (thus undermining the well-known Roman view of the Sabbath as a superstitious and detestable institution), Rabbi Akiva suggests he raise a dead person on the Sabbath, the one day of the week, the rabbi claims, when the dead do not come up. Tineus Rufus thus hires a necromancer to raise his own father, who duly appears every day but the Sabbath. After the Sabbath, though, the necromancer successfully presents the deceased father to his skeptical son:

> "Father, after you died, did you become a Jew? Why did you come up the other days of the week but not on the Sabbath?" He said to him, "Whoever did not observe the Sabbath of his own free will among you observes it against his will here." He said, "And what toil do you have there?" He said to him, "All the days of the week we are tortured (*niddônîm*), but on the Sabbath we rest (*ninnôḥîm*)." (Gen. Rab. 11:5)[45]

Leaving aside the possible presupposition that non-Jews, too, should observe the weekly holy day,[46] the text attests to a belief that punishment does not take place on the Sabbath. To be sure, unlike Adam in Pesiq. Rab. 46:2 or the Jewish idolater in Rabbi Yochanan's comment in b. Šabb. 118b, Tineus Rufus's father receives no acquittal or forgiveness. When the Sabbath is over, he must go back to his torment. Even so, it is noteworthy that it seems to have been violation of the Sabbath that landed him in the netherworld in the first place. Perhaps the point is this: had he observed the Sabbath among the living—as the Jews do, much to the annoyance of his son—he would not have had to learn of its special character in such a painful way after his death. Instead, he would have found his own existence one of "rest" every day of the week, as presumably the much-ridiculed Sabbath-observant Jews eventually will.

The conception of the Sabbath as averting the sufferings of the end-time is, in its various permutations, prominent in rabbinic literature, beginning from a fairly early date.[47] A statement in a Tannaitic midrash in the name of Rabbi Eliezer (late first–early second centuries CE), for example, reads, "If you merit to keep the Sabbath, you will be saved from three punishments: the Day of Gog, the afflictions preceding the advent of the messiah, and the Great Day of Judgment. Therefore it is said, 'Eat it today' (Exod 16:25)" (Mek. of Rabbi Ishmael, vayyassaʿ 5). Verbally, "today" (hayyôm) here picks up on "the Day (yômô) of Gog" and "the Great Day (yôm) of Judgment." The larger theological point, though, is to provide an eschatological explanation of the day on which Israel will enjoy the fruits of their observance of the sabbatical commandments. The Sabbath on which they eat the manna referenced in Exod 16:25 is, in a sense, yet to come. Its advent will be marked, among other things, by Israel's being spared the sufferings associated with the end-time. Once again, as in the story about Tineus Rufus, the practice of the Sabbath averts affliction.

In the rabbinic conception, in fact, Sabbath-observance does more than that: it constitutes a foretaste of the World-to-Come. An anonymous statement in the Talmud, for example, relates that "Sabbath is one-sixtieth of the World-to-Come"—not the whole thing, to be sure, but a significant and readily available earnest of it, just as, according to the same passage, "fire is one-sixtieth of Gehinnom [hell], honey is one-sixtieth of manna ... sleep is one-sixtieth of death, and a dream is one-sixtieth of prophecy" (b. Ber. 57b). The experience of the full reality of the World-to-Come has not yet arrived, but when it does, it will not be altogether unfamiliar. A taste of it comes one day every week.

Sarit Kattan Gribetz makes an important historical case for the rabbinic origin of this connection of Sabbath and future bliss. "The Mekhilta's linkage between the Sabbath and the World to Come," she writes, "does not draw on earlier traditions but rather advances an innovative interpretation about the Sabbath's relationship to the eschatological future World to Come, a connection that Christian texts make quite frequently." As an observation about the lack of such a connection in the surviving literature of Second Temple Judaism, this seems quite persuasive, and the emphasis on the actual practice of the Sabbath in the relevant rabbinic sources may well be, as she also argues, a response to Christian interpretations that "proposed that biblical references to the Sabbath might not indicate observance of a sacred day but rather a sacred era projected into the future."[48] If so, the linkage was one long waiting to be made. Surely a day of light and joy, a day of divine provision and sufficiency, a day without labor or anxiety about the future suggests nothing so much as the future bliss that the rabbis termed the "World-to-Come." Consider again the prediction at the very end of the book of Isaiah, with which we dealt for other purposes in chapter 2:[49]

²²For as the new heaven and the new earth
Which I will make
Shall endure by My will
  —declares the LORD—
So shall your seed and your name endure.
²³And new moon after new moon,
And sabbath after sabbath,
All flesh shall come to worship Me
  —said the LORD.
²⁴They shall go out and gaze
On the corpses of the men who rebelled against Me:
Their worms shall not die,
Nor their fire be quenched;
They shall be a horror
To all flesh. (Isa 66:22–24)[50]

The phrase "The new heaven and the new earth" in the first verse of this vision is almost certainly intended as an evocation of the opening words of the Torah, which tell of God's primordial creation of "heaven and earth" (Gen 1:1). This makes it all the more likely that the mention of recurring Sabbaths in the next verse in Isaiah is evoked by the seventh day of creation in Gen 2:1–3, the primordial (but as yet unnamed) Sabbath.[51] In the new and improved creation about to come, that is, those who survive the afflictions of the end-time will make a pilgrimage to God's rebuilt temple in Jerusalem on every Sabbath and every New Moon, thus testifying with their feet to the universality of his victory and his corollary reenthronement in the capital of the cosmos. That the faithful then gaze upon the endlessly burning and putrefying corpses of those who, by contrast, rebelled against him indicates the existence of a sharp moral differentiation in connection with the Sabbath in the future here envisaged. The obedient enjoy the Sabbath; the sinners do not. From such a vision, it is not far to the idea that the seventh day was, to revert to Gribetz's phrase, "a sacred era projected into the future," even though it was also very much "a sacred day" to be observed and not simply a spiritual state to be entered. If this is right, then the early rabbinic association of the Sabbath with the World-to-Come does indeed have Jewish antecedents. It should not be viewed *tout court* as a reaction to the early Christian revalorization of the Sabbath.

As the Mishnah would have it, this association dates to the time of the Temple itself. That is an association that we must now examine.

The Mishnah lists seven special songs that the Levites reportedly sang in the Temple, one on each day of the week. The list thus concludes with Psalm 92, which the Mishnah terms "a psalm, a song for the time to come, for the day that is entirely Sabbath and rest for eternal life" (m. Tamid 7:4). How ancient the Levitical singing of this psalm was is impossible to ascertain on the available evidence, but we can again say that the association of Psalm 92 with the Sabbath is explicit already in the biblical text (v. 1). It would thus not be unreasonable to see the specification of the other six psalms for their respective weekdays as a development out of this older liturgical use of the psalm for the Sabbath day. In fact, some scholars detect a liturgical character already within the psalm itself. "The mention of morning and evenings" (vs. 3)," writes Nahum M. Sarna, "suggests a connection with the daily sacrificial worship."[52]

But what precisely is Psalm 92 celebrating? The wording points to two possibilities. Together, they may actually reduce to one.

The first is creation, which, by testifying to the greatness in number or scope of God's actions and to the profundity of his thoughts, utterly overwhelms the psalmist:

> [5]You have gladdened me by Your deeds, O LORD;
> I shout for joy at Your handiwork.
> [6]How great are Your works, O LORD,
> how very profound Your designs! (Ps 92:5–6)[53]

But, as the poem continues, it becomes clear that part of that profundity consists of the moral lesson learned from a dramatic conflict—one from which, revealingly, God emerged triumphant:

> [7]A brutish man cannot know,
> a fool cannot understand this:
> [8]though the wicked sprout like grass,
> though all evildoers blossom,
> it is only that they may be destroyed forever.
> [9]But You are exalted, O LORD, for all time.
> [10]Surely, Your enemies, O LORD,
> surely, Your enemies perish;
> all evildoers are scattered. (Ps 92:7–10)

Lest we imagine that these lines constitute a change of subject after the evocation of creation in vv. 5–6, we should give careful attention to Sarna's proposal that v. 8 does not refer to the various and sundry historical events that scholars, "without a shred of supporting evidence," claim to detect here but rather to the LORD's cosmogonic victory. "Behind the literary composition lurks the popular creation myth of the Hebrew Bible," Sarna writes. "The myth controls the imagery and influences the very language and style of the psalm."[54] What the psalm recounts, in other words, is the combat myth well attested in the Hebrew Bible and much cognate literature of the ancient Near East as well. Hence "the association of the greatness of God's works and deeds with the overthrow of his enemies,"[55] and hence, we might add, the conclusion that as a result the LORD is "exalted . . . for all time."[56]

It is thus also appropriate that Psalm 92 closes with an image of the righteous flourishing within the LORD's temple, testifying to their God's moral probity:

> [13]The righteous bloom like a date-palm;
> they thrive like a cedar in Lebanon;
> [14]planted in the house of the LORD,
> they flourish in the courts of our God.
> [15]In old age they still produce fruit;
> they are full of sap and freshness,
> [16]attesting that the LORD is upright,
> my rock, in whom there is no wrong. (Ps 92:13–16)

The psalm for the Sabbath day thus ends where it began, with a hymnic affirmation of God's faithfulness and reliability. In the interim, however, we hear a familiar and dramatic story: the wicked rose in triumph for a time but only so that God might destroy them "forever," with the twofold result that he became "exalted . . . for all time" and the loyal votary who sings the psalm can have confidence that his own enemies will fall as well (Ps 92:8, 9, 12). In short, the LORD's victory is also the psalmist's, just as his Temple is also the secure residence of the preternaturally fruitful righteous who acclaim their God's uprightness (vv. 13–15).

It should not, then, be difficult to understand how, once transposed into the religious universe of the early rabbis, Psalm 92 could be understood to be "a song for the time to come, for the day that is entirely Sabbath and rest for eternal life," in those words of the Mishnah (m. Tamid 7:4). Given the rabbis' expectations for the end-time, the psalm can readily be understood to evoke a familiar pattern: the wicked wreak suffering on God's faithful for a time; he marches out to their defense, destroying their common enemy and vindicating their faith in him; he then establishes a sharp and unmistakable divide between the fates of the righteous and the wicked; finally, he is exalted for all eternity in his rebuilt Temple, in whose sacred precincts the faithful themselves are now securely planted; liberated from aging itself, like those who "in old age ... still produce fruit" (v. 15), and continually praising God, they experience the deathlessness of the resurrected.

The Talmud records a debate between two of those early rabbis about just why it is that Psalm 92 is designated for the Sabbath day (b. Roš Haš. 31a). In Rabbi Akiva's opinion, the reason is the prospective we have just presented: it is the psalm "for the day that is entirely Sabbath." Rabbi Nehemiah, by contrast, maintains that the designation is retrospective. "What grounds did the Sages have," he asks, "to make a division between these passages?" In other words, since even in Rabbi Akiva's view the six psalms listed for the weekdays all relate to the creation story with which the Torah opens, so should the one for the Sabbath: Psalm 92 is designated for that day because it was then that "he rested," his created labors now finished. In the background of this comment probably lies the psalmist's response to God's "handiwork" and "great works" (vv. 5–6), which presumably could not have filled him with such joy and awe were they not complete.

In a larger perspective, however, the difference between the primordial and the eschatological Sabbaths is minimal, and a psalm recalling the former is eminently appropriate for the latter as well. For as we saw in chapter 5, visions of the end-time tend to reflect the models of creation held by their authors.[57] In the case at hand, we should not be surprised to find that the day that consummated creation came to serve as a template for the era when all history would, in turn, reach its consummation.

As it happened, the notion that Psalm 92 relates not only to the weekly Sabbath but to the Sabbath-like existence of the World-to-Come diffused widely in the traditional Jewish sources, much aided, of course, by the Mishnaic text we have been discussing but also catalyzed by the key point of our present discussion—that in rabbinic culture, the Sabbath came to be seen both as rooted in Adam's paradisical existence and as foreshadowing the final redemption, when the righteous regain the lost paradise. One midrashic interpretation of the psalm's opening conveys this now familiar point with exceptional force. Spoken by Adam, "who was saved from the judgment of Gehinnom by the merit of the Sabbath," these words express his hope that as a result:

Through me all the generations will learn that whoever confesses (*yôdeh*) and takes leave of his sins is saved from the judgment of Gehinnom, as it is said, "It is good to confess (*ləhôdôt*) to the LORD / ... To proclaim Your steadfast love in the morning" (Ps 92:2, 3)—to all who come into the World-to-Come, which is like morning.... "You have gladdened me by Your deeds, O LORD" (v. 5). Said Adam, "The Holy One (blessed be He!) has gladdened me and brought me into the Garden of Eden." (Pirqe R. El. 19)[58]

In sum, the Sabbath both recalls the Garden of Eden and anticipates its return in the World-to-Come. Within the limits of the current world order, it ritualistically recreates the paradise that was lost but also provides a foretaste of the restored world that, so rabbinic tradition affirms, lies ahead. If this is "*the sanctification of time*," to use Heschel's term, it is also an act that is intended to afford a glimpse of a world beyond time and its depredations. In the memorable words with which Heschel ended his little book on the Sabbath, "Eternity utters a day."[59]

CHAPTER 8

Modern Life Challenges the Sabbath— and Vice Versa

FOR WELL OVER TWO MILLENNIA, the observance of the institution whose development we have traced in the previous seven chapters was a central, community-defining practice of the Jewish people. There were, of course, serious disagreements over its observance, as we discussed in detail in chapter six, and the challenge of defining what is compatible and what is incompatible with it goes on, as indeed it must. But until the last two and a half centuries or so, and despite the occasional deviant individual before then, Jewish communities throughout the world were firmly *šômēr šabbāt*, "Sabbath-observant."

The Christian case is in some ways less complicated but in others more so. One does not find much of an analogy to those continuing Jewish efforts to apply a well-articulated legal tradition to questions of sabbatical practice. One does, however, find considerable controversy about whether Christians are obligated by the covenantal law of the set of books that they, beginning in the mid-second century CE, have called the "Old Testament" and, if so, by how much of it and in what ways. In one of his earlier letters, Paul, the apostle to the Gentiles, seems to equate his correspondents' observance of special days with a reversion to the degraded superstition from which they have recently been converted:

> [8]Formerly, when you did not know God, you were enslaved to beings that by nature are not gods. [9]Now, however, that you have come to know God, or rather to be known by God, how can you turn back again to the weak and beggarly elements? How can you want to be enslaved to them again? [10]You are observing special days, and months, and seasons, and years. [11]I am afraid that my work for you may have been wasted. (Gal 4:8–11, NRSV)[1]

Paul's point is that if his Gentile correspondents accept the Jewish liturgical year and its attendant practices, they will actually be reenslaving themselves to the degrading and God-denying determinism from which their entry into the Church has freed them. If so, any observance of Torah-law as Torah-law (at least by Gentiles) stands in fundamental contradiction to the gospel itself. As the same apostle, speaking of another community-defining Jewish practice, puts it in the next chapter, "For in Christ Jesus neither circumcision nor uncircumcision counts for anything; the only thing that counts is faith working through love" (Gal 5:6, NRSV). Faith, love, grace, the spirit—these, and not adherence to the Mosaic commandments, is what God now desires.

This anti-sabbatical theology thus finds its meaning and derives much of its energy from a larger critique of Jewish Torah-observance widespread in the early Church and echoed in some Christian thought to this day, as we shall see. The apologist Justin, for example, who lived about a century after Paul, informs his Jewish debating opponent that the Sabbath was God's punishment, given "when your people showed itself wicked and ungrateful to God by molding a golden calf as an idol in the desert."[2] In this theology, God never really desired the observance of the Mosaic law at all: he imposed it as punishment. Neither Jews nor Gentiles should observe it.

In the case of these two early Christian writers and many others, the rage directed at traditional Jewish observances reflects willy-nilly the enduring appeal of such practices to their own Gentile readers. For one does not go to such lengths to belittle that which is self-evidently disgraceful and degrading and to warn people away from it. Rather, the practice so fiercely denounced exercises an appeal that the polemic now seeks to neutralize. And, indeed, given not only the importance of the Sabbath in the Jewish scriptures but also the evidence from the gospels that Jesus observed the Mosaic ordinances (if also at times claiming authority over them), it makes sense that some early Christians—and not just Jewish Christians—continued to observe the special day, however much Paul and his followers disapproved.[3] Hence, the decree of the Synod of Laodicea (363–364 CE):

> Christians shall not Judaize and be idle on Saturday, but shall work on that day; but the Lord's day they shall especially honour, and, as being Christians, shall, if possible, do no work on that day. If, however, they are found Judaizing, they shall be shut out from Christ. (Canon 29)[4]

There is no reason to assume that the Christians censured here observed the full range of Jewish law and certainly no reason to think they practiced the commandments of the Torah in accordance with rabbinic teaching. More likely, they simply read their Bible and piously sought to comply with its unqualified injunctions to cease from labor on the seventh day—a norm found, no less, in the Decalogue itself.[5]

In a text like this, we sense unqualified determination to oppose the enduring attraction of observing the seventh day of the week as a Sabbath, just as the Old Testament requires. Christians must not only cease to "be idle on Saturday"; they must also "work on that day." But this is, in a very revealing way, quite different from Paul's worry about his Gentile correspondents who "are observing special days, and months, and seasons, and years" (Gal 4:10). For no sooner do we hear the denunciation of ceasing from work on Saturday than we are told that Christians should "especially honour" something called "the Lord's day" and, if possible, abstain thereon from labor. In sum, here Old Testament law is not altogether superseded and replaced by love, faith, grace, or the actions of the spirit after all. Some aspects of the law, albeit reinterpreted, remain in force for Christians.

The most conspicuous reinterpretation is the transfer of sabbatical cessation of labor from Saturday to "the Lord's Day," which is how Christians came to refer to Sunday (the "Lord" in question being, of course, Jesus). Treating the first day of the week as one of rest was already a well-known norm by the time of Laodicea. The first Christian emperor, Constantine I, had so decreed in 321 CE. As for the cause of the transfer, the most obvious candidate would be the New Testament reports that Jesus rose from the dead on that day,[6] thus making ordinary Sundays into weekly counterparts to the annual Easter, as it were. If this hypothesis is valid, the change occurred at a relatively late date. For, as Samuele Bacchiocchi writes, "though the resurrection [of Jesus] is frequently mentioned both in the New Testament and in the early patristic literature, no suggestion is given that primitive Christians commemorated the event by a weekly or yearly Sunday service."[7] In fact, as Bacchiocchi sees it, when the change eventually took place, it "appears to have been motivated by the necessity to evidence a clear dissociation from the Jews," abetted, he thinks, by the "various Sun-cults ... predominant in ancient Rome" and the consequent "theme of Christ-the-Sun."[8] I would only add that in this instance the Christians' need to dissociate themselves from the Jews, whom they so often maligned in those days, was owing to more than social prejudice: it was owing as well to the continuing attraction of Judaism to their own flock and the attendant danger of a blurring or diminution of what they regarded as the central affirmations of their community. As we shall see, a similar worry exercised the rabbis in roughly the same centuries.

A text like Canon 29 of the Synod of Laodicea nicely evidences the tensions intrinsic to the classic Christian claim that the Church has inherited not only the Jews' Bible but also their unparalleled status as God's chosen people. On the one side, Christians must steer clear of the Scylla of "Judaizing," in the case at hand demonstrating their allegiance to the gospel by working on Saturday. On the other side, they must not come too close to the Charbydis of Marcionism, the now heretical theology that the gracious God of the gospel was altogether different from the putatively malevolent deity of the Jewish Bible, a set of books that the anathematized second-century theologian Marcion, not surprisingly, excluded without exception from his canon. The "orthodox" position that emerged from Marcion's challenge is one that insists that the God of Moses is the same as the God of Jesus and that the Jews' Bible is, in fact, the result of valid revelations that have never been repealed but have now been fulfilled and thus for some purposes rendered obsolete after all. The Jewish observance of Saturday as the Sabbath thus belongs to an older dispensation no longer in effect, however blind the Jews may be to this most momentous of shifts. But the organization of time into recurring seven-day units and the mandatory cessation of labor once a week remain entirely valid and must be respected. The Christian Sunday has indeed replaced the Jews' *šabbāt*, but not by means of simple historical progression. Rather, the change results from the higher revelation that does not renounce but instead definitively fulfills the earlier one.

Not surprisingly, then, even in some recent books by Christians who find the now very widespread neglect of Sunday as Sabbath troubling and thus urge their coreligionists to recover the Sabbath, unmistakable swipes at Judaism are in evidence. Earlier, we discussed examples in A. J. Swoboda's *Subversive Sabbath: The Surprising Power of Rest in a Nonstop World*.[9] Similarly, Mark Scarlata, while wisely cautioning his readers against "caricatures of the Jewish understanding of the law in the New Testament period," can still inform them on the very next page that "The Pharisees were trying to achieve righteousness by their outward obedience to the law, but Jesus offered grace through faith."[10] This reflects fairly well a certain polemic against the Pharisees in the gospels, but it does not take account of other sources of information about that Jewish sect. Nor does it reckon sufficiently with the Matthean Jesus's command to his disciples to "do whatever they teach you and follow it" (Matt 23:2) that we discussed in connection with Swoboda's use of the classical Christian anti-Pharisaic polemic. Finally, Scarlata fails to interrogate the sharp—and very Protestant—polarity between "outward obedience to the law," on the one hand, and "grace through faith," on the other, in order to assess whether the Pharisees actually subscribed to such thinking. The closest he comes lies in his correct observation that "not all Jews believed, or acted like, the Pharisees."[11] The possibility that the Pharisees did not believe, or act, like the ludicrously self-righteous hypocrites of New Testament polemic does not seem to have occurred to him.[12]

Adam Mabry, the author of another recent volume advocating a Christian recovery of the Sabbath, offers a comparable depiction: "Contrasting with Jesus' peaceful demeanor are the Pharisees—Jewish religious ninjas. I use that term because at this point in history they had constructed 39 rules around the practice of resting. That's right—these people came up with 39 ways to correctly do nothing. So when they saw that Jesus' disciples were rubbing grain in their hands to release the husk from the fruit on a Sabbath, they panicked."[13] What is curious here is the author's attitude toward the thirty-nine primary categories of prohibited labor. Apart from the historically dubious claim that this system and enumeration derive from the Pharisees and were known in the time of Jesus, Mabry's unqualified criticism seems at odds with a profound question that he poses a few pages earlier: "If you're concerned that by embracing regular Sabbath rest you're in danger of coming under some harsh legalism, simply ask yourself how *not* observing Sabbath rest is going for you."[14] This would seem to imply that the supposedly "harsh legalism" provides needed protection against something spiritually damaging. And if that is so, then is it not worthwhile to overcome whatever initial aversion to the system one may have in order to become aware of the spiritual reality it protects? Is a respectful inquiry not preferable to mockery about "Jewish religious ninjas" who were supposedly "panicking" because, as Mabry goes on to explain, Jesus "was openly defying their power and their position,"[15] as if there was nothing larger and deeper at stake for them than self-interest?

Behind this now-familiar disparagement of the Pharisees there again lies the classic Christian theology in which Jesus has fulfilled and thus suspended the commandments of the Torah. "I am simply making the case here that the Sabbath laws were fulfilled in Christ," Mabry writes, so much so, in fact, that he respectfully rejects the traditional Christian position "that you must rest one day every week, on a Sunday, because that is how we uphold God's commandments to keep the Sabbath day," though he does personally "take a day of rest each week, usually on Fridays."[16] Logically, none of this requires in the least that Christians engage in mockery of the Pharisees or other Jews or traditional Jewish practices or make historically groundless claims, such as Mabry's baffling assertion that before Jesus came, Jews could "fellowship with God" only on Saturday.[17] In his case and those of A. J. Swoboda and Mark Scarlata alike, what we are finding seems to be more than just the familiar mixture of classical Christian supersessionist theology and a deficiency of engagement with historical research into Christian origins. Note that all three authors are explicitly seeking to retrieve sabbatical practice for the Church, that is, to bring something characteristically associated with Judaism back into the consciousness and practice of their fellow Christians. Here, Bacchiocchi's words about the eventual emergence of a weekly Sunday service seem apposite. In their caricatures of the Pharisees, these books richly display the ancient and, for some, continuing Christian "necessity to evidence a clear dissociation from the Jews."[18] Their authors do not rest content with portraying the two traditions as different, though closely related, and proclaiming their own allegiance to the gospel. Instead, they must, to some degree, portray Judaism, at least in the time of Jesus, as self-evidently defective, even laughably so. For them, Judaism is both the source and the foil for what they advocate. In different ways and to different degrees, they treat it as simultaneously a rich spiritual resource and a defective religion in self-evident need of improvement.

It must be noted nonetheless that not all contemporary Christian advocates of retrieving the Sabbath continue the ancient tradition of disparaging Judaism. Practitioners of a fairer, more historically accurate, and more respectful approach are also in evidence.[19] And lest Jews become triumphalist in their indignation about the survival of that older, invidious treatment, it must also be remembered that disparaging a rival tradition, especially one with which one's own has much in common, is hardly unique to Christians. The presence of unflattering caricatures of competing ancient Near Eastern religions in Jewish sources from the Hebrew Bible through contemporary preaching and teaching is an apt, if necessarily imprecise, analogy.[20] The need for a foil seems to be a universal in human culture. Who exemplifies this need better than those who pride themselves on coming from a culture that, unlike its rivals, is free of it?

In Christendom, treating Sunday as a day of rest and abstention from one's occupation was quite common from the time of Constantine's decree of 321 CE until just a few generations ago. We have already seen it reflected in the young Charles Dickens's searing polemic of 1836 against British sabbatarian laws.[21] As for the United States, as Judith Shulevitz points out, "In 1908, strict Sunday-closing laws remained in force in seventeen states and in Indian territory," and many other states subscribed to less stringent versions of "blue laws," as they came to be called.[22] It bears mention that such laws almost inevitably discriminated against Sabbath-observant Jews, who, in addition to not working on Friday evening and Saturday, were now required to cease their labors on Sunday as well, missing two days a week whereas their Christian compatriots missed but one, and thus imperiling not only their income but sometimes their employment as well. In any event, a few decades ago, larger economic and social changes put the final nail into those discriminatory old ordinances. Now, stores, cultural institutions, and places of entertainment are generally open all week.

Concurrently, a new phenomenon has appeared on earth and spread far and wide: the "weekend."

It has not, however, replaced the Sabbath, nor can it. The oddly named "weekend" betrays the discontinuity between the two institutions. Biblically speaking, it combines the last day of one sabbatical week (Saturday) with the first (Sunday) of the next. Nothing, of course, ensures that either the Jewish "Sabbath" or the Christian "Lord's Day" will be observed during that two-day period. Unless individuals are religiously committed to one of those days, nothing will prevent them from shopping on both and otherwise acting in ways inconsistent with the Jewish or the Christian affirmations of the sanctity of the Sabbath as a unique and unparalleled period. As a public, legal institution, the Sabbath has been all but eliminated.

In an apostolic letter from 1998, Pope John Paul II put the difference between Sabbath and weekend well:

> The custom of the "weekend" has become more widespread, a weekly period of respite, spent perhaps far from home and often involving participation in cultural, political or sporting activities which are usually held on free days. This social and cultural phenomenon is by no means without its positive aspects if, while respecting true values, it can contribute to people's development and to the advancement of the life of society as a whole. All of this responds not only to the need for rest, but also to the need for celebration which is inherent in our humanity. Unfortunately, when Sunday loses its fundamental meaning and becomes merely part of a "weekend," it can happen that people stay locked within a horizon so limited that they can no longer see "the heavens." Hence, though ready to celebrate, they are really incapable of doing so. (*Dies Domini* 4)[23]

Put negatively, the loss of a Sabbath can, as Pope John Paul II puts it, reflect that drab spiritual state in which people "stay locked within a horizon so limited that they can no longer see 'the heavens.'" Put positively, it is one of the precious consequences of a lengthy historical process, one that long predates the particular social and economic changes that Shulevitz highlights in speaking of the repeal of blue laws. It derives, that is, from the Enlightenment (and, to cite a term from Jewish history, the correlative movement of the Emancipation) and its advocacy of freedom of religion and the separation of church and state. These historic changes took place, of course, in a highly uneven process at different paces and forms in different countries and are not by any means universal even now. But, in general, they have consistently and increasingly conduced to the privatization of religion: all religious organizations become voluntary associations. Individuals, whatever their upbringing or their ancestry, can join them or avoid them, participate in them or live independently of them, as they see fit. No longer can the religious traditions serve as the basis for social or political organization at large, whatever their authority for those who freely elect to join them.

As for the Sabbath in either its Jewish or Christian version, some members of those communities will continue to practice their holy day because of the inertial force of their early upbringing. But they don't have to, and in an increasingly mobile, interconnected, and socially diverse society, the opportunities and, yes, pressures to abandon it grow accordingly. This situation is, needless to say, light years away from the biblical law that treated desecration of the Sabbath as a capital offense (whatever the actual practice)[24] and even from the relatively recent sway of the American blue laws and kindred sabbatarian ordinances elsewhere. The new situation has thus unleashed a number of efforts among both Jews and Christians to *persuade* their communities to observe the Sabbath.

Among Jews, one early response was both radical and conservative. About two hundred years ago, some German Reform rabbis changed the day of the main weekly synagogue service from Saturday to Sunday, observed as the Sabbath (and not as a weekday, with its own service, like the other five). Needless to say, the loss of the seventh day and the assimilation to Christian practice constituted a major departure from millennia of tradition, but its rationale was to reenergize weekly worship among the many Jews who were already abandoning it for whatever reason, including, of course, the sheer inconvenience and financial sacrifice that Saturday observance was causing.[25] The change was not very widely adopted. Today it is mostly a historical curiosity, rendered obsolete, in part, by the emergence of the five-day workweek and its correlative, the weekend.

Another Jewish response to the loss of sabbatical observance is more subtle and thus has become more widespread. This one involves introducing and emphasizing a later service on Friday evening. Traditionally, the Friday evening service takes place around sunset (though it can be conducted somewhat earlier if the sabbatical restrictions are accepted earlier). Relative to the Saturday morning service, the traditional evening service is much shorter. Lacking, for example, a Torah reading or a sermon, it can today be over in thirty minutes, leaving the worshipers more time for the leisurely and celebratory feast that is the first of the three required meals of the day. But what happens in the winter when the sun sets early, in some locales even before five o'clock? How does one get home from work, finish the preparations for the Sabbath (traditionally, a major focus of Friday afternoon), and get off to the synagogue in time? The classical answer is, of course, that one should arrange one's schedule so as to avoid the conflict in the first place. But many liberal congregations chose another, and to their thinking more realistic, remedy. They moved the main service to a later time, say, 7:30 or 8:00 PM, so that people could get home from work, eat a quick meal, and be off to the synagogue without (or so it was thought) missing anything.

And what happens if people have to work on Saturday or choose to prioritize some other activity over synagogue attendance on that day? Here, too, the late-evening service on Friday can be of use. Given that one is unlikely to sit down to the traditional leisurely meal afterward, why not move some of the elements of the much longer Saturday morning service to Friday night, such as the readings from the Torah and the Prophets, a substantial sermon, and even life-cycle events, such as the bar or bat mitzvah ceremony? This new, vastly expanded evening service need not eliminate the morning service; it can be another option alongside the older one—but an option designed to attract those who will not or think they cannot conform to the traditional schedule of the Sabbath.

Whatever its merits, the introduction of the later and larger Friday evening service altered the rhythm and tenor of the traditional rabbinic Sabbath in very telling ways. For one thing, by accommodating those who sought to work on the day of rest, it necessarily pared the latter down and diminished its importance, even if, as was surely also the case, it enabled the participation of some who could not conform to the ancient norms. Now for many the Sabbath was shorter, beginning later and perhaps not even carrying over to the next morning. For another, it either eliminated or vastly truncated the lavish and leisurely family meal on Friday night, one that often included interpretations of the week's Torah portion or other spiritual insights offered by members of the family or guests. Instead, the focus of religious action, which had lain equally on home and synagogue, now shifted decisively to the latter. Like the Christian Sunday, Shabbat became principally a day of public worship. Participating in synagogue services took precedence over adherence to the classical rabbinic laws of the Sabbath.

But what if one couldn't make it to the synagogue simply because, in an age of increasingly suburbanization, one lived too far to walk there? Classical rabbinic law placed the obvious answer, driving (which had made the new situation possible), totally out of the question for several reasons, the most obvious being the second word in the phrase "internal combustion engine."[26] In 1950, the Committee on Jewish Law and Standards of the Conservative Movement issued a lengthy legal opinion to facilitate what the traditional halakhah, like Orthodox Judaism to this day, had always forbidden. (Since Reform Judaism did not consider itself bound by rabbinic law, the issue did not arise for that community.) Again, the motive was one of fortifying traditional practice in the face of momentous social and technological change. "To continue unmodified the traditional interdiction of riding on the Sabbath," the authors wrote, "is tantamount to rendering attendance at the synagogue on the Sabbath physically impossible for an increasing number of our people."[27] As for that longstanding prohibition, it cannot apply to the new technology precisely because, so the argument went, the technology is new: "The combustion of gasoline to produce power is a type of work that obviously could not have been prohibited, before its invention."[28] Therefore, the decision concludes, "When attendance at services is made unreasonably difficult, without the use of the automobile, such use shall not be regarded as being in violation of the Sabbath."[29]

As the first clause of that last sentence indicates, in this responsum driving on the Sabbath is not generally acceptable; it is permissible only for attendance at the synagogue. In a clarification a few years later, the Committee on Jewish Law and Standards would stress that the dispensation "does not include travel for other ends ... nor does it include travel to the synagogue to attend a Bar Mitzvah ceremony or reception, for the motivation here is not the service of God but the honor of man."[30] Otherwise, driving remains a violation. In sum, the Sabbath is not being downgraded; the synagogue service is being upgraded. And that is because today "[t]he average Jew's knowledge of Torah and his Jewish information are gained through the synagogue and in great measure," these rabbis go on to say, "through the sermon which both instructs and inspires our people to live in accordance with their faith." For this reason, the classical solution to the problem, praying at home, ideally in a group that included the ten men that traditional Jewish law requires for public prayer, has become unrealistic. For today, "the practice of private prayer has unfortunately fallen into such disuse that only the minimal number of people engage in prayer unless it be at a synagogue service."[31] Without the synagogue—and, importantly, the ability to drive to it—the survival of Judaism itself is imperiled.

In the same document, after another learned survey of the issue, the Committee on Jewish Law and Standards of the Conservative Movement declared the use of electricity on the Sabbath permissible. (Actually, the *use* of electricity was never an issue. The problem came with turning the electrical device on or off or otherwise adjusting it.) Here again, historical change played a major role in the decision:

> We think of Halachah as an instrument of the people, for the enrichment of the spiritual life of our people and not as an end of itself. Furthermore, in modern life the use of electricity is essential to the normal comforts of living. Great stress was laid in our tradition on the duty of having one's home brightly illuminated in honor of the Sabbath. There in the spirit of a living and developing Halachah responsive to the changing needs of our people, we declared it to be permitted to use electric lights on the Sabbath for the purpose of enhancing the enjoyment of the Sabbath, or reducing personal discomfort, or of helping in the performance of a mitzvah.[32]

In both these cases, the Committee regarded recent social changes and technological innovations as presenting insurmountable challenges to observing the traditional laws of the Sabbath. Either the law changes in a way that permits what had been forbidden or Judaism itself withers, a prisoner to out-moded strictures and the refusal of its contemporary authorities to authorize adjustments of the sort that the Committee believed their counterparts in earlier generations had made. As the quotation above shows, their reason-ing also assumes some degree of dichotomization and polarization between spirit and law, with the latter, of course, in the disfavored position. Its first sentence, for example, does not reckon with the possibility that adherence to divinely authorized halakhah "as an end in itself" might work powerfully "for the enrichment of the spiritual life of our people" and generate solutions to the new problems. Nor does it reckon with the prospect that eliminating two very obvious differences between Sabbath and weekdays by assimilating the for-mer to the latter might for that very reason lead to a diminution of sabbatical practice more generally. Finally, it bears mention that the two adjustments that the responsum makes also vastly reduce the difference between Sabbath-observant Jews and practicing Christians, who have, of course, no qualms about riding or turning lights on and off on their own Sabbath. This, in turn, encourages the perception that the two religious traditions are simply vari-ants of each other, two peas in the same Judeo-Christian pod, as it were. How far that perception can proceed without endangering not only Jewish obser-vance of the Sabbath but Jewish identity itself may not have seemed a major issue in 1950. But today, given the rates of intermarriage and assimilation, it has become a pressing question.

Half a century after this famous responsum was issued, Alan Mittleman, a professor at Jewish Theological Seminary, the flagship institution of the same Conservative Movement, reflected insightfully on what changes the legitima-tion of driving on the Sabbath had actually wrought:

> When Conservative Judaism approved of driving, it not only stretched the boundaries of observance, it diluted the ambiance of the Sabbath. Integral to the traditional ambiance is the walk to synagogue, with its slow and contemplative pace. The walk instantiates a total break with the car and all that it represents and evokes. Traditional Jews live within walking distance of a synagogue. They reclaim suburban streets for walk-ing and, on the way home, for socializing. By noontime on any given Sat-urday, the streets around a synagogue are full of women and men, baby strollers, groups of boys and girls. Cars have to slow down and navigate around groups of walkers, often to the annoyance of drivers. Because Orthodox Jews walk they must live within a reasonable radius from the synagogue, say one-and-a-half to two miles. Because lavish meals are also a part of the celebration of the Sabbath, they join together at one another's homes for the afternoon meal. Groups of people may be

found walking to and from lunch; children go to visit their friends in one another's houses. Despite the idea that the Sabbath is a day of rest, Orthodox neighborhoods are alive with social activity on Saturdays.[33]

Note the present tense of Mittleman's verbs. The old assumption that without the members' driving, synagogues would become moribund or empty on the Sabbath had already been disproven when he wrote over twenty years ago. Referring to the pioneering work of the sociologist Marshall Sklare, he describes the resurgence of Orthodox Judaism in America and the impact this largely unforeseen development has had on those who still held to the older assumptions:

> Their young—highly observant, motivated, and educated in Orthodoxy's network of day schools—went to the finest colleges. They pursued the liberal professions rather than business, combining high secular education and achievement with a highly traditional way of life. Secularization theory proved wrong. Baby-boomer Orthodox did not acculturate into Conservative Judaism. They created their own institutions and adapted them, without losing distinctive markers of religious observance, into the suburban milieu. Enabled by ever-expanding American religious tolerance and pluralism, they felt no need to mask their Jewish traditionalism. As anyone who lives in a major urban area today knows, an entire subculture of well-to-do modern Orthodox Jews exists in the upscale suburbs, complete with kosher pizzerias, Chinese restaurants, and high-quality private schools. The Orthodox resurgence is a leading cause of the felt malaise within Conservative Judaism.[34]

Here, to be sure, some qualifications are in order. Not all American Orthodox Jews, young or old, go to pricey colleges, of course, or live in upscale neighborhoods. But there is no question that pursuing a traditional halakhic life adds to the costs of both education and housing. Those whose children attend the day schools Mittleman mentions are also usually paying for the public schools that they do not utilize, and if the best deal on housing does not happen to lie within walking distance of an Orthodox synagogue, there, too, they will incur an added expense. In sum, quite apart from the other practical difficulties and limitations that come with identification as a traditional Jew, halakhic observance imposes its own financial sacrifices. What is remarkable is that increasing numbers of Jews—though the absolute numbers remain low—have nonetheless chosen the observant life over the alternatives on offer, as Mittleman notes. Given the social and religious history of American Judaism as it stood when the Conservative Movement issued the responsum on driving on the Sabbath in 1950, the grim prognosis of the document seemed eminently reasonable. In three quarters of a century's hindsight, the responsum seems to have overestimated the durability of the particular situation at the time it was issued and to have underestimated the vitality of the classical rabbinic tradition. It now comes across as defeatist.[35]

As for the observance of the Sabbath in Conservative Judaism itself (in which driving on the Sabbath has long ago ceased to be controversial), recent survey data reveal a pronounced movement in the opposite direction, with fewer young Conservative Jews committed to the practice of the seventh day. A comprehensive study issued in June 2020, which followed "a large sample of American and Canadian Jews since their bar/bat mitzvah rite of passage in 1995 (5755)," found that whereas in 1999 29 percent of the respondents reported that their families always did "something special/different on Friday night or Saturday because it is the Jewish Sabbath," the proportion of those who do so themselves had shrunk to 12 percent in 2018: "One-fourth of the cohort observes Shabbat always or usually. Yet, there is an increase in the share of those who never observe Shabbat (from 21% to 37%) and a decrease in those who sometimes observe Shabbat (from 51% to 36%). Busy family-life and intermarriage explain the erosion in Shabbat observance."[36] The damage intermarriage generally does to Jewish observance has been well-documented, including in the same study.[37] "Busy family-life" is a more complicated issue. A bar or bat mitzvah is the rite of passage that takes place for boys at the age of thirteen or for girls at twelve, respectively. By 2018, those who underwent these rites in 1995 would thus have been seventeen or sixteen in 1999 and thirty-six or thirty-five in 2018. That is indeed a busy age for family men and women, especially if they have multiple children. But was it less so for their families of origin when the respondents were in their early teens?[38] And is it less busy for the young Orthodox Jews whom Mittleman spotlights? The larger question is whether those who have abandoned or lessened the observances of the homes in which they grew up will return to them when things settle down. And what does it portend for the future of Conservative Judaism that increasing numbers of its own children are growing up with a diminished experience of Shabbat? Long-term and in the aggregate, the strategy to attract Jews to the practice of the Sabbath by lowering the standards of observance does not seem to work. Fortunately for Sabbath observance, it was not long before an alternative and countervailing approach became prominent.

The year after the "Responsum on the Sabbath: Driving & Electricity" was issued, Abraham Joshua Heschel, also a professor at Jewish Theological Seminary, published his famous and enduring little volume, *The Sabbath: Its Meaning for Modern Man*. For Heschel, too, the objective was to attract American

Jews back to the practice of the sacred seventh day, but his strategy for doing so was quite the opposite. Instead of seeking to accommodate sabbatical practice to modern technological life, thus lessening the contrast between the two, he made use of the traditional theology of the Sabbath to critique the over-reliance on technology and the spiritual threat presented by certain aspects of the thinking that it encourages. For Heschel, the Sabbath served as the spiritual antipode to modern materialism and the alienation that he believed to be inseparable from it. His critique was largely constructed, it will be recalled, on a stark polarization of time and space. "In technical civilization," he wrote, "we expend time to get space." By contrast, "The Sabbath is the day on which we learn the art of *surpassing* civilization." This is because "The Sabbath is the presence of God in the world, open to the soul of men"—in other words, "*Spirit in the form of time.*"[39]

In our previous discussion, we raised some problems with the stark space/time dichotomy on which Heschel, like others in his generation, relied.[40] In the present context, it is important to note that things of space—objects, sights, sounds, tastes, smells—are important to the practice of the Sabbath, and technology, if in some sense surpassed on that day, can still be very much present, as in the use of electric food warmers and lights and the timers with which one may, even according to Orthodox halakhah, turn the latter on and off. More fundamentally, the rabbinic laws of the Sabbath—the set of norms that give definition to the day—are intensely concerned with the organization of space. As David C. Kraemer puts it, "a person's personal space—the space that defines his Sabbath domain in the absence of other factors—is the space that she or he could control (the space that would be 'under him') without moving." So important is this dimension that, as anyone who has studied the Talmudic tractate ʿEruḇin knows well, "Every object must be categorized and then more finely categorized to determine its Sabbath map."[41]

But here I want to raise another issue about Heschel's apologetic strategy. Suppose one accepts his central conviction that there is a profound spiritual meaning to the Sabbath, one that humankind will ignore at their peril. How should they go about accepting it and operationalizing it?

To some Christian readers or those many non-Christians who instinctively think of religion in Christian terms, the Jewish answer is so obvious that the question will seem embarrassingly stupid: all humankind should convert to Judaism and practice the Jewish Sabbath. With this there is a grave problem: the answer is not very Jewish. As we have seen at some length, Judaism, at least in the rabbinic form bequeathed by antiquity, is not a missionary religion (though it can accept converts) and, it turns out, has grave reservations about Gentiles' observing the Sabbath if they have not converted.[42] Heschel's unqualifiedly universalistic language about the Sabbath as "the presence of

God in the world, open to the soul of men," and the like, collides head-on with the intense particularism of the holiday itself. It suffers from the inevitable shortcomings of any universalistic rationale for a particularistic practice.

The Christian pastor Adam Mabry offers one way forward, at least for his own community. Recall his reason for thinking there is nothing in the theology of the Sabbath that requires Christians to rest one day a week: "the Sabbath laws were fulfilled in Christ."[43] Here, like many Christians over the centuries, he cites the apparent identification of sabbatical "rest" with life in "Christ," as articulated in the New Testament book of Hebrews (Heb 4:1–11). In such a reading, "rest" is not a day, as in Jewish tradition, but a spiritual state, open only to those with faith in the Christian message:

> [9]So then, a sabbath rest still remains for the people of God; [10]for those who enter God's rest also cease from their labors as God did from his. [11]Let us therefore make every effort to enter that rest, so that no one may fall through such disobedience as theirs [that is, the disobedience of the rebellious Israelites of the wilderness wanderings]. (Heb 4:9–11, NRSV)

The Pauline or Deutero-Pauline book of Colossians, which Mabry also cites, removes all ambiguity about the alleged importance of an actual day observed as the Sabbath:

> [16]Therefore do not let anyone condemn you in matters of food and drink or of observing festivals, new moons, or sabbaths. [17]These are only a shadow of what is to come, but the substance belongs to Christ. (Col 2:16–17, NRSV)

In short, the Sabbath, like other observances characteristic of the Jews, was a prefiguration of redemption through Christ. As Mabry sees it, "... the point isn't the day. The point is the thing to which the Sabbath points—namely, our forever future with God."[44]

Here, too, there is an exclusive relationship between the Sabbath and the people of God—except now it is the Church (and ideally all humanity once they have joined the Church) that takes the role of the people of God, and the Sabbath is no longer a day (however wise it may be to observe one day a week as the Sabbath). It has been transformed into an existential stance severed from calendrical considerations.

From the vantagepoint of the Jewish Sabbath, Mabry's rather individualistic and subjective appropriation of it into Christianity is vulnerable to the same critique we made of Swoboda's.[45] As for Heschel, though he would obviously reject such Christological claims, for reasons we have already examined he would surely have no quarrel with the idea that the Sabbath is a foretaste of the World-to-Come, to use the ancient rabbinic language.[46] Nor would he have reservations about connecting the Sabbath with faith in God, recognition of him as the creator, finding his spirit available in ordinary life, or, for that matter, with the correlative downgrading of acquisition, production, domination of nature, commercial exchange, worldly success, social status, and the like, as the highest human achievements. But Heschel would just as surely have an enormous problem with devaluing the Sabbath as a calendrical event and recasting it as an atemporal spiritual state. For this would be to relinquish what for him is the key aspect of the whole institution—the sanctification of time. If the Sabbath is *"Spirit in the form of time,"*[47] surely it must involve something more recurrently realizable, predictable, and tangible, as it were, than simply "our forever future." However personally meaningful and spiritually rich Swoboda's Wednesday and Mabry's Friday may be, the Christian theology underlying those intended sabbatical days, like their rhythm and tenor, is instructively different from that of Abraham Joshua Heschel's conception of the Sabbath and the Jewish tradition that gave birth to it. It is also different from the Christian Sunday.

Pope John Paul II takes a less radical approach, one that is also somewhat more sympathetic to Jewish thinking on this issue. No Wednesday or Friday Sabbath or one-in-seven principle for him! Rather, the key point of his aforementioned letter is "the duty to keep Sunday holy,"[48] and his own citations of Hebrews 4 and the scriptural verses it midrashically exegetes are in the service of "the Lord's Day," the English translation of the name of the pope's letter:

> Already at the dawn of creation, therefore, the plan of God implied Christ's "cosmic mission." This *Christocentric perspective*, embracing the whole arc of time, filled God's well-pleased gaze when, ceasing from all his work, he "blessed the seventh day and made it holy" (Gen 2:3). According to the Priestly writer of the first biblical creation story, then was born the "Sabbath," so characteristic of the first Covenant, and which in some ways foretells the sacred day of the new and final Covenant. The theme of "God's rest" (cf. Gen 2:2) and the rest which he offered to the people of the Exodus when they entered the Promised Land (cf. Exod 33:14; Deut 3:20; 12:9; Jos 21:44; Ps 95:11) is re-read in the New Testament in the light of the definitive "Sabbath rest" (Heb 4:9) into which Christ himself has entered by his Resurrection. The People of God are called to enter into this same rest by persevering in Christ's example of filial obedience (cf. Heb 4:3–16). In order to grasp fully the meaning of Sunday, therefore, we must re-read the great story of creation and deepen our understanding of the theology of the "Sabbath." (*Dies Domini* 8)[49]

This, too, re-presents the classical Christian theology in which the Gospel fulfills and in at least some measure suspends the Torah. Thus, the Sabbath "in some ways foretells the sacred day of the new and final Covenant." Anyone seeking fairness in Jewish-Christian relations should pause to appreciate the qualifying phrase, "in some ways." The same applies to Pope John Paul II's use of the term "re-read" to describe the exegetical technique by which the theme of rest for God and for his chosen people in the Hebrew Bible provides the groundwork for the rest "into which Christ himself has entered by his Resurrection," according to the ancient Christian theology. Although *Dies Domini* never uses the word "midrash," it is clear that its author saw the Christian appropriation of the Sabbath as an instance of midrashic recontextualization. There is no implication here that ancient Jews themselves read the text that way or should have.[50]

Given these familiar Christological claims, Pope John Paul II goes on to explain the logic underlying the eventual replacement of Saturday by Sunday as the day that the Decalogue enjoins the faithful to remember and observe. Although, not surprisingly, as the pope saw it, "the practices of the Jewish Sabbath are gone, surpassed as they are by the 'fulfilment' which Sunday brings," he tells his fellow Roman Catholics, "the underlying reasons for keeping 'the Lord's Day' holy—inscribed solemnly in the Ten Commandments—remain valid, though they need to be reinterpreted in the light of the theology and spirituality of Sunday" (*Dies Domini* 62). Here, the Jewish Sabbath is not replaced by an existential stance or a random one day out of seven: the replacement in question remains solidly calendrical:

> Because the Third Commandment [that is, the Fourth according to most enumerations] depends upon the remembrance of God's saving works and because Christians saw the definitive time inaugurated by Christ as a new beginning, they made the first day after the Sabbath a festive day, for that was the day on which the Lord rose from the dead. The Paschal Mystery of Christ is the full revelation of the mystery of the world's origin, the climax of the history of salvation and the anticipation of the eschatological fulfilment of the world. What God accomplished in Creation and wrought for his People in the Exodus has found its fullest expression in Christ's Death and Resurrection, though its definitive fulfilment will not come until the *Parousia*, when Christ returns in glory. (*Dies Domini* 18)

Here again, one sees the delicate tightrope walk that Christians' appropriation of the Jewish Sabbath for their Lord's Day necessitates. To disregard the Sabbath commandment of the Decalogue would bring them perilously close to Marcionism; it would imply that the norms of the Old Testament had been altogether annulled. To reaffirm the sanctity of the seventh day of the week, as the Fourth Commandment plainly stipulates, however, might lead to Judaizing, for the Old Testament Sabbath has been suspended by dint of its fulfillment in Christ. In *Dies Domini*, as in Roman Catholic tradition for centuries beforehand, the two vectors converge in the message that attendance at Sunday mass, including participation in the Eucharist by those qualified for it, is the most appropriate observance of the reconfigured Sabbath. "The communal character of the Eucharist emerges in a special way," Pope John Paul II wrote, "when it is seen as the Easter banquet, in which Christ himself becomes our nourishment. . . . Obviously, the invitation to Eucharistic communion is more insistent in the case of Mass on Sundays and holy days" (*Dies Domini* 44). His message is unmistakable: however different the Jewish Sabbath and the Christian Lord's Day are—and they are quite different—something of the spiritual meaning and function of the former remains alive and available to Christians in the latter.

That the pope thinks Catholics should go to mass on Sunday is less than supremely newsworthy. In *Dies Domini* (1998), however, we sense that some new developments were endangering observance of the Christian Sabbath:

> There is a risk that the prodigious power over creation which God gives to man can lead him to forget that God is the Creator upon whom everything depends. It is all the more urgent to recognize this dependence in our own time, when science and technology have so incredibly increased the power which man exercises through his work. (*Dies Domini* 65)

With this, Pope John Paul II echoes half a century later the prescient thinking of Heschel (to whom he refers appreciatively[51]) on the spiritual impoverishment that technological progress can silently wreak upon those who have no established communal and creedal resources with which to resist it. For all the obvious and elementary differences between the two figures, there is an analogy between the ways they enlisted their respective Sabbaths in defense of their spiritual visions in the face of the potent new challenge.

In the last two decades or so, with the rapid growth of information technology and personal digital devices, the problem has only mushroomed. It now qualifies as a genuine crisis, as many have now noted. Shulevitz remarks that "It wasn't until the second half of the twentieth century that anyone noticed that all this time-saving didn't make us feel less rushed,"[52] but in the twenty-first the idea has become a commonplace. It has, she points out, brought into being something new under the sun:

And a secular Sabbath has emerged that is largely a way of curing an addiction to technology. Adherents to what's called a "technology Sabbath"—naturally, they stay in touch via the Internet—speak of themselves in language that evokes Alcoholics Anonymous testimonials: "I love technology. I'm not a Luddite. But I realized it was a problem when I would sit down to check my e-mail and it was almost like I would wake up six hours later and find I was watching videos of puppies on YouTube," Ariel Meadow Stallings, a blogger from Seattle, told the Reuters news agency in April 2008.[53]

In his own engaging volume about the Sabbath, Senator Joe Lieberman, a prominent American political leader and a practicing Orthodox Jew, brings the same point home:

> Let me make this personal: if there were not a divine law commanding me to rest, I would think of many good reasons to go about my normal routine on Friday night and Saturday. That's my nature. I am, for example, addicted to my Blackberry. . . . If there were no Sabbath law to keep me from sending and receiving email all day as I normally do, do you think I would be able to resist the temptation on the Sabbath? Not a chance. Laws have this way of setting us free.[54]

The affirmation that subjugation to God's Torah is liberating is an ancient one in Judaism. So is the polarity of service to God and service to worldly rulers that informs Lieberman's homiletical reflection on the effects of digital addiction: "Every generation has its own pharaoh and its own slave masters, uniquely based on the culture of the time," he observes. "Our pharaoh may be the electronic devices—computers, televisions, iPhones—that mesmerize us, dominating hour after hour of our lives."[55] The ancient story, it turns out, has acquired a renewed pertinence, and the ancient holy day that commemorates it, a renewed urgency.

Although electronic devices and working remotely have now made it vastly easier to labor seven days a week, as many people do, and to keep access to work as close as one's pocket, the deformation of our humanity in question involves more than just the overwork that the new technology facilitates. "The Sabbath forces us to pull our eyes away from the digital flow and rejoin the natural world, where communication is accomplished mainly through human voices speaking and human ears listening," Lieberman explains. "The genius of the Sabbath lies in the way it restricts us from certain activities and, thereby, frees us to experience others including conversations—big ones with God and less grand ones with our family and friends."[56] Could it be that Mabry's "Jewish religion ninjas ... [who] came up with 39 ways to correctly do nothing"[57] were on to something after all? For the unmistakable implication of a "technology Sabbath" is that people can disfigure and diminish their own humanity in far more ways than through over-dedication to gainful employment.

Lieberman's mention of conversations with God, family, and friends nicely captures both the vertical and the horizontal dimensions of the Jewish Sabbath. Whether all advocates of the "technology Sabbath" would be happy with his formulation is doubtful, however. Surely, people can unglue their eyes from the screen and engage in more traditional modes of communication without the theological dimension that has been central to Shabbat as far back as we can reconstruct. Even if we are to accept the famous claim of Alcoholics Anonymous that we must turn our lives over to a "Higher Power," are the capital letters strictly necessary? Must that higher power, that is, really have created the world, singled out the people Israel (or the Church, which has traditionally seen itself as bearing the fulfillment of the promises to Israel), and rescued them from Egyptian bondage? Are we actually to think that addicts who are not believers in Judaism or Christianity are doomed to lives of dependency?

Such questions point to a certain double directionality in the new "technology Sabbath." On the one hand, the term suggests there is a deep and needed wisdom in the traditional rabbinic halakhah and its limitation of technology, including electrical devices and not merely labor, on the sacred day. In that sense, the new phenomenon casts doubt on the idea that the answer to overwork in the broadest sense is a day off, and it powerfully echoes Heschel's worries about the spirit-sapping character of modern life. On the other hand, if all that is taken from the Jewish Sabbath is a recurring regimen of self-denial and self-reorientation, shorn of the larger theological and metaphysical framework in which halakhah is embedded, then the modern materialism Heschel critiqued and the alienation he believed to be its inevitable manifestation remain unchallenged. We are left instead with the familiar spectacle of a very modern, very secular, and very pared down appropriation of an ancient spiritual practice: Shabbat becomes the new yoga.

This is not to deny that such a regimen can help its practitioners achieve their stated goals or otherwise benefit them. Nor is it to deny that this particular regimen might even eventually lead some of them into a robust immersion in traditional Judaism. What there is ample room to question, however, is the durability of the "technological Sabbath." So long as we are talking about individuals undertaking a practice for self-improvement, in isolation or in small groups who make up their own rules as they go along, we are not talking about the mandatory, socially constituted and reinforced, and finely articulated institution that is the Jewish Sabbath. We are instead talking about a highly individualistic and idiosyncratic practice more akin to Swoboda's Wednesday or

Mabry's Friday (shorn, of course, of what is to them the most important rationale, Christian faith) or perhaps to a New Year's resolution.[58] Kelsey Osgood, author of the aptly titled "Why Your 'Digital Shabbat' Will Fail," puts it this way: "The observant Jewish community has successfully maintained Shabbat over thousands of years precisely *because* it's practiced in a community, one that operates with particular norms and expectations."[59] A major source of the astonishing survival of Shabbat over the millennia is precisely that it entails, and even continually brings into existence, a social body where there might otherwise have been only a collection of undefined or self-defined individuals, with their idiosyncratic spiritualities (or none at all); that it answers to norms and expectations rather than personal preferences and whims; that it is gratefully received rather than creatively devised to meet this or that generation's felt exigencies.

If the Sabbath is to come back with any force among Christians who have lost it, recovery is in my judgment likely to derive from more than a felt need to unplug and reconnect with one's inner self, with other people, with nature, or even with the divine. It will instead conform more closely to the thinking of Pope John Paul II: it will be communal rather than individualistic, focused on one day out of the seven-day week, and deeply rooted in a traditional and culturally resonant theological affirmation. Perhaps the new situation in which many people work seven days a week, some or all of them at home, will lead to a return of blue laws. Shulevitz, interestingly, considers this an "underrated" possibility.[60] Even were such an eventuality to come about, however—and the logistical obstacles alone are massive—there is much room to wonder whether the mandatory day off would really merit the name of "Sabbath," or have the longevity of the Jewish institution of Shabbat from which the term derives.

Without denying the existence of the subsidiary benefits of sabbatical observance, Osgood points to the most important cause for the survival of Shabbat when she identifies the foundational reason that traditional Jews practice it at all. "We do it," she writes, "for a very unfashionable, very simple, supremely awesome reason: because God told us to."[61]

Unfashionable it is, but so long as it endures, so will Israel's day of light and joy.

NOTES

Epigraph

This is the first line and the refrain in *Yôm Zeh Ləyiśrāʾēl*, ascribed to Rabbi Isaac Luria, a rabbinic authority and mystic living in Safed in the Galilee in the sixteenth century CE. The translation is by Sacks, *Koren Siddur*, 390.

Chapter 1

1. In Jewish discourse, it is preferable to avoid the familiar Christian term "Ten Commandments," since, according to the rabbinic enumeration, there are 613 commandments in the Torah and, however central or generative these ten are, they hardly supersede the others. Also, note that, according to rabbinic tradition, the first of the Ten Utterances is Exod 20:2 (=Deut 5:6), which, formally speaking, includes no commandment at all.

2. Henkin, *Week*, 13.

3. See pp. 59–61.

4. Tigay, "Notes," 112. It is possible that *šābûaʿ* in Gen 29:27, 28 refers not to the seven-day wedding feast (cf. Judg 14:12) but rather to the additional seven years of service that Jacob must fulfill, as argued, for example, by Jacob, *Das Buch Genesis*, 591–92. On the notoriously difficult passage Lev 23:15–16, which uses *šabbāt* (usually the word for the Sabbath), see Tigay, "Notes," 111, where he observes that it is unclear whether the unit of time intended is a sabbatical or nonsabbatical week. If the former, then we have here a biblical precedent for the rabbinic use of *šabbāt* to refer to the sabbatical week.

5. Hallo, "New Moons," 8.

6. See Hasel, "New Moon," 45–46.

7. Henkin, *Week*, 7.

8. Needless to say, the Neo-Babylonian date for the text is also problematic for any argument that it constitutes a source and not simply a (possible) dim parallel to the week, since the Israelite "seventh day" seems to have been well established before the end of the seventh century BCE.

9. Zerubavel, *Seven Day Circle*, 10–11. On some Israelite reflexes of this, see the next note.

10. Kamrin, "Telling Time." It is important to note that evidence has been adduced for an ancient Israelite calendar of 360 days consisting of twelve months of thirty days each, though there is no evidence that it served liturgical purposes or was widely known.

See Ben-Dov, "360-Day," 431–50. On the variant nonlunar calendar of the Priestly source (P) in the Pentateuch, see Guillaume, *Land and Calendar*, 42–45.

11. Anthony J. Spalinger, "Calendars," 224. On the Egyptian calendar, see also Neugebauer, *Exact Sciences*, 82, and Parker, "Calendars and Chronology," 13–26.

12. Murray, *Splendour*, 286. A decan is a ten-degree section of a zodiacal sign. Thus, there are 360 degrees in the yearly cycle, an ancient institution obviously reflected in the 360 degrees of the compass in use to this day. It has plausibly been suggested that the well-known late Talmudic tradition of the thirty-six righteous but occulted individuals who sustain the universe derives from the thirty-six decans of the heavenly cycle and thus reflects a distinct Jewish adaptation and transformation of the zodiacal system. On this, see Scholem, "Tradition," 252–53.

13. The form is morphologically plural but semantically singular, referring to one day.

14. See Balsdon, *Life and Leisure*, 59–61, and Zerubavel, *Seven Day Circle*, 45.

15. Balsdon, *Life and Leisure*, 60. Marcus Terentius Varro was an author and scholar of the first century BCE.

16. Ibid., 60–61.

17. See also Amos 8:4–10, though, for reasons that will be apparent in chap. 2, it is possible that the Sabbath here is not the weekly event to which the term comes exclusively to refer.

18. E.g., Shulchan Arukh, *Ḥôšen Mišpāṭ, Hilḳôt Dayyānîm* 5:1.

19. Balsdon, *Life and Leisure*, 64.

20. Ibid., 60, 63.

21. E.g., Exod 16:21–30.

22. Henkin, *Week*, 160. Given its Near Eastern origins and the contempt in which, as we shall see, some Roman intellectuals held the sabbatical week, the term "Western" is problematic in this context.

23. Zerubavel, *Seven Day Circle*, 49.

24. Ibid., 32.

25. Henkin, *Week*, 175.

26. Zerubavel, *Seven Day Circle*, 37.

27. Ibid., 36.

28. Henkin, *Week*, 175–76. Henkin points out that the Soviets had already abandoned the older Julian calendar, associated with Orthodox Church, immediately after the revolution (1917) and replaced it with the Gregorian (*Week*, 174–75).

29. See Colson, *Week*, 18–38; Hallo, "New Moons," 14, 17; and Zerubavel, *Seven Day Circle*, 12–18.

30. See the charts in Hallo, "New Moons," 17, and Zerubavel, *Seven Day Circle*, 18. A convenient online chart can be found at https://en.wikipedia.org/wiki/Planetary_hours.

31. The orbital period of Venus (224.7 days) is actually longer than that of Mars (87.969 days). See Zerubabel, *Seven Day Circle*, 15.

32. For possible explanations for this skipping of two planets in order to advance the third, see Colson, *Week*, 43–45 and Zerubavel, *Seven Day Circle*, 15–17. The question was addressed by the Roman historian and statesman Dio Cassius (ca. 155–ca. 235 CE) in *Hist. rom.* 27.18–19. On the Jewish literature relating to the interaction of the planetary week with the sabbatical week, see Gandz, "Origin," 223–24.

33. See pp. 207–8.

34. Colson, *Week*, 60. Colson is surely correct, but notice should be taken of the statement in the Talmud that "Not the constellation of the day but the constellation of the hour is the causative factor." b. Šabb. 156a.

35. See Gandz, "Origin," esp. 225–52.

36. See Klibansky, Panofsky, and Saxl, *Saturn and Melancholy*, 133–51. For a brief discussion of various speculations about a connection of the Sabbath with Saturn already in ancient Israel, see Robinson, *Origin and Development*, 33–34.

37. The translation is from Juster and Maltby, *Tibullus*, 15. On this passage, see also Schäfer, *Judeophobia*, 84–85, and on Greco-Roman attitudes toward the Sabbath in general, see pp. 82–92. Schäfer (86) observes that "the condemnation of resting on the Sabbath as idleness and indolence . . . seems distinctively Roman" and probably began with Seneca (mid-first century CE).

38. Colson, *Week*, 35.

39. Ibid.

40. E.g., Exod 16:23; 20:8; Deut 5:12; Neh 9:14.

41. Lewis, *Latin Dictionary*, 1610.

42. Given Tacitus's intense distaste for Jewish practice, "laziness" would probably be a better translation for *ignaviae* than "inactivity." As we shall see at length in chap. 6, in Second Temple and Rabbinic practice, the prohibition of work did not at all make the Jews "inactive" on the seventh day.

43. The idea seems to come up in Dio's account of a later capture of Jerusalem (37 BCE)—with whatever degree of historical veracity it may have—in 49:22. Note, however, that, against a longstanding consensus, Nadav Sharon has mounted a formidable case that Pompey's capture of Jerusalem occurred on Yom Kippur, not on an ordinary Sabbath. Sharon, "Conquests of Jerusalem," 196–97. For our purposes here, it suffices to note that even Sharon acknowledges that Dio Cassius regards the day in question as the Sabbath. See also Schäfer, *Judeophobia*, 88.

44. See pp. 151–55.

45. E.g., t. ʿEruḇ. 3:7; Sifre Deut 203; b. Šabb. 19a.

46. Efforts by various scholars of the ancient Near East to connect the Sabbath with Saturn were already recognized as speculative in the extreme nearly a century ago. See Kraeling, "Present State," 218–19.

47. Henkin, *Week*, 13.

48. See Gandz, "Origin," esp. 225–27 for the period under discussion. See also Stern, *Time and Process*, 64n14.

49. Klibansky, Panofsky, and Saxl, *Saturn and Melancholy*, 143. The words are theirs, not Vettius Valens's.

50. One might speculate that this Talmudic dispute echoes, probably unwittingly, a longstanding understanding of Saturn (including his Greek version, Kronos) as having the dual nature of a "benevolent god of agriculture" and a "gloomy, dethroned and solitary god," in the words of Klibansky, Panofsky, and Saxl, *Saturn and Melancholy*, 134.

51. It also occurs once in Late Biblical Hebrew (Qoh 12:3).

52. The coinage seems to have appeared in the same period as the Talmudic sages, though whether any of them is responsible for it and when the coinage took place is unknown. It has often been thought that *kîyûn* in Amos 5:26 refers to the planet Saturn, though this is uncertain.

53. Ibn Ezra, long commentary to Exod 20:13, translated from *Tôrat Ḥayîm*, 205–6. Since the rabbinic day, unlike the (pagan) Greco-Roman one, begins the night before, it is

Mars, associated with Tuesday, not Mercury, that governs what the rabbis call "Wednesday night." On the astrological system operative here, see Sela, "Abraham ibn Ezra," 28–31.

54. Sela, "Abraham ibn Ezra," 22–23.

55. Ibid., 29.

56. Ibid., 32.

57. For an argument that the actual observance of the Sabbath (and thus the sabbatical week) as a social institution—quite apart from the dates of compositions of the relevant texts—likely originated in the Hellenistic period, see Y. Adler, *Origins of Judaism*, 136–45.

58. Zerubabel, *Seven Day Circle*, 16.

Chapter 2

1. That the "Book of the Covenant" (or "Covenant Code" or "Covenant Collection"; all three terms are in use) is the oldest legal collection in the Hebrew Bible has long been a consensus among critical scholars, though one that also been the subject of critique, including in relatively recent years. For a thorough review of the history of the scholarship and a detailed and persuasive defense of a preexilic date for the collection, see Levinson, "Covenant Code," esp. 293–96, where Levinson dates the collection to the Neo-Assyrian period. More recently, David P. Wright, who argues for a heavy and deliberate dependence on, and motivation to revise, the "Laws of Hammurabi," dates the collection between 740 and 640 BCE. See D. P. Wright, *Inventing God's Law*, 96–106. Further complicating the issue is the possibility that the text in question has undergone a strongly theologically motivated process of redaction, with Exod 23:12 finding its place in a later stratum focused on Israelite experience and the *personae miserae*. On this, see Markl, "Redactional Theologization," esp. 55–56. The likelihood that Exod 23:12 is the earliest appearance of the Sabbath (here called "the seventh day) in a surviving collection of law cannot, of course, be taken as evidence that the institution originated at the time that this passage was composed.

2. In the Talmud (b. Meg. 12b), the ostensible ambiguity of the term produces a memorable midrash. In Esth 1:10, King Ahasuerus summons Queen Vashti "on the seventh day" of his banquet, which is its last day (v. 5), and her refusal to appear leads to her banishment and, conceivably, her death. In the midrash, however, he orders Vashti to appear naked, and her ill fate on that seventh day illustrates the principle that, ultimately, one receives what one gives. For from this, the midrash infers, we learn that "the wicked Vashti used to bring the daughters of Israel, strip them naked, and make them work on the Sabbath."

3. Robinson disputes this possibility on practical grounds, observing (specifically with respect to Deut 15:9 and 31:10 and reflecting their terminology) that "every individual could not have had his private *šᵉmiṭṭáh* in such a well-knit community as that of ancient Israel. Moreover, a little knowledge of primitive agriculture will show the impracticability of leaving a small piece of the land fallow for the use of the poor and the wild animals, when the surrounding fields are cultivated and ripe with crops." Robinson, *Origin and Development*, 116–17.

4. Zerubavel, *Seven Day Circle*, 37.

5. In the ensuing discussion, I am much indebted to Haag, *Vom Sabbat*, 12–16, and to Grund, *Entstehung*, 43–51.

6. Haag, *Vom Sabbat*, 7–11, argues that Exod 34:21 is the earlier text. The question of their relative chronology, however, need not detain us here. On the reason for the

placement of Exod 34:21 in the position in which it is now found, see Gesundheit, *Three Times a Year*, 21–22. Gesundheit's nicely reasoned redaction-critical discussion does not answer the question about the origins of the verse.

7. See the comprehensive tabulation in Robinson, "Idea of Rest," 37–39.

8. Robinson (*Origin and Development*, 248–49), by contrast, treats *mišbattehā* as referring to the Sabbath (which he understands as the fifteenth of the month and a day with strong royal associations): "the adversaries looked, they laughed about her sabbaths." The doubling of the final root consonant offers some support for his understanding of the otherwise unattested vocable.

9. Thus, BDB, 992, classifies *šebet* in this verse under the root *šbt* but indicates doubt and draws attention to the possibility that the root is actually *yšb*. See the helpful discussion of the issue and the bibliography in *HALOT*, 1409. Kaddari, *Dictionary*, 1054–55, which does not list entries according to roots, defines *šebet* here as "refraining, being restrained" (*himmānaʾût*) and classes it with the same word or variations of it in Exod 21:19, Isa 30:7, and 2 Sam 23:7. On Isa 30:7, see n. 13 below. It would seem most unlikely that the word in 2 Sam 23:7 derives from *šbt* rather than *yšb*. Note that BDB, 992, does not identify it as what it regards as the "dubious" word *šebet* in the sense of "cessation," and the translation "on the spot" (e.g., NRSV and NJPS) presumes a derivation from *yšb*.

10. In more technical terminology, the infinitive construct of the qal stem.

11. E.g., b. Ber. 20a.

12. Koehler and Baumgartner's confidence that the latter is "clearly the case" (*HALOT*, 1409) is unwarranted. Grund (*Entstehung*, 46n197), too, is skeptical about the existence of a noun *šebet* from the root *šbt*. If the word derives from *šbt*, one would also expect to see **šobtô* rather than the Masorah's *šibtô*.

13. In the case of Isa 30:7, it would be best to accept the emendation of the incomprehensible *rahab hēm šābet* to *rahab hammošbāt*, "Rahab who has been brought to an end," as has been suggested since the nineteenth century. See Gunkel, *Creation and Chaos*, 64. This is an English translation of Gunkel's highly influential *Schöpfung und Chaos*. Jastrow, "Original Character," 346, who accepts Gunkel's emendation, wants to translate this as "the quieted or appeased Rahab" but only because of his highly dubious notion that *šbt* originally had to do with pacification and propitiation. For other emendations that have been suggested, see Blenkinsopp, *Isaiah 1–39*, 413.

14. Grund (*Entstehung*, 44) gives the total number of occurrences of the qal of *šbt* without a sabbatical connection as fourteen, which she helpfully lists.

15. This form of the word is (as the asterisk indicates) not attested. All that we have is the suffixed plural, *mišbattehā*.

16. So Robinson, "Idea of Rest," 40: "Thus we find no instance in the pre-exilic texts and in the postexilic texts which are not related to the sabbath idea where the root *šbt* means 'rest,' 'sabbathize,' or 'feiern.'" As the next note shows, however, the dating is a matter of dispute. The same point about the alleged meaning of "rest" is made by Haag, *Vom Sabbat*, 16. See his larger discussion of the Hebrew verb *šābat* on pp. 12–18.

17. On this, see, e.g., Kratz, *Composition*, 100–114, which adheres to the classical critical attribution of a postexilic date; but also Israel Knohl, *Sanctuary of Silence*, 204–12, and Milgrom, *Leviticus 17–22*, 1361–64, both of whom support a preexilic dating, though without presuming that the Holiness Code was of uniform composition, lacking its own redaction history. Whether the appendix in Lev 27 is part of the Holiness Code, as some believe, is not germane to our discussion. Much good sense as well as healthy skepticism about the issue can be found in Blum, "Issues and Problems," 31–43.

18. The only other clear example is 2 Chr 36:21, which appears in a demonstrably late source and is obviously indebted to Lev 26:34–35, 43, which it connects midrashically to Jer 25:11–12 and 29:10. Exodus 16:30 is ambiguous: Does it mean "So the people observed the Sabbath (*vayyišbɔtû*) on the seventh day (rather like the NJPS, which renders the verb as "remained inactive") or "So the people stopped [gathering the manna] on the seventh day"? Given the occurrence of the noun *šabbāt* earlier in the narrative, including the previous verse, the former option seems likelier. It should be noted that, despite the emergence of a sense of the verb *šābat* to mean "observe the Sabbath, engage in sabbatical rest," the older sense of "to cease, desist" survives in the postexilic period (e.g., Neh 6:3) and cannot be said to have been displaced by the sabbatical sense of the word, whose distribution, again, was very limited.

19. See, e.g., Rechenmacher, "Šabbat[t]," 202.

20. Other etymologies, of course, have been proposed. See, for example, the survey in North, "Derivation of Sabbath," 184–87. Guillaume derives "the full moon bearing the Akkadian name *šapatum* from the root *šabaʿ* ('to be full') and not from *sebet* ('seven')" (Guillaume, *Land and Calendar*, 41).

21. Waltke and O'Connor, *Introduction*, 89. In n. 18, Waltke and O'Connor object to the terms "gemination" and "doubling" and endorse "lengthening" instead on the grounds that the phonetic realization of the "geminated" or "doubled" consonant is not really twice as long as that of the single one, but for our purposes, the conventional terminology need not be replaced. Waltke and O'Connor term this class of noun *nomen occupationis*. These words are, similarly, called *nomina opificum* in Joüon and Muraoka, *Grammar*, 231–32. As the latter work points out, etymologically, the second vowel was not long.

22. See Joüon and Muraoka, *Grammar*, 231–32, for these examples.

23. Note that it cannot be altogether ruled out that the geminated *t* is analogous to the gemination in the inflection of words like *gāmāl* (plural, *gɔmallîm*) or *qāṭān* (feminine, *qɔṭannâ*). For the general process, see Bauer and Leander, *Historische Grammatik*, 424 and 476. The word *mišbattehā* in Lam 1:7, for which there is no strong reason to suspect a connection with Akkadian *šabattu* (on which see below, esp. n. 26) adds some force to this latter possibility.

24. Rechenmacher, "Šabbat[t]," 200–201.

25. The connection is actually much older. See, for example, Jastrow, "Original Character," esp. 315–18. Note, however, that Jastrow thought *šabattu* corresponds, rather, to Hebrew *šabbātôn* (pp. 332–39). Recent examples include Robinson, "Idea of Rest," 40–41, who develops the idea much more in *Origin*, 34–37, 51–89, and Grund, *Entstehung*, 46–49. On the nature of the *šab/pattu*, see especially the latter volume, 106–17. More recently, see the two informative articles by J. L. Wright, "Shabbat of the Full Moon," and "How and When."

26. Rechenmacher, "Šabbat[t]," 202–3. The possibility that the Akkadian word *šab/pattu* itself ultimately derived from the Semitic root *šbt*, perhaps to indicate the day when the waxing of the moon was complete or came to an end, need not concern us. On this, see already Jastrow, "Original Character," 317, and also Robinson, "Idea of Rest," 40–41.

27. See Reiner, "Šapattu," 449–50, and Geller, "Šapattu," 25–27. The scholarly literature identifies the *šabattu* with the fifteenth, although, inasmuch as the synodical month is 29.5 days, either the fourteenth or the fifteenth would display a full moon. For a different view, see North, "Derivation of Sabbath," where he argues for an older etymology for *šabattu* and hence *šabbāt* from the dual for Semitic words for "seven," proposed in Landsberger, *Der kultische Kalender*, 131–36, here 134. On that understanding, the word

would be quite appropriate for "referring to the fourteenth or full-moon day" (North, "Derivation of Sabbath," 196). This etymology has not attracted much support. See, for example, Robinson, *Origin and Development*, 28–29.

28. Rechenmacher, "Šabbat(t)," 203. See also the reference to Bauer and Leander, *Historische Grammatik* in n. 23.

29. The text is CT XVIII 23, 1=K 4369. See Hrůša, *Die akkadische Synonymenliste*, 84. For an early but still valuable discussion, see Landsberger, *Der kultische Kalender*, 131–36. I thank Professor Peter Machinist for generously locating and sending me electronic copies of the Hrůša and Landsberger volumes and directing me to other relevant materials. Among the influential early studies of the *šab/pattu* ~ *šabbāt* issue are Jastrow, "Original Character"; Zimmern, "Sabbath," 199–202; Meinhold, *Sabbat und Woche*, esp. 3–13; and Meinhold, "Entstehung," 81–112, which surveyed a range of discussions of the issue to date. See also his later thoughts in Meinhold, "Zur Sabbathfrage," 121–38, a critique of Karl Budde, and the latter's reply in Budde, "Antwort," 138–45.

30. Jastrow, "Original Character," 316–17.

31. I have treated the concept of resurrection in this story in Levenson, *Resurrection*, 123–32.

32. See b. 'Erub. 51a. The figure derives from Num 35:5.

33. The words "in the biblical narrative" are important because no claim is being here made about chronological priority.

34. It is true that the Talmudic rabbis derive from the husband's words in 2 Kgs 4:23 the norm that "on the New Moon and Sabbath, a man is obligated to pay his respects to his rabbi [or teacher]" (b. Suk. 27b), but in context it is clear that the two individuals are living within the same community. The bereaved mother in this story, however, travels from Shunem to Mount Carmel (2 Kgs 4:25), a distance of a good twenty miles. Sensing the problem, Radaq (Rabbi David Qimchi, 1160–1235, Provence) glosses the husband's words creatively: "'Neither new moon nor sabbath' has passed since you saw him. Why do you have to go to him now?" (Radaq to 2 Kgs 4:23).

35. J. L. Wright, "Shabbat of the Full Moon." See also Robinson, *Origin and Development*, 65, where it is observed that in postexilic texts the Sabbath comes first, "thus maintaining the ascending order of the calendar reckoning."

36. On this passage and the next three to be discussed, see, e.g., Robinson, *Origin and Development*, 51–65; Haag, *Vom Sabbat*, 29–36; and Grund, *Entstehung*, 67–83.

37. Robinson, for example, speaks of the passage as stemming from Amos's school (*Origin and Development*, 54). Jörg Jeremias speaks of its "commentarial character" (Jeremias, *Book of Amos*, 146). Grund regards its secondary character as well recognized (*Entstehung*, 80).

38. I have set the NJPS translation into poetic lines.

39. The consensus is that Jer 17:19–27 is postexilic. See, e.g., Carroll, *Jeremiah*, 367–69; Grund, *Entstehung*, 84, 308; and Robinson, *Origin and Development*, 197–99.

40. As ably argued by Rhyder, "Sabbath and Sanctuary Cult," 731–32.

41. But see ibid., 731 for an argument that the hypothesized monthly *šabbāt* did not entail cessation from labor.

42. Robinson, *Origin and Development*, 56 (emphasis his).

43. The last case was pointed out to me by Allison Hurst.

44. I have put "festival," "new moon," "sabbath," and "festive season" in the singular to reflect the Hebrew more literally and to facilitate the ensuing discussion. The NJPS pluralizes each of them.

45. Wolff, *Hosea*, 38. To support the claim that the week-long festival of the vintage is the main festival of the year at this relatively early date, Wolff refers in n. 54 to Exod 23:16; Judg 21:19ff., and 1 Kgs 12:32. There is no doubt that the fall festival was of great importance, but these texts do not warrant the conclusion that the others, such as the Feast of Unleavened Bread, were of lesser significance.

46. See Hasel, "'New Moon,'" 41–42.

47. I have changed the NJPS "set times" in v. 4 to "fixed times" the better to reflect the identity of phrasing between v. 2 and v. 4.

48. Such a vision of an eschatological procession fits nicely with the universalistic thrust in postexilic and early Second Temple literature. On this, see Weinfeld, "Universalism," 228–42.

49. Note also its oft-remarked affinity with Isa 56:1–8, the beginning of the postexilic Third Isaiah, according to scholars who believe in such a division of the book. The affinity suggests a kind of *inclusio*, with the opening and closing of Third Isaiah both focused on the ritual incorporation of outsiders (whatever such incorporation was taken to entail) and the observance of the Sabbath.

50. Robinson (*Origin and Development*, 74–89) includes an elaborate discussion of two other passages in this category, 2 Kgs 11:4–12 and 16:18, but Grund (*Entstehung*, 89–92) is in my judgment on sounder ground in finding these texts too obscure to base anything on them.

51. So, for example, Robinson, *Origin and Development*, 166, and Grund, *Entstehung*, 176.

52. Whether the *šabattu/šapattu* fell on the fourteenth or fifteenth of the month has been contested among scholars. See North, "Derivation," 134, for an etymological argument that it coincided with the fourteenth of the month. As noted above (n. 27), this has not met with general acceptance.

53. See https://en.wikipedia.org/wiki/Time_zone.

54. Exod 31:15; 35:2; Lev 23:24; 16:31; 23:32; 23:39.

55. Also J. L. Wright, "Shabbat of the Full Moon."

56. J. L. Wright, "How and When." See also Wright's first essay in the sequence, "Shabbat."

57. Lev 23:39; Num 29:12.

58. Jastrow, "Original Character," 316.

59. Ibid., 318. A full account and critique of Jastrow's philological assumptions and arguments (e.g., about Hebrew *šabbātôn* as the actual cognate with Akkadian *šabattum*, the earlier and fuller form of *šabattu*, pp. 332–34) are not necessary here. Importantly, Geller ("Šapattu," 26) notes that only one text has been found for which Jastrow's understanding of the day as one of pacification of the god's anger is appropriate.

60. Jastrow, "Original Character," 324–26.

61. See Westermann, *Isaiah 40–66*, 336–37. But see also Childs, *Isaiah*, 478, where it is claimed that "the ritual of fasting is not rejected out of hand, but redefined by enlarging its parameters."

62. Jastrow, "Original Character," 324.

63. Num 29:7–11, which specifies the communal offerings for Yom Kippur, is read from a second Torah scroll between these two passages.

64. Jastrow, "Original Character," 324.

65. Ibid., 324–25. On the Puritan Sabbath, see Shulevitz, *Sabbath World*, 141–50.

66. See b. Ḥul. 111b.

67. See, for example, *Mekhilta de-Rabbi Ishmael, vayyassaʿ* 5, where the law is midrashically derived from the three appearances of *hayyôm* ("today") in Exod 16:25. Yitzhak Gilat points out that this enumeration actually comes from advancing the evening meal to a time before sunset, so that it is consumed during the Sabbath. Gilat, "On Fasting," 8n44. On the three mandatory meals, see below, pp. 147–50.

68. Gilat, "On Fasting."

69. On the Sabbath as a day of self-denial in Second Temple Judaism, see below, pp. 137–41 and note especially Simkovich, "Intimacy."

70. All translations from Jubilees in this book are taken from VanderKam, *Jubilees*, 1192. For more on this, see below, pp. 147–50.

71. Gilat, "On Fasting," 3–4.

72. He also makes no exception for other festive days, such as Passover, Rosh ha-Shanah, Sukkot, the Eighth Day of Assembly, Chanukkah, and Rosh Chodesh (the day of the new moon).

73. Gilat, "On Fasting," 5, with reference in particular to the passage also on b. Pesaḥ. 68b (as well as b. Beṣah 15b) that speaks of the dispute between Rabbi Eliezer and Rabbi Joshua. Gilat argues that the dispute is about the Sabbath and not only festivals (n. 18).

74. Gilat, "On Fasting," 11–15.

75. *Oraḥ Ḥayîm, Hilḵôt Šabbāt* 288:1.

76. "Mishnah" here may mean the study of the Oral Torah more broadly and not simply the collection that goes by that name. Helping the midrashist make his point (which is obviously not the plain sense of the verse) is the fact that the word after the last one he quotes is *vəḵibbadtô* ("and if you honor it"), which, out of context, can be understood as "you will honor Him." On the importance of copious and delectable food and drink on the Sabbath in (rabbinic) Jewish tradition, see Horowitz, "Sabbath Delights," 131–37.

77. See the observation of Geller, "Šapattu," 26, in n. 59 above.

78. Jastrow, "Original Character," 324.

79. Note, however, that as the forty-ninth day since the start of the previous month (if the latter had thirty days), it is, like the other numbers listed, divisible by seven.

80. Jastrow, "Original Character," 351. See also Zimmern, "Sabbath," 200–201.

81. North, "Derivation," 190.

82. For an explanation of what I mean by "covenantal monotheism," see Levenson, *Creation*, 135–39, and Levenson, *Love of God*, 1–58.

83. Jastrow, "Original Character," 319.

84. See Gilat, "On Fasting."

85. Achenbach, "*Lex Sacra*," 101. I have omitted the Hebrew words to gloss "new moon" and "*Shabbat*" and Achenbach's list of supporting verses, none of which actually establishes the identity of "*Shabbat*" that he assumes here.

86. Rhyder, "Sabbath and Sanctuary Cult," 731.

87. See, for example, Andreasen, *Rest and Redemption*, 27–28. Unfortunately, Andreasen's assumption that the Sabbath always and only referred to the concluding day of a seven-day unit is exactly what needs to be established. Note as well the unstinting judgment of Matitiahu Tsevat that "this speculation has led nowhere" in Tsevat, "Basic Meaning," 457n29. It would seem, however, that the speculation has led productively to a reasonable, if necessarily uncertain, etymology of *šabbāt*, though not—and this is a different matter—to a defensible claim that the weekly institution to which the word came exclusively to refer has a strong pre-Israelite antecedent in the Mesopotamian institution. See also Hasel, "'New Moon,'" 37–64.

88. E.g., Josh 10:13; 2 Kgs 4:6; Exod 23:5; Judg 15:7; 1 Sam 15:16; Ps 46:11.

89. Waltke and O'Connor, *Introduction*, 89.

90. Haag, *Vom Sabbat*, 41. On the use of the feminine for abstraction, see Waltke and O'Connor, *Introduction*, 102 and 104–5. No claim is made here that *šabbāt(t)* fits perfectly into any known Hebrew paradigm. See the critique of Haag in Rechenmacher, "Šabbat[t]," 199.

91. Here, an important caveat must be entered. It cannot be assumed that the calendar appearing in Lev 23 or in Priestly tradition more generally was lunar. The evidence for a solar calendar in use by those sources and elsewhere in ancient Israel before the late Second Temple period has been growing. See, for example, Guillaume, *Land and Calendar*, 42–45; Ben-Dov, "360-Day," 431–50; and Stackert, "Priestly Sabbath," 50–58.

92. Rabbinic tradition requires all Jews living in cities that were walled at the time of Joshua bin Nun to observe the fifteenth of the month, which is known as "Shushan Purim," and that Purim occur in the last month of the year, which, in the case of a leap year, means the thirteenth month (Adar II).

93. See pp. 52–53.

94. Hasel, "New Moon," 49, and Dahood, *Psalms 51–100*, 264. (Dahood uses the terminology "Passover" and "Tabernacles," though in the biblical nomenclature "Passover"/*pesah* refers to the sacrifice that *precedes* the Festival of Unleavened Bread / *maṣṣôt*.)

95. Hasel, "New Moon," 46–47.

96. Kraeling, "Present State," 224.

97. Weber, *Ancient Judaism*, 150.

Chapter 3

1. "Atra-ḫasis," *COS* 1.130:451.

2. See Hallo, "New Moons," 4–9, who notes a tendency, at least early on, not to take account for this purpose of the third lunar crescent (p. 6).

3. Ibid., 8.

4. See, e.g., Andreasen, *Rest and Redemption*, 13–14; Robinson, *Origin and Development*, 159–66; Wagner, *Profanität*, 21; Grund, *Entstehung*, 110–12.

5. The connection appears, e.g., in J. L. Wright, "How and When."

6. See pp. 8–12, 41.

7. Wagner, *Profanität*, 21; Nowack, *Schabbat*, 9–10.

8. See pp. 39–42.

9. Nowack, *Schabbat*, 9–10; Grund, *Entstehung*, 112n684.

10. E.g., Exod 12:18; Ezek 45:18–25.

11. Hallo, "New Moons," 11.

12. Ibid., 16.

13. A note in the NJPS explains that *vayqaṭṭēr*, "and he offered," has been changed to "to make offerings." Cf. LXX *ethumíon*, "they were burning incense."

14. Hallo, "New Moons," 10. On the same page, he speaks of "the terminal edge of a long evolution," which, though accurate, does not capture the violence of the process.

15. The same chronology appears in the schedule of sacrifices in Num 28:16–17 and 29:12.

16. Hallo, "New Moons," 10n47. See Ginsberg, *Israelian Heritage*, 44n59. Here, the relevant texts are Exod 13:4; 23:15; 34:18; and Deut 16:1, in all of which the expression *ḥōdeš hāʾābîb* signifies not the whole month of Aviv but rather its first day, the day of the

new moon. For the insight that the expression requires "an exact calendar date," Ginsberg credits Ehrlich, *Randglossen*, 312–13 (on Exod 13:4).

17. In this last case, the position is that of the House of Hillel. The House of Shammai dates the New Year for Trees (which has to do with tithing) to the first of Shevat instead.

18. See above, p. 232, n. 91.

19. In the solar calendar of the sort referred to in the previous note, the difference between 360 days (i.e., twelve months of thirty days each) and the solar year was mitigated by the addition of intercalary days inserted after every three months.

20. "Never" is a big word. No calendar perfectly matches the astronomical events, but the author is eminently confident that no adjustment of the Jewish calendar will take place in his lifetime or that of his likely readers, to whom he nonetheless wishes long lives.

21. See McCurley, "'After Six Days,'" 71–73, and Grund, *Entstehung*, 32–37.

22. "Gilgamesh," *COS* 1.132:459.

23. "Gilgamesh," *COS* 1.132:460. Foster (460n5) notes that the cuneiform for the name of the mountain could also be read as Niṣir, which appears in the latter's translation. On this passage, see Loewenstamm, "Seven-Day-Unit," 192–93, and Hallo, "Information," 178, who amassed evidence for what he considers "explicit references to an antediluvian week" in Mesopotamian sources (179). It would be more precise, however, to speak of a seven-day unit rather than a "week," given that the flow of time here is not routinely and without exception divided into successive units of seven days.

24. See, e.g., Heidel, *Gilgamesh*, 251–53.

25. See McCurley, "'After Six Days,'" 70–71.

26. See Loewenstamm, "Seven-Day-Unit," 193–204; Kapelrud, "Number Seven," 494–99; McCurley, "'After Six Days,'" 68–70; and Grund, *Entstehung*, 32–33.

27. "The Baʿlu Myth," *COS* 1.86:261.

28. Ibid., n. 174.

29. See Fisher, "Temple Quarter," 40–41; and Fisher, "Creation at Ugarit," 316–20.

30. Kapelrud, "Number Seven," 495.

31. Ibid., 498 (emphasis original).

32. Note that the pattern extends beyond the ancient Near East. It can, for example, be found in the Homeric epics as well; some instances appear in *Odyssey* 10.76–83; 12.397–402; and 14.249–52.

33. Smith, *Priestly Vision*, 88. The text is RS 1.003 (and the nearly identical RS 18.056). For a transliteration, translation, reconstruction, and discussion, see Pardee, *Ritual and Cult*, 56–67. For a fuller discussion, see Pardee, *Textes Rituels*, 143–213, and note the vocalization presented on 151–52.

34. Pardee, *Ritual and Cult*, 65. These are lines 47–48.

35. Ibid., 106n74.

36. Smith, *Priestly Vision*, 88.

37. See Goodfriend, "Seven."

38. "The Kirta Epic," *COS* 1.102:335.

39. See Goodfriend, "Seven."

40. E.g., Lev 8:33 and 9:1; 14:8–10, 23; 15:13–15; 15:28–30; 22:26–28; Num 6:9–12.

41. See chap. 2, n. 1.

42. On this passage, see especially Grund, *Entstehung*, 19–21.

43. The longstanding question of how, if at all, vv. 4–5 fit into this context need not occupy us here. My sense is that the principal connection is the danger of giving rein

to one's personal feelings without a proper, objective determination of the underlying facts, with the possible result that one gains financially at the expense of a potentially innocent person. Note also the concern for animals in the laws of the seventh year and of the seventh day that follow—wild animals in v. 11 and farm animals in v. 12. Whatever the compositional history of the whole chapter may be (and on that we are reduced to speculation), given the lexical echoes of these two verses in vv. 10–12 (see below), it would be unwise to treat vv. 4–5 as foreign bodies in their present location.

44. According to Jeffrey Stackert, "Although often read otherwise, Exod 23:10–11 does not command land fallowing. These verses actually require the planting and harvesting of the land in the seventh year and the donation of the seventh-year yield to the poor. Moreover, the accounting of years in the CC [i.e., "Covenant Collection/Code"] is not standard but instead applies to fields individually" (Stackert, "Sabbath of the Land," 244). Whether this is so depends on a number of questions, especially how we are to interpret the verbs *tišmᵊṭennāh ûnᵊṭaštāh* (rendered above as "you shall let it rest and lie fallow") in v. 11. The terms suggest relinquishment and abandonment. Nothing in the passage indicates that sowing and gathering are to take place in the seventh year, as in the previous six, or that an affirmative act of donation to the poor or wild beasts is to take place. Indeed, the fact that v. 11 begins with the noun *haššᵊbîʿît* ("in the seventh") suggests a contrast with the preceding verse, which speaks of sowing and gathering. With regard to *haššᵊbîʿît*, note the interesting suggestion of Rabbi Abraham ibn Ezra (twelfth century) in his longer commentary on Exodus, in which he draws attention to Neh 10:32, where "the seventh year" (*haššānâ haššᵊbîʿît*) is the object of the verb *niṭṭōš*. Ibn Ezra argues that, analogously, *haššᵊbîʿît* in Exod 23:11 is the object of *tišmᵊṭennāh ûnᵊṭaštāh*. In that case, it is the whole seventh year that is foregone. More likely in my opinion, this is an instance in which, as Gesenius puts it, "the suffix of the 3rd person singular feminine . . . refers in a general sense to the verbal idea contained in a preceding sentence." If so, then it is the activities of the previous clause (sowing and gathering) that are foregone in the seventh year (cf. *GKC*, 440). As for Stackert's claim that the norm "applies to fields individually," although this is the plain sense of Exod 23:10–11, it may not have been the practical expectation. See Robinson, *Origin and Development*, 116–17: "every individual could not have had his private *šᵊmiṭṭāh* in such a well-knit community as that of ancient Israel. Moreover, a little knowledge of primitive agriculture will show the impracticability of leaving a small piece of the land fallow for the use of the poor and the wild animals, when the surrounding fields are cultivated and ripe with crops." On both points, see Propp, *Exodus 19–40*, 280.

45. For a more detailed breakdown of the formal structure of the passage, see Grund, *Entstehung*, 23–24.

46. Ibid., 21.

47. Ibid., 22.

48. See Propp, *Exodus 19–40*, 186–88.

49. Grund, *Entstehung*, 51. My translation.

50. She also relies on Isa 32:17; 65:22; and Hab 3:17. Ibid., 26n42. It should be noted, however, that Isa 65:22 mentions building and not just planting and, more generally, that *maʿᵃśeh* can refer to other activities, such as those of a baker (Gen 40:17) and, again, a builder (Exod 5:4, 13).

51. *Entstehung*, 58–63. Grund is correct, though, in her rejection of the effort to connect the whole verse specifically with the Feast of Unleavened Bread mentioned in v. 18. On the early dating, see Robinson, *Origin and Development*, 126–34 and Haag, *Vom Sabbat,*

7–11. The latter argues that Exod 34:21 predates 23:12, but, as often in such matters, the evidence to sustain the argument is slim.

52. But note the Talmudic argument that Exod 34:21c actually refers to the sabbatical year in b. Roš Haš. 9a.

53. If one prefers to scan by accented syllables, the pattern remains the same: 3/3/3.

54. See, e.g., Arnold and Choi, *Guide*, 182–83.

55. Gesundheit, *Three Times a Year*, 36.

56. Ibid., 22.

57. Ibid., 21, adducing Leviticus 23 and Numbers 28–29 as evidence. The way that Lev 23:3 interrupts the list of holidays does offer a good analogy to the process Gesundheit hypothesizes to underlie Exodus 34, though it would seem that even there, the Priestly (or Holiness) source originally lacked mention of the Sabbath (hence, our word "interrupts"). In the case of Num 28–29, though, it would have been odd to omit mention of the Sabbath offerings (listed in 28:9–10) in a list that includes the sacrifices for all other days—weekdays, new moons, and festivals.

58. Ibid.

59. See pp. 129–31.

60. Exod 31:14–15; 35:2; Num 15:35.

61. De Vaux, *Ancient Israel*, 479–80. The French original was issued in 1958.

62. Grund, *Entstehung*, 164.

63. Although de Vaux was a Frenchman, my sense is that his position even then commanded more agreement in America or Israel than in Europe and that today it is the view of a distinct minority in all three places.

64. De Vaux, *Ancient Israel*, 479.

65. E. g., Baden, *Composition*.

66. Note also the contrast in 2 Macc 6:11 and the discussion of the differences in Goldstein, *II Maccabees*, 279–80. On the question of warfare on the Sabbath in Maccabees and Jubilees, see pp. 151–55, above.

67. See pp. 25–26, 45–46.

68. But note that in 2 Kgs 11:5, 7, and 9, the NJPS renders the word as "week."

69. See Robinson, *Origin and Development*, 74–89; Haag, *Vom Sabbat*, 30–34; Grund, *Entstehung*, 89–91. Whether the references are to a weekly or a monthly event is again unclear. On this, see Robinson, *Origin and Development*, 79–80. On the other hand, Robinson's conclusion that these allusions give evidence of a lunar cult connected to kingship goes well beyond what can be reliably inferred from the data we have.

70. See Hossfeld, *Dekalog*. Note his detailed discussion of variations on 21–162 and the summary of his overall reconstruction in his "Biography of the Decalogue" on 283–84. See also Weinfeld, *Deuteronomy 1–11*, 304–5.

71. See Cross, *Canaanite Myth*, 274–87.

72. Exod 31:14–15; 35:2; Num 15:35; Isa 56:2–8. I use "Priestly" here in the broader sense that includes the Holiness Source as a subset and recasting of Priestly tradition. On the Holiness Source as the origin of the first three passages, see Knohl, *Sanctuary of Silence*, 15–18, 53, but also Blum, "Issues and Problems."

73. See Grund, *Entstehung*, 95, on a putative but highly doubtful Assyrian reference.

74. A transcription, translation, and commentary are found in Dobbs-Allsopp, *Hebrew Inscriptions*, 358–70.

75. Ibid., 359. These are line 5 and the beginning of line 6. Pardee renders the sentence as "Your servant did his reaping, finished, and stored (the grain) a few days ago before

stopping (work)" ("The Meṣad Ḥashavyahu [Yavneh Yam] Ostracon," COS 3.41:77). For our interest, which involves only to the last two words of the inscription, the differences are immaterial.

76. Cross, "Epigraphic Notes," 44n45.

77. See pp. 20–21.

78. As pointed out by Dobbs-Allsopp, *Hebrew Inscriptions*, 362.

79. Grund, *Entstehung*, 94n559.

80. So also ibid., 94.

81. See Robinson, *Origin and Development*, 90–92; Grund, *Entstehung*, 92–95. Grund interprets *šbt* here as *šabbāt* but then sees the latter as largely a semantically neutral indication of time (95). That the laborer ceases his work just before *šabbāt* does not strike me, however, as semantically neutral. Granerød takes a similar position. "Provided that the phrase *lpny šbt* actually means 'before the Sabbath,'" he writes, "it cannot be said what kind of Sabbath the Yabneh-Yam ostracon referred to" (Granerød, *Dimensions of Yahwism*, 188). Given the ample biblical literature about the Sabbath from this period or possibly even earlier, such minimalism may be unwarranted.

82. See Granerød, *Dimensions of Yahwism*, 26–27, who wisely stresses that it is "important to state that any suggestion [as to the origin of the Elephantine Judean community] will have to be tentative because of the lack of data" (27).

83. Van der Toorn, *Becoming Diaspora Jews*, 30.

84. On the Sabbath at Elephantine, see, e.g., Porten, "Religion of the Jews," esp. 116–18; Doering, *Schabbat*, 23–42; Becking, "Sabbath at Elephantine," 177–89; Granerød, *Dimensions of Yahwism*, 182–206.

85. CG 44, concave side line 5. For transcription and discussion, see Lozachmeur, *Collection Clermont-Ganneau*, 1:214–16. For photos, see 2:pl. 123. Similarly for CG 186, convex side line 1 (see Lozachmeur, *Collection Clermont-Ganneau*, 1:335–37, and 2:pl. 216) and CG 204, convex side line 5. For transcription and discussion, see Lozachmeur, *Collection Clermont-Ganneau*, 1:352–53. For photos, see 2:pls. 228–229.

86. CG 152, concave side lines 1–5. See Lozachmeur, *Collection Clermont-Ganneau*, 1:303–5, and 2:pl. 190–91. The translation is from Porten, "Religion of the Jews," 116 (I have preserved only the words from the transliteration that are relevant to our discussion.) See also Rosenthal, *Aramaic Handbook*, 12–13. On the vexed question of the interpretation of this letter, see Doering, *Schabbat*, 29–32; and Becking, "Sabbath at Elephantine," 186.

87. For example, Doering, *Schabbat*, 30.

88. See pp. 26–27. The specific passages are Amos 8:4–7; Jer 17:19–27; and Neh 10:32 and 13:15–22. The last Nehemiah texts specifically mention foodstuffs.

89. Granerød, *Dimensions of Yahwism*, 195.

90. Y. Adler, *Origins of Judaism*, 144.

91. Porten, "Religion of the Jews," 117–18. More recently, Porten's position has been endorsed by Bloch, "Judean Identity," 57. Note Bloch's argument, based on comparative calendrical calculations, that Jews at Elephantine waited until after the Sabbath was over to sign contracts ("Judean Identity," 58–66). Also, especially relevant to the question of commerce on the Sabbath at Elephantine is CG 186. See Lozachmeur, *Collection Clermont-Ganneau*, 1:335–37, and 2:pls. 216 and 217. Porten's conclusion is that "the possible dispatch of fish and the individual's arrival before the day of the Sabbath may indicate a deliberate unwillingness to profane the Sabbath by travelling or dispatching an object on that day" (Porten, "Religion of the Jews," 118). Similarly, Dupont-Sommer sees

the key line of this ostracon (the first on the convex side) as stipulating that the delivery of the merchandise needs to be discharged before the Sabbath begins. See Dupont-Sommer, "Ostracon Araméen," 407–8.

92. Doering, *Schabbat*, 31–32, 34.

93. Ibid., 40–42.

94. See the relatively balanced view of Becking ("Sabbath at Elephantine," 186): "This ostracon indicates that on the day of the Sabbath, there obviously existed some trade in grocery ware. It might, however, be that this was a case of emergency.... Problematical in this interpretation is that the inscription does not hint at a case of emergency and that it contains no language of apology for trespassing the Sabbath. On the other hand, however, to conclude that this ostracon reflects standard procedures in Elephantine is premature. What can be adduced is the fact that at least a few Yehudites had no moral or religious problems with trade on a Sabbath." But has there ever been a time when *all* Yehudites/Jews had moral or religious problems with trade on the Sabbath?

95. Ezek 20:12–24; 22:6–31; 23:36–39.

96. See pp. 26–29.

97. Doering, *Schabbat*, 38. See his whole discussion on 36–39.

98. Granerød, *Dimensions of Yahwism*, 201.

99. Doering, *Schabbat*, 38–39.

100. Porten, "Religion of the Jews," 117.

101. Bloch, "Judean Identity," 46–52. Bloch is challenged on this by Tammuz, "Sabbath," 287–94, to whom he then replies in Bloch, "Was the Sabbath," 117–20.

102. Bloch, "Judean Identity," 55.

103. See chap. 2, n. 17, and McKay, "New Moon or Sabbath?," esp. 19–22.

104. Wellhausen, *Prolegomena*, 116. For a much more recent statement along the same lines, see, e.g., Robinson, *Origin and Development*, 166.

105. Grund, *Entstehung*, 306 (my translation).

106. Y. Adler, *Origins of Judaism*, 145.

107. Ezek 1:2. On the Sabbath in the Book of Ezekiel, see Robinson, *Origin and Development*, 202–15, and Haag, *Vom Sabbat*, 99–105.

108. See Robinson, *Origin and Development*, esp. 205–9, and Bauks, "Le Shabbat," 480–85.

109. I have dealt with this in part in Levenson, "When Did Judaism Begin?"

110. See Tsevat, "Basic Meaning," 447–59, and Brichto, *Names of God*, 399.

111. Grund, *Entstehung*, 25–26.

112. E.g., Lev 23:9–14.

113. Tsevat, "Basic Meaning," 455.

114. Num 18; Deut 18:1–5.

115. On this verse and its underlying conceptuality and rich repercussions in Judaism and Christianity alike, see Anderson, *Charity*.

116. E.g., Exod 16:23; 20:8; Deut 5:12; Ezek 44:24 (NJPS: "maintain the sanctity of My Sabbaths"); Neh 9:14.

Chapter 4

1. Exod 34:28; Deut 4:13 and 10:4.

2. See the useful charts in *Jewish Study Bible*, 141 and 357, and Sarna, *Exodus*, 108.

3. There is variation regarding the enumeration of verses in the Decalogues. Our references correspond to those in the NJPS.

4. The exception appears in the poem of Deut 33 (v. 2), where "Sinai" would seem to refer to an area to the southeast of the Land of Israel and not to the mountain of revelation.

5. The interpretation originates early in rabbinic tradition. See Mek. of Rabbi Ishmael, *baḥodeš* 7.

6. Such is the most common translation, though the NJPS, not without reason, reads "the LORD alone."

7. Again, altered from the NJPS to underscore the similarity of the Hebrew in the two verses.

8. See J. J. Cohen, "Order," 321–57. Pages 342–53 deal specifically with the hymn. On the elaborate mystical meanings of this deceptively simple poem, see Kimelman, *Mystical Meaning*. On the historical evolution and theological meaning of the larger ceremony of welcoming the Sabbath, see Green, "Some Aspects," 95–118. On the interpretation of the Sabbath as a foretaste of redemption, see chap. 7, below.

9. E.g., Exod 31:18; Deut 4:13; 1 Kgs 8:9.

10. Sarna, *Exodus*, 108. These are the figures for the version in Exodus, but the proportion would not be much different for Deuteronomy.

11. Reported in the longer commentary of Abraham ibn Ezra (on Exod 20:1).

12. See p. 18.

13. Childs, *Book of Exodus*, 394–95.

14. For a review of theories of the origin, development, and variations in the Decalogue(s), see Grund, *Entstehung*, 154–57, and Otto, *Deuteronomium 1–11*, 2:684–89.

15. Hossfeld, *Dekalog*, especially the detailed discussion of variations on pp. 21–162 and the summary of his overall reconstruction in the "Biography of the Decalogue" on pp. 283–84.

16. On the synoptic problem of the very different versions of the Sabbath commandment in particular, see ibid., 33–57.

17. Grund, *Entstehung*, 155–56.

18. Lohfink, "Decalogue," 251.

19. See Weinfeld, *Deuteronomy 1–11*, 305, for a convincing refutation of Hossfeld's view that the "citation formula" of Deut 5:12 actually refers to Exod 23:12 and 34:21.

20. Nelson, *Deuteronomy*, 82–83. I have taken the term "source citation formula" from Nelson.

21. Lohfink, *Theology*, 251.

22. I have changed "the stranger within your settlements" in Deut 5:14 (NJPS) to "the stranger who is within your settlements" to reflect the fact that the wording is identical to that of Exod 20:10. I have changed "to observe" in the NJPS rendering of Deut 5:15 to "to practice" in order to capture the fact that the verb (*'āśâ*) is not the same as the one with which this version of the commandment opens (*šāmar*). For an argument that supports the ultimate congruity of the two versions of the Decalogue, see Brichto, *Names of God*, 397–412.

23. I have changed the NJPS, which renders the second half colon as "remember to observe" precisely because of the gap in English between "remember" and "observe." My translation is more literal and brings out the overlap for which Weinfeld is arguing.

24. The point is stated nicely in Propp, *Exodus 19–40*, 175: "It seems, moreover, that the root illustrates the point well."

25. Weinfeld, *Deuteronomy 1–11*, 302–3.

26. See Deut 11:22; 13:19; 15:5; 24:8; 28:1, 13, 15; and 32:46.

27. Weinfeld, *Deuteronomy 1–11*, 303 (emphasis original).

28. Ibid.

29. Alluding to some version of the story now found in Num 12:1–15.

30. Lohfink, *Theology*, 252–53, who is followed by Nelson, *Deuteronomy*, 82. I have taken the diagram from Nelson, with adjustments to reflect the translation of the commandment that appears in our discussion and to highlight the correspondences.

31. This is all the more the case if we adopt the wording of a Dead Sea Scroll (4QDeut^n) and the Septuagint, which read something on the order of ləqaddəšô, "and keep it holy," at the end of v. 15. See Weinfeld, *Deuteronomy 1–11*, 281 and 304. Given the harmonistic character of 4QDeut^n, however, its worth as a text-critical witness is highly doubtful. See White, "4QDeut^n," 13–20. White concludes that 4QDeut^n is "a text made and used for some devotional and/or study purpose" (17) rather than a biblical manuscript. Similarly, see Eshel, "4QDeut^n," esp. 128–29.

32. Grund, *Entstehung*, 181.

33. The first two passages are Deut 6:4–9 and 11:13–21. The following line is inserted after Deut 6:4: "Blessed be the name of His glorious kingship forever and ever." In classical Jewish law, because the obligation as such is dependent on the time of day, it falls only on men.

34. On the dating of Deuteronomy, see Weinfeld, *Deuteronomy 1–11*, 16–19.

35. See pp. 59–61.

36. In Exod 23:12, the NJPS renders the phrase as "your ox and your ass," but the Hebrew wording is identical in the two verses.

37. See the examples cited in Weinfeld, *Deuteronomy 1–11*, 308.

38. See Deut 22:1–3; 22:10; and 28:31, in addition to the second appearance of the pair in the prohibition on coveting (5:18).

39. Lohfink, *Theology*, 255.

40. Ibid., 255–56.

41. Lohfink, *Theology*, 258.

42. Ibid., 256–57. See also Nelson, *Deuteronomy*, 81–82.

43. As delineated in Nelson, *Deuteronomy*, 82n7.

44. See n. 1, above.

45. See n. 2, above. This is true whether one follows the Jewish tradition that begins the second utterance at Deut 5:7 or the one that begins it at 5:8. In my judgment, the latter verse constitutes an interpolation that begins a new commandment, and vv. 9–10 originally referred to the "other gods" of v. 7. Perhaps Lohfink, a Jesuit priest, was influenced by the Roman Catholic tradition of treating vv. 6–10 as one unit.

46. See n. 38, above.

47. Lohfink, *Theology*, 264.

48. Ibid., 259.

49. See above, pp. 74–75.

50. I have changed "in the land" in Deut 5:16 to "on the land" in order to avoid a false contrast with the identical preposition in Exod 20:12.

51. Lohfink, *Theology*, 262.

52. Apart from the synonymous ʾăšer yîṭab lāk (Deut 4:40 and 6:3).

53. The three verses are Deut 12:25, 12:18, and 22:7. I thank Allison Hurst for this observation.

54. Lev 23:3, 24, 32, and 39. As noted earlier (see p. 30), the resumptive repetition in Lev 23:4 suggests that the sabbatical law of v. 3 was a later interpolation. This does not obviate the fact that no parallel alteration was made in Deuteronomy 16.

55. Grund, *Entstehung*, 171.

56. See pp. 68–69.

57. Idan Dershowitz, based on his work with the controversial Shapira fragments of Deuteronomy (which he believes to be authentic), argues that the two canonical versions of the Decalogue as well as the suspiciously parallel passage of Leviticus 19 have a common ancestor in the text preserved in those fragments. See the transcription of the sabbatical commandment in Dershowitz, *Valediction of Moses*, 73, 72–87.

58. I have changed "declared it holy" in the NJPS to Gen 2:3 to match the translation "hallowed" in Exod 20:11. Both verses use a piel of the root *qdš*.

59. See pp. 19–23.

60. The version that Dershowitz believes to be an authentic predecessor of the canonical Decalogues begins with *qdš*, "Sanctify." See Dershowitz, *Valediction of Moses*, 73.

61. See Levenson, *Hebrew Bible*, 62–81.

Chapter 5

1. Much of the discussion on this theme and throughout this chapter is an extension and refinement of my argument in Levenson, *Creation*. On the combat myth, see esp. pp. 3–50. The most famous discussion of the combat myth (German *Chaoskampf*) is Gunkel, *Schöpfung und Chaos*. Gunkel's classic appears in an English translation by William Whitney Jr., with a foreword by Peter Machinist, as *Creation and Chaos*.

2. See Clifford, "Hebrew Scriptures."

3. See "The Ba'alu Myth," *COS* 1.86:241–74. Gunkel discusses such passages at length in *Creation and Chaos*, 21–77, but, living before the great discovery of ancient Ugarit, he missed the West Semitic and disproportionately stressed the Mesopotamian origins of the motif.

4. I have developed the larger theological implications of this point at some length in *Creation*, 17–20.

5. A point I had to stress in the preface to the second edition of *Creation* (pp. xv–xxviii), against a dangerous (if currently convenient) misunderstanding of the first edition.

6. The translation is from Nickelsburg and VanderKam, *1 Enoch 2*, 233.

7. The translation is from Sacks, *Koren Siddur*, 767.

8. Classically analyzed in Gunkel, *Creation and Chaos*, 115–250. The identification of the dragon with the "serpent," "the Devil," and "Satan" appears in Rev 12:9.

9. See also Isa 66:22.

10. Ricoeur, *Symbolism of Evil*, 203.

11. NJPS reads "your channels," since the oracle is addressed to the monster.

12. This is not to deny, of course, that the sea monster was sometimes considered a creature of God and thus (at the moment) harmless. This is certainly the case in Ps 104, where we hear of "Leviathan that You formed to sport with" (v. 26), and it may be true of "the great sea monsters" (*hattannînîm haggədōlîm*) created on the fifth day of the primordial week in Gen 1:21 (the only specific species singled out for mention in the opening creation story of the Bible), as we shall soon observe. Our attention here lies, instead, on the more abundant texts in which the chaos monster remains, or can become, a threat to God's good order. On this, see Levenson, *Creation*, 14–25 and 53–55.

13. Adducing an analogy with the Babylonian New Year festival (*akitu*) is now conventional. On this, see Tadmor, "New Year," cols. 305–11.

14. Seligman et al., *Ritual*, 7, 8 (emphasis original). It is because the volume was "in every sense of the term, written by all the authors together . . . consensually" (x) that I simply use "Seligman" as shorthand for all four.

15. Ibid., 14.

16. Tambiah, *Performative Approach*, 124.

17. Ibid., 21, 22.

18. Ibid., 22.

19. Ibid., 25–26.

20. Ibid., 26.

21. Veyne, *Did the Greeks Believe*, 18.

22. See, e.g., Ps 26:1, 6, 11.

23. I have addressed this example in Levenson, "Response," 180–82.

24. Seligman, *Ritual*, 25–26.

25. Ibid.

26. Exod 23:14–17; 34:23; Deut 16:16–17.

27. On God's putative completion of the work on the seventh day, as Gen 2:2 has suggested to some over the centuries, see McCurley, "After Six Days," 81, and Jacob, *Das Buch Genesis*, 64–65.

28. Exod 23:12; 31:17.

29. See pp. 22–23.

30. Veyne, *Did the Greeks Believe*, 18.

31. The Mekhilta quotes Isa 58:13–14 in abbreviated form but, as often, probably intends the reference to be to the entire passage.

32. Saiman, *Halakhah*, 85.

33. Diddams, Surdyk, and Daniels, "Rediscovering Models," 4.

34. See the comment reported in the name of Bar Qappara in Gen. Rab. 1:5. It is a fine example of the painful collision of theological expectation with the stubborn reality of the scriptural text itself.

35. Middleton, "Creation," 61.

36. Enuma Elish IV:137–138. See Foster, *Before the Muses*, 462. On larger signs of indebtedness of the Priestly creation account to the Enuma Elish, see Speiser, *Genesis*, 9–10.

37. Albeit with a different verb, *bāqaʿ* as opposed to *hibdîl*. Source critics identify these verses with the same source as that of Gen 1:1–2:4a.

38. Levenson, *Creation*, 53–54. See also pp. 16–17.

39. Smith, *Priestly Vision*, 64.

40. Ibid., 60, citing a personal communication.

41. Ibid., 61.

42. The other occurrence is in Isa 34:11, where the pair is broken up into parallel poetic lines and the context is again one of the LORD's devastating anger as he wreaks judgment, this time upon Edom in recompense for its sins against Israel.

43. Like Gen 1:1–2:3, this verse has long been ascribed to P.

44. Smith, *Priestly Vision*, 64.

45. Seligman, *Ritual*, 7, 8 (emphasis original).

46. See Propp, *Exodus 19–40*, 675–76, and the ample bibliography he provides.

47. Janowski, "Tempel und Schöpfung," 40.

48. Ibid., 40–46. For a well-known Egyptian example of the connection of temple-building to creation, see "The Instruction Addressed to King Merikare," (which records [*AEL*, 106] that "[the god] subdued the water monster / . . . He slew his foes, reduced

his children, / When they thought of making rebellion . . . He has built his shrine around them / When they weep, he hears."

49. See, for example, Schäfer, "Tempel und Schöpfung," 122–33; Green, "Sabbath as Temple," 287–305; and Levenson, *Creation,* 90–99.

50. Foster, *Before the Muses,* 470.

51. Ibid., 471n2.

52. Enuma Elish VI:67–76.

53. Levenson, "Temple," 275–98; Levenson, "Jerusalem Temple," 51–57; and Levenson, *Creation,* 86–90.

54. On the religio-political background of the polemic, see Schramm, *Opponents.*

55. Isa 65:17–25 and Rev 21:1–2. See pp. 99–100, above.

56. The classic study of the latter is Cross, *Canaanite Myth,* 112–44.

57. On the interconnections of these three elements, see Weinfeld, "Sabbath," 501–12.

58. Rahlfs and Hanhart, *Septuaginta,* 2:102. The psalm appears as chap. 92.

59. This appears in the first blessing before the recitation of the Shemaʿ on the Sabbath morning. Note also ʾAḇot R. Nat. A, chap. 1. On this, see Weinfeld, "Sabbath," 508–10.

60. In both v. 13 and v. 14, the verb *ʾivvā* carries a strong sense of "choosing." It is not simply that the LORD has "desired" Zion, but, rather, he has singled it out for his throne, as the parallel with *bāḥar* in v. 13 would suggest.

61. Note the use of forms of *mənûḥâ* in 1 Chr 28:2, which has an obvious indebtedness to Ps 132. The same association with enthronement is probably also to be found in Isa 11:10.

62. See Schmidt, *Schöpfungsgeschichte,* 158–59; Weinfeld, "Sabbath," 501–2; Levenson, *Creation,* 101–8; and Walton, *Lost World,* 71–76.

63. See above, on Enuma Elish VI:49–54.

64. E.g., Pss 23:5–6 and 27:4–6. On this, see Levenson, "Jerusalem Temple," 39–46.

65. The classic essay on this is von Rad, "There Remains Still a Rest," 94–102.

66. In the Masoretic Text, these are vv. 43–45.

67. I have changed the NJPS rendering "a haven" to "rest" in v. 56 to facilitate the connection being made.

68. I have rendered *ləšiḇtəḵā* as "be enthroned" rather than "dwell" (NJPS) because of the Temple context and because Solomon explicitly questions whether his God can "dwell" (*yēšēḇ*) on earth at all (v. 27), thus nicely stating the paradox of divine presence as this stream of ancient Israelite thinking conceives it.

69. See especially Kearney, "Creation and Liturgy," 375–87, and Weinfeld, "Sabbath," 502. Kearney lists the speeches as beginning at Exod 25:1; 30:11: 30:17: 30:22; 30:34; 31:1; and 31:12 (p. 375).

70. The same point has been made about the seven years that it reportedly took to build Solomon's Temple (1 Kgs 6:38).

71. Kearney, "Creation and Liturgy," 375–78.

72. See Propp, *Exodus 19–40,* 484–85.

73. See Goodfriend, "Seven," for many examples.

74. See above, pp. 54–58.

75. See pp. 60–62.

76. On this source, see Knohl, *Sanctuary of Silence,* 16–17 on Exod 31:12–17, and Rhyder, "Sabbath and Sanctuary Cult," 727. Not all scholars attribute the passage to H, however. Grund (*Entstehung,* 277), for example, understands it as a Priestly composition

taking account of Lev 17–26. Stackert ("Sabbath of the Land," 241–42) regards *vayyinnāp̄aš* in Exod 31:17 as atypical of P and H and borrowed from Exod 23:12 and thus owing "to the Pentateuchal compiler, who by interpolating this verb seeks to harmonize the differing notions of Sabbath in the Torah sources." H, he notes, "never elsewhere indicates that rest and refreshment are essential characteristics of seventh-day Sabbath." See his discussion and proposed reconstruction of the strata in Stackert, "Priestly Sabbath," 58–59. Given the smallness of samples of references to the Sabbath in the reconstructed sources and kindred uncertainties, both the high degree of conjecture and the low degree of consensus on such matters are very likely to endure.

77. Blenkinsopp, *Prophecy and Canon*, 60–63; Weinfeld, "Sabbath," 502–3; Levenson, *Creation*, 84–86; Josipovici, *Book of God*, 101–6; Janowski, "Tempel und Schöpfung," 46; Middleton, *Liberating Image*, 81–88; Anderson, "Inauguration," 1–2.

78. I have departed from the NJPS translation of in Exod 40:33 to bring out the similarity with the Hebrew wording of Gen 2:2.

79. *Vəqiddaštā* appears in vv. 10, 11, and 13 as well and characterizes a key aspect of the completion of the process of devoting the accoutrements of the finished Tabernacle to divine service. Kearney ("Creation and Liturgy," 380–81) notes that the expression "(just) as the LORD commanded Moses" occurs a suggestive seven times in the reports of the manufacture of the priestly garments (Exod 39:1, 5, 7, 21, 26, 29, 31) and of the erection of the Tabernacle (Exod 40:19, 21, 23, 25, 27, 29, 32). For this and its further implications in the Priestly narrative, see Anderson, "Inauguration," esp. 6–7.

80. See Blenkinsopp, *Prophecy and Canon*, 59–69. I have departed from the NJPS rendering of the verse, which, by interpreting its last clause as the first clause of Josh 20:1, seems to me to obscure both the connection with what Blenkinsopp calls the "conclusion formula" (p. 60) and thus the connection with the creation of the world and the construction of the tent-shrine in the wilderness. The P version of the interlocking promises to Abraham appears in Genesis 17.

81. Westermann, *Genesis 1–11*, 88–90. For some conjectures about the prehistory of the passage, see Schmidt, *Schöpfungsgeschichte*, esp. 160–63.

82. See, e.g., Cassuto, *From Adam to Noah*, 5–6; Toeg, "Genesis 1," 291; Levenson, *Creation*, 66–68; and Middleton, *Liberating Image*, 83.

83. Cassuto, *From Adam to Noah*, 6.

84. Middleton, *Liberating Image*, 83.

85. Cassuto, *From Adam to Noah*, 6.

86. I thank Professor Gary A. Anderson for pointing me to the possibility that Cassuto was using the LXX version here. Interestingly, Cassuto renders the verse according to the MT and explicitly rejects an LXX reading in its second clause (*sunagōgēn* instead of *māqôm*). See *From Adam to Noah*, 20.

87. Ibid., 6.

88. Gen 1:10, 12, 25, and 31.

89. The awkwardness of that last clause suggests a deliberate effort to make up the deficit. Literally, it reads "because on it God ceased from all the work that God had created to do / by doing." It would have sounded much more natural if the second "God" had been eliminated (the verb alone would then mean "He created") along with the last verb ("to do / by doing").

90. Cassuto, *From Adam to Noah*, 6 (my translation).

91. Ibid., 6–8. Among scholars who subscribe to the Documentary Hypothesis, it was long the convention to attribute the first half of Gen 2:4 to the same source as

our passage (P), which would thus end with the words, "Such is the story of heaven and earth when they were created" (Gen 2:4a). The second half of the verse was, correlatively, interpreted as a temporal clause beginning the next—and very different—account of creation, attributed to the J source: "When the LORD God made earth and heaven" (Gen 2:4b). See, e.g., Speiser, *Genesis*, 3–5. If, however, the first half of the verse is included with Gen 1:1–2:3, the count of thirty-five words disappears from that seventh paragraph, and so does the figure of twenty-one for the appearances of "earth" (though it emerges for "heaven/sky"). For that reason, it would seem wiser to retain the traditional, or Masoretic, paragraphing, and to place a hard break after Gen 2:3. Whatever source-critical document may account for the following half-verse—even if it is P—Gen 1:1–2:3 constitute a unit, one to which justice cannot be done if we subsume it without qualification into the source in which it is now found. A different but complementary argument for the independence of Gen 2:4a from the P creation story is found in Cross, *Canaanite Myth*, 302.

92. Eliade, *Myth and Reality*, 21–38.

93. See Cassuto, *From Adam to Noah*, 8.

94. On Sinai as a wedding, see Levenson, *Love of God*, 130–39.

95. Prominent examples of this can be found in 1 Kgs 22:19–23; Isa 6; Job 1:6–12; 2:1–6.

96. I have departed from the translation of the NJPS to make the point that follows. Its rendering of the last two lines, "For in His image / Did God make man," obscures the fact that there is no indication of "His" in the Hebrew. Conceivably, we could read *ʾĕlōhîm* as doing double duty (or as the result of haplography): "For in the image of God God made man." This seems unlikely, however.

97. Middleton, *Liberating Image*, 58–59.

98. Ibid., 58 (emphasis original).

99. Radaq to Ps 8:6.

100. Middleton, *Liberating Image*, 51, 53 (emphasis original). He cites 1 Kgs 5:4; Ps 72:8; 110:2; Isa 14:6; and Ezek 34:4 as examples of the association of *rādâ* with kingship. A particularly telling case, it would seem, appears in Isa 41:2, which describes the LORD's empowering of Cyrus II. He (presumably the LORD) has "trodden sovereigns down" (*mᵊlākîm yard*). If Cyrus was, as he and other Achaemenid kings came to be titled, the "king of kings," it was, the prophet tells us, the LORD who made him that. Here I retain the MT and do not follow, as some do, 1QIsᵃ, which reads *yôrîd* ("brings down").

101. See the references in Middleton, *Liberating Image*, 27n37. To this can be added Bauks, "Le Shabbat," 486. The present author has discussed this in Levenson, *Creation*, 111–20.

102. That the term for "likeness" in Gen 1:26 and 5:3 (*dᵊmut*) could also carry this meaning can be very clearly shown from Isa 40:18–20.

103. See Levenson, *Sinai and Zion*, 71–72; idem, *Love*, 6–7 and Propp, *Exodus 19–40*, 157–60.

104. Middleton, *Liberating Image*, 204–5.

105. Ibid., 22.

106. Held, *Heart of Torah*, 8.

107. See n. 103, above.

108. See, e.g., Exodus 28–29.

109. Middleton (*Liberating Image*, 205) is "not convinced that Genesis 1 indeed derives from the same Priestly tradition that is responsible for the levitical laws." But

Genesis 17, which includes those promises that kings will descend from Abraham and Sarah (vv. 6, 16), is not part of any "levitical laws." Earlier in the same volume, Middleton expresses doubt about the exilic or postexilic date of the opening creation story of the Bible and even about our ability to reconstruct sources at all with any certainty (pp. 139–45). Scholars less skeptical on the latter point will properly be more skeptical of Middleton's egalitarian interpretation of the creation of humankind in the image of God.

110. On this, see, among others, Levenson, *Creation*, 101–4, and Middleton, *Liberating Image*, 209–12.

111. Enuma Elish VI:8–9 (Foster, *Before the Muses*, 469).

112. Lines 195–97, 240–41. See "Atra-Ḥasis," *COS* 1.130:451.

113. Meier, "Sabbath and Purification," 5, 6.

114. Middleton (*Liberating Image*, 212) also contests the idea that "Genesis 1:1–2:3 . . . constitutes the institution of the Sabbath" and "find[s] no justification within the rhetoric of the text itself for this reading." I would grant that the passage does not describe the "institution" of the Sabbath, but it does describe the *origin* of the Sabbath.

115. Note, in connection with the first occurrence of the noun "Sabbath" (Exod 16:23), the apparent recollection of some previous divine speech authorizing the institution. On the intimations of future Israelite practices within the P creation story in general, see Clifford, "Election," 7–22. On the adumbration of the Sabbath in particular, see 11–13.

116. The classic demonstration of this is Weinfeld, *Justice and Righteousness*. See also Levenson, *Creation*, 101–5.

117. Heschel, *Sabbath*. This is, in fact, the title of his first chapter.

118. Ibid., 8 (emphasis original). The "shrine" is the Day of Atonement.

119. Grund, *Entstehung*, 232. For a different demurral on Heschel's employment of the time-space dichotomy, see below, pp. 214–15.

Chapter 6

1. See, e.g., Swoboda, *Subversive Sabbath*, 34: "The fourth commandment, we must remember, only prohibits us from work on Sabbath. Nothing else is prohibited."

2. For a comprehensive and detailed discussion of sabbatical law in antiquity, see Doering, *Schabbat*.

3. Kugel, *Idea of Biblical Poetry*, 8 (emphasis original).

4. See pp. 62–64.

5. As suggested to me by Allison Hurst.

6. Often, these two passages are assigned to different sources. Verses 4–5 are ascribed to J, whereas vv. 22–30 are seen as part of the P text that dominates in the chapter. In 16:28, I have omitted the word "men" from the NJPS translation. Although the antecedent is masculine, no such word appears in the Hebrew.

7. Childs, *Book of Exodus*, 290–91, quoting Exod 16:28.

8. In the Bible, "Passover" (*pesaḥ*) generally refers to the sacrifice that immediately precedes the "Holiday of "Unleavened Bread" (*ḥag hammaṣṣôt*).

9. The translation is from VanderKam, *Jubilees*. The speaker is Moses. See also Jub. 2:17–33. On the list of sabbatical norms in the book, see Doering, *Schabbat*, 70–108.

10. See Doering, "Concept," 179–205, and Doering, *Schabbat*, 87–94. Interestingly, Doering points out that the author has structured his retelling of the patriarchs' journeys in Genesis in accordance with the prohibition of traveling on the Sabbath ("Concept," 183).

11. See VanderKam, *Jubilees*, 1207–8 and the references on 1208n76. Doering (*Schabbat*, 89) suggests that "go not your ways" (*mēʿăśôt dərākeykā*) in Isa 58:13 also played a role in the derivation of this law.

12. Doering ("Concept," 182) notes "the hypothesis that the author of *Jubilees* has utilized two (or three) lists of halakhic precepts and has incorporated them into his account."

13. Doering, *Schabbat*, 92–93.

14. CD X:21. On this limit, see Doering, *Schabbat*, 145–51.

15. E.g., m. Soṭah 5:3 and b. ʿErub. 51a. See the discussion of precedents in Doering, *Schabbat*, 151–54.

16. See b. ʿErub. 48a (for biblical antecedents, see Jer 17:19–27 and Neh 13:15–21). See also the expansionistic translation of the verse in Tg. Ps.-J., which combines both aspects of sabbatical practice. Needless to say, the rabbinic laws of traveling and carrying on the Sabbath are, as always, complex and not easily summarized. On the rabbinic innovation, see S. J. D. Cohen, "Judaean Legal Tradition," 128–29.

17. See Kugel, *Traditions*, 647–49. Kugel points out that "the distance involved here is apparently a little more than half a mile, that is, two thousand cubits" (648n10). I thank Professor Gary A. Anderson for drawing this example to my attention.

18. On the Sabbath in Josephus more generally, see Weiss, "Sabbath," 363–90.

19. 11Q19 XLVI:13–14.

20. See Deut 23:13–15.

21. Emanuel, "Give Them a 'Hand.'" Note especially this: "The crux of this matter is the question of whether the supposed Essene resistance to defecation on the Sabbath reflected an attempt to practice strict avoidance of labor, or an effort to remain pure on the seventh day" (pp. 13–14).

22. For example, it means "kindle" in Jer 7:18 but most likely signifies to "keep burning" in Neh 10:35. The corresponding passive (*pual*) of the same root clearly means "be burning" in Jer 36:22.

23. The Samaritan Pentateuch reads the *hiphil* rather than the *piel* here. This does not resolve the ambiguity, however.

24. Noam and Qimron, "Qumran Composition," 90. The discussion of the law in question appears on pp. 88–96. The texts at issue are 4Q264a and 4Q421.

25. But note that Noam and Qimron (ibid., 92), following the lead of Abraham Geiger in the nineteenth century, draw attention to the concern of the early or proto-rabbinic School of Shammai to limit "activities started before the Sabbath that are completed on their own on the Sabbath." See m. Šabb. 1:5–8. As they observe, starting a fire that will continue burning on its own on the Sabbath is not, interestingly, one of these activities.

26. Ibid., 91.

27. Propp, *Exodus 19–40*, 659.

28. In the twentieth century, the related questions of driving, which involved the use of the internal combustion engine, and using electricity came to divide traditionally observant Jews, with the Conservative Movement allowing these (within limits) and Orthodoxy forbidding them. The classic Conservative statement on this dates from 1950: "Responsum on the Sabbath," 1109–31. On the larger issues in a retrospective view, see Mittleman, "From Jewish Street," 29–37.

29. See the three speculations in Propp, *Exodus 19–40*, 659–60.

30. See above, pp. 136–37.

31. Mek. de-Rabbi Ishmael, *Baḥōdeš* 7. See pp. 106–7.

32. For a fuller demurral from Heschel's use of the time-space duality in connection with the Sabbath, see below, pp. 214–15.

33. Heschel, *Sabbath*, 3, 8, and 27 (his emphasis).

34. See b. Šabb. 18a and Shulchan Arukh, *'Ôraḥ Ḥayyîm* 246:1.

35. The influence of the Talmudic passage quoted here on *Lekha Dodi*, the song in which the congregation welcomes the Sabbath Queen, briefly discussed in chap. 4, is patent. See pp. 80–81.

36. It is also doubtful whether ancient Jews conceived of time as an abstract entity, as Heschel seems to assume they did. On this, see Stern, *Time and Process*, esp. 127: "In antiquity, the world-view of Hebrew- and Aramaic-speaking Jews remained completely process-related. Reality is seen as a succession of objects and events, whereas the notions of time as an entity in itself, a human resource, a continuous flow, or a structure or dimension of the created world, were simply non-existent."

37. See Doering, *Schabbat*, 96–97. Note that the Damascus Document makes it explicit that the exemption does not apply to an individual who would wish to bring an offering on the Sabbath (CD-A XI:17–18).

38. See pp. 26–27.

39. E.g., b. Pesaḥ. 68b.

40. Qimchi to Isa 58:13, citing b. Šabb. 113a.

41. On the Second Temple antecedents to rabbinic sabbatical law, see Doering, *Schabbat*, passim, and S. J. D. Cohen, "Judaean Legal Tradition," 128–30; 135–40.

42. On this, see Anderson, "Celibacy," esp. 129–36, and Doering, *Schabbat*, 79–83. Something of a parallel appears in CD XII 1–2, though the law seems to apply only to the temple city itself and thus to reflect the heightened purity expectations of the site. Note also that the punishment for violation is not capital (XII 3–6). On this, see also Simkovich, "Intimacy."

43. On the importance of marital relations on the Sabbath from the Middle Ages through the twentieth century, see Horowitz, "Sabbath Delights," 134–43. He notes that on this, Rabbanite practice stood in contrast to the Qaraite norm and may have drawn additional force from its usefulness in anti-Qaraite polemic.

44. See pp. 36–38.

45. Milgrom, "Concept of Impurity," 279–81.

46. Doering, "Concept of Impurity," 196. See also Doering, *Schabbat*, 66–67.

47. Note also the ritually polluting character of sexual intercourse as attested, for example, in Lev 15:18. It must be underscored that ritual pollution does *not* equate to moral failure in such a context.

48. VanderKam, *Jubilees*, 15.

49. Gribetz, *Time and Difference*, 121.

50. Jub. 50:13.

51. Jdt 8:6. See pp. 39–41. As pointed out there, the fasting in question probably took place only in the daytime.

52. See the previous note. The passage is b. Pesaḥ. 68b.

53. Gilat, "On Fasting," 5.

54. See above, pp. 36–39.

55. See pp. 40–41.

56. The presumption of three meals appears early in rabbinic tradition, for example, m. Šabb. 16:2 and 22:1.

57. See b. Šabb. 18a and Shulchan Arukh, ʾÔraḥ Ḥayyîm 246.

58. Goodenough, *Jewish Symbols*, 5:43. In a discussion that is as fascinating as it is speculative (pp. 41–53), Goodenough reconstructs the *cena pura* as especially focused on the eating of fish and invested with the various mystical and eschatological meanings associated with that dish.

59. On the Sabbath in 1 and 2 Macc, see Haag, *Vom Sabbat*, 118–24.

60. See pp. 67–68.

61. Exod 31:14–15; 35:2; Num 15:35.

62. On this passage, see Y. Adler, *Origins of Judaism*, 141–42.

63. See, for example, Robinson, *Origin and Development*, 247–59, and Grund, *Entstehung*, 308–9. So argues Y. Adler in some detail in *Origins of Judaism*, 136–45.

64. Note also Josephus's account of this in *Ant.* 12.274–78.

65. 2 Macc 5:25; 6:11; 8:25–28; and 12:38–39. See Y. Adler, *Origins of Judaism*, 140–41.

66. For a fuller text and discussion, see above pp. 10–11.

67. See p. 225, n. 43.

68. See also Josephus, *J.W.* 1.146, but note as well *J.W.* 2.517–18, in which Josephus speaks of Jews' abandoning the Sabbath and *eusebeias* ("religion," "piety") to score a victory against the Romans in the Great War. See also Weiss, "Sabbath," 376.

69. In some manuscripts, this appears as 3:7.

70. E.g., Mek., Neziqin 4; b. Yoma 85b.

71. See m. Yoma 8:6.

72. See b. Sanh. 74a–74b.

73. I have changed "for humankind" (NRSV) to "on account of humankind" in v. 27 (twice) in order to reflect the Greek more precisely. See also the parallels to this passage in Matt 12:1–8 and (with less expansion) Luke 6:1–5. Note that the account of David's actions in securing bread varies significantly from the text in 1 Sam 21:2–7 to which it is evidently intended to allude.

74. See b. Yoma 85a–85b.

75. See Bächer, *Agada*, 2:364n1.

76. Mek., Šabbataʾ 1.

77. On these issues, see Collins, *Mark*, 201–5.

78. 1 Sam 21:5; Exod 16:23; Neh 9:14.

79. Exod 16:22–30. See Milgrom, *Numbers*, esp. 408, and Project TABS Editors, "What Melacha Did." On the passage itself and its relationship to similar Pentateuchal texts, see Chavel, *Oracular Law*, 165–95.

80. See Exod 16:23.

81. Milgrom, *Numbers*, 408, and Levine, *Numbers 1–20*, 399.

82. Exod 31:14; 35:2.

83. See Sifre Num 114.

84. Chavel, *Oracular Law*, 180.

85. Milgrom, *Numbers*, 409. The reference to "Molech" is based on Lev 20:2–5, in which, similarly, the "the people of the land shall pelt [the worshiper of the false god] with stones" (v. 2).

86. As in Exod 31:14. Milgrom, *Numbers*, 409.

87. Hauptman, "New Interpretation," 323–24. Hauptman credits the translation to Shaye J. D. Cohen.

88. Hauptman, "New Interpretation," 328.

89. Ibid., 325.

90. As ordained, for example, in Exod 29 and 30:34–38.

91. See pp. 117–21.

92. See pp. 143–44.

93. See above, pp. 118–21.

94. Sarna, *Exodus*, 201. As argued above (pp. 142–43), there is, however, reason to resist the stark opposition of space and time reflected in this formulation, as well as the claim that Sabbath is about time in general as holy. At a more pedestrian level, Exod 31:12–17 and 35:1–3 comprise a *Wiederaufnahme* (a resumptive repetition) and thus jointly mark the interpolation and digression of chaps. 32–34.

95. Ibid.

96. Rashi to Exod 31:13.

97. For an accessible outline of contemporary sabbatical practice by an Orthodox rabbi, see Donin, *To Be a Jew*, 70–96.

98. On the halakhic issue in the Talmud and the subsequent history of Jewish jurisprudence, see E. Adler, "Sabbath Observing Gentile," 14–45. Adler explains the last statement here as referring to "the halakhic principle . . . which gives a Jewish court the legal right to administer capital punishment to gentiles who violate any of the Noahide laws" (18).

99. See pp. 21–23.

100. The question of the Gentile practitioner of the Sabbath is a part of the vexed question of the availability of Torah law to non-Jews in rabbinic thought. On the dangers of ahistorical generalization about this larger issue, see Hirshman, *Torah*.

101. Hertz, *Pentateuch and Haftorahs*, 298.

102. See b. Sanh. 58b, in the name of the late Babylonian sage Ravina.

103. See Rashi's comment to the quote from Ravina. In Mishneh Torah, *hilkôt məlākîm* 10:9, Maimonides makes it explicit that the violation occurs only if the Gentile treats the day in question as what E. Adler calls "a sanctified day of rest—a 'Sabbath'" and "manifest[s] a formal observance of sorts" (E. Adler, "Sabbath Observing Gentile," 22–23). I thank Professor Bernard Septimus for helping me to clarify my understanding of Maimonides on this issue.

104. In light of the origins of the week in the Israelite practice of the seventh day, which we explored in chap. 1, the ubiquitous term "weekend" is revealing, since the two days in question are comprised of what in origin were the last day of one week and the first of the next. With the attenuation of Sabbath-observance in once-Christian societies, the first workday (Monday) is now increasingly regarded as the beginning the week and Saturday and Sunday as its sixth and seventh days—a revealing departure from the biblical origin of the week that we explored in chap. 1.

105. Swoboda, *Subversive Sabbath*, 21–22.

106. Ibid., 8.

107. See above, pp. 155–57.

108. The question of Jesus's relationship to the Torah (including what would become the Oral Torah of the rabbis) commands a voluminous and growing literature. An accessible and still very instructive book on this is Sanders, *Jesus and Judaism*. On the question of the Sabbath, see pp. 264–67. As for the story of the disciples' picking grain, note Sanders's evaluation: "It is very likely that the entire pericope on plucking grain on the Sabbath (Matt. 12.1–8 // Mark 2.23–28 // Luke 6.1–5) is a creation of the church" (p. 266). For a more recent and admirably concise discussion of the question of "the Law" in the context of the New Testament and Second Temple and rabbinic Judaism, see Klawans, "Law," 515–18.

109. As the Markan Jesus explicitly charges in Mark 7:1–13 with particular reference to handwashing before meals (see also Matt 15:1–20). I thank Allison Hurst for bringing this parallel to my attention.

110. Swoboda, *Subversive Sabbath*, 57.

111. Ibid., 77.

112. Exod 20:10; Deut 5:14.

113. Swoboda, *Subversive Sabbath*, 201 (his italics).

114. Ibid., 56, 198.

115. See above, pp. 165–66.

116. The number of scholarly works dealing with this vexed subject is high and ever mounting. An early pioneer in the revision of traditional Christian interpretation of Paul, broadly speaking, was Krister Stendahl. See especially his early essay, "Apostle Paul," 199–215; reprinted in Stendahl, *Paul Among Jews*, 78–96. Note especially Stendahl's words of caution regarding Romans 7, whose misinterpretation is a major source of the anti-Jewish theology: "We should not read a trembling introspective conscience into a text which is so anxious to put the blame on Sin, and that in such a way that not only the law but the will and mind of man are declared good and are found to be on the side of God" (*Paul Among Jews*, 94). A major, thoroughgoing, and relatively early critique of the older view, still prominent and compelling in the main, is Sanders, *Paul and Palestinian Judaism*. For a reliable and up-to-date survey of the major trends and controversies in Pauline studies, see Zetterholm, *Approaches to Paul*. On the specific issue of Paul's relationship to Judaism, see esp. pp. 69–163, and McKnight and Oropeza, *Perspectives on Paul*, esp. 171–93. I thank Professor Giovanni B. Bazzana for directing me to Zetterholm and Andrew P. Hile for bringing McKnight and Oropeza to my attention.

117. On this, see Sanders, *Paul and Palestinian Judaism*, passim but esp. pp. 84–238 (on Tannaitic literature). On the Jewish conceptions, see Levenson, *Love of God*.

118. E.g., Pesiq. Raḇ Kah. 24, esp. 2 and 11.

119. ". . . as the Halakhah is a sweepingly comprehensive regula of daily life covering not only prayer and divine service, but equally food, drink, dress, sexual relations between man and wife, the rhythms of work and patterns of rest—it constitutes a way of life. And a way of life is not learned but rather absorbed. Its transmission is mimetic, imbibed from parents and friends, and patterned on conduct regularly observed in home and street, synagogue and school." Soloveitchik, "Rupture and Reconstruction," 1–2.

120. Rosenzweig, *On Jewish Learning*, 122 (emphasis original). The quote comes from a November 1924 letter to Martin Goldner, Nahum Glatzer, Hans Epstein, and Lotte Fürth. The editor (Glatzer) has given the letter, which appears on pp. 119–24, the title "The Commandments: Divine or Human?," although the literal translation of the German is "Divine and Human" (*Göttlich und menschlich*). In this quote, Rosenzweig was speaking about the Torah in general.

Chapter 7

1. For example, Exod 20:10; 34:21; 35:3; Num 15:32–36; Isa 58:13; Jer 17:19–27; and Neh 13:15–22.

2. For example, Exod 20:8; 31:13, 14, 16; Deut 5:12; Lev 19:3; Exod 23:12; Jer 17:22; Ezek 20:13; 22:8; and Isa 58:13.

3. Dickens, *Sunday*, chap. 3. Unpaginated source consulted at https://www.gutenberg .org/files/922/922-h/922-h.htm.

4. As specified in Exod 31:13.

5. Heschel, *Sabbath*, 15 (emphasis original).

6. On Gen. Rab. 11, see Hirshman, *Rivalry of Genius*, 43–54. Hirshman sees this chapter, which "essentially expounds" just one clause, "And God blessed the seventh day and declared it holy (Genesis 2:3)," as an Amoraic composition "well anchored in the tannaitic source of the first two centuries C.E." (43, 44). I thank Professor Hirshman for sharing his wisdom on this subject also in personal communications. On the versions and manuscript variations of this story, see Gribetz, *Time and Difference*, 288n165.

7. See pp. 113–14.

8. See m. Tamid 7:4 and Rahlfs and Hanhart, *Septuaginta*, 2:102. The psalm appears there as chap. 92.

9. See p. 114.

10. See Levenson, *Creation*, 53–65.

11. It is less than clear that this last root exists with that meaning in Biblical Hebrew, where the closest candidates (Ps 65:14; 73:6; and Job 23:9) seem rather to describe an act of covering rather than donning a garment.

12. See pp. 140–41.

13. Exod 3:1–6; 1 Kgs 17:8–16; 2 Kgs 4:1–7.

14. From a historical-critical perspective, one must note the possibility that "blessed" here is the result of a scribal error, as argued by Frankel, "Did God Bless Shabbat?" If so, this proved to be an extremely productive and theologically valuable error.

15. Tacitus, *Histories*, 5.4 (Moore, LCL). See pp. 9–10 and p. 225, n. 42.

16. The logic is reminiscent of the reassurance that the Israelite is given in Deut 15 that his observance of the septennial year of release will not actually result in a monetary loss: "For the LORD your God will bless (*bērakəkā*) you as He has promised you: you will extend loans to many nations, but require none yourself; you will dominate many nations, but they will not dominate you" (v. 6).

17. Tosafot to b. Šabb. 119a, on the basis of *ʿlt*, meaning "ladle" in b. ʿEruḇ. 53a.

18. Seligman, *Ritual*, 7, 8 (emphasis original). See above pp. 102–4.

19. See pp. 147–48.

20. Rosenzweig, *On Jewish Learning*, 122.

21. See Levenson, "Did God Forgive Adam?," 148–70.

22. On the text-critical variation, see Theodor and Albeck, *Midrash Bereshit Rabba*, 1:88.

23. See Sharvit, "Gutturals," 225–43, esp. the list of examples on pp. 226–33. I thank Professor Lewis H. Glinert for his help with bibliography on this issue.

24. Note the similar case of Gen 1:31, also involving what "they found written in Rabbi Meir's Torah" (Gen. Rab. 9:5).

25. For example, Targum Onqelos and Targum Pseudo-Jonathan, which both read *ləḇûšîn diqar*. See Kugel, *Traditions*, 132–35.

26. Gen 23:2; 25:9; 49:29–32; 50:13.

27. See b. ʿEruḇ. 53a.

28. See pp. 125–29.

29. On the dimensions of Adam in rabbinic literature and a proposal as to their deeper meaning, see Niditch, "Cosmic Adam," 137–46. On the earlier Jewish Adam literature (from the period 200 BCE–135 CE), see Levison, *Portraits of Adam*. Whatever scant precedent exists for the luminescence of Adam's body in this period, it and kindred notions become much more developed in rabbinic literature.

30. The translations are taken from Nickelsburg and VanderKam, *1 Enoch 2*, 64 and 81. On "the light of (many) days" in 1 En. 50:1, the translators observe "Perhaps one should read *the light of day*. One ms reads *the ancient of days*."

31. E.g., 1 Cor 15:22; Rom 5:12–21.

32. See, e.g., Wis 2:23–24; 4 Ezra (or 2 Esdras) 3:21–22; 4:30–32; 7:46–48. More generally, see Anderson, Stone, and Tromp, *Literature on Adam* and Levison, *Portraits of Adam*.

33. See Cohon, "Original Sin," 306–11.

34. Whether the original referent of "earliest ancestor" (ʾăḇîḵā hārîʾšôn) in Isa 43:27 is Adam is less than clear. For a well-reasoned argument that it may refer instead to Jacob, see, e.g., Blenkinsopp, *Isaiah 40–55*, 232. Note that the locution ʾādām hārîʾšôn as a name for Adam does not occur in the Bible.

35. On the whole question of imputed guilt and imputed merit in rabbinic tradition, see Cohon, "Original Sin," 311–21.

36. See n. 29 (above).

37. On this, see in a helpful, popular vein, Henze, *Mind the Gap*. Of course, the reverse is also true. Used appropriately, early Christian literature also helps us understand the Judaism of the time.

38. See Levenson, *Resurrection*, esp. 1–23 and 181–216, and Madigan and Levenson, *Resurrection*, 171–213.

39. Based on "The lifebreath [or, "'soul'"] of man (ʾādām) is the lamp of the LORD" (Prov 20:27a). A number of other noteworthy and instructively extravagant claims for Adam also appear in y. Šabb. 2:6.

40. See m. Roš Haš. 1:1.

41. On the translation "a body of troops," see Haberman, "Poetry," 31.

42. The manuscripts of Pesiq. Rab. vary widely. I have prepared this translation on the basis of the edition of Ish Shalom (Friedmann), *Pesiqta Rabbati*, 187b (see the notes and variants there), with assistance from the translation of Braude, *Pesikta Rabbati*, 2:791. Fortunately, the text-critical variation does not affect our point here. I have translated Ps 92:1 and Gen 2:2 in accordance with the understanding of these two verses in this midrash.

43. Seligman, *Ritual*, 7 and 8. See above pp. 102–3.

44. On this fascinating little story, see Hirshman, *Rivalry of Genius*, 44–49, and Gribetz, *Time and Difference*, 124–28.

45. On the translation "tortured," see Lieberman, *Texts and Studies*, 32–33 and 521.

46. See Hirshman, *Rivalry of Genius*, 48: "Is this some general prescription, as if the father were retorting in kind—'*You* become a Jew while you are still alive'—or is this a matter of calling on gentiles to observe the Sabbath?" Hirshman is "inclined to endorse" the former interpretation. Gribetz, on the other hand, writes, "The participation of a non-Jew in Sabbath observance in Genesis Rabbah may also be understood in a context in which Christian and non-Christian Romans continued to attend synagogue services on the Sabbath even though Sunday was now officially recognized as a sacred day by the empire" (*Time and Difference*, 126). (This, of course, dates the story to a time after Constantine I decreed such recognition in 321 CE.) "The story," Gribetz concludes, "ends with an ironic twist—as much as imperial officials struggle with the Sabbath, they cannot contain its observance by those who are not Jewish; and even those who deride the idea of the Sabbath rest and refuse to celebrate it in this world will be obliged to observe Sabbath rhythms in the World to Come" (127).

47. For some repercussions of this in later Jewish folklore, see Schwartz, *Tree of Souls*, 238 and 242.

48. Gribetz, *Time and Difference*, 115. The idea appears as early as Heb 4:1–11.

49. See p. 32.

50. In Jewish practice, it is customary to end by repeating v. 22 in order not to conclude the book on a negative note.

51. On the possibility that *šabbāt* here refers instead to the hypothetical Israelite day of the full moon, see above, pp. 32–33.

52. Sarna, *Studies*, 397–98. Sarna is endorsing a suggestion of N. H. Snaith here. The specification of sacrifice for each morning and evening is found in Exod 29:38–42.

53. I have substituted the NJPS alternative "profound" for "subtle" for ʿāmǝqû in v. 6.

54. Sarna, *Studies*, 399.

55. Ibid., 403. On the combat myth, see above, pp. 96–99.

56. The fact that this poem precedes Ps 93, which presents similar images and even similar language (e.g., *mārôm* in 92:6 and 93:4), adds to the probability of Sarna's proposal. See above, pp. 113–15. It bears mention that in Qabbalistic circles in the late sixteenth century, Ps 92 became the seventh psalm in another sequence as well, the seven psalms in the ceremony with which the Sabbath is greeted on Friday night. About this, Arthur Green insightfully comments, "They represent the powerful arrival of God or 'the kingdom of heaven,' the scattering of God's foes, and the universal joy at His arrival. It is interesting to see how close the kabbalists are here to the original meaning of these psalms, although they have now applied them to they own mythic context." Green, "Some Aspects," 106.

57. See pp. 99–100.

58. I have altered the NJPS translation of vv. 2 and 3 to facilitate the midrashic point being made.

59. Heschel, *Sabbath*, 101. The phrase *"the sanctification of time"* is found (with italics) on p. 8. On the limitations of this formulation, see above, pp. 142–43.

Chapter 8

1. In v. 10, I have changed NRSV's "elemental spirits of the world" to "elements," which is more faithful to the Greek *stoicheia* in general and in this passage in particular. Nonetheless, *stoicheia tou kosmou*, best rendered "elements of the world," which appears just above (v. 3), should be understood as the referent here as well.

2. Justin Martyr, *Dialogue*, 32.

3. See Bacchiocchi, *From Sabbath to Sunday*, 17–73.

4. Hefele, *History of the Councils*, 2:316, quoted from https://www.ecatholic2000.com/councils/untitled-21.shtml#_Toc385946536.

5. Exod 20:8–11; Deut 5:12–15.

6. Mark 16:1–8; Matt 28:1–10; Luke 24:1–27; John 20:1–18.

7. Bacchiocchi, *From Sabbath to Sunday*, 84. See his exhaustive review of the supposed evidence to the contrary on pp. 74–131.

8. Ibid., 234, 268. On "Sun-Worship and the Origins of Sunday," see pp. 236–69.

9. See pp. 167–70.

10. Scarlata, *Sabbath Rest*, 18 and 19.

11. Ibid., 18.

12. On the historical questions, see Sievers and Levine, *Pharisees*, esp. chap. 12 by Jens Schröter, "How Close Were Jesus and the Pharisees?" I thank Allison Hurst for bringing this book to my attention.

13. Mabry, *Art of Rest*, 62 (commenting on Luke 6:1–5).

14. Ibid., 48 (emphasis original).

15. Ibid., 63. Elsewhere (p. 71) he also makes the odd claim that "Pharisees were Jewish religious nationalists."

16. Ibid., 113, 112, 116. This differs only slightly from the positions of Swoboda and Scarlata, who think the particular day is not important so long as one day out of every seven is designated for sabbatical rest. Swoboda, *Subversive Sabbath*, 201, and Scarlata, *Sabbath Rest*, 201.

17. Mabry, *Art of Rest*, 114.

18. Bacchiocchi, *From Sabbath to Sunday*, 234, 268.

19. An outstanding example is Wirzba, *Living the Sabbath*.

20. See Levenson, "Is There a Counterpart," 159–78.

21. See pp. 175–76.

22. Shulevitz, *Sabbath World*, 189. Her whole discussion of the subject (pp. 188–94) is quite informative.

23. John Paul II, "*Dies Domini*," https://www.vatican.va/content/john-paul-ii/en/apost_letters/1998/documents/hf_jp-ii_apl_05071998_dies-domini.html. The numbers in the citations refer to paragraphs in the letter.

24. Exod 31:14–15; 35:2; Num 15:35.

25. See "Ask the Expert: Sunday Services," https://www.myjewishlearning.com/article/ask-the-expert-sunday-services/.

26. See pp. 140–42.

27. Adler, Agus, and Friedman, "Responsum," 3:1118.

28. Ibid., 3:1127.

29. Ibid., 3:1129.

30. Ibid., 3:1188. See also the forceful "Reevaluation of the Responsum on the Sabbath" by Rabbi Theodore Friedman, one of its authors, on pp. 1186–87.

31. Ibid., 3:1120.

32. Ibid., 3:1127.

33. Mittleman, "From Jewish Street," 36. With regard to "the walk to synagogue, with its slow and contemplative pace," note that the more punctilious are likely to walk briskly to services—in order not to be late and to exemplify their eagerness to participate in communal prayer—but more slowly in the return home, when time is not of the essence and socialization is more appropriate.

34. Ibid., 35. See Sklare, *Conservative Judaism*, 261–67.

35. Note Mittleman, "From Jewish Street," 29: "The rabbis were not so much making bold innovations as putting a brave face on defeat." One should not take the new situation Mittleman describes as warranting Orthodox triumphalism. Not only is the percentage of Sabbath-observers in American Jewry (and Diaspora Jewry generally) still low, but the attrition rate among Orthodox Jews seems to be about 33%. The problem was the subject of a symposium in *Jewish Action*, the magazine of the (modern) Orthodox Union, "The View from Pew." It also bears mention that it is not unusual for Orthodox synagogues quietly to tolerate members who drive to and from services. The difference with the Conservative Movement lies not only with the proportion of regular members who do so but also, and for our purposes more importantly, with the difference between nonjudgmentally accepting those who deviate from the norm, on the one hand, and amending the norm so as to provide communal legitimation for the quondam deviation, on the other. Finally, the prospect must not be discounted

that large-scale political, economic, or social changes (such as the resurgence of anti-Semitism in the wake of the Hamas-Israel war in 2023) might reverse the reinvigoration of Orthodoxy of the last sixty years or so and restore a more accommodationist model of Jewish practice.

36. Keysar and Kosmin, "Bar/Bat Mitzvah," 15. I thank Professor Jack Wertheimer for bringing this important study to my attention. Marshall Sklare had already observed the decline over half a century ago: "The available evidence suggests that the Conservative strategy of liberalization, innovation, and beautification has been a failure; it underlies the fact that the majority of Conservative Jews do not follow even the most basic Sabbath observances" (Sklare, *Conservative Judaism*, 273).

37. See ibid., 36.

38. I suppose, though, that we cannot rule out the possibility that many of their families had only temporarily done "something special/different on Friday night or Saturday [a low bar, by the way] because it is the Jewish Sabbath" in anticipation of the upcoming bar/bat mitzvah, but that seems unlikely.

39. Heschel, *Sabbath*, 3, 27, 60, and 75 (italics in the original).

40. See p. 132 and pp. 142–43.

41. Kraemer, "Sabbath as a Sanctuary," 82 and 87. For a defense by Heschel of his employment of the time-space dichotomy (though against a very different critique from Kraemer's), see Heschel, "Space, Time, and Reality," 263–69. The essay ably responds to Weiss-Rosmarin, "Time and Space," 277–78.

42. See pp. 165–67.

43. Mabry, *Art of Rest*, 113.

44. Ibid.

45. See pp. 169–72.

46. See pp. 196–201.

47. Heschel, *Sabbath*, 75 (italics in the original).

48. John Paul II, *Dies Domini*, paragraph 7.

49. I have changed the punctuation and the abbreviations for biblical books so as to conform to the style of this volume. The italics are in the original.

50. Compare Mabry, *Art of Rest*, 113: "Doing no work every Saturday was, for the Jewish believers before Christ came, a sign pointing them to Jesus."

51. John Paul II, *Dies Domini*, n. 13.

52. Shulevitz, *Sabbath World*, 21.

53. Ibid., 204. The Reuters story, "Texting while driving? Time to unplug," by Jill Serjeant, can be found in *Technology News*, April 17, 2008 (https://www.reuters.com/article/idINIndia-33106220080418). The synonym "digital Sabbath" now seems commonplace.

54. Lieberman and Klinghoffer, *Gift of Rest*, 28.

55. Ibid., 29.

56. Ibid., 95.

57. Mabry, *Art of Rest*, 62.

58. A few of which do work.

59. Osgood, "Why Your 'Digital Shabbat' Will Fail" (italics in the original).

60. Shulevitz, *Sabbath World*, 206.

61. Osgood, "Why Your 'Digital Shabbat' Will Fail."

BIBLIOGRAPHY

Achenbach, Reinhard. "*Lex Sacra* and Sabbath in the Pentateuch." *Zeitschrift für altorientalische und biblische Rechtgeschichte* 22 (2016): 101–10.

Adler, Elchanan. "The Sabbath Observing Gentile: Halakhic, Hashkafic and Liturgical Perspectives." *Tradition* 36.3 (2002): 14–45.

Adler, Morris, Jacob Agus, and Theodore Friedman. "Responsum on the Sabbath: Driving and Electricity." Pages 1109–31 in *Proceedings of the Committee on Jewish Law and Standards of the Conservative Movement, 1927–1970*. Edited by David Golinkin. New York: The Rabbinical Assembly and Institute of Applied Halakhah, 1997.

Adler, Yonatan. *The Origins of Judaism: An Archaeological-Historical Reappraisal*. AYBRL. New Haven, CT: Yale University Press, 2022.

Anderson, Gary A. "Celibacy or Consummation in the Garden? Reflections on Early Jewish and Christian Interpretations of the Garden of Eden." *HTR* 82 (1989): 121–48.

———. *Charity: The Place of the Poor in the Biblical Tradition*. New Haven, CT: Yale University Press, 2013.

———. "Inauguration of the Tabernacle Service at Sinai." Pages 1–15 in *The Temple of Jerusalem: From Moses to the Messiah; In Honor of Professor Louis H. Feldman*. Edited by Steven Fine. Brill Reference Library of Judaism 29. Leiden: Brill, 2011.

Anderson, Gary A., Michael E. Stone, and Johannes Tromp, eds. *Literature on Adam and Eve: Collected Essays*. Studia in Veteris Testamenti Pseudepigrapha 15. Leiden: Brill, 2000.

Andreasen, Niels-Erik A. *Rest and Redemption: A Study of the Biblical Sabbath*. Andrews University Monographs 11. Berrien Springs, MI: Andrews University Press, 1978.

Arnold, Bill T., and John H. Choi. *A Guide to Biblical Hebrew Syntax*. 2nd ed. Cambridge: Cambridge University Press, 2018.

Bacchiocchi, Samuele. *From Sabbath to Sunday: A Historical Investigation of the Rise of Sunday Observance in Early Christianity*. Rome: Pontifical Gregorian University Press, 1977.

———. "Remembering the Sabbath: The Creation-Sabbath in Jewish and Christian History." Pages 69–97 in *The Sabbath in Jewish and Christian Traditions*. Edited by Tamar Eskenazi, Daniel J. Harrington, and William H. Shea. New York: Crossroad, 1991.

Bächer, Wilhelm. *Die Agada der Tannaiten.* 2 vols. Strassburg: Karl J. Trübner, 1899.

Baden, Joel S. *The Composition of the Pentateuch: Renewing the Documentary Hypothesis.* AYBRL. New Haven, CT: Yale University Press, 2012.

Balkan, Kemal. "The Old Assyrian Week." Pages 159–74 in *Studies in Honor of Benno Landsberger on His Seventy-Fifth Birthday, April 21, 1965.* Assyriological Studies 16. Chicago: University of Chicago Press, 1965.

Balsdon, J. P. V. D. *Life and Leisure in Ancient Rome.* London: Phoenix, 1969.

Bauer, Hans, and Pontus Leander. *Historische Grammatik der hebräischen Sprache des Alten Testaments.* Hildesheim: Olms, 1962.

Bauks, Michaela. "Le Shabbat: Un temple dans le temps." *Études théologiques et religieuses* 77 (2002): 473–90.

Becking, Bob. "Sabbath at Elephantine: A Short Episode in the Construction of Jewish Identity." Pages 118–27 in *Ezra, Nehemiah, and the Construction of Early Jewish Identity.* FAT 80. Tübingen: Mohr Siebeck, 2011.

Ben-Dov, Jonathan. "A 360-Day Administrative Year in Ancient Israel: Judahite Portable Calendars and the Flood Account." *HTR* 114 (2021): 431–50.

Berlin, Adele, and Marc Zvi Brettler, eds. *The Jewish Study Bible.* New York: Oxford University Press, 2014.

Blenkinsopp, Joseph. *Isaiah 1–39.* AB 19. New Haven, CT: Yale University Press, 2000.

———. *Isaiah 40–55: A New Translation with Introduction and Commentary.* AB 19A. New York: Doubleday, 2002.

———. *Prophecy and Canon: A Contribution to the Study of Jewish Origins.* University of Notre Dame Center for the Study of Judaism and Christianity in Antiquity 3. Notre Dame, IN: University of Notre Dame Press, 1977.

Bloch, Yigal. "Judean Identity during the Exile: Concluding Deals on a Sabbath in Babylonia and Egypt Under the Neo-Babylonian and the Achaemenid Empires." Pages 43–69 in *A Question of Identity: Social, Political, and Historical Aspects of Identity Dynamics in Jewish and Other Contexts.* Edited by Dikla Rivlin Katz, Noah Hacham, Geoffrey Herman, and Lilach Sagiv. Munich: de Gruyter Oldenbourg, 2019.

———. "Was the Sabbath Observed in Āl-Yāḫūdu in the Early Decades of the Babylonian Exile?" *ZAW* 132.1 (2020): 117–20.

Blomberg, Craig. "The Sabbath as Fulfilled in Christ: A Response to S. Bacchiocchi and J. Primus." Pages 122–28 in *The Sabbath in Jewish and Christian Traditions.* Edited by Tamar Eskenazi, Daniel J. Harrington, and William H. Shea. New York: Crossroad, 1991.

Blum, Erhard. "Issues and Problems in the Contemporary Debate Regarding the Priestly Writings." Pages 31–43 in *The Strata of the Priestly Writings: Contemporary Debate and Future Directions.* Edited by Sarah Shectman and Joel S. Baden. Abhandlungen zur Theologie des Alten und Neuen Testaments 95. Zürich: Theologischer Verlag Zürich, 2009.

Braude, William G. *Pesikta Rabbati: Discourses for Feasts, Fasts, and Special Sabbaths.* Yale Judaica Series 18. New Haven, CT: Yale University Press, 1968.

Brichto, Herbert Chanan. *The Names of God: Poetic Readings in Biblical Beginnings.* New York: Oxford University Press, 1998.

Brown, Francis, S. R. Driver, and Charles A. Briggs. *A Hebrew and English Lexicon of the Old Testament.* Peabody, MA: Hendrickson, 1906.

Budde, Karl. "Antwort auf Johannes Meinholds 'Zur Sabbathfrage.'" *ZAW* 48 (1930): 138–45.

Carroll, Robert P. *Jeremiah: A Commentary*. OTL. Philadelphia: Westminster, 1986.

Cassius Dio Cocceianus. *Dio's Roman History*. Translated by Earnest Cary and Herbert Baldwin Foster. LCL 32. Cambridge, MA: Harvard University Press, 1970.

Cassuto, Umberto. *A Commentary on the Book of Genesis. Part 1, From Adam to Noah*. Translated by Israel Abrahams. Jerusalem: Magnes Press, 1961.

———. *From Adam to Noah: A Commentary on Genesis I–V*. 3rd ed. Jerusalem: Magnes Press, 1959.

Chavel, Simeon. *Oracular Law and Priestly Historiography in the Torah*. FAT 2/71. Tübingen: Mohr Siebeck, 2014.

Childs, Brevard S. *The Book of Exodus: A Critical, Theological Commentary*. OTL. Philadelphia: Westminster, 1974.

———. *Isaiah*. OTL. Louisville, KY: Westminster John Knox, 2001.

Clifford, Richard J. "Election in Genesis 1." Pages 7–22 in *The Call of Abraham: Essays on the Election of Israel in Honor of Jon D. Levenson*. Edited by Gary A. Anderson and Joel S. Kaminsky. Christianity and Judaism in Antiquity. Notre Dame, IN: University of Notre Dame Press, 2013.

———. "The Hebrew Scriptures and the Theology of Creation." *Theological Studies* 46 (1985): 507–23.

Cohen, J. Joseph. "The Order of the Friday Evening Service and the 'Lecho Dodi'— A Comparative Liturgical Study." Pages 321–57 in *Adam-Noah Braun Memorial Volume: Essays in Jewish Studies*. Edited by Shear-Yashuv Cohen and Hayim Lifshitz. Jerusalem: Weiss Press, 1969.

Cohen, Shaye J. D. "The Judaean Legal Tradition and the Halakhah of the Mishnah." Pages 121–43 in *The Cambridge Companion to the Talmud and Rabbinic Literature*. Cambridge: Cambridge University Press, 2007.

Cohon, Samuel S. "Original Sin." *HUCA* 21 (1948): 275–330.

Collins, A. Yarbro. *Mark: A Commentary*. Hermeneia. Minneapolis: Augsburg Fortress, 2007.

Colson, F. H. *The Week: An Essay on the Origin and Development of the Seven-Day Cycle*. Westport, CT: Greenwood, 1974.

Cross, Frank Moore. *Canaanite Myth and Hebrew Epic: Essays in the History of the Religion of Israel*. Cambridge, MA: Harvard University Press, 1973.

———. "Epigraphic Notes on Hebrew Documents of the Eighth-Sixth Centuries B.C.: II. The Murabbaʿât Papyrus and the Letter Found near Yabneh-Yam." *BASOR* 165 (1962): 34–46.

Dahood, Mitchell. *Psalms 51–100*. AB 17. Garden City, NY: Doubleday, 1968.

Dershowitz, Idan. *The Valediction of Moses*. FAT 145. Tübingen: Mohr Siebeck, 2021.

Dickens, Charles. *Sunday Under Three Heads*. London: Chapman & Hall, 1836.

Diddams, M., L. K. Surdyk, and D. Daniels. "Rediscovering Models of Sabbath Keeping: Implications for Psychological Well-Being." *Journal of Psychology and Theology* 32.1 (2004): 3–11.

Dobbs-Allsopp, F. W., ed. *Hebrew Inscriptions: Texts from the Biblical Period of the Monarchy with Concordance*. New Haven, CT: Yale University Press, 2005.

Doering, Lutz. "The Concept of the Sabbath in the Book of Jubilees." Pages 179–205 in *Studies in the Book of Jubilees*. Edited by Matthias Albani, Jörg Frey, and Armin Lange. TSAJ 65. Tübingen: Mohr Siebeck, 1997.

————. *Schabbat: Sabbathalacha und -praxis im antiken Judentum und Urchristentum.* TSAJ 78. Tübingen: Mohr Siebeck, 1999.

Donin, Hayim Halevy. *To Be a Jew.* New York: Basic Books, 1972.

Dupont-Sommer, A. "Un Ostracon Araméen Inédit d'Éléphantine (Collection Clermont-Ganneau N° 186)." *Rivista degli studi orientali* 32 (1952): 403–9.

Ehrlich, Arnold B. *Randglossen zur Hebräischen Bibel; Textkritisches, Sprachliches und Sachliches.* Leipzig: J. C. Hinrichs, 1908.

Eliade, Mircea. *Myth and Reality.* New York: Harper & Row, 1963.

Emanuel, Jeffrey P. "Give Them a 'Hand': An Archaeo-Literary Study of Toilet Practices at Khirbet Qumran and Their Implications" presented at the Proceedings of the Society of Biblical Literature 2012 International Meeting. Amsterdam, 22 July 2012.

Eshel, Esther. "4QDeut^n—A Text That Has Undergone Harmonistic Editing." *HUCA* 62 (1991): 117–54.

Fisher, Loren R. "Creation at Ugarit and in the Old Testament." *VT* 15 (1965): 313–24.

————. "The Temple Quarter." *Journal of Semitic Studies* 8.1 (1963): 34–41.

Foster, Benjamin R. *Before the Muses: An Anthology of Akkadian Literature.* 3rd ed. Bethesda, MD: CDL Press, 2005.

Frankel, David. "Did God Bless Shabbat?" TheTorah.Com, 2016. https://thetorah .com/did-god-bless-shabbat/.

Gandz, Solomon. "The Origin of the Planetary Week or the Planetary Week in Hebrew Literature." *PAAJR* 18 (1948): 213–54.

Geller, M. J. "Šapattu." *Reallexikon der Assyriologie und Vorderasiatischen Archäologie* 12:25–27.

Gesenius, Wilhelm. *Gesenius' Hebrew Grammar.* Edited by E. Kautsch. 2nd ed. Oxford: Clarendon, 1910.

Gesundheit, Shimon. *Three Times a Year: Studies in Festival Legislation in the Pentateuch.* FAT 82. Tübingen: Mohr Siebeck, 2012.

Gilat, Yitzhak. "On Fasting on the Sabbath." *Tarbiz* 15 (1982): 1–15.

————. "On the Development of the Labors Forbidden on the Sabbath." *PAAJR* 49 (1982): 9–21.

Ginsberg, H. Louis. *The Israelian Heritage of Jerusalem.* Texts and Studies of the Jewish Theological Seminary of America 24. New York: The Jewish Theological Seminary of America, 1982.

Goldenberg, Robert. "The Jewish Sabbath in the Roman World up to the Time of Constantine the Great." Pages 414–47 in *Aufstieg und Niedergang der Römischen Welt.* Berlin: de Gruyter, 1979.

————. "The Place of the Sabbath in Rabbinic Judaism." Pages 31–44 in *The Sabbath in Jewish and Christian Traditions.* Edited by Tamar Eskenazi, Daniel J. Harrington, and William H. Shea. New York: Crossroad, 1991.

Goldstein, Jonathan A. *II Maccabees.* AB 41A. Garden City, NY: Doubleday, 1983.

Goodenough, Erwin R. *Jewish Symbols in the Greco-Roman Period.* Vol. 5 of *Bollingen Series* 37. New York: Pantheon Books, 1956.

Goodfriend, Elaine. "Seven, the Biblical Number." TheTorah.Com, 2021. https:// www.thetorah.com/article/seven-the-biblical-number.

Granerød, Gard. *Dimensions of Yahwism in the Persian Period: Studies in the Religion and Society of the Judaean Community at Elephantine.* BZAW 488. Berlin: de Gruyter, 2016.

Green, Arthur. "Sabbath as Temple: Some Thoughts on Space and Time in Judaism." Pages 287–305 in *Go and Study: Essays and Studies in Honor of Alfred Jospe*. Edited by Raphael Jospe and Samuel Z. Fishman. Washington, DC: Bnai Brith Hillel Foundations, 1980.

———. "Some Aspects of Qabbalat Shabbat." Pages 95–118 in *Sabbath: Idea, History, Reality*. Edited by Gerald J. Blidstein. The Goldstein-Goren Library of Jewish Thought 1. Beer Sheva: Ben-Gurion University of the Negev Press, 2004.

Gribetz, Sarit Kattan. *Time and Difference in Rabbinic Judaism*. Princeton, NJ: Princeton University Press, 2020.

Grund, Alexandra. *Die Entstehung des Sabbats: Seine Bedeutung für Israels Zeitkonzept und Errinerungskultur*. FAT 75. Tübingen: Mohr Siebeck, 2011.

Guillaume, Philippe. *Land and Calendar: The Priestly Document from Genesis 1 to Joshua 18*. The Library of Hebrew Bible / Old Testament Studies 391. New York: T&T Clark, 2009.

Gunkel, Hermann. *Creation and Chaos in the Primeval Era and the Eschaton: A Religio-Historical Study of Genesis 1 and Revelation 12*. Bible Resource Series. Grand Rapids, MI: Eerdmans, 2006.

———. *Schöpfung und Chaos in Urzeit und Endzeit: eine religionsgeschichtliche Untersuchung über Gen. 1 und Ap. Joh 12*. Göttingen: Vandenhoeck und Ruprecht, 1895.

Haag, Ernst. *Vom Sabbat zum Sonntag: Eine Bibeltheologische Studie*. Trierer Theologische Studien 52. Trier: Paulinus, 1991.

Haberman, Avraham Meir. "Poetry as a Preserve for Forgotten Words and Meanings." Pages 29–34 in *P'raqim: Yearbook of the Schocken Institute for Jewish Research of the Jewish Theological Seminary of America*. Edited by Eliezer Shimshon Rozental. Jerusalem: Schocken, 1967.

Hallo, William W. *Archival Documents from the Biblical World*. Vol. 3 of *The Context of Scripture*. Leiden: Brill, 1997.

———. *Canonical Compositions from the Biblical World*. Vol. 1 of *The Context of Scripture*. Leiden: Brill, 1997.

———. "Information from Before the Flood: Antediluvian Notes from Babylonia and Israel." *MAARAV* 7 (1991): 173–81.

———. "New Moons and Sabbaths: A Case-Study in the Contrastive Approach." *HUCA* 48 (1977): 1–18.

Hasel, Gerhard F. "'New Moon and Sabbath' in Eight Century Israelite Prophetic Writings (Isa 1:13; Hos 2:13; Amos 8:5)." Pages 37–64 in *Wünschet Jerusalem Frieden*. Edited by Matthias Augustin and Klaus-Dietrich Schnuck. Frankfurt am Main: Peter Lang, 1988.

Hauptman, Judith. "39 Melachot of Shabbat: What Is the Function of This List?" TheTorah.Com, 13 February 2020. https://www.thetorah.com/article/seven-the-biblical-number.

———. "A New Interpretation of the Thirty-Nine Forbidden Labors." Pages 323–37 in *The Faces of Torah: Studies in the Texts and Contexts of Ancient Judaism in Honor of Steven Fraade*. Edited by Michal Bar-Asher Siegal, Tzvi Novick, and Christine Hayes. Göttingen: Vandenhoeck & Ruprecht, 2017.

Hefele, Charles Joseph. *A History of the Councils of the Church: From the Original Documents*. 5 vols. Edinburgh: T&T Clark, 1867.

Heidel, Alexander. *The Babylonian Genesis: The Story of Creation*. Chicago: University of Chicago Press, 1942.

————. *The Gilgamesh Epic and Old Testament Parallels*. Chicago: The University of Chicago Press, 1946.

Held, Shai. *The Heart of Torah: Essays on the Weekly Torah Portion: Genesis and Exodus*. Vol. 1. Philadelphia: The Jewish Publication Society, 2017.

Henkin, David M. *The Week: A History of the Unnatural Rhythms That Made Us Who We Are*. New Haven, CT: Yale University Press, 2021.

Henze, Martin. *Mind the Gap: How the Jewish Writings Between the Old and New Testament Help Us Understand Jesus*. Minneapolis: Fortress Press, 2017.

Hertz, J. H., ed. *The Pentateuch and Haftorahs*. 2nd ed. London: Soncino, 1979.

Heschel, Abraham Joshua. *The Sabbath*. New York: Farrar, Straus & Giroux, 1951.

————. "Space, Time, and Reality: The Centrality of Time in the Biblical World-View." *Judaism* 1 (1952): 263–69.

Hirshman, Marc. *A Rivalry of Genius: Jewish and Christian Biblical Interpretation in Late Antiquity*. State University of New York Series in Judaica. Albany: State University of New York Press, 1996.

————. *Torah for the Entire World*. Tel-Aviv: Hakibbutz Hameuchad, 1999.

Horowitz, Elliott. "Sabbath Delights: Toward a Social History." Pages 131–58 in *Sabbath: Idea, History, Reality*. Edited by Gerald J. Blidstein. The Goldstein-Goren Library of Jewish Thought 1. Beer Sheva: Ben-Gurion University of the Negev Press, 2004.

Hossfeld, Frank-Lothar. *Der Dekalog: Seine Späten Fassungen, die originale Komposition und seine Vorstufen*. Orbis Biblicus et Orientalis 45. Freiburg: Universitätsverlag; Göttingen: Vandenhoeck & Ruprecht, 1982.

Hrůša, Ivan. *Die akkadische Synonymenliste, malku = šarru: Eine Textedition mit Übersetzung und Kommentar*. AOAT 50. Münster: Ugarit-Verlag, 2010.

Huizinga, Johan. *Homo Ludens: A Study of the Play-Element in Culture*. Boston: Beacon, 1950.

Ignatius of Rome. "Epistle to the Magnesians." *Christian Classics Ethereal Library*, n.d. https://www.ccel.org/ccel/schaff/anf01.v.iii.i.html.

Ish Shalom (Friedmann), Meir. *Pesiqta Rabbati*. Vienna: publisher not identified, 1880.

Jacob, Benno. *Das Buch Genesis*. Stuttgart: Calwer Verlag, 2000.

Janowski, Bernd. "Tempel und Schöpfung: Schöpfungstheologische Aspekte der Priesterschriftlichen Heiligtumskonzeption." *Jahrbuch für Biblische Theologie* 5 (1990): 37–69.

Jastrow, Morris. "The Original Character of the Hebrew Sabbath." *American Journal of Theology* 2 (1898): 312–52.

Jeremias, Jörg. *The Book of Amos: A Commentary*. OTL. Louisville, KY: Westminster John Knox, 1998.

John Paul II. Apostolic Letter. "*Dies Domini*." Apostolic Letter, 31 May 1998. https://www.vatican.va/content/john-paul-ii/en/apost_letters/1998/documents/hf_jp-ii_apl_05071998_dies-domini.html.

Josephus. Translated by Henry St. J. Thackeray et al. 10 vols. LCL. Cambridge, MA: Harvard University Press, 1926–1965.

Josipovici, Gabriel. *The Book of God: A Response to the Bible*. New Haven, CT: Yale University Press, 1988.

Joüon, P, and T. Muraoka. *A Grammar of Biblical Hebrew*. 2nd ed. Rome: Gregorian and Pontifical Press, 2011.

Juster, A. M., and Robert Maltby, eds. *Tibullus: Elegies.* Oxford World's Classics. Oxford: Oxford University Press, 2012.

Justin Martyr. *Dialogue with Trypho.* Translated by Thomas B. Falls. Edited by Michael Slusser. Selections from the Fathers of the Church 3. Washington, DC: Catholic University of American Press, 2012.

Kaddari, Menaḥem Zevi. *A Dictionary of Biblical Hebrew.* Ramat-Gan: Bar-Ilan University Press 2017. [Hebrew]

Kamrin, Janice. "Telling Time in Ancient Egypt." *Heilbrunn Timeline of Art History.* New York: The Metropolitan Museum of Art, 2017. https://www.metmuseum.org/toah/hd/tell/hd_tell.html.

Kapelrud, Arvid S. "The Number Seven in Ugaritic Texts." *VT* 18 (1968): 494–99.

Kaplan, Jonathan. "The Credibility of Liberty: The Plausibility of the Jubilee Legislation of Leviticus 25 in Ancient Israel and Judah." *CBQ* 81 (2019): 183–203.

Kaye, Lynn. *Time in the Babylonian Talmud: Natural and Imagined Times in Jewish Law and Narrative.* New York: Cambridge University Press, 2018.

Kearney, Peter J. "Creation and Liturgy: The P Redaction of Ex 25–40." *ZAW* 89 (1977): 375–87.

Kennedy, Dennis. "A Response to S. Bacchiocchi and J. Primus." Pages 129–36 in *The Sabbath in Jewish and Christian Traditions.* Edited by Tamar Eskenazi, Daniel J. Harrington, and William H. Shea. New York: Crossroad, 1991.

Keysar, Ariela, and Barry A. Kosmin. "The Bar/Bat Mitzvah Class of 5755: Tracking Jewish Connections over Two Decades 1995–2019." New York: Jewish Theological Seminary, 2020.

Kimelman, Reuven. *The Mystical Meaning of Lekhah Dodi and Kabbalat Shabbat.* Sources and Studies in the Literature of Jewish Mysticism 9. Jerusalem: Magnes, 2003.

Klawans, Jonathan. "The Law." Pages 515–18 in *The Jewish Annotated New Testament.* Edited by Amy-Jill Levine and Marc Zvi Brettler. New York: Oxford University Press, 2011.

Klibansky, Raymond, Erwin Panofsky, and Fritz Saxl. *Saturn and Melancholy: Studies in the History of Natural Philosophy, Religion and Art.* London: Thomas Nelson, 1964.

Knohl, Israel. *The Sanctuary of Silence: The Priestly School and the Holiness School.* Minneapolis: Augsburg Fortress, 1995.

Koehler, Ludwig, and Walter Baumgartner. *The Hebrew and Aramaic Lexicon of the Old Testament.* Leiden: Brill, 2001.

Kraeling, Emil G. "The Present State of the Sabbath Question." *American Journal of Semitic Languages and Literatures* 49 (1933): 218–29.

Kraemer, David C. "Interpreting the Rabbinic Sabbath: The 'Forty Minus One' Forbidden Labors of Mishnah Shabbat 7:2." Pages 385–93 in *The Faces of Torah: Studies in the Texts and Contexts of Ancient Judaism in Honor of Steven Fraade.* Edited by Michal Bar-Asher Siegal, Tzvi Novick, and Christine Hayes. Göttingen: Vandenhoeck & Ruprecht, 2017.

———. "The Sabbath as a Sanctuary in Space." Pages 79–91 in *Tiferet LeYisrael: Jubilee Volume in Honor of Israel Frankus.* Edited by Joel Roth, Menachem Schmelzer, and Yaacov Francus. New York: Jewish Theological Seminary, 2010.

Kratz, Reinhard G. *The Composition of the Narrative Books of the Old Testament.* London: T&T Clark, 2005.

Kugel, James L. *The Idea of Biblical Poetry: Parallelism and Its History.* New Haven, CT: Yale University Press, 1981.

——. *Traditions of the Bible: A Guide to the Bible as It Was at the Start of the Common Era.* Cambridge, MA: Harvard University Press, 1998.

Landsberger, Benno. *Der kultische Kalender der Babylonier und Assyrer.* Leipzig: A. Pries, 1914.

Levenson, Jon D. *Creation and the Persistence of Evil: The Jewish Drama of Divine Omnipotence.* 2nd ed. Princeton, NJ: Princeton University Press, 1994.

——. "Did God Forgive Adam? An Exercise in Comparative Midrash." Pages 148–70 in *Jews and Christians: People of God.* Edited by Carl E. Braaten and Robert Jenson. Grand Rapids, MI: Eerdmans, 2003.

——. *The Hebrew Bible, the Old Testament, and Historical Criticism: Jews and Christians in Biblical Studies.* Louisville, KY: Westminster John Knox, 1993.

——. "Is There a Counterpart in the Hebrew Bible to New Testament Anti-Semitism?" Pages 159–78 in *Divine Doppelgängers: [The LORD's] Ancient Look-Alikes.* Edited by Collin Cornell. University Park, PA: Eisenbrauns, 2020.

——. "The Jerusalem Temple in Devotional and Visionary Experience." Pages 32–61 in *Jewish Spirituality from the Bible Through the Middle Ages.* Edited by A. Green. New York: Crossroad, 1986.

——. *The Love of God: Divine Gift, Human Gratitude, and Mutual Faithfulness in Judaism.* LJI. Princeton, NJ: Princeton University Press, 2016.

——. "Response: Natural and Supernatural Justice." Pages 177–85 in *Judaism and Ecology: Created World and Revealed Word.* Edited by Hava Tirosh-Samuelson. Cambridge, MA: Center for the Study of World Religions, Harvard Divinity School, 2002.

——. *Resurrection and the Restoration of Israel: The Ultimate Victory of the God of Life.* New Haven, CT: Yale University Press, 2006.

——. *Sinai and Zion.* New York: HarperOne, 1987.

——. "The Temple and the World." *Journal of Religion* 64 (1984): 275–98.

——. "When Did Judaism Begin? A Review of Yonatan Adler, *The Origins of Judaism: An Archaeological-Historical Reappraisal.*" *Mosaic,* 28 November 2022. https://mosaicmagazine.com/observation/history-ideas/2022/11/when-did-judaism-begin/.

Levine, Amy-Jill, and Marc Zvi Brettler, eds. *The Jewish Annotated New Testament: New Revised Standard Version.* New York: Oxford University Press, 2011.

Levine, Baruch. *Numbers 1–20.* AB 4A. New York: Doubleday, 1993.

Levinson, Bernard. "Is the Covenant Code an Exilic Composition? A Response to John Van Seters." Pages 272–325 in *In Search of Pre-Exilic Israel.* Edited by John Day. JSOTSup 406. London: T&T Clark, 2004.

Levison, John R. *Portraits of Adam in Early Judaism.* Journal for the Study of the Pseudepigrapha Supplement Series 1. Sheffield: Sheffield Academic, 1988.

Lewis, Charlton T. *A Latin Dictionary.* Oxford: Clarendon, 1879.

Lichtheim, Miriam. *The Old and Middle Kingdoms.* Vol. 1 of *Ancient Egyptian Literature.* Berkeley: University of California Press, 1975.

Lieberman, Joe, and David Klinghoffer. *The Gift of Rest: Rediscovering the Beauty of the Sabbath.* New York: Howard Books, 2011.

Lieberman, Saul. *Texts and Studies.* New York: Ktav, 1974.

Loewenstamm, Samuel E. "The Seven-Day-Unit in Ugaritic Epic Literature." Pages 192–209 in *Comparative Studies in Biblical and Ancient Oriental Literatures.* AOAT 204. Kevelaer: Butzon & Bercker; Neukirchen-Vluyn: Neukirchener Verlag, 1980.

Lohfink, Norbert. "The Decalogue in Deuteronomy 5." *Theology of the Pentateuch: Themes of the Priestly Narrative and Deuteronomy.* Minneapolis: Fortress, 1994.

———. *Theology of the Pentateuch: Themes of the Priestly Narrative and Deuteronomy.* Minneapolis: Fortress, 1994.

Lozachmeur, Hélène. *La Collection Clermont-Ganneau: Ostraca, epigraphes sur jarre, etiquettes de bois.* 2 vols. Mémoires de l'Académie des Inscriptions et Belles-Lettres 35. Paris: de Boccard, 2006.

Mabry, Adam. *The Art of Rest: Faith to Hit Pause in a World That Never Stops.* Epsom, UK: The Good Book, 2018.

Madigan, Kevin J., and Jon D. Levenson. *Resurrection: The Power of God for Christians and Jews.* New Haven, CT: Yale University Press, 2008.

Markl, Dominik. "The Redactional Theologization of the Book of the Covenant: A Study in Criteriology." *Biblische Notizen* 181 (2019): 47–61.

Matt, Daniel. *The Zohar: Pritzker Edition.* Vol. 1. Stanford, CA: Stanford University Press, 2007.

McCurley, Foster. R. "'After Six Days' (Mark 9:2): A Semitic Literary Device." *JBL* 93 (1974): 67–81.

McKay, Heather A. "New Moon or Sabbath?" Pages 12–27 in *The Sabbath in Jewish and Christian Traditions.* Edited by Tamar Eskenazi, Daniel J. Harrington, and William H. Shea. New York: Crossroad, 1991.

———. *Sabbath and Synagogue: The Question of Sabbath Worship in Ancient Judaism.* Religions in the Graeco-Roman World 122. Leiden: Brill, 1994.

McKnight, Scot, and B. J. Oropeza, eds. *Perspectives on Paul: Five Views.* Grand Rapids, MI: Baker Academic, 2020.

Meier, Samuel A. "The Sabbath and Purification Cycles." Pages 3–11 in *The Sabbath in Jewish and Christian Traditions.* Edited by Tamar Eskenazi, Daniel J. Harrington, and William H. Shea. New York: Crossroad, 1991.

Meinhold, Johannes. "Die Entstehung des Sabbats." *ZAW* 29 (1909): 81–112.

———. *Sabbat und Woche im Alten Testament: Eine Untersuchung.* Forschungen zur Religion und Literatur des Alten und Neuen Testaments 5. Göttingen: Vandenhoeck & Ruprecht, 1905.

———. "Zur Sabbathfrage." *ZAW* 48 (1930): 121–38.

Meyers, Carol. *Exodus.* Cambridge Bible Commentary. Cambridge: Cambridge University Press, 2005.

———. "Household Religion." Pages 118–34 in *Religious Diversity in Ancient Israel and Judah.* Edited by Francesca Stavrakopoulou and John Barton. London: T&T Clark, 2010.

Middleton, J. Richard. "Creation Founded in Love: Breaking Rhetorical Expectations in Genesis 1:1–2:3." Pages 47–85 in *Sacred Text, Secular Times: The Hebrew Bible in the Modern World.* Edited by Leonard Jay Greenspoon and Bryan F. LeBeau. Omaha, NE: Creighton University Press, 2000.

———. *The Liberating Image: The Imago Dei in Genesis 1.* Cedar Rapids, MI: Brazos, 2005.

Milgrom, Jacob. "The Concept of Impurity in Jubilees and the Temple Scroll." *Revue de Qumran* 16 (1993): 277–84.

———. *The JPS Torah Commentary: Numbers.* Philadelphia: The Jewish Publication Society, 1990.

———. *Leviticus 17–22.* AB 3A. New York: Doubleday, 2000.

Mittleman, Alan. "From Jewish Street to Public Square." *First Things* 125 (2002): 29–37.

Moberly, R. W. L. "Review of Middleton, *The Liberating Image*." *Theology Today* 64 (2007): 365–66.

Murray, Margaret A. *The Splendour That Was Egypt: A General Survey of Egyptian Culture and Civilisation*. London: Sidgwick & Jackson, 1949.

Nelson, Richard D. *Deuteronomy*. OTL. Louisville, KY: Westminster John Knox, 2002.

Neugebauer, Otto. *The Exact Sciences in Antiquity*. 2nd ed. Acta Historica Scientiarum Naturalium et Medicalium. Copenhagen: University Library, 1957.

Nickelsburg, George W. E., and James C. VanderKam. *1 Enoch 2: A Commentary on the Book of 1 Enoch, Chapters 37–82*. Edited by Klaus Baltzer. Hermeneia. Minneapolis: Fortress, 2012.

Niditch, Susan. "The Cosmic Adam: Man as Mediator in Rabbinic Literature." *Journal of Jewish Studies* 34 (1983): 137–46.

Nihan, Christophe. *From Priestly Torah to Pentateuch: A Study in the Composition of the Book of Leviticus*. FAT 2/25. Tübingen: Mohr Siebeck, 2007.

Noam, Vered, and Elisha Qimron. "A Qumran Composition of Sabbath Laws and Its Contribution to the Study of Early Halakah." *Dead Sea Discoveries* 16 (2009): 55–96.

North, Robert. "The Derivation of Sabbath." *Biblica* 36 (1955): 182–201.

Nowack, Wilhelm. *Schabbat*. Gießen: Alfred Töpelmann, 1924.

Osgood, Kelsey. "Why Your 'Digital Shabbat' Will Fail." *Wired*, 15 April 2022. https://www.wired.com/story/digital-shabbat-screen-time-psychology/.

Otto, Eckart. *Deuteronomium 1–11*. Freiburg: Herder, 2012.

Pardee, Dennis. *Ritual and Cult at Ugarit*. Edited by Theodore J. Lewis. Writings from the Ancient World 10. Atlanta: SBL Press, 2002.

———. *Les Textes Rituels*. Ras Shamra 12. Paris: Éditions Recherche sur les Civilisations, 2000.

Parker, Richard A. "The Calendars and Chronology." Pages 13–26 in *The Legacy of Egypt*. Edited by John Richard Harris. 2nd ed. Oxford: Oxford University Press, 1971.

Peli, Pinchas H. *Shabbat Shalom*. Washington, DC: Bnai Brith Books, 1988.

Philo. *The Special Laws*. Translated by F. H. Colson. LCL 320. Cambridge, MA: Harvard University Press, 1937.

Pieper, Josef. *Leisure: The Basis of Culture*. San Francisco: Ignatius, 1963.

Polak, Frank H. "Poetic Style and Parallelism in the Creation Account (Genesis 1.1–2.3)." Pages 2–31 in *Creation in Jewish and Christian Tradition*. Edited by Yair Hoffman and Graf Reventlow. JSOTSup 319. Sheffield: Sheffield Academic, 2002.

Porten, Bezalel. "The Religion of the Jews of Elephantine in Light of the Hermopolis Papyri." *Journal of Near Eastern Studies* (1969): 116–21.

Primus, John H. "Sunday: The Lord's Day as a Sabbath—Protestant Perspectives on the Sabbath." Pages 98–122 in *The Sabbath in Jewish and Christian Traditions*. Edited by Tamar Eskenazi, Daniel J. Harrington, and William H. Shea. New York: Crossroad, 1991.

Pritchard, James B., ed. *Ancient Near Eastern Texts Relating to the Old Testament*. 3rd ed. Princeton, NJ: Princeton University Press, 1969.

Project TABS Editors. "What Melacha Did the Wood Gatherer Violate?" TheTorah. Com, 12 June 2014. https://www.thetorah.com/article/what-melacha-did-the -wood-gatherer-violate.

Propp, William H. C. *Exodus 19–40*. AB 2A. New York: Doubleday, 2006.

Rad, Gerhard von. *Deuteronomy: A Commentary*. OTL. Philadelphia: Westminster, 1966.

———. "There Remains Still a Rest for the People of God: An Investigation of a Whole Biblical Conception." Pages 94–102 in *The Problem of the Hexateuch and Other Essays*. New York: McGraw-Hill, 1966.

Rahlfs, Alfred, and Robert Hanhart, eds. *Septuaginta*. 2nd ed. Stuttgart: Deutsche Bibelgesellshaft, 2006.

Rechenmacher, Hans. "Šabbat[t]—Nominalform und Etymologie." *Zeitschrift für Althebräistik* 9 (1996): 199–203.

Reiner, Erica. "Šapattu." Pages 449–50 in *The Assyrian Dictionary of the Oriental Institute of the University of Chicago*. Edited by John A. Brinkman et al. Chicago: Oriental Institute of the University of Chicago, 1989.

Rhyder, Julia. "Sabbath and Sanctuary Cult in the Holiness Legislation: A Reassessment." *JBL* 138 (2019): 721–40.

Ricoeur, Paul. *The Symbolism of Evil*. Boston: Beacon, 1969.

Robinson, Gnana. "The Idea of Rest in the Old Testament and the Search for the Basic Character of the Sabbath." *ZAW* 92 (32–42): 1980.

———. *The Origin and Development of the Old Testament Sabbath*. Beiträge zur biblischen Exegese und Theologie 21. Frankfurt am Main: Lang, 1988.

Rosenthal, Franz, ed. *An Aramaic Handbook*. Porta Linguarum Orientalium. Wiesbaden: Harrassowitz, 1967.

Rosenzweig, Franz. *On Jewish Learning*. Edited by N. N. Glatzer. Modern Jewish Philosophy and Religion. Madison: University of Wisconsin Press, 1955.

Ruppert, Lothar. "Die Ruhe Gottes im Priesterschriftlichen Schöpfungsbericht Gen I und die 'Zufriedene Ruhe' des Ptaḥ im Denkmal Memphitischer Theologie." Pages 110–23 in *Studien zur Literaturgeschichte des Alten Testamentes*. Stuttgarter biblische Aufsatzbände 18. Stuttgart: Verlag Katholisches Bibelwerk, 1994.

Sacks, Jonathan. *Covenant and Conversation: A Weekly Reading of the Jewish Bible Exodus: The Book of Redemption*. New Milford, CT: Maggid & The Orthodox Union, 2010.

———. *The Koren Siddur*. 2nd ed. Jerusalem: Koren Publishers, 2015.

Saiman, Chaim N. *Halakhah: The Rabbinic Idea of Law*. LJI. Princeton, NJ: Princeton University Press, 2018.

Sanders, E. P. *Jesus and Judaism*. Philadelphia: Fortress, 1985.

———. *Paul and Palestinian Judaism: A Comparison of Patterns of Religion*. Philadelphia: Fortress, 1977.

Sarna, Nahum M. *Exodus*. JPS Torah Commentary. Philadelphia: The Jewish Publication Society, 1991.

———. *Studies in Biblical Interpretation*. JPS Scholar of Distinction Series. Philadelphia: The Jewish Publication Society, 2000.

Scarlata, Mark. *Sabbath Rest: The Beauty of God's Rhythm for a Digital Age*. London: SCM, 2019.

Schäfer, Peter. *Judeophobia: Attitudes Toward the Jews in the Ancient World*. Cambridge, MA: Harvard University Press, 1997.

———. "Tempel und Schöpfung: Zur Interpretation einiger Heiligtumstraditionen in der rabbinischer Literatur." *Kairós* 16 (1974): 122–33.

Schmidt, Werner H. *Die Schöpfungsgeschichte der Priesterschrift.* Wissenschaftliche Monographien zum Alten und Neuen Testament 17. Neukirchen-Vluyn: Neukirchener, 1964.

Scholem, Gershom. *The Messianic Idea in Judaism and Other Essays on Jewish Spirituality.* New York: Schocken, 1971.

———. "The Tradition of the Thirty-Six Just Men." Pages 251–56 in *The Messianic Idea in Judaism and Other Essays on Jewish Spirituality.* New York: Schocken, 1971.

Schramm, Brooks. *The Opponents of Third Isaiah: Reconstructing the Political History of the Restoration.* London: Bloomsbury, 2009.

Schwartz, Howard. *Tree of Souls: The Mythology of Judaism.* New York: Oxford University Press, 2004.

Schweid, Eliezer. *The Jewish Experience of Time: Philosophical Dimensions of the Jewish Holy Days.* Northvale, NJ: Jason Aronson, 2000.

Sela, Shlomo. "Abraham Ibn Ezra's Appropriation of Saturn." *Kabbalah* 10 (2004): 21–53.

———. "Saturn and the Jews." *Herbert D. Katz Center for Advanced Judaic Studies,* 10 November 2017. https://katz.sas.upenn.edu/resources/blog/saturn-and-jews.

Seligman, Adam B., Robert P. Weller, Michael J. Puett, and Bennett Simon. *Ritual and Its Consequences: An Essay on the Limits of Sincerity.* New York: Oxford University Press, 2008.

Sharon, Nadav. "The Conquests of Jerusalem by Pompey and Herod: On Sabbath or 'Sabbath of Sabbaths'?" *Jewish Studies Quarterly* 21 (2014): 193–220.

Sharvit, Shim'on. "Gutturals in Rabbinic Hebrew." Pages 225–43 in *Studies in the Hebrew Language and the Talmudic Literature Dedicated to the Memory of Dr. Menaḥem Moreshet.* Edited by Menaḥem Zevi Kaddari and Shim'on Sharvit. Ramat-Gan: Bar-Ilan Press, 1989.

Shulevitz, Judith. "Bring Back the Sabbath." *New York Times Magazine,* 2 March 2003.

———. *The Sabbath World: Glimpses of a Different Order of Time.* New York: Random House, 2010.

Sievers, Joseph, and Amy-Jill Levine, eds. *The Pharisees.* Grand Rapids, MI: Eerdmans, 2021.

Simkovich, Malka Z. "Intimacy on Shabbat: Was It Always a Mitzvah?" TheTorah. Com, 20 January 2014. https://www.thetorah.com/article/intimacy-on-shabbat.

Sklare, Marshall. *Conservative Judaism: An American Religious Movement.* New York: Schocken, 1972.

Smith, Mark S. *The Priestly Vision of Genesis 1.* Minneapolis: Fortress, 2010.

Soloveitchik, Haym. "Rupture and Reconstruction: The Transformation of Contemporary Orthodoxy." *Tradition* 28.4 (1994): 1–36.

Spalinger, Anthony J. "Calendars." Pages 224–27 in *The Oxford Encyclopedia of Ancient Egypt.* Edited by Donald B. Redford. Oxford: Oxford University Press, 2001. https://www.oxfordreference.com/display/10.1093/acref/9780195102345.001.0001 /acref-9780195102345-e-0115;jsessionid=DC3559AC91F374D4E79072A9CB2FD385 ?rskey=A6hIus&result=116.

Speiser, E. A. *Genesis.* AB 1. Garden City, NY: Doubleday, 1964.

Stackert, Jeffrey. "The Priestly Sabbath and the Calendar: Between Literature and Material Culture." Pages 49–64 in *Contextualizing Jewish Temples.* Edited by Tova

Ganzel and Shalom E. Holtz. Brill Reference Library of Judaism 64. Leiden: Brill, 2020.

———. "The Sabbath of the Land in the Holiness Legislation: Combining Priestly and Non-Priestly Perspectives." *CBQ* 73 (2011): 239–50.

Steiner, Richard C. "On the Dating of Hebrew Sound Changes (*Ḥ>Ḥ and *Ġ>ʿ) and Greek Translations (2 Esdras and Judith)." *JBL* 124 (2005): 229–67.

Stendahl, Krister. "The Apostle Paul and the Introspective Conscience of the West." *HTR* 56 (1963): 199–215.

———. *Paul Among Jews and Gentiles and Other Essays*. Philadelphia: Fortress, 1976.

Stern, Sacha. *Time and Process in Ancient Judaism*. Portland, OR: The Littman Library of Jewish Civilization, 2003.

Swoboda, A. J. *Subversive Sabbath: The Surprising Power of Rest in a Nonstop World*. Grand Rapids, MI: Brazos, 2018.

Tacitus. *The Histories, Books IV–V*. Translated by Clifford H. Moore. LCL 249. Cambridge, MA: Harvard University Press, 1931.

Tadmor, Hayim. "The New Year in Mesopotamia." *Encyclopaedia Biblica* 7:305–11.

Tambiah, Stanley J. "The Magical Power of Words." *Man* 3 (1968): 175–208.

———. *A Performative Approach to Ritual*. Radcliffe-Brown Lecture in Social Anthropology. London: British Academy, 1981.

Tammuz, Oded. "The Sabbath as the Seventh Day of the Week and a Day of Rest: Since When?" *ZAW* 131 (2019): 287–94.

Theodor, J., and C. Albeck. *Midrash Bereshit Rabba: Critical Edition with Notes and Commentary*. 3 vols. Jerusalem: Wahrmann Books, 1965.

Tigay, Jeffrey H. "Notes on the Development of the Jewish Week." *Eretz-Israel* 14 (1978): 111–21.

Toeg, Aryeh. "Genesis 1 and the Sabbath." *Beth Miqra'* 50 (1972): 288–96.

Toorn, Karel van der. *Becoming Diaspora Jews: Behind the Story of Elephantine*. AYBRL. New Haven, CT: Yale University Press, 2019.

Tôrat Ḥayîm: Ḥamiššâ Ḥumšê Tôrâ, Sēfer Šəmôt. Vol. 1. Jerusalem: Mossad HaRaḇ, 1993.

Tsevat, Matitiahu. "The Basic Meaning of the Biblical Sabbath." *ZAW* 84 (1972): 447–59.

VanderKam, James C. *Jubilees: A Commentary on the Book of Jubilees*. Minneapolis: Fortress, 2018.

Vaux, Roland de. *Ancient Israel*. Vol. 2. New York: McGraw-Hill, 1965.

Veyne, Paul. *Did the Greeks Believe in Their Myths? An Essay on the Constitutive Imagination*. Chicago: University of Chicago Press, 1988.

"The View from Pew: Where Do We Go from Here?" *Jewish Action*, 2021. https://jewishaction.com/jewish-world/where-do-we-go-from-here/.

Wagner, Volker. *Profanität und Sakralisierung im Alten Testament*. BZAW 351. Berlin: de Gruyter, 2005.

Waltke, Bruce K., and Michael P. O'Connor. *An Introduction to Biblical Hebrew Syntax*. Winona Lake, IN: Eisenbrauns, 1990.

Walton, John H. *The Lost World of Genesis One: Ancient Cosmology and the Origins Debate*. Downers Grove, IL: IVP Academic, 2009.

Weber, Max. *Ancient Judaism*. New York: The Free Press, 1952.

Weinfeld, Moshe. *Deuteronomy 1–11*. AB 5. New York: Doubleday, 1991.

———. *Justice and Righteousness in Israel and the Nations*. Jerusalem: Magnes, 1985.

———. "Sabbath, Temple and the Enthronement of the Lord—The Problem of the Sitz im Leben of Genesis 1:1–2:3." Pages 501–12 in *Mélanges bibliques et orientaux en l'honneur de M. Henri Cazelles*. Edited by André Caquot and Mathias Delcor. AOAT 212. Kevelaer: Butzon & Bercker; Neukirchen-Vluyn: Neukirchener Verlag, 1981.

———. "Universalism and Particularism in the Period of Exile and Restoration." *Tarbiz* 33 (1964): 228–42.

Weiss, Herold. "The Sabbath in the Writings of Josephus." *Journal for the Study of Judaism in the Persian, Hellenistic, and Roman Periods* 29 (1988): 363–90.

Weiss-Rosmarin, Trude. "Time and Space." *Judaism* 1 (1952): 277–78.

Wellhausen, Julius. *Prolegomena to the History of Ancient Israel*. Gloucester, MA: Peter Smith, 1973.

Westermann, Claus. *Genesis 1–11: A Commentary*. Minneapolis: Augsburg, 1984.

———. *Isaiah 40–66: A Commentary*. OTL. Philadelphia: Westminster, 1969.

White, Sidnie Ann. "4QDt^n: Biblical Manuscript or Excerpted Text?" Pages 13–20 in *Of Scribes and Scrolls: Studies on the Hebrew Bible, Intertestamental Judaism, and Christian Origins Presented to John Strugnell on the Occasion of His Sixtieth Birthday*. Edited by Harold W. Attridge et al. College Theology Society Resources in Religion 5. Lanham, MD: University Press of America, 1990.

Wirzba, Norman. *Living the Sabbath: Discovering the Rhythms of Rest and Delight*. Grand Rapids, MI: Brazos, 2006.

Wolde, Ellen van. "The Text as an Eloquent Guide: Rhetorical, Linguistic and Literary Features in Genesis 1." Pages 134–51 in *Literary Structure and Rhetorical Strategies in the Hebrew Bible*. Edited by L. J. de Regt, Jan de Waard, and J. P. Fokkelman. Assen: van Gorcum; Winona Lake, IN: Eisenbrauns, 1996.

Wolff, Hans Walter. *Hosea: A Commentary on the Book of the Prophet Hosea*. Hermeneia. Philadelphia: Fortress, 1974.

Wright, David P. *Inventing God's Law: How the Covenant Code of the Bible Used and Revised the Laws of Hammurabi*. New York: Oxford University Press, 2009.

Wright, Jacob L. "How and When the Seventh Day Became Shabbat." TheTorah. Com, 13 April 2015. https://thetorah.com/how-and-when-the-seventh-day -became-shabbat/.

———. "Shabbat of the Full Moon: And the Origins of the Seven-Day Week." TheTorah.Com, 11 March 2015. https://thetorah.com/shabbat-of-the-full -moon/.

Wurzberger, Walter S. "A Jewish Theology and Philosophy of the Sabbath." Pages 139–48 in *The Sabbath in Jewish and Christian Traditions*. Edited by Tamar Eskenazi, Daniel J. Harrington, and William H. Shea. New York: Crossroad, 1991.

Zerubavel, Eviatar. *The Seven Day Circle: The History and Meaning of the Week*. New York: The Free Press, 1985.

Zetterholm, Magnus. *Approaches to Paul: A Student's Guide to Recent Scholarship*. Minneapolis: Fortress, 2009.

Zimmern, Heinrich. "Sabbath." *Zeitschrift für deutschen morgenländischen Gesellschaft* 58 (1904): 199–202.

ANCIENT SOURCE INDEX